Mothers, Sisters, Resisters

Mothers, Sisters, Resisters

Oral Histories of Women

Who Survived the Holocaust

🌷 *edited by*

Brana Gurewitsch

The University of Alabama Press

Tuscaloosa and London

JUDAIC STUDIES SERIES
Leon J. Weinberger
General Editor

∞

The paper on which this book is printed meets the minimum requirements of
American National Standard for Information Science-Permanence of Paper for
Printed Library Materials, ANSI Z39.48-1984.

The following interviews were published previously in the *Newsletter* of the
Center for Holocaust Studies and are reprinted here with corrections, revi-
sions, and/or the addition of footnotes: Nina Matathias, Took Heroma, Emilie
Schindler, Zenia Malecki, Aida Brydbord, Anna Heilman, and Rose Meth. Permission has been granted by the Museum of Jewish Heritage to publish all the
interviews in this volume, save the interview with Gertrud Groag, which is published with the permission of the Oral History Division of the Institute of Contemporary Jewry at Hebrew University, Jerusalem.

Library of Congress Cataloging-in-Publication Data

Mothers, sisters, resisters : oral histories of women who survived the
Holocaust / edited by Brana Gurewitsch.
    p. cm. — (Judaic studies series)
  Includes bibliographical references (p.   ).
  ISBN 0–8173–0931–4
  ISBN 0–8173–0952–7 (pbk.)
  1. Jewish women in the Holocaust. 2. Holocaust, Jewish
(1939–1945)—Personal narratives. 3. Holocaust survivors—United
States—Interviews. 4. World War, 1939–1945—Jewish resistance. I.
Gurewitsch, Bonnie. II. Series: Judaic studies series (Unnumbered)
  D804.47 .M67 1998
  940.53′18′0922—ddc21

                                                          98–19753

British Library Cataloguing-in-Publication Data available

❦ Contents

# ❦ Acknowledgments

A book of this nature is the result of the participation and cooperation of many people. Foremost are the Holocaust survivors, who found the strength to record their testimonies and graciously cooperated with the editorial process.

Most of the oral histories are from the Yaffa Eliach Collection, donated by the Center for Holocaust Studies to the Museum of Jewish Heritage, New York. Staff members and volunteers of the center conducted some of the interviews; did some of the initial transcribing, verification, and translation; and provided the clerical support for the initial publication of some of the interviews in the center's *Newsletters*.

With the merger of the center into the Museum of Jewish Heritage—A Living Memorial to the Holocaust in 1990, the center's oral history collection and I found a new home and continuity in the museum's oral history project. I have enjoyed warm support for this publication from the museum's director, Dr. David Altshuler, and my colleagues on the museum staff, and I was encouraged to make use of the museum's interviews, some of which appear in the book.

I was cordially assisted at the Avraham Harman Institute of Contemporary Jewry at the Hebrew University, Jerusalem. I am grateful to Professor Dov Levin, Ricki Garti, and Mira Levine. I also appreciate the cooperation and interest of Dr. Willi Groag, son of Gertrud Groag, and Jerzy Warman, son of Marysia Warman. Dr. Vojtech Blodig of the Terezin Museum sent me useful information relating to the Groag interview. The librarians at New York's Fashion Institute of Technology guided me to useful reference works on the process of making cloth from flax.

Jeshayahu Pery and Alfred Gruenspecht did sensitive, competent translations for me, and my cousin, Dr. Gisela Gross, was always available to guide me through the pitfalls of the German language. Judy Engelberg and Evelyn Unterberg did the excellent transcriptions, which are the core of the book, working with speed, accuracy, and much devotion to the material.

Ray Kaner and Esther Juni's suggestions of specific interviews were constructive and very much appreciated. Dr. Myrna Goldenberg and Dr. Barbara

Galli read the manuscript and offered insightful and useful suggestions that have enhanced the book. I am grateful to Kathy Swain of the University of Alabama Press for her meticulous and sensitive copyediting.

Finally, my family has cheered me on, advised and encouraged me, shared countless dilemmas, and never lost faith in the viability of this project. Arne, you made it possible. Thank you for your love and support.

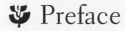 Preface

In the summer of 1972 I was teaching Hebrew and Jewish history in the education program of Camp Ramah in the Berkshires, one of several Jewish summer camps that provides both formal and informal Jewish education to its campers. I was fortunate to experience what so rarely happens between teenagers and a teacher. A wonderful "chemistry" developed with my group, and within three weeks they had devoured the Jewish history material that usually sufficed for an entire eight-week course. Eager to sustain the high level of enthusiasm within the group, I explained that we needed to move on to another topic and asked them what they wanted to learn. "The Holocaust" was their immediate answer. I was taken aback. I felt unprepared, emotionally and academically, to teach the Holocaust. When the teaching supervisor insisted that it was my responsibility to fulfill the students' request, I went to the camp library and did my best to prepare lessons for a four-week course on the Holocaust. To my relief and surprise, I found that when I approached the material analytically rather than emotionally, as I had in the past, it no longer frightened me. The group responded to my rather crudely presented material with more than enthusiasm. I sensed a huge hunger in these teenagers, an almost visceral need to know about the Holocaust. Realizing my own inadequate preparation for teaching the material, I used the months before the following summer for intensive study of the Holocaust, preparing curriculum materials and lesson plans. During the next two summers I taught an intensive eight-week course on the Holocaust at Camp Ramah. Of all the courses I have taught, the Holocaust engaged students most. It has also demanded continued study on my part.

I first became involved with the Center for Holocaust Studies, Documentation and Research as a volunteer researcher in the spring of 1977. The center's founder and director, Professor Yaffa Eliach, recognized, in 1974, the urgency of recording, in a systematic manner, the testimonies of Holocaust survivors and other eyewitnesses to the Holocaust. She decided to approach the interviews as the raw material of historical documentation. Gaps in the historical record were identified; specific groups of eyewitnesses were identified whose testimony would help fill those gaps without duplicating oral history projects already under way. At the time, Holocaust oral history was conducted only in Israel. Questionnaires were developed that would guide interviewers to elicit factual information that could be verified with existing documentation.

In the fall of 1977 I assumed the responsibilities of research librarian at the Center for Holocaust Studies and eventually qualified as a Certified Archivist in order to care properly for the center's growing collection of recorded interviews and archival material. Between 1978 and 1990, when the center merged into the Museum of Jewish Heritage—A Living Memorial to the Holocaust (New York), the oral history collection grew from three hundred to approximately three thousand recorded interviews, with related archival materials consisting of artifacts, documents, photographs, manuscripts, and personal papers.

I began my work with the process of verifying information offered by interviewees in their interviews. It became apparent to me that because of their traumatic nature, the experiences of the Holocaust were indelibly etched into memory. Events that had occurred thirty-five years before were as vivid as they were when they occurred. By using the methodology of the historian, oral histories could be verified and the testimony trusted.

The eyewitnesses, however, who had encountered ignorance of and indifference to their experiences, were wary of sharing memories that brought them pain and nightmares. Would they be believed now, after such a long time? When they first arrived in the United States as refugees after World War II their need to tell about their experiences was met with disbelief and insensitivity. "We had a hard time here during the war; sugar was rationed," and "Forget about the past; get on with your life" were typical reactions of American families and acquaintances.

In 1976 the publication of a book of Holocaust denial by Dr. Arthur Butz, a professor of electrical engineering at Northwestern University, galvanized many eyewitnesses into recording their testimonies. They felt the need and obligation to put their memories into the historical record, to add their testimony to the body of already existing evidence that would refute Butz and other deniers. The airing of the NBC "Holocaust" miniseries in 1978 aroused the interest of students, teachers, and the media and gave impetus to curriculum development efforts. These events sparked a growing interest in the Holocaust at many levels. Other Holocaust resource centers and oral history projects were established with the cooperation and participation of Holocaust survivors and other eyewitnesses. All these efforts encouraged many eyewitnesses to come forward.

The methodology of recording and processing oral histories at the Center for Holocaust Studies evolved in response to necessity and to the material itself. Interviewing techniques were refined, and topical questionnaires were developed that aided interviewers in eliciting verifiable, factual information. Researchers were trained to apply a rigorous verification process to the interviews in which the researcher determines whether the events described can be corroborated by other sources. Dates of events, names of places and people, and other quantifiable data are compared with information in primary and secondary sources as well as with information in other oral histories. Aida Brydbord's mention of Dr. Olia Goldfein, who served on the *Judenrat* in Pruzhany, is corroborated in the Pruzhany *Yizkor* book, which also adds fascinating material about the woman doctor's background and Holocaust experiences that give added insight into women's history.[1] As part of this verification process, I developed a detailed subject catalog that facilitated research at the Center for Holocaust Studies.

As a result of the particular focus of the interviewing projects at the center, thematic cataloging developed that reflected not only the facts of the Holocaust experience but also its human dimension. The oral history project that explored the experiences of Hasidic communities led to subject cataloging that reflected the response of all Jews as Jews during the Holocaust: religious observance, the use of ritual objects, loyalty to religious and cultural values. The project that focused on the experiences of young children led to cataloging the experiences of families and human relationships during the Holocaust. These two projects were particularly important for exploring the experiences of women in the Holocaust.

In 1985 two women, Rose Meth and Anna Heilman, visited the Center for Holocaust Studies. They were actively involved in the effort to erect a monument at Yad Vashem in Jerusalem to honor the memory of four Jewish women. These women were hanged in Birkenau on January 6, 1945, for their participation in the smuggling of gunpowder from the Weichsel Union Werke factory where they worked to the men of the Auschwitz resistance. The smuggling of explosives, in which Mmes. Meth and Heilman were also involved, resulted in the explosion and burning of gas chambers and contributed to the eventual cessation of gassings in Birkenau. Of the four women who were hanged, only the name of Roza Robota, the runner who actually transferred the gunpowder to the men, had been published in historical accounts. Mmes. Meth and Heilman and other women survivors of Auschwitz were determined to assure that the names of the other three women, Alla Gaertner, Regina Saperstein, and Esther Wajcblum, would be entered into the historical record. Their efforts were successful, and a monument to the four women now stands at Yad Vashem. Interviews recorded at the Center for Holocaust Studies with Rose Meth and Anna Heilman (see "Resisters") revealed the fascinating story of how ordinary women from traditional Jewish backgrounds rose to extraordinary heights of courage that impacted on the course of events at Auschwitz. Although other factors, such as the proximity of the Allies, were probably more significant influences on German policy, the psychological impact of the resistance activities on other prisoners was enormous.

Another interview, with Zenia Malecki, member of the FPO (Jewish resistance group) in Vilna, also revealed significant historical data that had not been previously published. Her oral history fills a small but interesting gap in the story of the surrender of Yizhak Witenberg, leader of the FPO, to the Gestapo. Once again, a woman's role was crucial.

The 1990 issue of the Center for Holocaust Studies *Newsletter*, published in magazine format, was devoted to the topic of Jewish women and resistance activities during the Holocaust. As editor of the *Newsletter*, I decided to include material that would broaden the field, adding to the seven edited oral histories from the center's collection eight short biographical sketches of women whose resistance activities were relatively unknown. In preparing this issue of the *Newsletter* it was clear to me that I had but scratched the surface of a vast field of inquiry into the Holocaust experiences of women, the raw material for which was in the three thousand oral histories of the center's collection.

The themes I selected for this book asserted themselves in the interviews. They are rough definitions, rather than rigid categories, and each interview may have characteristics of more than one category. All of the women resisted their fates. They supported each other like sisters and nurtured each other like mothers. The division of themes is designed to highlight one dominant aspect of each experience: of mother/child relationships, of siblings, or of those who engaged in organized, physical resistance.

"Mothers" and "sisters" are biologically determined. To a certain extent, women's Holocaust experiences were determined by their gender and their roles in families. When the invading Germans shot Jewish leadership shortly after occupation, Jewish communities were shorn of their most active and experienced men. In an attempt to evade forced labor, Jewish men fled east, leaving women and children, usually treated more humanely by civilized occupying forces, alone. Selections for forced labor in ghettos and then in concentration camps were usually gender- and age-based, separating able-bodied males and females and condemning mothers with their very young children, or the aged, to death. The Nazis, unlike other modern warriors, had genocidal plans for all Jews, including women and children, whose labor was not worth exploiting even temporarily. Women who joined resistance groups may have come as individuals, but in the social structure of partisan groups women often found protectors among the men and established relationships that later often became stable marriages. These women filled nurturing and supporting roles, like Aida Brydbord, who nursed the sick and wounded even though she had a gun and was trained to use it. Marysia Warman, like other women in resistance groups, exploited the stereotypical view of women held by the Nazis to serve as a courier and in other roles in which Jewish men would have been more easily detected. In concentration camps strict separation of the sexes was the rule. Women were forced to rely on their own resources, developing leadership roles and loyalties to each other. After liberation, women spoke almost universally of their fear of rape by Soviet soldiers, who did not distinguish among civilians, Jewish victims, and defeated Germans in their rush to enjoy the fruits of victory.

In another sense women, like men, influenced their own destinies by taking action unrelated to gender. *None* of the women was passive. Each acted and reacted to events, evading, hiding, resisting, making choices, taking initiatives, fighting the death that was intended for them. By refusing to be separated, mothers and daughters or sisters resisted the isolation that was the first step in the dehumanization process. By taking risks for each other they fought the system and their own despair. By remaining true to their Jewish identities even when they were "passing" as Aryans, Jewish women drew spiritual and moral strength that contributed to their survival and assured Jewish continuity after the Holocaust.

All of the women, regardless of how old they were during the Holocaust, knew that they suffered because they were Jews. This understanding, instinctively felt and clearly articulated, governed their responses and reactions. European Jews were conditioned by more than a thousand years of anti-Semitism. Their coping mechanisms were ingrained, put into operation as soon as they felt threatened. Escaping from advancing German armies, hiding from *Aktions*, bribing or negotiating with officials, obtaining false documents that would give them Aryan identities, and seeking refuge within a church or with Christians whose sympathies could be trusted or purchased were all survival techniques that had served Jewish communities and individuals in the past. These survival techniques appear in many of the experiences described in this book. They were used by Jewish women and men; sometimes the consequences were different for each gender.

Escape, the classic and immediate response to physical danger, was particularly difficult for Jews. In the prewar years the decision to try to leave Germany required almost prophetic foreknowledge of a destructive fate that had not yet been decided. Restrictive immigration policies in most western countries during the 1930s effectively closed off avenues of escape for German and Austrian Jews who did not begin their emigration efforts very early. Even in the late 1930s Jews in other countries did not feel threatened. After World War II began and passenger ships stopped crossing the Atlantic, most European Jews were trapped. The Final Solution developed gradually, using the traditional forms of anti-Semitism that Jews had coped with for generations. The Germans used secrecy, euphemism, and the natural skepticism of civilized people who could not believe that genocide was the goal to confound resistance to the process of destruction. Jews who were forced into ghettos obeyed German decrees on one level, but like Gertrud Groag and the Jewish leadership at Terezin, they used the time-tested techniques of bribery, negotiation, evasion, and secrecy to create resources, institutions, and protective devices that sustained them individually and as communities. By using capital punishments or by sending those who assisted Jews to concentration camps, the Germans succeeded in terrorizing local populations, preventing most would-be sympathizers from risking their lives to help Jews. Churches were not exempt from this policy. Together with a tradition of indigenous anti-Semitism, particularly in eastern Europe where the Jewish population was largest, all these factors resulted in minimizing opportunities for Jews to escape the Final Solution and allowed the systematic process to proceed inexorably.

An important characteristic of Jewish society was the primacy of the Jewish family. Loyalty to and responsibility for family members is a basic Jewish value, which prevented many Jews from leaving their families to engage in resistance activities. Aida Brydbord did not leave the ghetto for the forests with her fiancé until her father gave his consent and arranged for their clandestine marriage. Only after mass deportations destroyed family structure did remaining Jews feel free to join resistance groups. Marysia Warman did not leave the Warsaw ghetto to work for the resistance on the Aryan side until after her mother was deported, and she managed to arrange a haven for her sister. Often, families that had risked much to stay together were deported together to their deaths. After Jews were deported to concentration camps, they were practically doomed. There were a few successful individual escapes and exceptional uprisings in Treblinka, Sobibor, and Auschwitz. But Jewish fugitives were in as much danger of being shot or turned in by the local population as they were of capture by German or collaborationist military units. In the camps, as all vestiges of their human identities were stripped from them, Jews could retain only what remained in their minds and souls.

Jewish women, like Jewish men, had strong identities as Jews. Even those who were not particularly observant of religious laws acted and reacted as Jews. Trying to behave in accordance with Jewish values, keeping track of the Jewish calendar, risking their lives to save other Jews, particularly children, and retaining a sense of decency even when opportunities for revenge arose at liberation are a few examples of such behavior. Although prewar Jewish life may have been nominally patriarchal, with men dominating the public sphere, it may be argued that values were transmitted in the Jewish home equally by both parents. Girls learned acts of charity by sharing their mothers' philanthropic activities and by participating in activities sponsored by their Jewish school or after-school youth group. They learned a standard of proper behavior, distinguishing right and wrong.

One experience that particularly threatened Jewish women was the ordeal of undressing as part of the intake procedure or selection in concentration camps. "Almost every woman referred to the humiliating feelings and experiences surrounding her entrance to the camp . . . being nude, being shaved all over . . . being observed by men. . . . These stories demonstrate shared fears about and experiences of sexual vulnerability as women, not only about mortal danger as Jews."[2] Personal modesty was ingrained in Jewish women from childhood, even between mothers and daughters. Edith Horowitz had never seen her mother unclothed. Rachel Silberman reports that her sister, "not quite fourteen years old," was subjected to an internal examination on their arrival at Stutthof on the pretext that the Jewish women were hiding money or valuables. Rachel Silberman articulates her outrage: "My mother nearly pulled her hair out. . . . German men were doing the examining. Men!" To undress in front of strange men was unthinkable, a dreadful, disorienting shock and threat to their personal integrity. In spite of this ordeal, which was repeated throughout the camp experience, Jewish women continued to try to protect themselves from sexual attack. Ironically, the re-ligious environments in which many Jewish women grew up sheltered them from knowledge of sexual matters. Helen Foxman's husband had to explain to her what a lesbian was. Edith Horowitz reports that one of the SS women might have been a lesbian, but her perception is probably that of an adult looking back because at the time, she points out, "nobody ever talked about things like this." Sara Silber was asked by a civilian worker in the factory where she was a forced laborer: "You look like you come from a respectable home. Why did you become a prostitute?" Silber did not know the meaning of the word, but the civilian could not imagine any other crime for which a woman would be imprisoned.[3] Edith Horowitz reports that in the labor camp at Zillertal German workers would ask the Jewish slave laborers of what crimes they were guilty. The Jewish girls would respond, "I'm not guilty; I'm still a virgin!" Edith understands the implication of this exchange only in retrospect. Similarly, Miriam Rosenthal reports that when she was being transferred on a civilian train to the Kaufering camp, a German woman as-sumed that Rosenthal's shaved head was an indication of a sexual offense. The contrast between reality and the stereotyped reaction of the German woman is stark.

After liberation, when chaos reigned and all women were considered fair game by Soviet liberators, women survivors took extraordinary measures to avoid rape. Sonia, an older married woman, protected teenaged Sara Rigler by offering herself instead of the younger woman, whose earlier experiences with Russians are a series of narrow escapes from rape. Rozalia Berke de-scribes the fear of the local German population of the Russian occupiers, and Cesia Brandstatter describes how she and her camp sisters barricaded them-selves with tables and chairs to prevent the Russians from entering their bar-racks. They violated the Sabbath, escaping by train, but the train was also invaded by drunk Russian soldiers who had to be forcibly removed by an officer from the laps of the girls.

Actively resisting their fate and maintaining Jewish identity are not reac-tions unique to women, although these actions may dispel some stereotypi-cal views of Jewish women. One reaction that seems to be uniquely femi-nine, however, is the tendency of women to form close and long-lasting relationships that become a source of mutual assistance and strength.[4] The term *Lager Schwestern* (Camp Sisters), coined by women in concentration camps, is unique to women. A parallel term, describing male friendships as "brotherly," does not exist for men, indicating that whereas men may have been loyal to family members or friends, they did not perceive the relationship either as "brotherly" or unique to the camp experience.

Although close relationships between brothers or between fathers and sons did exist, it seems to me that they were not as prevalent as those between sisters or between mothers and their children. Fathers may have been more apt than mothers to send their sons out on their own, thinking that the agility, courage, and physical strength of youth would help the boys survive if they were not hampered by the presence of an older, perhaps weaker, parent. Although men who were not family relations assisted each other in concentration camps, the assistance was more likely to have been a single instance, a moment of advice or a physical gesture, rather than a long-term relationship of mutual trust and caring. In contrast, men in partisan groups, organized with quasi-military discipline, encouraged and supported mutual assistance, but there the loyalty was to the group, its leader, or ideology, rather than to one or two close friends.

Women, however, sustained sisterly and quasi-sisterly relationships for extended periods of time. Mothers and daughters, such as Hannah Rigler and her mother and sister, sometimes forged close attachments with other mothers and daughters. Sometimes the women were relatives, such as Miriam Rosenthal and her cousins. Some women, such as Cesia Brandstatter and her camp sisters, bonded with prewar friends. Others, such as Rose Meth and Esther Wajcblum, found each other in the concentration camp. "Small groups of women in the same barracks or work crews, formed 'little families' and bonded together for mutual help."[5] In the winter of 1944–1945 the Nazis collected seven pregnant Jewish women from various labor camps and brought them to Landsberg, Germany, to the Kaufering I concentration camp, where they were allowed to give birth and keep their babies.[6] The women were "attended" in childbirth by a Jewish doctor who was also a prisoner. His only equipment was hot water and a *tallit*, which he was given to use as an apron. These seven women, strangers to each other, helped each other recuperate, a stronger woman nursing the weaker women's babies, and physically and morally supported each other. All seven women and babies survived and were liberated after a death march to Dachau. Some of these women are still in touch with each other. Women who were unrelated adopted each other, called each other sisters, and sustained the relationships throughout their camp experiences and often after liberation and until today.

It is interesting to note that none of the women considers her survival a result of particular behavior or choices on her part. Some attribute their survival to the support and assistance of others: their mothers, sisters, or camp sisters. Some say it was divine intervention, and others say it was simply good luck. None considers herself heroic; each simply struggled for survival as best she could. It is important to note that the interviewees are frank in their descriptions of human behavior. Extreme behavior of the Nazis and their collaborators created intolerable conditions and behavior among the victims that reached extremes of both bestiality and saintliness. Interviewees are anxious for this aspect of the Holocaust to be known. They want the reader to know that they experienced both inexplicable horror and ineffable kindness. In order to avoid mythologizing the Holocaust, it is crucial to include all aspects of the experience as the eyewitnesses describe it.

The women stress the importance of the credibility of their testimonies. They want to be believed in spite of the unbelievable nature of their experiences. The extent to which I was able to verify and corroborate the information in the interviews is revealed in the notes, which sometimes add fascinating details to the material in the interviews. When information offered in the interview seems to contradict documented fact, the note indicates the discrepancy. Although not all material is verifiable, an interview that is generally factual and consistent with other accounts should be read as reliable testimony. All interviewees have participated in the oral history project voluntarily, and those who were alive during the editing process reviewed and approved the edited text of their interviews for this publication. Their names are used in order to give added credence to the testimonies; the interviewees want the reader to know that "this is what really happened to me."

Editing the transcripts of interviews with Holocaust survivors, whose native language is not English, poses some special challenges. The primary objective is to let the voice of the interviewee speak directly to the reader, with as little editorial intervention as possible. Traumatic portions of the narration, however, may have been expressed in the speaker's native language. The speakers often "free associate," disturbing the chronological flow of the story. The flow of the story may be interrupted with answers to questions that clarify and add more detail. In editing the transcripts I have excised interviewers' questions, restored chronological order, translated foreign language material, and moved paragraphs in order to facilitate the full description of each episode.

In preparing the material for publication I have tried to preserve as much of the original narrative as can be readily understood in the speaker's own words. Grammatical errors, which are an embarrassment to the narrator, have been corrected, and the run-on sentences that rush out in the emotional heat of the interview have been divided into more manageable segments. It should be noted that most interviewees, as they reviewed the edited transcripts, paid scrupulous attention to grammar and spelling, not wishing to appear inarticulate in English. Because of the historical and cultural weight of terminology that describes aspects of Jewish experience or of the Holocaust experience, such terminology appears in its original language, as used by the interviewees. Individual words are defined in the glossary, and phrases or sentences are defined immediately in parentheses. Where the foreign language was not intrinsic to the material it has been translated and is indistinguishable from the rest of the narrative. In each case, I have tried to preserve the voice of the interviewee, and her approval of the text would indicate that she is comfortable with the result.

Interviewers' names and the date of the interview are listed at the end of each interview. Where I was the interviewer I am listed as Bonnie Gurewitsch. That is the name by which I am known at work and in the records of the Center for Holocaust Studies and Museum of Jewish Heritage.

Editing these interviews has been a challenge and a privilege. I have been challenged to use many skills to present these oral histories as the credible testimony of reliable witnesses who have testified thirty, forty, or fifty years later to events that are seared indelibly into their memories. Knowing that each testimony is a reflection of selective memory, a composite effort of interviewer, interviewee, and interview guidelines that seek particular kinds of information, I am utterly convinced that these interviewees are relating the truth as they remember it, and I have found that this truth can be corroborated in much of its detail.

I feel privileged to have been part of the effort to record these extraordinary testimonies. It has been a privilege to meet and speak with women who have suffered great adversity and pain and yet express hope, love, and faith in humanity and God and quietly derive deep satisfaction from living productive, useful lives. These women have paid a terrible price for being Jewish; they continue to be proud and active Jews. For the interviewees, recording their oral histories was part of the experience of *Iberleben*, of physical survival. Editing this book has been my effort to share their oral histories with future generations.

Mothers, Sisters, Resisters

Mothers

Motherhood, women's most gender-determined characteristic, posed particular challenges during the Holocaust. At the simplest level, it was the mother's responsibility to keep her children alive. In a wartime situation, when consumer goods were scarce and the physical environment threatening, providing food, clothing, and shelter was a challenge to all mothers. But during the Holocaust, Nazi ideology decreed that all Jewish lives were worthless. Jewish women and children were treated as enemies of the Nazi state rather than as noncombatants. The challenge of survival for Jewish mothers and children became almost insurmountable. In the ghettos, Jewish children were sometimes specifically targeted in special children's *Aktions* in which they were rounded up and sent to their deaths. In the death camps, men and women were segregated; young children and their mothers were usually selected for immediate death. In spite of ingenuity, daring, and defiance of Nazi decrees, circumstances prevented the survival of millions of mothers and children. Sometimes geography contributed to survival, sometimes the age of the child influenced the chances for survival, and sometimes fates were determined by the nature of the particular camp to which they were sent. Occasionally roles reversed, and children took responsibility for their mothers, sometimes succeeding, but often failing to insure their survival.

The interviews in this section show how mothers faced this challenge in varying situations, with differing degrees of success, and demonstrate the overwhelming odds against the survival of Jewish children in the Holocaust. The interviews are arranged in an order that reflects an increasing degree of danger to mothers and children, from escape of occupied territory, to internment, to hiding in more or less protected circumstances, to the experiences of mothers and children in concentration camps.

Escape, the most instinctive reaction of a parent to danger, and the classic first reaction of Jews to persecution, is the theme of

Rywka Diament's interview. The Diament family's escape and survival as a unit was made possible by geography and the fortunate whim of the Swiss government, which allowed them to enter Switzerland. Had they been living in eastern Europe they would have been fatally trapped by German occupation. Rywka Diament's marriage to a poor Yiddish writer in Paris revealed a latent streak of independence in the young Polish orphan from a small town who arrived penniless in Paris to live with her brother and sister-in-law after the death of her parents. Although she clearly deferred to her husband, whose intellectual skills she admired, she assumed responsibility for her children and acted independently to bring them to the relative safety of Nice, in the Italian zone, and later to place them in a convent until arrangements could be made to smuggle the family across the border into Switzerland. There, too, she took the initiative to regain custody of the children after they were put in foster care. She benefited from the connections and reputation of her husband, but it was clearly she who managed the children's care and protection.

Rita Grunbaum was with her husband and mother when she was deported from her home in Rotterdam with her baby. The arrangements they had made to protect their child did not work out, and it was Fred Grunbaum who snatched the baby and put her on Rita's lap in the bus that took them to Westerbork. Here, too, geography and political circumstances helped to determine the survival of the Grunbaum family. As an internment camp, Westerbork had an environment that was relatively benign; it provided a subsistence diet, allowed people to use the clothing and provisions they brought along, and provided decent medical care. The Grunbaums also sought to escape from Europe, applying for entry to Palestine, then under the British Mandate. The British government, following the White Papers of 1929 and 1939, severely curtailed legal Jewish immigration to Palestine,[1] but relatives of the

Grunbaums succeeded in obtaining the valuable Palestine immigration certificates for the Grunbaum family.[2] Because they had the certificates they were not deported from Westerbork to Auschwitz, where mother's and baby's fate would have been sealed; instead, they went to the camp for exchange prisoners at Bergen Belsen, which was not yet designated a concentration camp. There the regime was more moderate than at concentration camps, and even the minimal medical care and rations were enough to sustain life. Throughout the ordeal, Rita Grunbaum, a social worker trained to observe and keep records of human behavior, focused her attention on her child, keeping a diary of the baby's physical, social, and intellectual development and recording her illnesses and her maturation for future reference in the hope of their survival. This diary of her child's development is an indication that Rita Grunbaum's role of mother was all-consuming, even in the abnormal conditions of internment. Perhaps her involvement in this traditional woman's role was a factor in sustaining her. "Women's work"—activities centering around food, children, clothing, shelter, social relations, warmth, and cleanliness—may be regarded as the only meaningful labor in a time of such dire necessity.[3] Although her husband was interned in the same camps, men and women were separated, and it was Rita who cared for her child and gave moral support to her own mother.

Escape and hiding were the tactics used by Nina Matathias and her husband in Greece. Like the Diaments, geography was in their favor. They lived in an area of Greece that was occupied by the Italians, who did not implement the Final Solution. When the Germans occupied their town of Volos, the rabbi of the community sensed the mortal danger and signaled the need to escape. The remote mountain village where they hid was very primitive; life was difficult but possible. Giving birth during a German raid, Nina was fortunate to have a healthy child and struggled to sustain him with very little and to create a Jewish household. The sight of her with her child softened the heart of a German soldier who was searching for partisans, and their lives were spared. The first thing the Matathiases did when they were liberated was to arrange for a *brit milah*, ritual circumcision, for their son in affirmation of their Jewish identity. The family is the central focus of Nina Matathias's world, and the loss of her extended family in the Holocaust is one that hurts her even today.

Pregnancy and childbirth during the Holocaust were doubly dangerous for Jewish women, who had to cope not only with wartime shortages and dangers but also with their vulnerability as Jews. Nina Matathias was fortunate to have an easy birth and the assistance of kind neighbors who did not betray her. The German soldier who did not arrest her acted instinctively, reacting emotionally to the sight of mother and infant. Nina points out that he was not Gestapo, indicating that he was not ideologically motivated to investigate who she was. Perhaps he was young or inexperienced. In Siauliai, Lithuania, pregnancy and childbirth were forbidden.[4] In Auschwitz, pregnant women were selected for death or medical experiments or were subjected to forced abortions.[5] Several interviewees describe childbirth in concentration camps, but none of the babies was allowed to live. The episode of the *Schwenger Kommando* in Landsberg, described in Miriam Rosenthal's interview, is rare.

Some Jews trapped in German-occupied territories in eastern Europe first tried escaping to Russian-held territory. Helen Foxman gave birth in such an area. She had a hemorrhage and other postpartum problems but attributes the hardships she and her husband suffered during the Communist occupation to their refugee status, not to their Jewish identities. The loss of their possessions was particularly difficult for her as a mother, leaving her and her infant with six diapers and no indoor plumbing. Like

Rywka Diament she deferred to her husband in the major decisions that they faced, but it was she who remained on the outside
while he and the child were in hiding. It was she who provided
food and made arrangements for her husband's shelter. Like the
biblical Miriam, Helen Foxman remained close to her child when
he was adopted by their Polish nursemaid. Here the vulnerability
of Jewish men is particularly apparent. Blonde, blue-eyed Mrs.
Fuksman was able to masquerade as a Polish woman, while Mr.
Fuksman was completely at the mercy of the people who were
paid to protect him; so was their little boy, whose Jewishness was
known and whose protector raised him as a devout Catholic as the
Jewish mother watched. After the war, in the United States, Mr.
Foxman once again assumed the dominant role in the family, but
Mrs. Foxman did not remain passive, working and sharing the role
of the provider and taking over his business when he could no
longer work.

Hannah Bannett and her husband also suffered first during
the Russian occupation of the eastern part of Poland. Their house
and many of their possessions were confiscated by the Russian
commissar. With their two young children, they were eventually
forced to seek refuge in a smaller town. When the Germans invaded, Hannah realized that her "Aryan" looks and fluent German
were advantages that would help her protect herself and the children. Her husband, a religious, bearded Jew, hid from the constant roundups and massacres. She maintained contact with non-
Jews and took action to protect the family. It was she, assisted by
her mother and sisters, who arranged hiding places and false documents for herself and her children, but there were interim periods
when arrangements had to be changed, when she was left alone
with the children and had to improvise safe space for them. The
images of Hannah and her two children homeless, eating sandwiches on a park bench or whiling away the daylight hours in a

movie theater, emphasize the vulnerability of a woman with children as well as the innocent picture they must have presented to strangers. As soon as she found reasonable arrangements for herself and the children, she tried to assist her husband; his arrest and death in the Cracow prison point up the lack of options for men, who could not hide their Jewish identity. Circumstances did not allow her the luxury of grieving for her husband; she had to carry on her masquerade at work, and she had to be strong for her children. Throughout the time Hannah hid her Jewish identity she was also vulnerable to the advances of the men she worked for, so she changed jobs often. Because of her religious convictions, the option of consenting to a relationship was unthinkable. She stresses that she tried to behave and dress as unobtrusively as possible to avoid calling attention to herself. Like Rita Grunbaum, caring for her children gave structure and meaning to her everyday life. Like Rywka Diament, she did things on instinct, reacting to dreams, hunches, and gut feelings. She never lost faith in God, and prayer was a significant factor in maintaining her equilibrium, even if she prayed in a church.

Edith Horowitz and Rachel Silberman are daughters who experienced the Holocaust together with their mothers. Edith was a young child and adolescent, Rachel a young woman. Both testimonies provide insight into the relationships of mothers and daughters and into the difference between experiencing the Holocaust as an individual or as part of a closely knit pair. Throughout Edith Horowitz's testimony she repeats "I had a mother" almost as a mantra. Sometimes the sentence refers to the advantage Edith had because her mother protected her. Sometimes it refers to the responsibility Edith felt for her mother. Her mother provided for her when her father was killed, smuggling and dealing on the black market. She wanted to accompany her own mother to deportation but acquiesced when her mother insisted, "You have children. You have to live." In the labor camp Edith's mother worked in the kitchen and could have arranged for Edith to work with her. Twelve-year-old Edith, in an act of adolescent rebellion that even the Holocaust did not stifle, refused, yet her mother still gave her extra bread in the morning when Edith could not stomach the soup. Thrust into the harsh reality of the slave labor factory, Edith hardly understood the nuances of crude speech and behavior among the prisoners, but she appreciated the efforts her mother made to create little "moments of reprieve" when she lit Sabbath or Ḥanukkah candles. Given a choice to stay behind and cast her lot with the non-Jewish factory workers, Edith chose to go on the forced march with her mother: "I couldn't run. I had a mother, and my mother didn't want to." Her bond with her mother was her most precious advantage; nothing could sever it. Throughout the experience her mother tried to shelter Edith from immoral behavior, not relinquishing prewar standards. Neither volunteered to go with the officers in Nordhausen who demanded company. In the cattle car on the way to Mauthausen, another woman encouraged her daughter to do what she could to obtain the favor of the male *Kapo*. Edith's mother told her not to look, and when another *Kapo* offered to help Edith escape with him, her mother reminded her that being under a man's protection meant giving in to his demands. In Italy Edith's mother protected her from an unsuitable marriage proposal. Edith finally did separate from her mother to join a Zionist group traveling to Palestine and was interned with them by the British on Cyprus. By then she was seventeen and finally started maturing physically. When her mother, in Palestine, learned that Edith was in Cyprus, she resumed the role of provider, sending her a package with soap and a brassiere, knowing instinctively what her daughter must need. Edith recognizes that in having her mother she had a precious advantage in the Holocaust; she also recognizes that she did not have a childhood.

She has not come to terms with this, although she has established her own family. The Holocaust is with her always. Edith has another interesting insight into the experiences of women. It seems to her that women, because of their domestic skills, coped somewhat better than men: "The men were unshaven, filthy, with torn clothes. A woman did whatever she could; she would sew her clothes together. . . . But the men, it was pitiful."[6]

Rachel Silberman was older and more mature than Edith. She was left alone with her mother and sister and other female relatives in Siauliai, Lithuania, when the men in their family were arrested soon after the German occupation in June 1941. She was traumatized by the loss of her brother's children in the children's *Aktion* of November 5, 1943, but could not properly grieve for them because she had to continue working at various forced labor assignments. Rachel's mother chose to remain in the ghetto rather than escape to the forests because she wanted to be there when her daughters returned. The three women were deported together when their ghetto was liquidated, and their consecutive numbers attest to their physical closeness when they were given concentration camp numbers. Like Edith Horowitz, Rachel describes the shock of undressing in front of German men and the horror of the internal examination inflicted on her fourteen-year-old sister. Rachel describes how her mother and other "older" women kept up the spirits of the other women prisoners, drawing on traditional Jewish resources and reminding the women of miracles that happened to Jews in the past, suggesting that there would be continued miracles for them as well. Rachel's mother kept track of the Jewish calendar in order to determine the date of *Yom Kippur*, the holiest day of the year. Learning of an error in her calculation, Rachel's mother became bitter and disillusioned at the thought that they might have eaten on that holy fast day, thus negating what was for her an act of spiritual resistance to the dehumaniza-

tion process. In spite of their success in staying together and supporting each other in several camps, Rachel and her sister were unable to protect their mother from the murderous blows of the German guard who fatally beat her. Her death was particularly painful
because it came just moments before liberation, and it underlines
the basic tragedy of the Holocaust, that regardless of the best efforts of people to resist their fates, Jews were at the mercy of their
murderers.

Brandla Small also resisted the fate that was determined for
her child. Hiding with her child during the infamous *Gehsperre
Aktion* in the Lodz ghetto, in which children and the elderly were
selected and deported to their deaths, Brandla prevented her
daughter's deportation. She hid her after the *Aktion* as well to
avoid the prying questions and enmity of those whose children
were taken. After her husband was caught in an *Aktion* Brandla
had to provide for her child alone. In order to qualify for food rations, she did piecework at home, scrounging for some of the supplies like the Children of Israel during their slavery in Egypt. But
all her efforts and suffering in the ghetto were in vain. Her daughter was snatched from her arms at the Auschwitz arrival platform,
and in Auschwitz children were automatically sent to the gas
chambers. Although she rebuilt her life after the Holocaust, remar-
rying and raising a new family that brings her much satisfaction,
Brandla is still searching for her little girl, keeping track of the
years, missed birthdays, and the child's unfulfilled potential. The
child is still with Brandla, the pain of her loss still fresh, mourning
unresolved, motherhood thwarted.

Rywka Diament

Rywka Diament grew up in the small town of Konin, Poland. She was the youngest of seven children; her father[1] was a melamed, a religious studies teacher for young children. The family was strictly Orthodox and quite poor. Although Rywka's formal education stopped when she was fourteen and one-half, she was a voracious reader, patronizing the Jewish libraries in town[2] and continuing her education on her own. In 1927 both her parents died within ten weeks of each other, and Rywka, at nineteen, was left alone. Her older siblings decided that she should join a brother and his family in Paris, and she arrived there, penniless, in 1928.

Life with her brother and sister-in-law was not easy. She quickly found work doing hand finishing in a garment factory and tried to withstand constant pressure from her sister-in-law to choose a suitable husband from the candidates whom she presented. When she was introduced by a friend to Zajwel Diament, a Yiddish writer, whose intellectual interests were compatible with her own, she married him despite her sister-in-law's disapproval.

The newlyweds were poor but happy. They started their own garment business and persuaded their landlord to let them live on the premises to save the expense of paying a second rent. Rywka was content within the circle of Yiddish writers who were their friends and associates. Her husband had a story published in a Yiddish newspaper; Rywka served as his editor. Their son Henri was born in 1933, and their son Paul was born in 1938.

When World War II began Rywka was traumatized by the need to spend nights in a bomb shelter with her children. Her husband arranged for her to be evacuated from Paris to St. Leger des Vignes, in central France, with other women and children. He remained in Paris and volunteered for the French army, but because he was a Polish citizen he was referred to the Polish army, where he worked as a carpenter. Even in

St. Leger des Vignes Rywka felt insecure, and after a year her husband
sent a friend to help her return to Paris. There they were assisted finan-
cially by the Kehillah, which gave them a stipend because Mr. Diament
was a Yiddish writer. In May 1941 the first of many roundups of Jews oc-
curred. Rywka's brother and Mr. Diament went into hiding, afraid that
they would be caught and interned with other Jewish men who were not
French citizens.

In the spring of 1941 Mr. Diament was called to go to a labor camp.
His sister-in-law helped him make contact with a French mailman who
belonged to the Resistance. With their assistance Mr. Diament escaped
over the Pyrenees and then crossed into the Free Zone of France, to
Nice, then under Italian occupation, where there was a community of
Jewish refugees and Yiddish writers.[3] Mr. Diament immediately wrote to
his wife and urged her to come to Nice. Her friends thought he was
crazy. "Who would take women and children?" they asked, and advised
her to stay home and not to travel, which was more dangerous. Rywka
enlisted the assistance of the head of the Kehillah, who gave her some
money, and she sent her husband's sewing machine to Nice so he could
earn some money with it.

I felt it was my destiny, and I started to prepare for the trip to go to my
husband. I went to someone who helped people cross to the Free Zone,
and I told him I would pay him well. He asked me how old my children
were, and when I told him he said, "I can't do it for your small child. Your
older son will understand, but not the baby. If he starts to cry, the whole
group will go to a concentration camp. I can't do it. The travel will not be
in a pullman; it is very exhausting, and if the child cries you know what
will happen." Paul was then two and one-half years old. The man refused,
but he gave me the address of a French lady who he said would do it another way.

I dressed the children very nicely, and I put a colored kerchief on my
head so I wouldn't be recognized. We traveled by train. I had to provide food
for the children. I went to a cafe and asked for milk for the children; the
people understood very well what was going on, but they were helpful. When
I came to the French lady's address she wasn't home. I waited for her. It was
five o'clock in the evening; I couldn't go to a hotel, I couldn't go any place.
Finally she came. She said, "Maybe it's still possible today. There are eleven
kilometers to walk in a forest. It will be dark. If they don't recognize me

because of the dark, they will shoot me." There was no electricity because of the blackout. I said, "Let's go, let's go." She gave me her baby's carriage for Paul, and then she said I was not dressed like a peasant, so she gave me some used clothing to put on over my clothes, and she said we would go.

She said, "I will keep a little distance from you. If I see that the Germans are near, I will signal to you to go quickly, deeper into the forest, and I will not acknowledge you at all. But let's hope that it will be OK." So we all marched all those kilometers. It was in the fresh air, in the forest. Paul was happy because he was sitting in the carriage; Henri understood everything, and he was excited and didn't complain, and so we arrived. When there was only one-half a kilometer more to go, she said, "I am not going with you to the end. You go by yourself because it is dark already." I offered her an umbrella that I had, but she said, "I don't want to take even this from you." She told me to go straight, and I would be in the Free Zone, where I would find the Underground people. I should identify myself to them, and they would give me a place to sleep.

When I arrived there with the children I found a group of Jewish Scouts.[4] They were all tired from their day's activities. There were also other refugees like myself. The Scout leader gave the children milk and didn't ask for money. We were safe there, but the next day we had to take a bus and go to Lyon, further into the zone. There was still the danger of French collaborators checking the bus for foreigners. Paul was on my lap, and Henri was next to me, and I told him not to talk to me because of my poor accent. At one point a *gendarme* asked the driver if there were strangers on the bus. The driver told him no, and when he asked, "Are you sure?" he said, "You can go in and check." The *gendarme* asked him, "Why did you take so many people?" and he said, "I took as many as were waiting for the bus."

At Lyon we took a train toward Nice. My husband told me to take the train to Antibes, one station before Nice.[5] He met us there; we arrived safely, and we took a taxi to his hotel in Nice. It was the first time we saw the Mediterranean Sea; it was blue. All of us slept in one big bed that night. There were lots of mosquitoes; we covered ourselves with a net for protection.

The next day we started to look for a place to live because it was dangerous for four people to stay in a hotel room. First we went to a Jewish writer and his wife, and we stayed with them. It was hard to get food. You had to buy it on the black market. Legally you could only get what was allowed on your ration cards. The writer's wife went to the *Kehillah* to ask them to help us.[6] They fed us, and they helped us find an empty apartment belonging to tourists who did not come during wartime.[7] We got an apartment upstairs in a very nice villa, the home of a former Russian prince who had escaped from the Russian Revolution. In the same house there was a Jewish musician, a violinist. Henri used to go to his room to see his instruments; he was very interested. We bought Henri a violin, and the musician started teaching him. We paid him in food; I cooked for him. Every month you could get a portion of wine. I used to give my wine to the bakery, and the baker gave me bread, so I had enough to give the musician. My husband worked as a tailor in order to make a living. It was very hard work for him, especially the ironing. He got sick. There was not enough food. The little one had his glass of milk; I tried my best for the child. I went to a field to dig out some carrots, which I exchanged for other food. Once one of the nuns from the nearby church gave us eggs; she helped us later, too, knowing that we were Jews.

For two years we were under Italian occupation. My husband wrote essays and poetry. His book, *Under the Swastika*, was published in Paris later, when we were in Switzerland. All the Jewish writers met in the school. Everybody read from his writings. My husband was part of it, one of the organizers of the group. We could listen to the English radio, learning about concentration camps and about the Germans liquidating the Jews. Everyone who had a chance listened to the radio, although it was forbidden. We used to cover it and listen at night. My husband reported to the other Jewish writers what he heard on the British radio about the extermination of the Jews. The writer Vevyorka reacted: "Please stop telling those kinds of stories. It is unbelievable that Jews are being exterminated." This Vevyorka and his entire family were caught by the Germans and taken to a concentration camp. All of them perished.

In September 1943 we saw that the Italians were retreating.[8] The *Kehillah* and the Scouts suggested that we go to Switzerland.[9] The Scouts gave us false French identity cards in the name of Blanc, which we could use to travel in France.[10] I had to learn all the details of our false identity by heart. We decided not to tell Henri to avoid tension in the child. We believed that if we succeeded in crossing the border to Switzerland no one would question him.[11]

When the Germans first came in we prepared a hiding place, which we used for four weeks. Before we decided to try to get to Switzerland we decided that whatever happened to us, we wanted the children to be safe, so I dressed them nicely and took them to the convent. I didn't ask in advance; I just took the children with me in a *fiacre* to the convent. The nun said that they could take our children for a while because the children who were usually there were still on vacation. When I told the nun that it was a temporary arrangement until we could take the children with us to Switzerland, she said, "I can understand that you are going to take a risk for your husband and yourself, but how can you expose the children to such danger?" I said, "I hope it will be good." "From where do you have this conviction that it will be good?" I said that my husband had had a dream in which his father came to him and told him to take road number 44. The dream was a sign that we should go, and I believed that we would succeed. She said, "Your father-in-law was probably a good Catholic!" [Laughing] "Excuse me," I said, "He was a very good Jew!" I was convinced that we would arrive safely.

Paul was very unhappy about the separation. Henri was happy and excited; for him it was an adventure. After ten days we had our false papers, and we took the children out of the convent. *Erev Yom-Kippur*[12] I lit the candles before *Kol Nidrei,* and I prayed for our safe arrival in Switzerland. On the train my husband refused to sit with us. He was afraid that if he was caught they would take us, too. I called him over, and I said, "Sit with us. Whatever happens to you will happen to us." The train stopped often because of bombing, and the lights went off.[13]

We arrived in Annemasse.[14] There we were told that we could not cross the border that day. We waited in a cafe that was full of Germans, so the owner put us in a storage room. Later, we started walking toward the border.[15] We were guided by some Jews who knew how to smuggle across the border. They walked in front of us, and we had to follow them. We didn't have good shoes; our feet were wet,[16] but we continued to follow them. My husband walked ahead with Henri, and I walked with Paul. My husband returned to see what was happening with me and took Paul in his hands and helped me move forward. We did not know where we were. The Swiss soldiers said, "This is Switzerland; you can't enter." But we said we were escaping from real danger, so they lifted the barbed wire and helped us cross the border.[17]

They took us to a police station, and they asked us who we were. I asked them to give us scissors so we could cut open our coats and take out our real papers.[18] They separated the men from the women and children and started asking questions. They interviewed us separately, but our answers were the same, mine and my husband's. They gave us something to drink and some food and took us to a refugee camp.[19] Henri was with my husband, with the men, and Paul was with me, with the women. We slept on straw, no covers; they didn't give us anything. Men and women were also separated for eating while they continued to investigate us.[20] They moved us to three or four refugee camps,[21] and finally my husband was assisted by a professor from the University of Geneva who knew him as a writer. We were released because of my husband's poor health.

Three weeks later my husband had a heart attack and was in the hospital for seven weeks. He had the best doctors, and the professor used to visit him. About two weeks after we arrived in Switzerland the children had to leave us; they were sent to foster families. The *Kehillah* asked the local Swiss Jews to take care of the refugee children, but they refused to take them, so the government appealed to the non-Jews to take Jewish children, promising that the refugees and their children would leave Switzerland immediately after the war. So our children had to stay with *goyim*. We wanted Henri to stay with a family where there was a musician because he played the violin. He went to a family where the father was a professor of music at the university. But the girls in that family didn't treat him nicely. They used to torment him: "You are a refugee child, you are so poor, you have nothing, what will happen to you? You will be a beggar near a church!"[22]

Paul refused to leave us, but we explained to him that he must. I took him to the train that would take him from Geneva to Basel. He had a placard around his neck with an address and his name. There were other Jewish refugee children there and some supervisors. Paul was smiling but sad. He asked me, "When will we be together again?" I said, "Very soon, very soon." He wanted me to tell him how many days it would be. When the train whistled Paul became white as paper. I felt very bad and was assisted by two refugees from our camp to overcome the pain of separation from my child.

After my husband was released from the hospital he was told that we were free to leave the camp. The professor found us an apartment in Geneva and gave us some old furniture: a desk; chairs; a wide, comfortable sofa that three of us could sleep on; and a little bed for Paul. The apartment had a kitchen and an additional small room. The Joint[23] paid the rent.

As soon as my husband left the hospital I went to the authorities and made efforts to get my children back. They said that as long as the children were with the foster families they didn't have to pay; if the children were with us they would have to give us money. In fact, the money came from the Joint, not from the Swiss government.

Once my husband had to give a speech in Basel, so we visited the children together. We found out that the children had the right to go to a rabbi for religious studies. Once a week they used to give Paul money for the train, and they sent him by himself to the rabbi. Once, when my husband was in Basel he went to the train stop, hoping to see Paul. He heard a child crying and recognized Paul's voice. He took the child in his arms and kissed him, and Paul told him that he was crying because he lost his money. My husband took him back to the foster family. They treated Paul very nicely.

This unexpected meeting of my husband with the crying child was, for us, a sign from God. I fought to get the children back. I told the authorities that Henri must join us, that they must consider the dangerous escape that we made, and that at his age we must take care of his education. Henri came back to us after a year, and Paul came back after fourteen months. Henri went to *ḥeder*, but he didn't learn too much there. There was much assimilation in Switzerland. We became more religious, going to *shul* on *yomim tovim* and fasting on *Yom Kippur*. It was difficult to be religious; I promised myself that as soon as we got to America we would completely change our lifestyle.

Henri and Paul attended Swiss schools. At the end of the war Rywka was devastated to learn of the fate of the Jews in the Holocaust. Except for the brother who lived in Paris, none of her family survived. The Diament family arrived in the United States in July 1948, sponsored by the Joint. Mr. and Mrs. Diament both worked in the garment industry. After a number of years, in poor health, Mr. Diament left the garment industry and worked on the Yiddish Lexicon *in New York. He died in 1963. Henri is now a professor of French and linguistics; Paul is a professor of electrical engineering. Rywka Diament has four grandchildren and four great-grandchildren.*

—Interviewed by Bonnie Gurewitsch, May 4, 1988, and May 10, 1988. Yiddish portions of the interview translated by J. Pery.

Rita Grunbaum

When World War II began Rita and Manfred Grunbaum were living in Rotterdam, the Netherlands. Rita was a social worker; Fred was a vice-president in an export-import business. Their daughter, Dorien, was born in 1942.

At midnight on September 29, 1943,[1] the night before *erev Rosh Hashanah*, the bell rang. Two German SS and one Dutch Nazi were at the door.[2] We had thirty minutes to get ready. We had been prepared for the past six months; rucksack and suitcase were packed. Then Fred found out that Dorien was not on the list. What to do? She was thirteen months old. We could not leave her with our neighbors; that would have jeopardized them. We decided to take her with us. I carried her through the dark night surrounded by three Nazis. All our friends were there at the German headquarters. It was the roundup of the last remaining Dutch Jews. Fred persuaded the commander to allow some Gentile ladies who had been arrested by mistake to take Dorien with them when they were released because she was not on the deportation list. Fred gave the ladies the address of our very close Gentile friends who would take care of Dorien. We left Dorien in her stroller and proceeded to the waiting bus. I was numb, letting Fred make the decisions. Then, just when the bus was about to leave, Fred ran out to look once more at Dorien, and there she was, sitting in her stroller, surrounded by all those SS men, screaming at the top of her lungs. Fred grabbed her and took her with him and put her on my lap. What a relief. It was the best thing we could have done. We often talked later about what went through his mind that night, the concern for us and what the future had in store for us. Fortunately, we did not know. From then on, we always said, "It cannot get any worse," but it got worse until the very end.

We were sent to Westerbork, one of the Dutch concentration camps, also a transit camp for deportation to Poland.[3] Men and women were separated [in different rooms] but lived in the same barracks. Mothers with children under three did not have to work, so I was exempted.[4] My mother and Fred had to work. Tuesday was a day of great anxiety. It was the day when two to three thousand people were transported to Poland packed together in cattle cars. You never knew who would be selected, but as soon as the transport left, people resumed their "normal" lives. The fight for survival became the law. We knew that families were separated after arrival in Poland. It was not until a year later that we learned what really was going on.[5]

[On November 13 Dorien became very sick.[6] She had a temperature for several days; it went higher and higher until that night it was 103. The doctor[7] checked her three times for polio, which had been diagnosed three days earlier in several cases.[8] Luckily, all her reflexes were alright. Two days later a running ear. One week later, on November 22, they had to puncture her left ear.[9] Now, on December 12, both ears are still running, but Dorien is as active as ever. She lost a lot of weight but gained it all back. Dorien now walks behind the stroller and between two people. She also got two molars during this time.]

[In January 1944 I was asked to take care of the household of Dr. Biale, who lived in a little house by himself.[10] The woman who took care of it was put on transport. This was good for Dorien, who started to walk much better, holding on to the furniture. After a few days she did not mind not seeing me when I was in the kitchen and she in the living room. It was a much more normal way of life. Unfortunately, it soon became too much for me, and I had to stop.]

[On February 4 suddenly again a high fever. Dorien had had a cold for quite a while. At night in the barrack Dr. Benavante[11] pierced both of her eardrums. The next morning the temperature was normal, but the ears were not running. Dr. Benavante does not examine anymore because he is leaving on transport on Tuesday. The temperature remains normal; so do the ears. At the same time Dorien has diarrhea, which has caused her to lose one pound in three weeks. That is a pity because she becomes weaker and walks less well. Before that she gained regularly. She now has four molars and four cutting teeth.]

On February 14, 1944, we were sent in a long train to Bergen Belsen.[12] The minute we got into the train Dorien developed an ear infection. [Her right ear is running. She cries a lot because of the pain and the nervous tension in the train. The nurse came to clean the ear and gave me cotton and peroxide, which ran out during the journey. Dorien ate well and fell asleep, changing between my lap and Fred's. She slept until 6 A.M., when we arrived in Celle.[13]]

People were nervous, not knowing what to expect. The welcome was not very encouraging. Many SS officers with police dogs were at the station.[14] Most people had to walk the ten kilometers to the camp. [It was very cold, rain and snow. Mothers with children and old people were allowed to ride in trucks to our destination. When we arrived, Dorien was deposited roughly on the ground. It was terribly cold the whole day; the stove was without fire, and only at night were we given hot soup.]

Men and women lived in separate barracks.[15] At first we were one to a bed. We slept on straw mattresses in wooden bunks two and three high. Each barrack had a huge iron stove to try to keep the people warm and to help dry clothes and warm food. [Fred and Mother and most of this transport have to live in quarantine. We speak to each other through barbed wire. During the next few days the weather becomes radiant, but we can't get the children warm. Dorien eats like a woodcutter, two pieces of bread and hot cereal in the morning, at noon a good dinner, and in the evening again two or three sandwiches with hot cereal. You can see her gain weight. She is not very happy; she screams when I have to leave, until she befriends Marguerite Reiss, a six-month-old baby, and her mother, Yvonne. Things are now improving, but she is not as happy as in Westerbork.[16]]

As long as possible we ate our evening meals together until Fred was too weak to walk. Fortunately, I was able to see him every day and help him. Until then he did all kinds of work: carried the heavy food containers, dug ditches, painted, and for a while was a night watchman. Once a *Kapo* beat Fred up severely because he did not perform fast enough. Fred was terribly angry that he couldn't hit back. That was even worse than the blow.

Except for mothers with children under three and the sick, everyone else had to stand *Appell* every morning at 6 A.M. and every evening after work.[17] It was a counting of heads. The inmates had to stand in a big field, rain or shine, in the bitter cold, and under the burning sun. When the Germans were in a bad mood this sometimes went on for ten hours.

In March 1944 Dorien came down with pneumonia. The doctor wanted her to be cared for in a hospital there. We agreed with this if I were allowed to go along to take care of her myself. On the first night in the hospital a baby died in the same room. It made me feel terrible that I could not have saved her. Dorien was quite sick and lost a lot of weight, but with the proper medication she recovered soon. The quiet of the hospital and the rest from the very noisy barrack with hundreds of people was good for both of us. Those two weeks were like a vacation. Dorien's friends would parade in front of the window, which delighted her.

[April 13, 1944. Today Dorien could sit on the table in the sun, nice and warm. She loves to get out of bed for a little while, but she is not yet allowed to walk. We progress very slowly and carefully, trying not to overdo it, taking into account the many deaths due to pneumonia. Dorien now knows how to drink from a cup when she feels like it, which means when she is thirsty. Otherwise she takes it from a spoon.]

[She starts having temper tantrums again. She knows, of course, that here in the hospital I cannot let her scream. She does not like hot cereal made with bread and gets very angry when I try to make her eat it. Best of all she likes dinner at noon; she eats part of it before her nap and the rest after her nap. I will start toilet training her again, of course on the potty.[18] Before she became sick she did her bowel movement for two weeks on the potty, and often wee-wee. Now we have to start all over again.]

[April 14, 1944. Dorien is doing well. She sits in her bed and plays while she sings. She is her own self; she can concentrate on her toys. She plays for the first time with toy animals. She likes the little babies and is very friendly with everybody, especially with the *Sanitater*. Other people have told me this, because when he comes I have to be in our barrack for roll call.]

[April 25, 1944. Dorien has been out of the hospital for a week, suddenly discharged although she had not yet been out of bed. She immediately adjusted well in the barrack, walks around holding on, plays with the other children. Sometimes she will stand by herself and the other day even took a few steps by herself. She understands much more; she will carry out a request. One can see that she has grown mentally during her illness. She now understands very well when I put her on the potty; she will do most of her duties on it when I watch her carefully. She drinks regularly now out of a cup, eats a lot, everything, even pea soup. She has gained well in this one week.]

[Yesterday she started singing the song Mrs. Lehman taught her; she sang it completely in tune. She plays very nicely with Marguerite, as if she were her younger sister. They laugh together, sing together, and fight together. When Dorien hits her, Marguerite laughs.]

[The big fontanel is not yet closed; it takes a long time. She also has a large tummy. Let's hope that all will be taken care of later!]

[May 1, 1944. This week Dorien did her bowel movements on the potty. I gave her a piece of paper. She took it and wiped herself.]

It was remarkable that in those extraordinary circumstances most children seemed to develop normally. She had many friends and lots of fun of sorts. Only in the morning, when the *Kapo* came for barrack inspection with his whistle and shouted *"Achtung!"* did she become frightened. When the barrack leader gave her her whistle to blow, she was able to overcome this fright. The first word she spoke was *Achtung*. That summer Dorien suddenly started to walk by herself and to speak full sentences.

There were highlights, too, like the beautiful sunsets on the wide heather fields. It made you feel miles and miles away from the camp. A concert was given during Ḥanukkah week in the Hungarian[19] barrack on a Sunday afternoon. I was so hungry for music that I went over myself. It was festive. The only thing I remember of the program was the "Ave Maria" sung by a young woman I knew from Rotterdam. She sang it as an encore. It was so breathtakingly beautiful that I still cannot hear it today without tears. She was sent to Auschwitz and never came back.

In the spring and summer of 1944 the prisoner population of Bergen Belsen gradually increased, and with the arrival of a new commandant, Josef Kramer, on December 2, 1944, it was formally classified as a concentration camp. Kramer, who had been the commandant of Auschwitz, instituted a harsh and punitive regime, and as large transports of prisoners from other camps were sent to Belsen, conditions deteriorated and became chaotic.

Where 120 people had lived in one barrack, there were now 500. We had to change barracks many times, in the end carrying our own bunkbeds, and usually this had to be done in one hour. The impossible always became possible. We used to say, "It cannot become worse," but it did. In the beginning, food was adequate, and there were extra rations for the children. Now it was one piece of bread a day and one pint of water containing turnips and potato peels, a so-called soup. People became weaker and weaker. Hunger became the enemy.

We learned to recognize the true nature of people. I saw with my own eyes how men came sneaking around when their wives and children were asleep to steal their bread ration.[20] Women stole from their neighbors. Some people became saints while others turned into beasts. Some gave up. When that happened you were sure they would die within days. Many friendships were formed. In order to fight hunger and the thought of food, professionals started to give lectures. Fred heard talks on many interesting topics, especially Jewish subjects.[21] In the women's barracks many recipes were exchanged and collected.

In January 1945 Red Cross packages were distributed. We received three packages sent by our relatives in Mexico.[22] They were invaluable in content as well as in emotional support. It was good to know that there were people outside who cared.

During those years I learned what it meant to be an Orthodox Jew. I observed from close by the fervor with which services were conducted, the intense trust and belief in God. There was a young schoolteacher from North Africa who came to Bergen Belsen with several hundred North African Jews.[23] His name was Labi. He and his people lived like their forefathers a thousand years ago. Their religion taught them that one was not allowed to eat certain foods. Our daily soup sometimes contained small pieces of horse-meat, one of the things one was not allowed to eat, so Labi would not eat that soup. Nobody could convince him to eat it in order to survive. He said it was forbidden; this was the law. He lived by the law and would not disobey, no matter what happened. He would only do what was right.

We celebrated the Holy Days. The tables were covered with white sheets. Twice, a *seder* was conducted in every barrack.[24] The first year the rabbis gave permission to eat bread instead of *matzot*, but many would not hear of it. The second year there was no more food and no bread either. So *matzah* was made from flour and water from the kitchen, a little piece for each. People were all around the table or on the bunk beds, low and high, listening to the *Haggadah*. The whole scene was lit by two candles. We understood when we were told that our ancestors were slaves. We were slaves now, and God would save us from our enemies. History had become reality.

After January 1945 most people were too weak to work. My mother now lived in the old-age barrack where people died one after the other. Death was everywhere. It came almost as a friend, as a relief, yet we continued to fight. Hygienic conditions were at their lowest point; people could no longer walk to the outdoor latrine. In the morning everything had to be cleaned up before the ten o'clock inspection. I will spare you the horror of further details.[25]

At this time my mother said to me, "I can't anymore; I can count on my fingers how many more days I will live." I bawled her out, "We came here together, and we will go home together!" and this gave her the strength to hold on.

On April 9, 1945, the Grunbaums were put on a transport that was headed for Theresienstadt,[26] but they never reached it. After traveling for two weeks the train reached Troebitz, Germany, where the SS disappeared, and the prisoners were liberated by the Russians. The Grunbaums' joy was short-lived, for first Rita and then Fred became ill with spotted typhoid fever. Dorien was cared for by friends while her parents were ill. On July 1, 1945, Rita, Fred, Dorien, and Rita's mother arrived in Maastricht, Netherlands, on an ambulance train. Their dear Dutch friend, Gerrit, met them and invited them into his home to stay until they recuperated and they could live independently. The Grunbaums immigrated to the United States in 1946. Rita worked as a freelance photographer and then as a social worker until her retirement.

What have I learned from these years? That a person can withstand much more than you can imagine. That even in your darkest moments there are always some bright spots. We always found something to laugh about. The tremendous respect instilled in me for Orthodox Jews. To make the best of every day, and I've done that very consciously ever after. Above all, that at certain moments in our lives things happen that we cannot comprehend, but we have to accept them without questioning.

—*Interviewed by Ruth Bloch, March 29, 1979*

Nina Matathias

Nina Matathias was born in Salonika, Greece, in 1920. Her family was traditionally observant. Like most Sephardic Jews in Salonika, the men attended synagogue on Shabbat and holidays, and Shabbat and kashrut were observed at home. Nina joined a Zionist organization as a teenager and attended a Greek high school where she was the only Jewish student. Nina's father was disabled by arthritis. Nina was the oldest of the five children in the family, and she and her sister Mathilda worked in a factory to support the family. Although she never personally experienced anti-Semitism, Nina describes a pattern of persecution of Jews in Salonika in the 1930s that made her feel insecure.[1]

I had no social life. *Nothing, nothing.* We did not have enough to eat and to wear, certainly not enough to have a social life. You don't know what it meant to live in Greece. Do you see how the African people suffer now? We suffered so much; we saw people dying of hunger in the streets; they used to pick up the corpses like you pick up the garbage here. Many, many families were in our situation. They had to work very hard just to have enough to eat. In Salonika there were very, very rich Jews and very poor. The middle class had it worst of all. We had a Jewish community center, *Le Communita*, that took care of the poor people. If you went there and said, "I'm poor, I don't have this, I don't have that," they used to give you a home to live in, some kind of assistance. But we were from a very good family. In those years you didn't go begging. You had pride; you suffered, and you didn't ask for anything.

Before the war we heard what was happening in Berlin, with Germans forcing Jews to sweep the streets or beating them, and we heard about *Kristallnacht.* We read all these things in the newspaper. The government of Greece sympathized with the Germans at that time, so we were afraid. We were expecting something to happen to us in Greece too. But even if someone had warned us, we had no means to leave, to run away. With what? We could go to our relatives in another city, but we had no money for the train or to take something with us.

On a very hot day in July, the Germans came in and ordered all the Jewish men to assemble in a square.[2] These Jews had to stand there for hours. Not to move at all. If they tried to move or to scratch or to mop the sweat from their faces, the Germans beat them, sent the dogs after them. The Jews suffered a lot. A couple of weeks later they ordered all the able-bodied men to report to work.[3] They sent the Jews to work in the street, fixing the railroad. Many of those Jews died at that time because they were not accustomed to that kind of work.

My sister Mathilda and I continued to work. My brothers were young. One brother was fourteen at that time, and the other was nine. My father was an old man, fifty years old, not in this category to go to work. Still, we were afraid; we felt sorry for our friends, for our relatives. But we didn't know what to do. We had no money, nothing.

We stayed in Salonika until I got married, in September 1942. My husband was from Volos,[4] near Trikala, south of Salonika. This part of Greece was occupied by the Italians.[5] I had a wedding in the bigger synagogue in Salonika, in a beautiful synagogue. My husband paid for everything: for my gown, for everything, because my family had no money. After the wedding we stayed one week in Salonika, and then we left, and I never saw my parents again.

In the beginning we corresponded. Three months after my wedding, my sister-in-law was preparing to get married, and I sent for my sister Maddy (Mathilda) to come to the wedding. So she came to Volos for the wedding, and that was how she survived. After the wedding was finished, my father wrote us a letter saying, "We are very sick in fear, don't let Maddy come back because she's going to catch the disease." So we understood, and we kept her with us.[6]

We knew what was happening in Salonika because my husband was friends with people who worked on the railroad. We sent one person to try to find my family, and he arranged to bring them to Volos on the next train, but by the time he got there all the Jews were concentrated in the ghetto, and my family couldn't move from Salonika.[7] They couldn't go out anymore. My mother gave him her jewelry to give to my sister, that's all. After that we didn't know what happened to them until the end of the war. We tried to send a letter; we tried to send packages because they said they needed warm clothes, matches, candles, but we didn't know if they received those things or not.

Our friend said he didn't find anybody at my family's address, but he left the package that we sent with him. We didn't know if it was true or if he just took the package. In those days you didn't ask too much. You were afraid maybe he would do something bad to you, you know?

In Volos we lived well under the Italians; the whole region had a curfew, but the Italians didn't bother the Jews. But in March 1943, when we learned about the Jews in Salonika, we were afraid.[8] We went to the mountains right away.

We went to a small village in the mountains called Ios Lavrendios, St. Lavrendios. One Jewish family in this village was from Salonika. One or two other Jewish families were from Volos. Many Jews didn't leave Volos when we left. When the Germans came in, they went to Rabbi Moshe Pessah and asked him for the names of the Jews.[9] He immediately sent a message to each family, "Leave Volos because I'm leaving too. If you stay, you're going to be caught by the Germans." Because of that, most of the Jews of Volos survived. Rabbi Pessah was a very, very wise man.

We rented a room, and we lived in Ios Lavrendios. My husband used to go down to Volos to buy things and sell them to the peasants in the villages to make a living. We didn't have plenty, but we had enough to eat. There were other Jews in the village who escaped there just like we did. The local people were all Greeks, but they hid us. By that time, I had my first child.

It was December 3, 1943, about ten o'clock at night. It was snowing; it was very cold. As I was giving birth to my son, the village people came running and crying, "The Germans are coming, the Germans are coming!"[10] So we ran a few meters out of the village, and we found a little hiding place, and we stayed over there. I was screaming with the pains, and a neighbor was with me, and she said, "Don't worry, don't worry, we are here. Just hold my arm. Squeeze my arm when you have the pains." I was screaming, just holding on and making the arm of this lady black and blue until my son was born. My husband was present with his scissors, and he cut the umbilical cord. Thank God nothing happened.

Everybody tried to help at that time with blankets and everything. When they called, "The Germans are coming," nobody thought about anything but their own lives. Nobody tried to take anything. We just ran. After a couple of hours we came back, with an infant. I had so much pain. . . . I was not myself. I thought it was only a bad dream, you know? Afterward, when you think of what you went through, you think, "Me, I did this?" But at the time, you don't think. One, two, three, you do things without knowing. Sometimes they say, "This person is a hero," but circumstances make you a hero even if you don't want to be one.

No one helped me give birth; he came out by himself. Thank God for that, no problem. We had no means to make a *bris*. After eleven months, when we were liberated, we came down to Volos, and we had the *bris*.[11]

We were aware of the Jewish holidays. My husband used to have two holy books with him; he carried these books with him all the time. My husband is very religious even now. But then, we managed as well as we could. We knew when it was *Shabbat*, so we didn't cook, we didn't clean. That's all. We couldn't observe anything. We had no candles, nothing. We had no sugar, but in the village they used to make like a maple syrup. We used this to make a little cake with flour, not with almonds or walnuts, just things that grew in the village, something to say this is our holiday so we should not forget.[12]

Each Jewish family tried to keep to itself; we did not want to show that there were too many Jews in one village. The first year, when we were up there in the mountains, an old man said, "We have to get together and read from the *Torah*." That first year it was not so bad. They gathered together to read without a *sefer* or anything else, just to be together. On *Yom Kippur* each one stayed home. We fasted, that's all.

The first year we were in hiding we were able to go down to Volos and buy flour, and we made our own *matzah* for Passover. But the second year was very, very bad because of the Germans. They used to come to the villages to look for Jews or for partisans, and they came on Passover. My husband and his brother flew out of the village, and my brother-in-law was hit by a German bullet, but thank God the bullet wound was not so bad.

It was not possible for Jewish women to go to the *mikvah*.[13] Where would we go? We tried, after we took a bath, to put cold water on.[14] It was not easy even to take a bath at that time because we didn't have bathrooms, we didn't have showers, we didn't have anything. We had to warm the water and put a big washtub in the middle of the room, and we could wash ourselves, that's all. Primitive. Even when we were in our homes, we didn't have bathrooms with baths. Even to wash dishes we had to warm the water. For that reason there was not too much time for socializing. Only the very, very rich people had these luxuries.

My sister-in-law's husband fought in the Resistance. They used to go out on missions to blow up the Germans' trucks, and they would come back to the village. For that the Germans used to come and look for them in the village. All the men, even the Greeks, used to go out to the wilderness so as to not be caught in the village; otherwise, they would be killed. In our village the Germans never disturbed the women and the children.

When my son was about two months old the Germans came to look for partisans. My husband ran away with the other men, but I stayed with the infant. A German came into my room and saw the baby, and he said to me with his hands, "I have one like this in Germany." If they were not Gestapo they were not interested in Jews.

There was not too much to do in the village. Most of our time was spent looking for something to eat because there was not too much available. My husband used to go around the village selling things, like material for making pants or shirts, and I used to clean the house and go out to look for something to eat, to cook. There was not too much variety.

When I got up in the morning I used coal to make a fire. I fed the baby, and I had to warm the water to wash the diapers. There was no washing machine, no running water. I brought the water from the pump in the street. I had to wash so many diapers every day, and if it was bad weather I had to think of how I was going to dry those diapers and how I was going to make supper or fix something for the baby. The time went by quickly. There was no time to think about what I was going to do. Now, life is different. You have too much time on your hands. You say, "I have to belong some place to pass the time." In those years my life was full.

Once the Germans came, and they caught all the people they found in the square. My father-in-law was among them, and I had the courage to go to the square to see about him. I left the baby with a neighbor, and I went and I pleaded with my hands with a German to let him go because he was an old man and sick. They said to me, "Go home. He's going to come home. Don't worry." That time, nothing happened to him. They held the men for a couple of hours standing in the square, and then they sent him home.

There was a radio in the village. Every night I used to go into a cave where they had the radio hidden. We listened to the news on the BBC from London. The broadcasts told us what was going on, but we didn't hear anything about the Jews, nothing. When D day came, we heard about it. I left my baby with my husband because he used to tell me, "You are so aware of the news, go and listen. You listen better." When I came home everybody used to come to our room to hear the news from me because there was no room in the cave for many people. I used to sneak into the cave all the time;

I was very small. I don't know who the radio belonged to, probably someone from the village.

In October of 1944 we heard the people who came from Volos say, "We are liberated, we are liberated."[15] So we came down with our possessions. My father-in-law used to have a big house, and we used to live in one of its apartments. Our apartment was occupied by Greeks, so when we came down we had no place to go, even though it was *our* home. We said, "Give us at least one room until you find a place." But they said, "No, we're not going anywhere." There was no government, nothing; only the partisans took care of things. They sent somebody who said to the Greeks, "Out. You go and you leave these people. They suffered enough. They have no place to stay." And we were in *our* home. We had some of our furniture, like the bed and a few other things with us because when we left, under the Italians, we rented a truck, and we took everything with us. When we came back, we brought those things back.

We came home in October, and in November we had the *bris* for my son. At that time there was no money. We had to give things to pay for the *bris*. I remember we gave three big boxes of cigarettes to the *mohel* to come and make the *bris*. At that time cigarettes were like gold. We did this because we thought this was the most important thing for us to do.

Life was very difficult for Nina and her husband after liberation. At first Mr. Matathias supported the family by buying and selling merchandise. A month after Nina's second child was born, in 1945, Mr. Matathias was drafted into the Greek army. Nina lived on meager rations from the Greek government and the United Nations Relief and Refugee Agency, but her situation was so desperate that her husband threatened to desert the army in order to rescue his family. His commanding officer, a Greek general, arranged for the family to live at the army base and to receive army food. After three years, when Mr. Matathias was discharged from the army, the family went to live in Trikala, Mr. Matathias's birthplace, where they were assisted by the Joint (the American Joint Distribution Committee). A third child was born in 1952. In 1956 they immigrated to the United States, where they suffered the loss of a child to leukemia and had a fourth child. In the United States Mr. Matathias worked at various occupations until his retirement. Nina also worked in their grocery store. Two of their children are teachers; one is a doctor. Nina and her husband have seven grandchildren.

I think life was harder for us after the war than during the war. During the war we were young; we didn't know what was going on; we tried to survive. When you're young you don't think too much. But after suffering so much, we were just not a happy family. It was very hard for our children, not having aunts and uncles and grandparents, not having cousins, not having anybody. It is still hard for us because we have no relatives to depend on. We have friends, but still it's not the same as *family, family.*

—*Interviewed by Rosalind Fenster, January 30, 1986*

Helen Foxman

Helen Radoshycka grew up in Warsaw. She finished her studies at the Gymnasium and then worked in her mother's business until 1935, when she married Joseph Fuksman. When Germany attacked Poland on September 1, 1939, Helen was pregnant. Her husband was visiting a sick brother in Baranowice, which was occupied by the Russians.

I didn't know anything about him. I only knew that he was at his parents' house. Mama sent me out of Warsaw. She said, "Go!" I was ready to make a cleaning[1] because he was there, I was here. They were bombing us, the war was going on. What was I to do? One of my older brothers came with me. It took us four weeks to cross the Russian border. We were sent back from the border three times by the Germans under the guns. Finally, we crossed the border separately. I stayed with my in-laws in Baranowice until my son was born.[2]

My in-laws were very wealthy people. When the Russians came, they gave my husband's parents a lot of trouble. They took away everything from them. They arrested my father-in-law several times. My husband and I were in a different danger. We were refugees because we came from Warsaw to Baranowice. So when the child was born we had to escape; otherwise they would arrest us and send us to Russia. Right after I gave birth, I had a hemorrhage, and when I came home from the hospital, they were picking up Jews and other refugees and sending them to Russia.

They came to take me, but I had a letter from a doctor that they were not supposed to touch me because of the hemorrhage, and they didn't take me and the child away. My husband ran out to hide somewhere. But we knew we had to get away from Baranowice.

It was a very difficult time because I couldn't feed the baby, and I had to get a woman to take care of him. This postponed our going away for two months. Finally, it was so dangerous to stay there that we had to leave everything. We went to Slonim, where we were strangers. It wasn't far away. Of course we struggled a lot there.

We had next to nothing. We took my child and a few little things; how much could I carry? We took whatever my husband could take with him. Everything we had was confiscated by the Russians in Baranowice. The house was confiscated, as were all of our belongings. *Everything* was taken away from us.

In Slonim my husband started to work for the Russians, of course, as a bookkeeper. I was staying alone with the baby in the worst possible facilities. A cousin of his had pity, and she found us a room. The room belonged to her son. He was a dental technician, and all the stuff from his work was in that room. The plaster, everything. There was no water in the room. I had to bring up water from downstairs and take the dirty water down to the basement. [Crying] No crib, no carriage, no diapers. I had six diapers, three triangles and three squares. I used to boil them every day on the primus.[3] Bring *up* the water, take *out* the water.

I could never go down with the baby because I couldn't carry him. I was too weak after the hemorrhages, but I had to go every day to pick up his food. There was a place where they used to give you bottles of food for the children. When I went out, the cousin of my husband used to take care of the baby, hold him. He was a wonderful child, and this made it a lot easier for us. There were no refrigerators to keep the food. People who knew who I was used to give me some pieces of ice to keep his food and gave kerosene to help me. You couldn't get those things anywhere. Food was very scarce. You had to buy everything at the market, but the prices . . .

We lived for almost a year in these circumstances, and it was very hard. The baby was sick; with every new tooth he had pneumonia. My husband was working in a forest far away. He used to come home for Saturday, and Saturday night he used to go back. He *walked* back. There was no transportation. I had to do everything myself. My husband wasn't well already at this time because of the shock he had after his mother's death and the trouble with our living as refugees.

My brother came from Vilna, and he talked us into going to Vilna. When he came, the baby was sick again with pneumonia. My brother said, "How long can you live like this? If you come to Vilna your situation will change a lot." But you couldn't just walk to Vilna; you had to smuggle over the border again.[4] I couldn't go immediately because they wouldn't let my husband go. It took a few months. I went first with the child only because my husband had been promised that they would let him go. He got some papers from the Russian doctor at his workplace that he had to go to Vilna to see a specialist.

He came to Vilna just a few days before Hitler came in.[5] We were not allowed to live in Vilna itself, so we got an apartment eight miles away from the city. The baby was a year old already. I couldn't take care of him because I had to go to work. Somebody recommended a woman to me who took care of young children. She watched him, and I used to commute every day to work.

Soon they established ghettos in Vilna.[6] Since we lived farther away from Vilna, we postponed moving into the ghetto until we settled what to do with the baby. We packed up our stuff to move into the ghetto. Bronya, the woman who watched the baby, saw us packing, and she asked, "What's going to be with the child?" I answered her, "Whatever happens to us will happen to the child." Then she said, "Give him to me. I'll take him." I just looked at my husband to see what he would say, and he said, "OK. Take him."

Everything was done on the spur of the moment. You couldn't think. I couldn't talk it over with my husband. But if he said yes, I understood that he knew better than I. He was a very educated person. As we packed we separated everything because we could only take a little bit on our shoulders or whatever you could carry in your hand and three hundred rubles for each person. The following day she took away all our stuff, all our belongings, in a few wagons. We gave her everything we had, and after she was through, she took away the baby. By this time, I had a baby carriage that somebody gave me. It was cold . . . autumn already. So she dressed him warmly, and she walked away with him, and we just looked through the edges of the curtains.

We didn't go to the ghetto right away. The Polish neighbors tried to convince us that we should remain in this place. "You don't have to go into the ghetto. We'll help you." I didn't know. I didn't think I was so stupid, but when they said it, I trusted them. When I spoke to my husband, he said, "No, we have to go to the ghetto. We cannot trust them. They think we have a lot of money; they'll keep us for a while, and later on they'll take hold of us and give us up."

It was late when we came to the ghetto. It was ten days later.[7] We couldn't walk on the sidewalks[8]; we had to walk in the gutters. I was afraid they would arrest us or kill us on the spot. My husband said to me, "We'll rent a horse and wagon, and I will bandage my ear around my head as if I have a mastoid infection, and I will lay down on the wagon, and this is the way we will go to the ghetto." So I walked after him like you walk after a dead person.

We came into the ghetto with 180 rubles for the two of us. We moved into the bigger ghetto.[9] As we came close to the gates of the ghetto, my husband got out of the wagon. They let us in, and we started to search for a place to live. The first thing . . . people who knew us were going on like this . . . "You see?" they said in Yiddish, "that *Ois vorf* (scoundrel, outcast)! The mother left her child outside and came in to save her life." [Crying]

We kept going, searching for a place to lay down our heads. Wherever we went there were people living, fifteen, twenty people in a room. Every place was taken.[10] In one place my husband met a woman who knew him from Baranowice. He opened the door, and she said, "Oh, Fuksman." He said, "Maybe you have a place for us?" And she said, "If I don't have, would I let you go?" She had a store with a long table in it. She said to us, "This is the place I can give you. Can both of you sleep here?" My husband said, "Whatever it is, we'll manage."

Soon after we came into the ghetto we had to go to work. My husband was placed in a factory not far away from the ghetto, in Szpitalna 23. He worked there not as a regular worker but as a slave for Hitler.[11] The factory produced all kinds of makeup and perfumes and women's delicacies. Later they made soap and shoe paste and floor paste. My husband didn't let me go to work. There was a reason for this. He said, "Sometimes maybe you'll have to go out and see how the child is."

As soon as Bronya found out where Joseph was (I don't remember how), she started to come to his work place. She got in touch with him. She gave him her address, and she started to nag him for a written statement that we were giving away the child to her as her own child. So, on the spot, my husband wrote a few words that he was giving her the child. The following day she came back and threw the paper at him and said, "What did you give me? This is nothing! Throw it out! Where is Helen's signature? What do you mean, you gave me the child? And the mother will come and ask for him back?" He said, "I'll bring it tomorrow." He came home, I gave him the signature, and the following day he gave her the paper that said the child belonged to her. She took him, baptized him a day or two later, and gave him a different name, of course.

Then she started to come for money. She came to the gates of the ghetto. The police[12] knew where everybody was, and they told her where we were. Every time she came, he had to give her money. No amount was enough for her. He had to give her whatever she demanded. So he agreed with her that he would give her five thousand rubles every month. It was a lot of money.

First of all you had to live. The Germans hardly gave you any food. They gave you a half a kilo, a pound of bread for a week. This was next to nothing. So Jews started to smuggle food into the ghetto. A lot of Poles used to sell them food because it was good business. The Jews would buy flour and bread and potatoes and sometimes butter, whatever the ghetto needed. This way my husband used to make money. It's not easy to tell you what kind of trouble we had in the ghetto. Every night hiding from *Aktions. Every night* was a cleaning. *Every night. Aktions.* Yeah. You had to be on the run. Only in the morning when the people went out to work, then it was quiet.[13]

They gave the men who worked documents called Pink *Scheins* for their families.[14] My husband had one for me and one for a child. He didn't know what was going to happen. In case we had to take back our child we had to have a child listed on the slip. Because we had a child listed on the pass, twice we took a child from the family we lived with during the *Aktion.* But later on the mother didn't want to give us the child anymore. She said, "If they take me, they'll have to take my children too. I don't want any of them to remain alone in this world."

My husband belonged to the Revisionist group in the Underground, to the Glazman company.[15] He worked with them, but there was not much they could do.[16] Glazman was killed in the forest.[17] We were lucky that we didn't go away. A few months after we came to the ghetto we heard about the place where I was supposed to stay with my husband. A few rich Jews remained there. They were killed by the same *goyim* who were living there who promised them the stars from the sky. The *goyim* took away their belongings and buried them in the forest in ditches. So my husband was right. He said, "You see, the same would happen to us." I didn't say no because, whatever he said, I never said no. I understood that he knew what was going on.

Sometimes I used to get some letters from Warsaw through somebody who came.[18] After we went into the ghetto I had one note. But then it stopped. News came in 1943 that the ghetto in Warsaw was being liquidated and fighting was going on.[19] It was hard to believe because my whole family was there. [Crying] My husband heard it through the Underground. He didn't want to hurt me, but eventually I had to know. I don't even know where my family was killed.

My youngest brother was being hidden by a Gentile woman in a small town on the outskirts of Vilna. There was a trial going on in that town. A young boy was tried and sentenced to jail for stealing a cow. He got up and said, "You're going to put me in jail for stealing a cow, and you're not doing anything for hiding Jews? I know where people are saving Jews!" They took away the son of the Gentile woman, and they brought my brother to the Vilna ghetto. The Gestapo in Vilna sent him out to work as a slave in Ponar.[20] About ninety people, Jews, were working at Ponar, burning the dead bodies.[21] These Jews built a tunnel from Ponar to outside the ghetto. It took them months.[22] As the last day approached, they disappeared through the tunnel. But they were not lucky enough to save their lives. From around ninety people, eleven were saved. The rest were killed. After this they needed new people out in Ponar to burn the bodies. Because my brother was guilty of hiding, he was taken out there. His hands and feet were chained. This is where he was killed.[23]

It's not easy to describe the situation in the ghetto. All day you were under fire. *Every five minutes* there was something else. Every half an hour another group of Gestapo came in, and the streets got *empty*; you didn't see a soul. Everybody was hiding; people were afraid to put their heads out. They were searching around, looking, looking. . . . They knew that the Jews were living there, they were smuggling in food and doing business. This was the only way to survive.

I used to go out of the ghetto almost every week to see the baby. I never wore the star when I went out. I used to take it off and walk out of the ghetto with a group of workers and get on the sidewalk and walk to Bronya's house. She lived far away, somewhere behind the city. I walked; I didn't care. It was important for me to see how the baby was taken care of. Well, he recognized me, but he didn't know me. He was afraid of me. I wasn't allowed to go near him and to kiss him. She would say, "Ah, you're starting in already. You want him to know who you are?" He called *her* "Mama." He called me by my name.

They liquidated the rest of the people from the ghetto in autumn, 1943.[24] It happened on the last Saturday in September. They were sending all the men to a camp; Klooga it was called.[25] That same day my husband said to me, "It's not good. We have to be prepared to separate." I said, "Why are you talking like this?" He said, "Well, I am picked out to go to the train station to clean out the cars. I'll see how it is going to be.

"I will not come back into the ghetto," he said. "If it is possible, I'll send you a note, and I'll tell you where I am." At one o'clock in the morning somebody knocked at the door, called me, and gave me a little note. The note said, "I'm going out to the place where I work. Don't wait for me. Try to do everything to get out of the ghetto." This was it. Now I knew where he was. He wasn't under a roof anyplace, he was just under the blue skies, out in a back yard. Only women were left in the ghetto by then.

The only excuse for leaving the ghetto was to buy bread. I bribed someone, and I got out of the ghetto.[26] I went to the place where my husband used to work. It was an open field. I sat down on a stone. I didn't know what I was waiting for. I wondered, should I go into the factory and ask? I *had* to. So I opened up the door of the factory and asked whoever came out, "Was my husband here?" He said, "Yes, he was here this morning. The director called him in and gave him a shaver to shave his beard off.[27] He gave him his belongings and some breakfast, and he told him that for his own safety he could not keep him here because the whole factory is in jeopardy." The director of the factory was *Volksdeutsch*. Some of them were nice fellows.

I was sitting there in that empty field, and there was a night watchman in this place, a *shikker*, a *goy*. He knew my husband very well. As he walked over near me he threw down a note. The note said, "Come when it's dark and I'll show you where your husband is." I had to sit and wait. In the meantime, about an hour later, she came along with the baby. The *goya*.

She knew that the ghetto was cleaned out. She always knew what was going on in the city. She knew where my husband worked. She didn't know that she was going to see me because she had no idea that I would ever get out. She came around, and she said, "Why are you sitting here?" I said, "Where shall I go?" She said, "Where is Joseph?" I said, "I don't know, but I will come back in the evening, and the super will tell me where he is." So she said, "Come home," and I went home with her. In the evening I went to see my husband. He was hiding. How do I explain it to you? There was an empty little house. Maybe it had one room. Empty, open doors. There was a loft on the top under the roof. He was sitting in this loft with two other people, a brother and a sister. The super brought me over and said, "Here is your Joseph." My husband and the other man came down from the loft, and because there were no stairs to go up, they made stairs out of themselves and I walked up and I slept over that night.

Every night I brought him something to eat. In the beginning Bronya was very good. She wouldn't let me go without taking something for them to eat. You could not, God forbid, stand or sit in that place. You had to lie on that straw. It was an attic, a very low attic. At five o'clock, before it started to get light, I would slip down from there and go home, without a document, without anything. There was a curfew. You wouldn't see a soul in the street.

I looked like a *goya*. My hair was light brown, straight, and I had no lipstick, *nothing* on my face.[28] She lived on the ground floor. One of her windows faced the street. When I returned in the morning I knocked on the window, and she let me in. This went on for a few weeks.

The neighbors used to see me, but they didn't know who I was. Then she started to work on getting me papers. I had no documents. She got me a birth certificate from a friend of hers, which said I was eighteen or twenty years older. With this birth certificate she went with me out to a small place to get documents. I got them with the signature of the police, and with these papers I applied for a job.

She got a place to live on the outskirts of Vilna, and I went to live with her. I got a job in a bookbinding place. It had been a Jewish factory, and the Germans were running it. The women who worked there were all Polish, and I was among them. What did I gain there? I had ration cards. They paid a few hundred rubles a month, I think, and every day they gave you soup for lunch, and that was it. But it was good for me because I was staying with her.

Later on, the super from the factory took my husband into his home, to his apartment, because it got very cold. They had absolutely no facilities in that loft. They had to go down at night, out in the field, to do their personal things. Vegetables were growing in the field, and they used to take some vegetables without washing them and eat them. That was their food. She wouldn't give me enough food for three people. Then the super took Joseph into his house. He gave him a place, a small room. My husband slept on the floor.

He paid the super five thousand rubles a month from the money he made while he was working outside the ghetto and bringing stuff into the ghetto to sell.[29] With the money we saved he used to buy pieces of gold. I couldn't keep this in the ghetto, and he couldn't hold it either. In the factory there was a guy whom he trusted. When he saw that the time in the ghetto was short, he gave him the money. He said to this guy, "Eventually, they'll get rid of us. If something happens to me, and my wife is alive, you'll give her whatever she needs whenever she comes." That's how it was.

When he was in hiding and I was free because I had Gentile papers and I was working, whenever I needed money I came to him, and he sold the gold for me and gave me rubles. I had to pay for upkeep of my husband's room. All he got there was the floor, the bare floor. If I didn't bring him bread, he wouldn't have anything to eat. All he ate was dry bread. I used to risk my life to go out to the market at six o'clock in the morning to buy the bread and bring it to him. Sometimes I used to bring him a head of garlic. In the place he was hiding they had everything, but the wife would never say, "Joseph, here is something to eat." Never. But when she was gone and the man was at the house he would bring him a glass of sweet, hot tea. That was it. How many times did my husband tell me that on Saturday or Sunday when they went out they always left a dish of food for the dog and cat. He would take a little food from that dish [crying]. Only when he knew that they were not around did he go out to the toilet. He didn't want to disturb them. And he was such a spotless person.[30] . . . That's how it was.

She [Bronya] did plenty of harm to me. She was a very sick, vicious woman. She was a lesbian. I didn't know it. I didn't know what was wrong with her. She disliked my husband from the beginning. She kept calling him, "that Jew," "that stubborn Jew," and "Jew" and "Jew" all the time. One day when I went to my husband where he was hiding I said to him, "What is going on with that woman?" I didn't sleep through any night. I had to get up in the morning at six o'clock and go to work, and she wouldn't let me sleep. She wouldn't let me touch my child, who was lying with her next to my bed. My husband said, "She's a lesbian. She doesn't like men." I didn't know what that meant, so he explained it to me. She used to get up in the morning, wild. She would take away my documents, undress the child: "Get out with him! Get out!" I took the child, and I went. She had some friends there, so I went to her friends. Her friends had a nephew, a Gestapo guy. He knew that the child was Jewish and that she was raising him. When I walked in with the child, the woman said, "What happened?" I said, "Nothing. She threw me out with the child." In a moment she said, "Julek is coming." She saw him from the window and said, "Run away!" I said, "And him?" She said, "Leave him to me." So I ran out of the house. Julek was going wild; he almost killed the child. She said to him, "Why do you want to kill him? Because he doesn't have parents? What do you want from him? Leave him alone!" Julek said, "He's a Jewish bastard." So she said, "So what? She's raising him as her child. What do you want from her and from him?" That's how it was until he calmed down. Every few days Bronya got so crazy that she threw me out of the house. That's what I went through with her for more than a year.

All the time I lived with her I kept paying her. I gave her whatever she needed. There were so many miracles. That she didn't search my purses. . . .

She didn't follow me when I went out. She didn't come to the factory every day. She could have come. She was three, four houses away from the factory. What would I have done if she waited until I walked out of the factory and followed me and saw where I went every day? There were a lot of miracles.

She treated my son well. But if he leaned a little to me, she would spank him. . . . His tushy would be swollen like a balloon. "You were feeling something for her!" she would say. Sometimes she would give him a bath and wash his face and get soap in his eyes. He was only a child, he couldn't take it, so he would say "Let Helah wash me." That's all he would have to say. He would get a spanking, and how. Otherwise, she fed him well, she kept him clean. He called her Mama. I don't know what was in him, but he felt that she was the one who was saving him. He was afraid of her, but he was very close to her. He hugged her, he kissed her. When she got so crazy, he would cry and beg her, "Mama, Mama."

Everybody knew that he was a Jewish child. She didn't deny it. He was taken to the Gestapo three times. She told them that the Russians took away the child's parents and that she had promised herself that she was going to raise him and save him. Toward the end, she wanted to make a priest of him. She took him to church every day. He wore a holy medallion around his neck. Whenever he passed a church he would cross himself. Even after the war, when my husband walked with him to the main *shul* in Vilna on Sukkot,[31] when they passed the big, old church he would say, "Let me cross myself, Daddy," and he would. My husband let him. That's how he was raised by her. At first he denied that he was Jewish. On the first day after the war, when my husband was saying his prayers in the morning and Abie saw the *siddur*, he said, "Throw it out!" to my husband. My husband said, "Why should I throw it out?" "Because this is Jewish." Little by little my husband would tell him, "But you are Jewish." He would say, "No, I'm not." But he learned very soon.

After the war was over my husband came out of hiding. The day all the Germans were gone my husband came back to our place. He came up, he walked up the stairs, and first he greeted her. He didn't greet me because he knew whom he was dealing with. The child was afraid to go to him because all this time, although my son knew that he existed, he knew him with a different name and did not know him as his father. So when my husband walked over and kissed him, the child got very pale; he was scared. And she became crazy. She really didn't know that he was alive all that time. One day I had to tell her that Joseph was gone so she wouldn't follow him. I knew that if she knew that he was alive, she would do everything to get rid of him. When he showed up suddenly, she got crazy. The first thing she said was, "Now, you're going to live with Joseph, and I'll go with Henry." I looked at her, and I said to her, "Bronya, what's the matter with you? Aren't you happy that Joseph is alive? Didn't you pray all the time that one of the men would survive and be able to help us in our hard life?" "No."

My husband went out to rent an apartment and to buy what we needed. We lived together a year: I, my husband, and the child, and she was with us. She was like part of the family. After all, she saved the child. We started to live like *menschen*. My husband was called back to the factory where he used to work as a slave. He became the director of the factory. One day there was an announcement in Vilna that all the people had to come and register for documents. My husband went to the police station and gave them his name and my name, and he said we had a child. "Where is the child's paper?" they asked. He told them what happened, that we gave him away, that he was listed in the woman's name, and that we didn't have any document of his. Even if we had, we could not use it. So the chief of the police said this was a very strange case. He said that we would never be able to get the child back. "You have to go to court with this case."

That's how it started. There were three trials about him in Vilna. It took us a year. The stones in the street were crying with us for what we were going through with her and with that child. At the first trial the court acknowledged that he was our child. It was the first trial about a saved Jewish child. They sent fifty lawyers from Moscow to witness this trial. She said, "No." She was not going to give him up. He belonged to her. She brought us to a second trial, and she lost again. She went on to a third one, and she lost him on that one. But officially we couldn't get him because she was against it; then the court said to her, "Well, there is nothing that you can do." She said, "I will go to Stalin. He'll help me. This child belongs to me." What didn't she say against us! She said that we were not a peaceful couple, that we fought. That a child like that should have decent parents. That we were bad people. But the *goyim* who worked with my husband during Hitler's time in the factory were our best witnesses. They came into the court as our witnesses. We also had witnesses who said that we paid her for keeping the child because she denied that we paid her. The witnesses said that many times we borrowed money from them to pay her.

After the third trial the judge called my husband to the side, and he said to him, "You're a Polish citizen, aren't you?" My husband said, "Yes." So he said, "Why don't you get away from her? She'll kill you. She's not going to leave you alone." My husband said, "We are registered to go back to Poland,[32] but our number is too far away. They're sending the first numbers." The judge said to him, "Bring me the number. I'll see what I can do." He helped us get away as soon as possible. And this judge was a Lithuanian *goy*. Not a Russian or a Pole or a Jew. Abie started to cry, and he started to hug her and kiss her, so they gave him chocolates, and they said, "Go with Joseph." He was so beautiful and so good when he was a little one, with a golden head of hair and blue eyes and fair skin.

The judge sped up our number to leave Vilna. We left her everything, all our belongings. We took with us only what was necessary so as to not carry too much. I begged her, "Come with us. You have nobody, Joseph has nobody. You'll be like our mother. You'll be in our family. Wherever we'll go you'll go with us." "No, I will never go with Jews anymore." We felt grateful to her because she saved the child, and indirectly she saved us because if the child had been with us we would have never saved ourselves and not him. Never. We knew what happened to others. We knew of Jewish children who were taken to Gentile people and they survived and the parents were killed. We wanted to take two of these children with us when we left Vilna. The people didn't want to give them to us. They said, "If the parents come, we'll give them back." The same thing would have happened to our child.

We left Vilna at the end of 1945. We went to Lodz, Poland. We didn't go to Warsaw, didn't go to see where my family lived. I didn't go to see the cemetery where my father was buried because we had to rush out of Poland. She was after us. She heard that in Poland it was okay to kill Jews. A friend of hers who lived in Lodz told us, "You'd better get away because Bronya is coming." So we tried to get away as soon as possible. It wasn't easy. You couldn't go traveling on your own. You were dependent on organizations, and you had to smuggle over the borders again and again. We had to pay to be smuggled across the borders. But the Revisionists were helpful to us; they gave us priority to go before other groups because they knew that we were in danger.[33]

We came to the American zone; we were in DP [displaced persons] camps three and one-half years. My husband was already sick, and Abie was four years old, four and one-half years old. To go to Israel [Palestine], you had to be smuggled over borders and cross the mountains to Italy.[34] My husband said it would be a disgrace to his father's grave for him to go to the United States. We were waiting, waiting, waiting [for Palestine immigration certificates]. My husband was the head of the camp in Bad Gastein; he was the first to vote in the plebiscite of the Anglo-American Committee of Inquiry about immigrating to Palestine.[35] A lot of Jews went illegally at that time. But we couldn't go that way because of his health, and Abie was still a small child; we couldn't schlep him over the mountains. So we waited for a certificate that never came. Then we received papers from my husband's relatives in New York.

When the papers came from America, my husband didn't want to sign. He sent them back. The papers came a second time. He didn't want to sign them. They came a third time, and I said to him, "Sign the papers. This is the last chance. If you send them back now, you won't get them again. Wherever we are, if you get the certificate to go to Israel, we'll go to Israel." We never got the certificate. You know when we got the certificate to go to Israel? Before we got married, in 1935. He was in Baranowice, and I was in Warsaw, and he wrote me a letter that he got a certificate for the two of us to go to Israel. I was very attached to my mother because my father died very young and my mother was left with nine children. I was very angry, and I answered him in a letter, "If you want to go to Israel you marry somebody else and go. I'm not going. I'm not leaving Mama." And we didn't go.

In New York, the family lived in a fifth floor walk-up on Cannon Street on the Lower East Side. Joseph had several factory jobs in succession, with difficult working conditions that were ruining his fragile health. When an opportunity arose to buy a farm in Tom's River, New Jersey, they did, thinking that the environment would be healthier, but they could not support themselves on the farm. Joseph returned to his old factory job in New York City and commuted to the farm for weekends.

I was on the farm with Abie. He was going to *yeshiva* there, and he used to help me with the farm. He would come home from school, put away his books, and come out to help me feed the chickens, collect the eggs, and close the chicken coops in the evening. My husband came for Saturday and Sunday only. He didn't have a place to stay in New York because he couldn't pay rent for an apartment, so for a whole year he slept on a cutting table in the factory. One night the police saw a light in the factory building at night and thought there was a fire in the building. When they came into the building and saw him they thought he was a thief. He explained why he was there, and they told him that it was too dangerous for him to stay in the building alone at night. He said he would go home to his wife on Friday and that she would find him a place.

I did. I went to relatives of my brother's and told them what was going on, and they said, "What's the matter with you! Did he have to sleep a year in the factory on a table?" It took a few months to sell the farm, and we moved to Brooklyn. Then that factory closed, and my husband was very sick. He developed asthma and was in and out of hospitals. Finally he got a job in the YIVO,[36] and he worked there for five or six years. When he was laid off because they were short of money he worked at CYCO, a Yiddish publishing house. The dust in that place was killing him. There was no air conditioner, no fan, so I bought him an air conditioner, and he started to breathe a little easier. When that became too much for him he started doing business from the house. He sold Yiddish books. He sent out bulletins to libraries and universities. I still do it.

One day I went to buy something with Abie, and he saw a sign in the window of the Barton's office on 33rd Street.[37] I couldn't speak English; I couldn't open my mouth. Abie said, "Mamshie, would you like to put in an application?" I said, "I won't be able to fill out the application because I don't know how to write English." He said, "Let's go in." We went in, and he filled out the application, and they hired me. I started as a greenhorn at eighty-five cents an hour, and after five years I was made assistant manager and then manager. I worked fifty-five and sixty hours a week because they were open Saturday night and Sunday.[38] I worked because I *had* to work. I couldn't let my husband slave. I did the shopping and cooking and cleaning. I made everything myself, gefilte fish every week, because we needed everything. I didn't have a cleaning woman until now. After twenty years they wouldn't let me go to work anymore. My husband and Abie, they nagged me, "Ma, stop!" So I stopped.

Abraham Foxman is now national director of the Anti-Defamation League of B'nai B'rith. Mrs. Foxman died in 1993.

—*Interviewed by Bonnie Gurewitsch, July 28, 1983*

Rywka Diament and her son Paul, St. Leger des Vignes, France, 1940. *(Rywka Diament File, Yaffa Eliach Collection, donated by the Center for Holocaust Studies, Museum of Jewish Heritage, New York)*

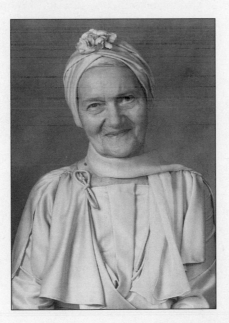

Rywka Diament at the wedding of a granddaughter, Rye, New York, September 1986. *(Courtesy Edith and Joshua Gurewitsch)*

Rita Grunbaum and her daughter, Dorien, Rotterdam, Netherlands, June 1943. *(Courtesy Rita Grunbaum)*

Rita Grunbaum, Larchmont, New York, April 1995. *(Photo by
Mark Seliger)*

Nina Attoun Matathias and her fiancé, Jack, Ios Lavrendios, Greece, 1939. *(Nina Matathias File, Yaffa Eliach Collection, donated by the Center for Holocaust Studies, Museum of Jewish Heritage, New York)*

Helen Fuksman, her son, Abraham, and husband, Joseph, Bad Gastein Displaced Persons Camp, Austria, 1947. *(Courtesy Abe Foxman)*

Hannah Marcus Bannett, pre–World War II, Poland. *(Courtesy Nehama Teichtal)*

Hannah Marcus Bannett at the wedding of a granddaughter, Tel Aviv, Israel, 1987. *(Courtesy Nehama Teichtal)*

Left to right: Edith Rymald Horowitz, her mother, Hella Fabrikant Rymald, and her brother, Adolf Rymald, Dortmund, Germany, 1938. *(Courtesy Edith Horowitz)*

Right, Edith Horowitz and her mother, Hella Rymald, Queens, New York, 1998. *(Courtesy Edith Horowitz)*

Rachel Silberman's family. *First row:* her sister, Masha. *Second row, left to right:* her father, Azriel Rosmites; Rachel; her mother, Henna Rosmites. *Third row, left to right:* her brothers Zeev and Zvi (Grisha). Siauliai, Lithuania, ca. 1932. *(Courtesy Rachel Silberman)*

Left, Rachel Silberman and her sister, Masha Roter, at the Western Wall, Jerusalem, Israel, 1967. *(Courtesy Rachel Silberman)*

Hannah Bannett

The third of five children in a middle-class Orthodox family in Cracow, Poland, Hannah graduated from the Gymnasium. She attended university in Cracow, where she studied literature, and in Berlin, where she studied Oriental cultures. Hannah's paternal grandfather, Rabbi Aaron Marcus, an enlightened German Jew who had studied at the university in Berlin,[1] became interested in Hasidism, moved to Cracow, and became a follower of the Radomsker rebbe.[2] He was also a Zionist and attended the first Zionist Congress in Basel, Switzerland, in 1897. This blend of cultural influences, in which the religious and secular coexisted, provided Hannah with the strong faith, language skills, and cultural sophistication that later served her as survival skills.

Hannah married in 1935 and went to live in Tarnopol, where her husband was a successful businessman. In 1935 the couple purchased a house in Haifa and planned to go to Palestine to live but were not able to liquidate the business successfully before World War II broke out. Hannah gave birth to their daughter, Nehama, in 1938, and in August 1939 their son, Yeheskel, was born.

When the war broke out in 1939 the Russians took over the eastern part of Poland. They came into our house. We had built it; it was modern, the fanciest house in Tarnopol. The Russian commissar, a woman named Tarasova, moved into my house with her husband and daughter. Because I had the two babies, they let us stay in the house. We lived together in my apartment. They adored my children, but they couldn't tolerate the fact that we were wealthy. They constantly stole things from us, promising to return them after the war.

My mother-in-law had her small apartment in the same house. We were able, very quietly, to celebrate the Jewish holidays in her apartment, but more important for us was that *shehita* was forbidden. One day I heard the commissar screaming at her husband, *"Zhid!"* and I realized that he was Jewish. That explained his nice attitude to us. One day I spoke to him, very nicely, and asked him if he would mind, because we could not eat nonkosher food, if the *shohet* came and slaughtered in our basement. He answered me in good Yiddish that I should make sure that the *shohet* cleaned up the basement meticulously after he finished. So the *shohet* used to come every week and slaughter for us.

After eight months they chased us out. Most of the rich Jews were sent to Siberia, but these Russians liked us, so they "exiled" us to a smaller town, and since many wealthy Jews had gone to Brzezany and living conditions there were not bad, we went there too.

In Brzezany things were relatively better for us because we were freer, although my husband had to leave the house often because of actions against the capitalists. There was a rabbi who lived nearby who helped with questions of *kashrut*. There was a synagogue with regular prayers. My husband was a religious man who prayed daily, and we observed *kashrut* strictly.

In 1941, when the Germans came in,[3] I saw battles for the first time between two major military powers. There were thousands of casualties. After a few days a group of German soldiers *(Wehrmacht)* came into the house where we lived and asked if they could rest in our garden. They saw my children and were charmed when I responded to them in German. They showed me pictures of their children and gave my children rolls and candies, which was a great treat. Then they told us that the Ukrainians were searching for Jews. They did not identify us as Jewish because of our blond hair and blue eyes, which are characteristic of my family. I was also considered to be pretty.

That same day, when the German soldiers slept in our yard, a group of Ukrainians came in with their sticks and some merchants from the town, and there was great camaraderie between them and the German soldiers, real brotherhood. I ran into the house and told my husband to jump out the window quickly (we were on the ground floor) and hide near the German soldiers in the yard. Those Jews who didn't escape quickly enough were caught and forced to clean the streets that had been the scene of bloody battles and heavy bombardments.

There were terrible *Aktions*. They chose *Yom Kippur*, the most holy day, for an *Aktion*.[4] They demanded that all the Jewish men from ages sixteen to sixty-five report, on pain of death, to the school or to the city hall. I had a good friend from Tarnopol, Tamara, whose husband was a lawyer, who came to ask what to do. My husband also wondered what he should do. I begged him not to go. An internal voice, a terrible fear, warned me. I thought, if they are commanding all the Jews to report to the same place on such a holy day, nothing good will come of it. I told my husband that he must hide in our attic. Our non-Jewish landlady, who was very friendly to us, had no objection. He climbed up, taking the *maḥzor* for *Yom Kippur* with him and stayed in the attic the entire day. The landlady removed the ladder. Many other Jews reported, several hundred people, including Tamara's husband, and none of them returned, not one.

That night our landlady's sister, Mrs. Zilinska, a very pious Catholic woman, came and told us that the Ukrainians had been talking about rumors that all the Jews would be killed. She went to the forest and, hiding behind some trees, witnessed the entire *Aktion*. The Jews were taken to the forest outside the city and massacred in deep pits that they had to dig. They threw dirt over the bodies, and those who remained alive were taken away. Mrs. Zilinska saw that the earth was still moving over the mounds of bodies long after the Germans left the scene. She was shaken to the depths of her soul by these murders.

There were other Jews like us who said, "It's *Yom Kippur*" and decided to hide and pray to God to pity us and see our misfortune and hope that God would protect us. We remained alive. After each *Aktion* there was a period of relative quiet.

The first decree had been to hand in all valuables to the Nazis, including furs.[5] Of course, we hid some things so that we would be able to survive. I still had rings, diamonds, and other valuables. We gave the furs to the Germans, but we gave one very valuable fur coat of my husband's that he got for our wedding to a non-Jewish woman who arranged to give it to a priest for safekeeping with the understanding that he would return it after the war.

After the *Yom Kippur Aktion* there was an *Aktion* not only for men but for all Jews,[6] so I escaped with my children to the church, where the Germans never searched. We entered the church; it was 4 or 5 A.M., still dark, and the children were shivering in the bitter cold. We sat there and waited; services had not yet begun. All of a sudden I saw the priest who had received my husband's fur coat, and I had the feeling that he was not our friend. He approached me and said that he was responsible for what happened in his church, and he demanded that I leave. So I said, "Anyone may enter the church to pray. You know who I am. Why are you doing this to me? I also want to live. You know what is written in our Bible, which is also the Bible of the Catholics: 'Love thy neighbor as thyself.' " He stared at me and left. We waited until Mrs. Zilinska appeared with a hot drink for the children and said that the *Aktion* was over. Then we went home.

Our landlady gave us permission to deepen a storage space under some boards in the kitchen so that in case of emergency we could hide there with the children. My husband dug it out, and we prepared blankets and other supplies there. My husband begged me to test it to see if there was enough air for us, but I said I would not crawl into my grave. I could not do it. Then Mrs. Zilinska came to tell us that on a certain day there would be another *Aktion*.[7] When Mrs. Zilinska saw that I would not get into the bunker, she said, "It is clear to me that God wants you to live. We have a sister in Lvov. Her husband is an older man, unemployed, and her daughters are students in the *Gymnasia*. If you can pay them handsomely you can hide there." This offer was for me and the children. It was hard to hide the children. My son wasn't talking yet, and every time he wanted something he cried loudly.

The German district commander announced that Jews who paid a large ransom would be able to stay alive and work at forced labor. My husband paid a large sum of money and was accepted as a gardener for the German district commander. My landlady and Mrs. Zilinska took this as a clear sign that God wanted us to survive and wrote immediately to their sister in Lvov. I went to Lvov with the children immediately and paid the sister and her husband a lot of money.

There we had a tough time because the two daughters, one age seventeen and the other age eighteen, were always hungry and ate up all the food I bought. Whenever I bought charcoal for the stove in my room they opened the door of my room so the heat would warm up the old man. The younger daughter always brought home the news and insisted that I come into their room to hear it: "Today they hung Jews whom they caught masquerading as non-Jews." It was torture. After a few months they told me that the neighbors suspected them of hiding Jews in the apartment because their standard of living was too high, so they asked us to leave.

I went with my children to look for Bernstein Street, where I knew that an uncle of mine was living. I didn't know where the street was, so I approached a newspaper vendor in a kiosk to ask directions. He volunteered to take me there, but soon showed me a badge that indicated that he worked for the Gestapo. He suspected that because I was looking for a street in a Jewish neighborhood I might be Jewish. I was scared to death; I thought I was lost for sure. In my winter coat I had sewn in twenty gold dollars and a supply of

Polish zlotys. But how could I bribe a Gestapo agent? He said I must go to the Gestapo with him, and I said, "What are you talking about? What do you want from me?" He said that if I was not Jewish they would release me. Meanwhile, my son was crying, "Let's go home, I'm hungry," and I said to the man, "What do you want from me? Even if I were Jewish, Jews have a right to live. What do you want? My child is tired and hungry. Let us go!" He took the money I held out to him and told me to get lost.

It's hard to describe what we experienced during that period of time. Whenever I tried to rent a room, even if the room was available, the owners would not rent to someone without an identity card. It was very dangerous. I did not wear the yellow star because I was masquerading as a non-Jew. I was in touch with my husband regularly. He sent letters to the Polish woman in Lvov, and I received them. My mother and sisters had remained in Cracow, and my sister Bronia wrote that they were living as Aryans with forged papers, and she was trying to obtain such papers for us so we could hide our identities that way. I went to a suburb of Lvov, called Kulparkow, near a mental hospital that the Germans were using for their casualties, and I found an apartment in the home of a Polish woman named Domaniewska. I told her that my children were sick and that I was coming to the hospital for a few days for a consultation so that she would take me in without an identity card. When she saw that a week or two had passed and that I wasn't leaving, she started to suspect that I was Jewish. Her daughter told her that if she hid Jews she would be endangering her life. She had to chase us away; there was no alternative. God was great and was always very kind to me. Just then, my sister Bronia came and brought the false papers for me.

It was in 1942. I moved to Cracow, where my mother, who was such a pious, religious woman, was also living as a non-Jew.[8] My brother-in-law, who was also hiding his identity, said that emotionally he could not stand the strain. He was ready to enter the ghetto voluntarily. My husband wrote that the situation in Brzezany had worsened; from time to time friends of his were taken away and never returned. He didn't know what to do. Perhaps we could find a way to transfer him to Cracow and hide him someplace.

My sister Lydia said that I could not stay with my mother too long because it was very dangerous for all of us to be together. So during the days I went walking with my children, almost until evening. I would sit in the public park with them or go to a twenty-four-hour movie theater where I could sit for many hours. I fed the children sandwiches, and they slept in the movie theater. I was deathly afraid of the usher with his flashlight. My blood would freeze with fear that he was searching for me. I spent two or three weeks of hell that way. I didn't have food ration stamps because I wasn't a registered resident, but thank God I still had money and could buy food on the black market.

In order to be a registered resident I needed an address, either a residence or a job. First I found a job as a housekeeper for a bachelor. His name was Sep Wirth, and he was a good friend of Hans Frank,[9] the governor general of Poland. Another servant also worked there, a young woman, and it turned out that she was also Jewish. Wirth always complimented my style and my good taste. He told me he could tell that I was from a wealthy home, that I was so intelligent and I spoke excellent German and that I knew how to conduct myself so well at the parties he made for the Gestapo and other important people. I knew how to set a festive table. I worked there for a while, and then Wirth made advances toward me, and I knew I had to leave.

My sister brought me a newspaper with an advertisement for a housekeeper for a family of four. I answered the advertisement, and the lady of the house was a pleasant woman. She said she had two sons and asked me how much I wanted to be paid. She said I certainly did not give the impression that I was a servant, but if I wanted the job she would hire me. I told her that before the war I was not a servant but that my husband, a Polish officer, was missing in action, I had no means of support, and I needed the job. I told her that I would work for very little if she would take me with my little girl. She said she had to consult her husband and told me I should come back the next day for an answer.

I went home to my mother, who had been praying for my success. I said I hoped God would help me succeed. When I went back the next day the husband, Dr. Professor Helmut Sop, made a very good impression on me. The wife told me that her father-in-law was also a doctor; there were many doctors in the family. The professor was from Bielefeld in Germany. He was a psychiatrist, director of a hospital for physically and mentally sick people. He, too, asked me if I could supervise the household independently, including the cooking. I told him that I could and that he could determine the salary because he would be supporting me and my daughter. They told me to move in the next day and to start work in two days.

Meanwhile, my sister Lydia placed my son in the home of a Polish teacher who demanded a lot of money, which we paid. He hid my son in his home. The child was miserable. That was the worst tragedy of my life. When I came to visit him every Sunday afternoon when I was free, the child was actually not normal. "Mommy, take me away. I can't stand it. They beat me so much. . . . Why can my sister be with you and not me?" One day when I came the child was so agitated and absolutely did not let me leave. [Crying] So I said to him that I would ask Aunt Lydia to come and take him that very day. "Take me just for one day to be with you," he begged me, "then you can bring me back." "You are circumcised," I explained to him, "and in the house where I work there are two boys. If you are in the same house with them they will discover that you are Jewish." Children have a sixth sense when they are in danger, and he said, "Mommy, I will take two pairs of pajamas and sleep under your bed; they won't even know that I am there." (Thank God I can talk about this now. For *years* I couldn't.) That Sunday, when I left his house I sensed a terrible, mortal danger. I cried in the street, and it was forbidden to cry in the street because only Jews did that, so I went into a church that was open because it was Sunday. I sat in the corner and prayed to the Almighty, blessed be He, with all my heart, that he should pity me. "What should I do, Master of the Universe? There is nothing to do." I found Lydia and told her that she must take the child for a day or two. She took him, and it turned out that it was my son's fate to survive because that same night they took away a second Jewish boy whom this Pole was hiding, unknown to us. Either someone informed, or possibly the Pole gave him up for the reward money. It was a miracle from God, impossible to figure out. Both my children are so pious, so religious; it was absolutely not a coincidence.

Lydia could not make other arrangements for my son. He spent two days with Bronia, two days here, two days there. It was a worse nightmare than ever. We never knew what the next moment would bring, if someone would inform. Lydia was being blackmailed by the daughter of the concierge of the building where we used to live in Cracow, who recognized her and demanded a huge sum of money so she would not denounce Lydia and the entire family, whom she imagined were also hiding. Lydia was very frightened.

One day Dr. Sop asked me why I always dressed so plainly and suggested that I indulge myself in a new, more stylish dress. I was afraid that he intended something personal toward me and jokingly reminded him that he had a young, pretty wife and children. Besides, there was a steady stream of young women who came to see him. But I took the opportunity to tell him that I couldn't think of buying a new dress because I was supporting a son who was being cared for by relatives in the country, and they told me that they could no longer keep him. I begged him to do me the great kindness of allowing my son to come to live with me, and God was with me in this. As a result of this conversation my son came to stay with me in the house of the professor.

Several times a month there were parties, with Gestapo attending. Dr. Sop also invited his Polish medical colleagues, and there were always high officers of the SS. I always prepared everything, and they were very satisfied with me.

My husband wrote that the situation in Brzezany was very dangerous,[10] and Lydia helped me make arrangements to transfer him to Cracow. There was a non-Jewish woman, Mrs. Grochowska, who would help people cross over to the Aryan side for a large sum of money. We paid in advance, and she prepared the clothing of a railroad worker for him to wear, and in that disguise she planned to bring him via Lvov to Cracow. She told me to be at her place at 8 A.M., and I said I would be there with my daughter because it was dangerous for me to walk around with my son. The night before this appointment I had horrible nightmares. I saw my husband, bloody, shadowy figures cutting his flesh; he was praying to me to come and rescue him. I went into the bathroom and splashed my face with cold water, not wanting anyone to see me in that distraught condition. As soon as I returned to bed and closed my eyes the same visions returned, and I was absolutely crazy with grief. Why should I be dreaming such nightmares? What happened? In the morning I rose very early. I ran to my sister to tell the Polish woman not to go get my husband, that I didn't want her to go. But she had already left. I was half dead with worry.

Professor Sop's wife was named Tonia; she liked me very much and confided in me about the lack of understanding between her and her husband. She said he had once found her with a friend of his, and since then their relationship was quite cool. He also had extramarital relationships. With them, the marital bond was not taken so seriously. When I came to her because I wanted to go get my husband at 8 A.M., she said I couldn't go because they expected an important general for lunch and I had to go do the shopping. I had no choice; I went shopping with her, my heart full of tears, under terrible stress, still under the influence of the nightmare. Finally, at 10 A.M. I went with my little girl, so petrified that I thought I would lose control of myself in the tram. When I finally arrived at the address of Mrs. Grochowska I saw a group of people congregated outside, talking among themselves, but I fearfully crossed the yard toward Mrs. Grochowska's apartment. Then I saw her husband, carrying the blue leather suitcase that my husband took to Brzezany. It held all our personal treasures. I didn't have time to ask him anything, but when I got to the apartment and Mrs. Grochowska saw me with my little girl, she told me to run away immediately. Five minutes ago the Gestapo had come and taken my husband; someone had informed on him. So I said, "You believe in God; what did you do?" She said if I had come five minutes earlier they would have taken me, too. They came at eight and waited for me. When they saw that I wasn't coming, they took my husband and left. God protected me. It was a divine signal that God wanted my daughter and me to survive. I never saw my husband again.

My husband was taken to the prison on Montelupich Street,[11] where they took all the Jews who were caught hiding with Aryan papers. It was well-known that the Nazis tortured Jews to death there to find out who else was hiding; they would promise to release the prisoner if he would tell them. The tortures were so severe that some people actually informed on others. After a while Lydia's landlady, who was friendly with the prison guards, told her that they tortured my husband until he died. He was such an honest and dear person, like the other six million holy martyrs.

At Helmut Sop's house the guests, who sometimes included Hans Frank, always said that they envied him for having such an excellent, reliable, and honest housekeeper. They praised me highly. There was one Ukrainian officer in German uniform who always made me very nervous. One day he came into the kitchen; whenever there were big parties there was a lot of work in the kitchen and Tonia always helped me. He said to her in German, "Tony, today you must give me plenty of alcohol to drink. There was a *Juden Aktion*, and one woman would not let go of her child. She clutched the child to her. We said the younger women were going to work, but she would not let go of the child. I shot her and the child, and those Jewish eyes are haunting me." He thought I was so busy that I would not pay attention, but I heard every word. I went into the bathroom, trembling with distress, until I could compose myself.

Tonia would frequently travel with the children to visit friends for the weekend. Then Helmut would be alone in the house. One day he told me that since he was alone he would eat at the hospital and that I did not have to prepare his meals. I went into the living room to straighten up, and I saw the Gestapo man, sprawled on the sofa, half dressed. I had a real shock. He said to me that he couldn't find his wallet. I said, "You are among friends; it must be here someplace" and started to search for it under the armchairs, under the sofa. Then, with a sadistic smile, he said, "Oh, I'm sorry. I found it in my trouser pocket." I turned to leave the room, and he demanded some food. I went to get him food, wanting to get out of there, when he demanded that I keep him company while he ate. You can imagine my fear when he began to interrogate me about my "husband" and his military service. I had no idea how to respond to his questions, but God was with me and told me to beg his pardon, that Tonia and the children were due back in a few hours and that I had to prepare lunch for them. "Well done," he said, and then I understood that he knew I was Jewish.

Mother told me not to keep kosher in the house where I worked because of the war, that any rabbi would forgive me because it was a matter of saving my life. I ate only dairy foods there and said I was a vegetarian from before the war and never ate meat. Tonia was satisfied because meat was expensive, but she always offered it to me.

When my husband was killed my mother and sister Lydia did not tell me because they saw how distressed I was, how hard I was working. Lydia was better at "managing" under the circumstances, and I asked her how I could send my husband a parcel in prison. She didn't answer me directly and tried to comfort me, saying that so many husbands were killed, including hers, and mine was only in prison. I didn't give up on the idea, and a few days later I took advantage of Dr. Sop's satisfaction with my work in the kitchen (eating well was very important to him) and approached him with a request. I told him that I had a Polish friend, a non-Jew who married a Jew. Her husband was caught hiding as an Aryan and was now in the Montelupich prison. Since Dr. Sop was the prison doctor, I was wondering if it was possible to send the prisoner a sum of money. Dr. Sop replied that he would look into the matter and give me an answer in two days. After two days, when I served him his food, he was cold as ice. He had always been very cordial to me, well mannered; now he acted like a totally different person. I sensed a great danger, that he knew something. He told me that I could give him a sum of money, but no food was permitted.

I didn't have much money and asked Lydia to take up a collection among Jews whom she knew in hiding. Lydia and my mother could no longer restrain themselves and said, "Good God, what have you done? Don't you realize that your false papers are in the name of Anna Kwiatkowski and your husband's false papers are for Mytoslaw Kwiatkowski? You'd better run away immediately!" I begged her, "Mother, where will I go? What are you telling me to do, now that both children are with me?" I was so broken I prayed to God, "What do you want to do? If you want to destroy us, do it! If Sop will have a drop of feeling in his soul, he will be silent."

I hoped that after the conversation with the Ukrainian about the *Juden Aktion* that perhaps Sop was having second thoughts about the Nazis. Maybe I would be spared. I stayed at my job, and he was polite. Maybe he thought that protecting a Jewish woman and her children would provide him with a safeguard after the war since he knew that Germany was losing. Wasn't it a miracle, that this Nazi, Hans Frank's friend, let me stay with my children? He only had to say one word, and I would be lost.

Before the Russians entered Cracow there was an evacuation of women and children. Before she left, Tonia kissed me and said that it looked like the Germans were losing. Dr. Sop said that I could not remain in the apartment because he had to return the apartment to the Housing Department. I begged him to let me keep my own room. He agreed and kindly said that I could take the provisions that Tonia left, as well as the supply of charcoal that was in the cellar. I was happy, and I remained there till the end. He said he was going to live at the hospital where he worked. I remained in the apartment till the end, and by then I didn't even have enough money for a tram ticket.

I heard that in Germany there were committees helping refugees, especially the Joint,[12] and also an illegal *aliyah* organization to help people get to Palestine.[13] Since I had a house in Haifa, I hoped I would get an immigration certificate.[14] I traveled to Hannover in the spring of 1945. There I worked for UNRRA[15] as a clerk, and I waited to get the certificate. I got the certificate and sailed with my children on the *Providence* from Marseilles on *Sukkot*, 1947. Providence means God's protection!

God has been so good to me, giving me long years and wonderful children, grandchildren, and a great-grandchild, perhaps so that I should tell this story.

In 1949 Hannah married Yitzhak Bannett. She is now widowed and lives in Tel Aviv. In 1987 her book, B'tzel Korato Shel Nazi *[Refuge in the Nazi's House], was published in Israel. It is dedicated to the memory of her grandfather, Rabbi Aaron Marcus. In her introduction she pays tribute to the moral education she received from her parents and grandparents and to the faith that she learned from them in which the principle of "Love thy neighbor as thyself" governs human behavior.*

—*Interviewed by Bonnie Gurewitsch, February 25, 1987; translated from Hebrew by Bonnie Gurewitsch*

Edith Horowitz

Edith Rymald Horowitz was born in 1930 into an upper-middle-class family in Dortmund, Germany. She had an older brother, whom she admired as talented and highly intelligent. The family lived "uptown"; they had servants, and Edith was well dressed. Edith's father came from Lyzhansk, a Galician town that was the home of a prominent early Hasidic master, Rabbi Elimelekh of Lyzhansk. Although the family was traditionally observant, Edith did not experience an intensive Jewish religious atmosphere as a young child.

In 1933, when Hitler came to power, Edith's parents sold everything and moved the family to Metz, France, but could not stay there as refugees, who were encouraged by the French authorities to immigrate to the French colonies or to Palestine. Colonial life was not acceptable to Edith's mother, so they returned to Dortmund in 1935, hoping they could live quietly.

In October 1938, they expelled the Jews.[1] I remember it vividly. It was a Thursday. The fish was cooked, and the chicken was out in preparation for *Shabbat*. At ten o'clock at night a policeman knocked at our door. He told us that we all had to go to the police station. He was kind enough to permit us to get dressed, and he decently turned around when my mother dressed. My mother was able to take her pocketbook along, which I think was unfortunate, as I will tell you later. They took us to the railroad station, and we were sent to Zbaszyn, no-man's land between Poland and Germany. The Germans threw us out, and Poles did not let us in. Unluckily, I think, my mother had enough money in her purse to buy train tickets to Cieszyn, where her mother lived. If we had remained in Zbaszyn, my brother might have survived because some children were sent to England or the United States.[2]

Coming from Germany to Poland was a trauma for us, like coming from America to Poland. In Germany we lived a modern life. We had a gas oven and indoor heating. In Poland people had outhouses. I had beautiful clothing. Everybody picked up my dress to look underneath. In Poland children came to school barefoot. Cieszyn was a beautiful place, not a *shtetl* with unpaved streets. There was a nice Jewish life. There were *shuls* in Germany, but nothing like this. People wore *shtreim'lekh, Poilishe hits,* black socks. I was eight years old, and because I didn't know how to speak Polish they put me into third grade in the Polish school. It was horrible. I also attended the *Bais Yakov* school, which I liked.[3]

Then the war broke out. The Germans were welcomed with flags flying. I recall it like it was today. The Germans came in and saw me dressed in my German clothes, with my long blond hair in braids. A German officer asked me where they could rest. I answered him in German, and he asked us to bring out water for the soldiers. We had to pump the water. Whenever a pail of water was brought out I had to drink from it to test it to see if it was poisoned. When *yom tov* came[4] they burned the synagogues. We lived next to a synagogue. It was an inferno, at night. It was terrible. Three months later Cieszyn had to be *Judenrein,*[5] so we went to Jaworzno, where my grandmother was born.

Jaworzno was smaller and more primitive than Cieszyn. Two or three families lived in one apartment. Edith's father eked out a living by selling cloth to the Polish peasants. In 1941 he was taken to a forced labor camp. On the fifth day of Kislev, 1941, the family received a telegram that he had died in Auschwitz of pneumonia.

They sent us his ashes; they sent us his clothes. The pants were torn in strips. A bloody, wet handkerchief was in the pocket. It looked like he was beaten to death. This was in December; I was eleven in January. My mother gave away my father's clothes. The water carrier got his jacket; I saw it every day when he brought the water. People were not permitted to congregate, but for a full year we had a *minyan* in our room, and my brother said *kaddish.* My mother begged the men not to come because if they were caught they would be killed, with their families, but they came. In the winter I heard their footsteps.

After my father died I was very bitter. I rarely entered my friends' houses where there were still two parents because they still had a normal life. My mother and I had to smuggle for a living. Many times I walked from Jaworzno to Chrzanow with cloth wrapped around me, with a little cape covering it. My mother used to go from Jaworzno to Sosnowiec and back, in one day, to buy gloves and stockings and bring back the merchandise to sell to the farmers. Jews were not permitted to go out before seven in the morning, but she did. Once she fell asleep on the train because she had to wake up at three o'clock in the morning to catch the train. The Germans came on the train, looking for smugglers. Everybody else ran out of the car and didn't wake my mother, so the Germans caught her with the goods and took her to the police station.

For two days my brother and I didn't know where our mother was, and we had just lost our father. There was no telephone; I was eleven years old. When the Jews of Jaworzno heard that a woman named Rymald had been arrested, they bribed the police with a kilo of coffee and a kilo of tea, and she was released. I begged her, "Mother, please don't do that anymore." She said, "What will we live on?"

In the summer of 1942 Moshe Merin, Judenalteste of Sosnowiec,[6] came to Jaworzno several times. He selected young people to go to work camps, and older people were "resettled," sent to Auschwitz.[7] Edith and her brother hid in the cellar of their apartment building to avoid being caught on the street, but they were caught after three days. Her brother escaped; Edith and her mother were sent to Bedzin, where Jews were concentrated in a ghetto/labor camp.

My brother escaped from Jaworzno to Sosnowiec. He went to Merin and asked him to save his mother and sister and grandmother. Merin said he would save me and my mother but not my grandmother.[8] They took all the old people to the trains, and my mother said to her mother, "I'm coming with you." She didn't know where. My grandmother was sixty-seven years old. She said, "Hella, you can't. You have children. You have to live." I saw my grandmother walking into the wagon. How can I describe her? She looked Italian. She was like a contessa. She always wore long, black clothes. She was in mourning all her life for her husband, who died when she was young. She wore a *sheitl*, and on top of the *sheitl* she wore a mantilla, in either gray or black. She was a very aristocratic lady; she spoke three or four languages. In Cieszyn she always sat by the window reading the *Tzena U'rena*. When a Gentile passed by on the street, he would always take off his hat to her.

In addition to Edith's grandmother, the body of her great aunt, who had died, was placed on the deportation train to take the place of a living

person. Edith and her mother were taken to the ghetto in Srodula, a sub-
urb of Sosnowiec. Edith worked in a toy factory.

Whatever my mother had, she sold. We ate frozen potatoes. They tasted very sweet, like sweet potatoes. Three families were living in one apartment. There was a bed, but there were red bedbugs, which flew from the ceiling. It was impossible to sleep in the bed, impossible, so my mother and I slept on the table. Can you imagine it?

In the spring, my brother heard that in two days there would be a "reset-tlement," taking away the children from Srodula, so he begged my mother to volunteer to go to a work camp and to take me along. I was twelve and one-half years old, as big as I am now. My mother was forty-two years old. We were sent to Zillertal,[9] in Riesengebirge.[10] It was a new camp, a brand new barrack. We brought along our clothing. We got a straw mattress and a sheet, a blanket, and a pillow. My mother was the cook; she could choose her assis-tants, but I didn't want to work with her. I didn't want the girls to say that because my mother was the cook I could work in the kitchen.

I was the youngest in the camp. I had to learn to weave[11] within three days, a procedure that usually takes months; otherwise I would have been sent to Auschwitz. The girls loved me. I was blond, with long braids. We worked from six to six. The foreman, *Herr* Meister, was the cruelest bastard. He especially hated children. He was six feet, four inches. I had never seen such a tall man. The minute he came to see if you were working or to fix a machine near you he greeted you by stepping on your foot. His biggest pleas-ure was to eat in front of us: an orange, an apple, bread, show it to us, let us smell it. He teased the younger girls especially. The youngest were sixteen or seventeen; nobody was as young as I was.

We had to get up at five in the morning. My mother gave me a piece of bread from her food; I couldn't eat the soup in the morning. I still cannot eat in the morning, to this day. I had to weave. I was very conscientious. I was afraid not to be. The head of the camp hated me because I would never compliment her. Other girls cleaned her shoes or watered her flowers. I never did. I just couldn't. The work was very hard. When we had to carry those big boxes with yarn for weaving, if a French prisoner[12] came over to help me, the foreman slapped him. Some of the German coworkers were very nice to us. Sometimes they brought us a piece of apple. They always asked us, "Why are you here? What did you do? What crime did you com-mit? The German prisoners are murderers; they killed children, they killed mothers. Why are you here?" In German they would ask, "*Bist du shuldig?*" [Are you guilty?] My friend would answer in Yiddish, "*Ich bin unschuldig. Ich bin nor ein besula!*" [I'm not guilty. I'm still a virgin!] [Laughter] The diet was eight hundred calories a day, and there was the hard work. We all developed terrible skin rashes. You could see the girls shrink from day to day. I didn't have my period. I was too young. The other girls didn't have theirs either.[13]

> *Edith describes bombing raids in which the Jewish prisoners were not per-*
> *mitted to seek shelter and had to continue working. She describes the ar-*
> *rival of prisoners of war of many European nationalities from whom the*
> *Jewish prisoners would glean bits of news about the progress of the war.*
> *In 1944 a transport of Jewish women arrived from Auschwitz. They were*
> *like "monkeys," Edith says, "hundreds of women with grey dresses, com-*
> *pletely shaven." These women, Hungarian and Czech Jews, told the oth-*
> *ers about the gassings in Auschwitz. There was animosity between the*
> *Hungarian women and the Polish women because the Hungarians*
> *blamed the Poles for working in the Auschwitz gas chambers.[14] "Your*
> *people killed my people, my parents." The girls didn't know what they*
> *were talking about.*

Among the Hungarian ladies there were a lot of sophisticated women, especially the ones from Budapest and Kosice. Women from the small towns, like Maramures, were religious; the ones from Budapest were not religious.[15] One girl who was religious had an old calendar, and we always observed the *yomim tovim*. We fasted on *Yom Kippur*. On *Pesaḥ* we hid the bread; we ate only potatoes. It was a rough week, believe me. On *Shabbos* we had to go to work. Since we worked in a factory that made cloth, the girls brought my mother thread, and she made wicks and *bentched* the "candles." My mother asked a woman who returned to the town at night if she would bring her a candle after Christmas from the Christmas tree. My mother lit this candle, made the *brakha*, and blew it out, every week, for *Shabbos*. I used to yell at her, "Mother, they're going to kill you!" She said that the girls insisted. Everybody was waiting, watching her, and she did it. On Ḥanukkah she lit "candles" every night.[16] We used pieces of yarn because we didn't have many candles. She kept those "candles" for two years.

I listened to the stories the women would tell. Oh, the stories! I got an education. There was a woman who was a teacher. From her we learned *Torah Be'Al Peh*[17]: geography, history. There were girls who wrote poetry. We used to dance. (Later on we had to dance for the Germans; we had to perform.) We thought that there were no Jewish men left, that only we were alive, like Lot in the Bible.[18] Once a dentist came, a Jewish man. He told us that other Jewish men were alive.

A Hungarian lady from Kosice told my mother, "I'm pregnant. Do you have a girdle to give me so I can pull in my belly, so I will be able to work?" My mother had a girdle. What woman didn't wear a girdle in those years? She gave her the girdle and a little bit of extra food every day.[19] One week I was working the night shift. My mother came running to the barrack and said to me, "Edith, I have scissors someplace. Come with me; take the scissors into the barrack. The girl is giving birth, and people are afraid." I put the scissors on the stove to heat it up, and I put a little bit of alcohol on it that someone had hidden. It was the first time I saw a birth. We put the girl down on newspapers, rags, whatever there was. It was an easy birth. She couldn't scream; it wasn't permitted. Nobody was allowed to know about it. No. She wanted to keep the baby. My mother said to her, "You are a young girl. Maybe the war will end, and you will find your husband. Don't feed the baby. Leave it. We'll just put it down here. Don't feed it. Leave it." But the baby cried. The Germans found out, and they came to take the baby away. She said, "No," so they sent someone specially from Auschwitz to pick her up and bring her to Auschwitz. She didn't survive. I don't know her name, but I will never forget such a thing.

I think one of the SS women was a lesbian. She liked to invite young girls to her room. Nobody ever talked about things like that. She was a young, stunning woman. When the cat in the kitchen was in labor and had trouble delivering, this SS woman helped the cat. She had so much compassion. Then the next day she caught a girl with a peach in her hand; she almost beat her to death. I think the German women were much crueler than the men. I can't understand it now when I see Jewish people driving Mercedes cars.

Before they evacuated us from the camp it became a concentration camp. The SS guarding us became much stricter. If people took something or spoke to the Germans in the factory, they got a beating, or they shaved our hair. We had to produce more.

In January 1945, when the Russians came closer, they evacuated us. I could have remained. The workers in the factory said to me, "Edith, we'll take you. You look like one of us; we'll hide you. Please stay; don't go." But I had a mother who looked like a real Jewess, like Rebecca, with black hair and dark eyes. My mother insisted that we take along whatever we had, and we started to walk. Some of us ran away, but I couldn't run. I had a mother, and my mother didn't want to. It was winter; we walked in the snow. We walked and we walked until we came to a camp named Nordhausen.[20]

Nordhausen was a real concentration camp. We saw people with the striped uniforms, mostly men. They brought us into a big room and took away our clothes. I'd never seen my mother naked.[21] For three days there were thousands of naked women in that building, supposedly for delousing. The building had a glass roof, and on top of the roof there were officers looking at us. If they asked for volunteers, girls would go with them. For two days there was no food, nothing to drink, nothing. Then it started, terrible, traumatic things. They took us to waiting cattle cars, a hundred people in one car. Some of the Nordhausen *Kapos* became our *Kapos*.[22] They were German prisoners.

The only way to survive was if you had elbows. Whoever pushed harder survived. There was a mother with two daughters. The mother encouraged one of the girls to do whatever she could. My mother just begged me, "Don't look." At night, the *Kapo* opened the door of the cattle car; I was sitting in front of the door. The mother said to us, "Let my daughter escape with the *Kapo* because she could be pregnant," so the three of them escaped. Today they are very wealthy, renowned, refined, nice people. I have never forgotten this scene.

There was one *Kapo* who told me that he came from my city, Dortmund. He was a homosexual. One night he said to me, "Tonight I will open the door, and I will take you, but I will not take your mother." My mother said to me, "Edith, I want you to escape, but can you imagine what he will do to you? And then he will leave you someplace. It's up to you." I wouldn't leave my mother anyway, but she was not for it. Then they hooked our train onto a train carrying ammunition and tanks. American or English planes came very low and started to shoot. When I woke up, my mother was on top of me, covering me with her body so that nothing would happen to me. The girl next to me was shot in both legs. Part of my hair and part of my eyebrows were gray from fright. I have a scar from the shrapnel.

You know, it's a funny thing. When women deteriorated, they deteriorated terribly, but not the way men did. There was a physical difference. The men were unshaven, filthy, with torn clothes. A woman did whatever she could; she would sew her clothes together, sew something. But the men, it was just pitiful. When we were in those closed wagons it was snowing and raining, and we were crowded together. We had to push to get to the bucket. No toilet, nothing. It was *bad*. But then we looked through the little hole. I saw how the men were transferred in open cars, in the snow, the ice, the wetness.

We came to Mauthausen.[23] We walked from the station up the hill. If I hadn't known better I would have thought it was a military school. Big! I saw barracks and barracks, miles and miles of camp. They put us in barracks with thousands of women. There was no room to lie down, only to sit. We had to carry those big stones, bring them up the steps, and when we were up, they said "We don't want them. Bring them down." Whoever couldn't do it was pushed.[24] For me, carrying fifty pounds was a lot. We all had lice and were sick with dysentery. People ate the skin of potatoes; there was nothing else. In Mauthausen I saw a corpse lying on the floor, and a man went over and took off his pants and left him completely naked. But this was not enough. The man cut off a piece of the corpse's behind and lit a fire and broiled it. That's the reason I don't eat veal. It reminds me of the white meat.

In March they transferred us and the men to Gunskirchen.[25] We walked. It seemed like days and days. Whoever couldn't walk was shot in the neck. I wanted to escape, but my mother couldn't. I would never do it on my own. As we passed by on the streets of towns, Austrian people would throw garbage, urine, and excrement on us from their windows. They saw that we were Jews, prisoners. We had Stars of David sewn on the front and back of our clothing. Some wore the striped prisoner's garb; we still had the rags we had been wearing for three or four years. We had wooden shoes; we could hardly walk. They called it *Todes March*, the **March of Death**.

We arrived in Gunskirchen. It was still winter, and the snow started to melt, so there was mud up to our knees. We occupied barracks where horses had lived. Straw was scattered around. Men and women were in the same barracks. There was no water. People licked the mud with their tongues. My mother did it too. I begged her, "Please don't!" The next day they all got diarrhea, and the majority died. Then the Red Cross representatives came,[26] and they gave the children food packages. My mother exchanged most of the crackers for soap. To her, a bar of soap was so precious. She was hoping that someplace there would be a shower or water where we could wash ourselves. I wonder which is worse—to be eaten up by lice or to be hungry? At least when you wash yourself, you feel like a human being, not like an animal. What I have against this whole experience is that they tried to dehumanize us.

After Gunskirchen I remember very little. I got the sleeping sickness. Other people got dysentery; I slept. I slept standing, sitting; I just fell asleep.

Edith describes an American Jewish soldier on a jeep who entered the camp at liberation and the turmoil of prisoners grabbing for the food provided by the Americans. Her mother did not permit Edith to eat any of that rich food, giving her some of the crackers from the Red Cross package. At night they slept in an Austrian farmer's house requisitioned for survivors by the Americans, and Edith remembers with regret that she was too weak to take revenge on the Austrians. Edith and her mother stayed in Wels, Austria, for a few weeks until Edith was strong enough to travel.

The two started walking toward Linz, Austria, intending to return to Germany to look for Edith's brother. One night, in a survivor camp, soldiers from the Jewish Brigade[27] encouraged them to join a group of survivors who were immigrating to Palestine. Edith's mother was reluctant, anxious to seek her son.

It wasn't that they were forcing us, but who would start up with a soldier in uniform? We still had the prisoner mentality. A uniform meant SS, Gestapo, or, worse still, the Polish police, whom I was more frightened of than any others except the Germans. It took me years after I came to the United States to ask a policeman for directions. The Jewish Brigade soldiers said, "We need Jews in Israel. When you come to Israel we will help you look for your son, and if your son is alive, we'll do anything for you. The boat is waiting in Italy."

They organized us into a group of forty or fifty people and brought us to Innsbruck. There I met thousands of young people. I was so happy to see that there were so many survivors. Then we were taken by train to Italy. We stayed in a refugee camp in Modena. It was paradise for us. The Americans fed us three times a day. Minestrone soup. I was with a group of kids who were eighteen, nineteen years old. There were not many fifteen-year-olds. Everybody knew me; I was the girl with the braids. Nobody had long hair; most of the women had very short hair because their hair had been shaved and had just started to grow. I traveled around with my friends through Italy, but I always came back to Modena, to my mother.

One young man, Monek, was in the Polish army.[28] He was my boyfriend. He was nineteen or twenty. He was very nice. He never took advantage of me. He sent me two English pounds in a letter. It was a lot of money then. I changed it on the black market and bought myself a raincoat and two sweaters. I was still a little girl. I had a mother. I was fifteen years old, not physically developed. I didn't have my period.

When we were in southern Italy the United Nations Relief and Refugee Agency brought us into empty houses in Santa Cesarea, on the beach. I had never seen an ocean before. I was sitting there on the highest rock, and I had just washed my hair. I had a mania about washing because there had been months when I couldn't wash my hair. It was quite long, and I was drying it, sitting on the rock with my hair down, like Lady Godiva. Suddenly someone approached me from behind and kissed me. I turned around; a gorgeous young man was standing there. I went pale, and he burst out crying. He thought I was his sister. We became very good friends. One day he asked me how old I was, and I told him and that was the last time I saw him. He said, "I need a woman, not a child." He cried, and I cried with him because I felt so bad. I really wished I could be his sister. Everybody always said to me, "You're so fortunate to have a mother." Very few people had somebody. They were all alone. There were herds of kids and youngsters, all alone. That's why there were so many marriages, sometimes really strange marriages that never would have happened before the war. But we always thought we were the last Jews. Who knew if there were any other Jews left? People were afraid that if you didn't grab a partner then you wouldn't have one.

In Santa Cesarea I met Sephardic Jews, Greeks, mostly from Salonika. They spoke Ladino among themselves. Many of them were castrated or sterilized as a result of the experiments that were done in Auschwitz.[29] They were a nice group. One of the youngsters befriended me. He told me about it; I didn't know what he was talking about. How would I know about castration? His name was Michael. He proposed marriage to me, and he spoke to my mother. My mother said that I still played with dolls. I was sixteen and one-half. I didn't really play with dolls, but I surely wasn't ready to get married. I had a mother, but the majority had nobody, and they wanted to have somebody.

Representatives of Zionist youth groups came to Santa Cesarea from Palestine to train the youngsters for immigration to Palestine. They lived together, and Edith separated from her mother to join this group. A group of fifty were taken on a small fishing boat and brought to Genoa, where they stayed a few months with a group of four or five hundred Jewish

*youngsters, prepared for the effort of running the British blockade of Pal-
estine. By then, Edith was seventeen years old.*

I don't know how long we were on the boat. The water ran out; we
started to drink salt water and ate dry biscuits, and in order to kill the taste
they gave us cigarettes. Since then I have smoked. When we came to Haifa
we were surrounded by the British, but we did not leave the boat without a
fight. They had to drag us down from the boat one by one. We fought back.
I hit a soldier; he hit me. I got hold of a frying pan, and I hit him on the head.
Of course, I got a good kick. I flew. But I was not going to be sent someplace
again and not fight back. Even now, when I think about it I get the chills. We
saw the Holy Land. We were there overnight. We refused to get off the boat.
The population of Haifa came out to greet us. They sang the *Hatikvah*, and
we sang it, too. We were taken down one by one to a military boat that was
waiting for us. The British soldiers were angry. They behaved toward us like
Nazis, like SS in white gloves.

*The youngsters from the "illegal" boat were taken to Cyprus, to camp
number 66, one of many established to house the "illegal" immigrants
until they could be admitted to Palestine under the limited Jewish immigration quota established by the British. After a year, when the names of
the youngsters in these camps were publicized in the Palestine newspapers and radio, Edith's mother, who had arrived in Palestine by then,
found out where she was.*

My mother found out where I was, and she immediately sent me a package with sneakers and a brassiere, a toothbrush and toothpaste, and of course
soap. She must have known that I must have been old enough to wear a
brassiere; I didn't have one. This was the worst thing for me, when I started
to develop, to walk around without a brassiere.

*When the British authorized fifteen hundred immigration certificates for
youngsters who were under age seventeen or who had a parent in Palestine, Edith was included in the transport. She arrived in Palestine in
1947.*

I had my mother's address in Tel Aviv. Can you imagine the reaction
when I knocked on her door and walked in? Everyone who lived in the house

came down. That night my mother took me to the beach and bought me the ice cream and watermelon that I loved. In Italy we ate tons of it. Life was hard in Tel Aviv. My mother shared the room with another woman from Cieszyn. There were only two beds; underneath the beds there were boxes for the bedding. I slept in the box with the bedding. I was very disappointed. I just didn't like the place. I was afraid of it; I don't know why. My mother didn't speak Hebrew. She worked in a dentist's office cleaning the instruments. They paid her a little. When I walked in and saw my mother doing the jobs that our maid had always done. . . . We were not so terribly wealthy, but there was a certain standard of living in Germany. Here she was cleaning the floor for another Jew. But my mother was very happy.

Edith went to Ayanot, a boarding school run by Aliyat Hanoar, an organization that assisted in the rehabilitation, absorption, and education of young immigrants to Israel. She had a difficult time adjusting and remembers the kindness and patience of the staff and the native-born Jewish students. Edith worked in the kitchen and in a hospital. The siege of Jerusalem during Israel's War of Independence prevented her from studying nursing at Hadassah Hospital in Jerusalem, so she took a job in a factory. Edith's mother married a man from New York who had come to Tel Aviv on a visit. She left Israel with him. Edith was eager to join her mother and stepfather in New York and delayed her own marriage because of that trip. She returned to Israel in 1951 and married the fellow who had courted her. They came to the United States and had three sons.

My husband and I became religious again. Continuation of Judaism is the most important thing in our lives. I still have nightmares. I always dream that I'm falling, falling, every time there is anti-Semitism or I watch a show about it. It must be self-punishment. I always dream that I'm back in camp. I am trying to forget, but I will never forgive.

Did you ever attend a wedding or *simḥah* in the family of a Holocaust survivor? There are hundreds of people, and there is hardly one table of family. I have a mother, that's all. I have my husband's family, but they are in Israel, and I have a cousin here with whom I am not very close. That's all.

I never had a childhood. My husband is nine and one-half years older than me; I recognized immediately that he could take care of me. He is a very responsible person. I could move to Africa; I didn't have to be afraid. I would always be fed and always be clothed. He is a man who takes care. When I was eleven or twelve I had to help my mother with a livelihood and with food. I didn't want that responsibility anymore.

It has been so many years from 1945 to today, 1983. Not a day passes when I don't think about it. Many times, especially when I feel guilty about smoking, I say to myself, "Edith, you really should try to live as long as you can, not for yourself, but to be a witness. If somebody would write a book that [said] it didn't happen, you should step forward and say, 'I am living proof.'"

Like many others, I survived by sheer luck. Survival of the fittest, is that the expression? Very refined, delicate people did not survive. You couldn't. Elbow grease. You had to push; either be pushed or push.

—*Interviewed by Aviva Segall, October 13, 1983*

Rachel Silberman

Rachel Silberman was born in 1922 in Siauliai, Lithuania, into a mid-
dle-class family. Both her parents worked. She had two older brothers
and a younger sister. After finishing the Hebrew elementary school in
Siauliai, Rachel attended ORT[1] school, where she learned dressmaking
and needlework. She was a member of HaShomer HaTzair, the Social-
ist Zionist youth movement.

On June 26, 1941, after the Russian retreat from Siauliai,[2] the Ger-
mans occupied the town and immediately looted the possessions of
Rachel's family. Her father and two brothers were arrested in the first
wave of arrests, and only her oldest brother was released. Her father and
second brother were shot in a massacre of men in the forest nearby.[3]
Rachel, her mother, and her younger sister, as well as her sister-in-law
and her two children, were given a single room in the Kaukazas ghetto.[4]
Food was scarce, and community resources were insufficient to supply
an adequate diet. From time to time a Lithuanian woman friend would
smuggle some food to Rachel's mother. Rachel and her younger sister
were taken to forced labor at the Zokniai airfield, then to the Radviliskis
camp to dig peat, and then to the work camp at Panevyzs to again dig
peat. After each of these assignments they would be brought back to the
ghetto.

I still had my friends there, in the ghetto, who belonged to *HaShomer.* We used to have informal get-togethers, not official meetings. We would sing Hebrew songs, and they also tried to put on little plays, very sad ones, unfortunately. We tried to keep our morale up. The young people lived with hope. We never gave up. We didn't hear anything from outside, no. There was very little news, but hope was always there, the *pinteleh yid* was always strong.

Towards the end when we returned to the Trakai ghetto,[5] my mother told me that they had come for everybody older than fifty and under fourteen, and they took my brother's two children.[6] My mother witnessed that. When I came back to the ghetto and the children weren't there, it was a very sad time. Losing my father was the first blow for us, but when the children were taken away I almost fell to pieces. I walked around with hope, day after day, thinking that maybe I'd see our children creeping out from somewhere. It hurt me a lot. They were my mother's first grandchildren. I'll never get over it. Those children somehow never got out of my system.

The brother who was released from jail escaped to the forests with his wife and joined the partisans. Before Rachel and her mother and sister were deported to Germany, this brother pleaded with their mother to join him in the forests, but she refused, saying that she would not abandon her two daughters. In July 1944 the three women were deported with the remaining Jews of Siauliai.[7] They were transported "like cattle," arriving a few days later at the Stutthof camp in Germany.[8]

First, there was the most beautiful scene when we got there; I'll never forget it. When we got off the trains there was a pond with swans, and you had the impression that you were going to some kind of a resort.[9] I'll never forget that scene. I often wondered, a swan is a peaceful bird . . . What was the idea of having those swans there?

Then we stood in long, long lines where they tattooed the numbers, but by the time we reached the front, they were out of tattoo, so they wrote it down with indelible pencil on the arm, 48043. I was always the first one, so my number was first, my mother's was next, and then my sister's. Before they brought us into the barrack, they took us into the showers, which dripped cold water. I should tell you it wasn't enough to wash an arm, certainly not the body. There were gynecology chairs, where every tenth or every fifteenth woman was examined. Who should they pick on? My sister, who was not quite fourteen years old. They said that women were supposedly hiding some valuables. My mother nearly pulled her hair out when she saw that. It was out in the open. We didn't realize what was happening until we got close to it. My sister was yelling so; it was like somebody was going to kill her. German men were doing the examining. Men! There was just plain hysteria among the women. We walked out of the shower naked onto the street. On the street were tables like you see in a market, piled with clothes, and everybody had to grab whatever. So a big woman grabbed short shoes. We started to trade among ourselves, and the Germans were chasing and beating.

Then they brought us into the barracks, and the real bad things started. Stutthof was jammed with people. There were a lot of Ukrainian girls, old-timers already. Those Ukrainian girls were in charge. Either they slept around, or they smacked, or they talked to you, if they were in the mood, with a good word. The confusion was so great that you didn't know what to do, how to behave. We were put in wooden barracks with wooden bunk beds. There were three layers of bunks. And all over the walls and beds we found writing: *"Ich heis Sorah . . . "* [I'm called Sarah . . . "] We found an awful lot of messages all over: stay away from that barrack, this is a death camp,[10] don't go to this, hints. Don't speak back to anybody, just keep quiet if you want to stay alive, poems, all kinds of messages written down.

We did not work in Stutthof. We had to get up in the morning and stand in line for *Appell,* and they would count us twenty times, until you passed out from the sun. . . . Hours. Hours weren't enough. People used to pass out; there were all kinds of incidents. A woman had a baby who wasn't developed; she was just at the beginning of her pregnancy. There were sick people who couldn't stand in line, and they passed out.

In Europe people would keep a big wooden box outside where they threw kitchen garbage. In Stutthof they had it in a big square section of the yard. There was our food: whole cabbage heads were boiled, and grass was boiled, poison ivy. We found whole sticks with leaves on them, whole beets. One person got a chunk of this, and one got the water. There was a big ladle, and as you walked by with your *schissel* they would spoon it into your *schissel,* and that was it. I think we ate twice a day.

At this point I was still with my mother and younger sister, who was five years younger than me. Our biggest problem was the lice. When we came, we did not have lice, but the women who were there already were full of lice, and it didn't take long for it to spread. That was our biggest problem. The minute somebody got ill, they were taken out. If somebody had a fever, we wouldn't tell anybody. Sure, everybody tried because we knew what the end was. The minute they caught somebody sick, he was out. They didn't shoot them in front of us, but we knew what happened. If they took them across to the other side of the camp, they didn't come back, we knew.[11]

They wanted a certain girl to sing, and she said, "Not now." Maybe she had a sore throat, or she wasn't in the mood, whatever, so they came over with a pail of water and stood her in the corner, and they spilled the water on her. Whoever it was in that corner got it with the cold water.

My mother kept our spirits up. She used to sing *zemirot,* distracting the girls; she told them stories about how miracles had happened, so why not to us? There were other women like that, mostly the "older" women. My mother didn't live to be forty-five. These women really kept up our spirits. There was one little girl, and she was hidden for a few weeks, and one day she got caught. A German passed by on a motorcycle and insisted he saw a child. I remember that incident. That little girl was taken away. There was another child with our group. Her stepmother kept her. She was also taken away.

After a few weeks, transports of a few hundred women started leaving Stutthof. Each time Rachel's mother was not selected, Rachel and her sister would run back to be with their mother. Finally, they all passed the selection and were put on a train that traveled into Germany, stopping often at farms to discharge a few women. Rachel, her mother, and her sister were taken to work for a farmer in Platenhof, where there were also three French prisoners of war and two Polish women. They were all given separate living quarters.

Here you would call it a maid's room, a back room. The three of us were always together. The French war prisoners were very nice. They used to get packages from the Red Cross, and they would help us along. Once they gave us some raisins; once they gave us a piece of chocolate. They used to push the food under the door to us; they were nice to us. I used to sew for the Polish girls sometimes, repairing or mending, so they would throw us a couple of tomatoes once in a while. We used to get a bread every day for the three of us. They gave us food, but we worked very hard. We did general farm work, fertilizing the fields, picking fruit, picking tomatoes.

Once we were in the field, and my mother saw another Jewish woman working on another farm close to the field where we were working. My mother started a conversation with her about when *Yom Kippur* was going to be. My mother thought it was going to be the next night, and the other woman said, "Tonight is *Yom Kippur*." And all of a sudden my mother became very bitter, very bitter.[12] She had figured out the calendar, more or less, and she figured out that it was *Yom Kippur*, and she told us not to say anything so that the farmer wouldn't know anything. We started to think that maybe we should ask him for time off from work or something, but she thought that it was better that he didn't even know. She said as long as we knew, that was enough. And by heart, she said a little prayer with us; I don't even remember what. But it meant a lot to her. It hurt my mother a lot. She suffered a lot from losing my father. She just didn't want to be alive without my father; her life didn't mean anything to her. She just lived for us. She became very bitter, very bitter.

Rachel and her mother and sister worked at that farm until the end of the summer, when the farmer took them back to the train that returned them to Stutthof. From there the three were taken to Stubhoi, near Elbing,[13] where Rachel was chosen to work in the kitchen.

Cooking was in German hands. Jews did only the cleaning of the potatoes, carrots, sugar beets, whatever there was. My mother had dysentery, and one of the women told me that I should steal a couple of potatoes, bring them into the kitchen, cut them in slices, and bake them for my mother on the stove, and that would help her stomach. I did it, but I guess I wasn't a good thief, and I got caught. There was one German, *yimaḥ shemo*, an *Oberscharführer*, who had a rubber hand. He used to kill with that hand. He used to beat the hell out of us. He caught me. He saw me with those potatoes and told me to follow him. While I walked behind him, I kept dropping potatoes because I had about six. I left only two so that I wouldn't be caught with more than two. But he realized what I had done. He butchered me. He nearly killed me, and then he let me go. . . . It only hurt him because I tricked him. I lied, I stole the potatoes, I had more than those two. But by the time I had to show him what I had, I had only two, and this bothered him terribly.

Then he told me to go. So I left, and my mother and my sister immediately realized that something had happened. I was all red, with a swollen face, and he came back after me. The man who brought the potatoes called me to stand up. He shouted that I lied to him and that I was the one who did God knows what to him. He shouted at me the whole day long. Finally, we went home to the barracks. That was Christmas day. On Christmas night at *Appell* he called out the numbers of five prisoners to come to the center. One of the numbers was mine. It was a bitterly cold night, full of snow, but the most beautiful dry weather. . . . My mother started to fight with me. She wanted to go. We looked alike. I looked very much like my mother, and she thought we could get away with it because we were only one number apart. We started to argue, and finally I went. I stepped out, and he called the five girls to the center. There was a big milk can, and everybody had to lie down, and he started hitting with a stick. I was the last one. He gave me twenty. I don't know how, but I walked out of the center. I was thrown into the snow, and I got up. My mother and my sister came for me right away, and they took me to the barrack. My mother wanted to see how beaten up I was. She wanted to see if my body was all right.

On top of this, that night another German caught two Hungarian Jewish girls who stole two beets and hid them. At night they went out to get the beets, and he noticed them. That German took the door off our barrack, and he beat them so. It wasn't human. Then the snow came into the barrack, and we were all cold, we were full of snow. What can I tell you? It was a night to remember. The women themselves tucked the girls in, covered them, helped them. We helped each other. I must say, in the bad times people didn't care, like my mother didn't care, whether it was me or it was another girl. There was another mother and three daughters, and we were close together and if anything happened to anybody, we would all help each other.

There were sometimes incidents such as, "I don't like you. You are a *Litvak*, that's why you did that." It was normal; it didn't mean anything. But there was also a Hungarian woman doctor, a thin, tall lady. You could see she was an educated, fine woman. She went around and said to the girls, "Don't eat what they gave today. Don't eat it. This is poison." She was right; there was something wrong. They gave us raw salami, not cooked thoroughly, and she said, "You will all get sick from it." And those who ate did get sick. That woman was so sick herself, but she walked around and watched and tried to help whoever she could.

I don't remember exactly how long we were in Stubhoi, but it seemed like a lifetime because it was very bad. Whenever a girl would cry because she was sick or bitterly cold, my mother, may she rest in peace, would comfort her. She used to tell stories. Most of the women her age were like that, calming us down when we cried. I think that there was quite a bit of *aḥdus* there. People were more good than bad. There were incidents where people got into fights, but it was because of the bad life. Somebody hid a little container of cold milk, and they got into a fight, and they spilled it right onto my back. It wasn't very pleasant, what should I tell you? I got up, and I was so angry, and my mother said, "This isn't the time for anger. We get beaten so much from all over. It happens, so what can you do about it?" I was ready to fight because I was the one who got wet. But that wasn't enough that we should say that Jews behaved badly among themselves, not true.

In February 1945 Rachel, her mother, and her sister were brought back to Stutthof with the other women from Stubhoi. From Stutthof they were

*taken out on a death march. A minimal amount of food was provided
for the prisoners by civilians along the way.*

Near Kolkowo,[14] where we were liberated, they said to stand in line and
everybody would get a hot potato. My mother, my sister, and I were the last
ones in the line because of my mother. She couldn't walk, and we stood last
with her. All the people who already had gotten a potato came back near
us to stand in line to get another one, and the German got very angry and
started to hit us over the heads with a club. He hit my mother, even though
she did not stand a second time, and he split her head. She was bleeding
badly, and we hadn't gotten the potato yet. We stood at the side looking for
something to stop the blood: paper, *shmattes*, whatever we could find. There
were French prisoners; they came over with white paper bandages, and they
started to wrap the bandages around her head, but the German came over,
and he hit them all again. They took some water, and they kept washing
the blood off, and he kept hitting them, and they stood there, and they just
finished wrapping her head up.

Then women came with sandwiches, but we couldn't eat them because
we couldn't tolerate what had happened to our mother. There was so much
food; we never saw so much food in those years. But we just couldn't eat, and
my sister was crying, and I was just concentrating on my mother. We saw that
it was bad because the skin was completely split. Then we got into Kolkowo,
and in a barn in Kolkowo she was finished already. That was the end. She
kept repeating, "I'm not surviving, as you can see. When you survive, remember these addresses of my brothers and my sister in the United States." She
had a sister and two brothers. She kept repeating: remember those addresses,
remember those addresses, and we didn't want any part of it because we kept
telling her, "Oh, you'll survive with us. You'll be alright." But we knew that
she wouldn't survive. That was on the tenth of March, and at five o'clock in
the morning on the eleventh, we were liberated.

The Russians came in. We got up in the morning, and the door opened,
and a Russian came in. He said, "Don't be afraid. We have liberated you.
You're liberated people now. Get up!" And then he yelled out at somebody,
"My God, look what's going on in here!" We were all full of worms, full of
flies, sick. Most of us had to be carried out. My sister was very sick. I washed
her a little and dressed her, and she fell to the feet of the Russian soldier, and
she started to kiss his feet and to cry, "Why didn't you help my mother? Why
didn't you come a day earlier?" She got very hysterical, and he picked her up

and said, "Don't kiss my shoes. You survived; you're a newborn child." He said, "Go and help who you can. We can't stay here. We have to advance. The war isn't finished. We have to see who else we can liberate, others like you." They were very nice to us; they really were nice to us.

Then they started to put all the people who survived in the German hospitals, but there was not enough room in the hospitals, so they put us in houses. Five girls were in our house, and the Russians used to come with medication. One Polish Jewish girl was delirious; she had high fever. I was completely out, like in a daze. The Russian said to me, "We can't come anymore to you because we have to go on. We can't pamper you now. This is the address of the hospital, and whoever feels better will have to go to town and bring medication for the others." My sister was feeling better, and she went to town for the medication. A Russian soldier brought her back; she had fainted. "Does she belong here?" I said, "Yes, it's my sister. What happened?" He said, "I don't know. I mentioned a name to her, and she passed out." When she revived she gave us the medicine and told this story. She was sitting on the side of the road on her way back, and that Russian came by with a horse and buggy and offered her a ride. She was afraid to get in, but he said, "Look, I don't need you. I see that you're Jewish and you're sick. You want a ride? I'll give you a ride. Don't be afraid of me." So she got in. He asked her where she was from, so she said she was from Lithuania, Siauliai. "Oh," he said, "I know. I fought there." Then he mentioned the woods where he fought, and she said, "God knows if my brother is alive. He was a partisan, I don't know whether he's alive or not." He said, "I doubt that your brother is alive. There is only one Jew who survived; his name is Grisha. I used to go with the Jewish soldiers because he already had a house." So she passed out. It was my brother, Zvi. He was the only Jew who survived at that time. He was the first one to get back to Siauliai. That's how we knew that my brother was alive. We started to write letters; every day we wrote a letter. And we started to go home.

Rachel and her sister returned to Siauliai by train. Her sister immediately started school. Rachel and a girlfriend went to Lodz, where they joined the kibbutz Yihud, *planning to immigrate to Palestine. Their group consisted of about fifty young people. Supported by the Joint Distribution Committee and organized by the* Briha, *they went to France. From there they began an odyssey of crossing borders illegally on their way to Italy's port cities. They walked a good part of the way, climbing*

over rocky mountain passes and crossing streams until they came to
Milan.

In Milan, the Hebrew Immigrant Aid Society (an American group)
and other Jewish organizations helped the refugees contact their relatives
in the United States. Rachel's uncle offered her an affidavit to come to
the United States. In Milan, Rachel met and married Leon Silberman,
and they decided to go to the United States. Her sister immigrated to
Israel in 1967, and her brother went in 1976. Rachel and Leon's son was
born in 1948, and their grandson was born in 1983. They recently retired
from a successful dressmaking business that they conducted together.

We came to the United States through the Joint; the Jewish Family Service in northern New Jersey sponsored us. They were very nice. We would
have done nothing wrong if we would have taken a little charity. When we
came they gave me $25.00. It was November, and I didn't have a coat, only
a dress. The woman said, "Don't be ashamed to take it. We're paying for your
room for the week, and here is $5.00 to buy food for the night, and when you
come on Tuesday, we'll give you more money." This was on a Thursday I
think. Leon had an address of a *landsman*, so he went there, and the *lands-*
man gave him a job immediately. He made $35.00 a week. There was a cold-
water flat available for $25.00 a month in New York. Leon said we could take
the rooms, we'd move in, we'd survive. I never went back to the Jewish Family Service after that. Leon brought home a couple of dollars; I made an
apron; I made a hem for 50 cents, here and there. No one realized how poor
we were; at that time I didn't realize that. I thought things would pass, it
would be better; you know, you always hope for better. So we bought jars of
baby food for Alan, and we drank from the jars instead of from glasses. We
survived. I was so anxious to learn English. Every penny that I had I spent on
necessities. Whenever I had some change, I used to buy those little Golden
Books with the pictures, like bears and Goldilocks, and when there were
words that I didn't know, I used to try to help myself, to learn that way. I didn't
have any help from my relatives. My old aunt is still alive. I call her up once
in a while; how do you do? I make sure when I'm on vacation to go there
and have lunch with her. I'm proud that Hitler did not accomplish what he
wanted. I'm not bitter.

—Interviewed by Bonnie Gurewitsch, July 31, 1978

Brandla Small

*Brandla Small was one of ten children in a working-class Jewish fam-
ily. When World War II began she was living in Lodz, engaged to be
married. In 1940 a small private marriage ceremony was performed
by the rabbi in her father-in-law's synagogue in the Lodz ghetto. In
1941 her daughter Rose was born. The family lived together in the
Lodz ghetto until 1944.*

They asked us to give up the children,[1] but I didn't. I was fighting.
How I did it? That is a miracle. Yes. The Nazis came in about six
o'clock in the morning. Jewish police were there too. They were
called by the command and were told to go upstairs to the rooms to make
everybody leave the house, to go downstairs to the courtyard. There was a big
truck, and they took away the kids.[2]

One of my neighbors was a ghetto policeman picked by Chaim Rumkowski. His name was Goldberg. This Mr. Goldberg and a few other policemen came up, and they said, "You have to leave the house. We are here to
see to it that the rooms are empty. Everybody must go downstairs," and everyone went down to the selection. My husband was not there; I think he
went to work that time, and I was left with my daughter.

After the Jewish police came into my room to tell me to go down, they
went upstairs. While they went upstairs I sneaked downstairs. I went into my
neighbor's room with the baby. I held my baby in my arms. The beds were
not made; the blankets were hanging down on both sides of the bed with the
pillows on the sides of the bed. I said to myself, "Whatever will be, I'll take
the risk." I pushed myself down under the bed, stretched myself out, put the
baby on my chest, and said, "God be with me." I gave the baby a piece of
hard bread because I didn't want her to cry. If she should cry maybe the
Nazis would find me. So she was lying quietly; a miracle made me try to
save her.

I heard the Nazis coming up the steps, *klopping* with those heavy boots with the iron things on the sides. I could hear every step. I heard, I heard, I felt terrible. I said, "Whatever happens, I have no choice." They were on the steps in the front. I pulled down the blankets all together because I wanted to see something too. I heard them coming, and I saw them come to the door, which was wide open. They were checking and looking all over. They saw that it was quiet, and they believed the Jewish police who said, "Nobody is there anymore."

Then I heard them go down with their boots with the iron things in the back of the heels. And the baby was quiet, as if she knew something was going on. Then I went down the steps to the main floor, and I opened a door, but I didn't go out because the people were already all outside, and the police were out there too, waiting with those trucks.

I opened the door of a room, and I sneaked in. In the old country, they used to hang stuff, clothes, on the doors. I went behind the door, and I put the coats over me. I opened the door until it touched the wall, and I stayed there pressed tight against the wall with my daughter. I was quiet, waiting until everybody left. I held my daughter tight in my arms, and she was quiet, holding the little piece of dry bread.

Then I heard the trucks leave, and it was quiet; they had taken a lot of people, the older people, the sick, and the children. When the truck left I heard quiet. No talking, no Nazis yelling and screaming, "*Farfluchter, far-fluchter*" and other dirty words that I don't want to repeat. So I went out of there, and I went back up to my room. That time I saved my child.

My husband was working at Lagienicka 36 in the *Schneider Resort*, working for those Nazi murderers there.[3] When they caught him on the street and took him I was left with my child. What could I do? No food, nothing for the baby.[4] I needed food for the baby.

I used to work at home braiding rags into carpets for the Nazis. They gave me production to do in the house.[5] I had to tear up old rags in small pieces. Some old stuff they gave me, and some of it I had to find on my own in order to have enough. I had to produce a measure of three hundred yards to get a ration card for soup. Three times a week I had to produce this. When I delivered my production I got a ration card to get soup every day, that little bit of water, whatever they gave us. I shared this little bit of soup with my daughter.

You can imagine what kind of childhood a child could have at a time like this. She didn't have much. I had no toys for her; I played with her. I tried to give her whatever I could. I couldn't take her out to show that I had my child safe after the *wysiedlenie*. I hid her from the other parents. They were jealous. I don't blame them. I would be the same way. They asked me how I saved her. I hid her so the other parents wouldn't see her. Many parents did give away their children; they couldn't help it.

Another time in an attic a few mothers were hiding with infants, and they didn't want to give away the children to the Nazis.[6] The women didn't have food to give the children to keep them quiet. This same neighbor, Mr. Goldberg, made a hiding place for us in the wall; I was in that wall. The children started to cry in the attic, in the hiding place. The mothers didn't want the crying to betray us. Infants, you know, couldn't understand "sha," be quiet, don't cry. So the mothers didn't want to satisfy those Nazis, to give away the babies with their own hands because we knew what the Nazis would do with the kids, so they did it themselves. They killed their own children, a couple of kids, yes. I saw it.

In August 1944 I volunteered for the last *wysiedlenie*.[7] I had no food for my child, nothing. They took us to the train tracks, and they gave us each a whole little bread, a little margarine. Before this, Chaim Rumkowski said, "*Kinder*, if you are in camps, you'll work there," to talk us into going.[8]

So I said, "Whatever will be, will be." You can imagine a mother's heart without a little food to give to her child. So they put us on cattle trucks. Like animals we were sitting there, like in a chicken coop, with the little babies, no toilet, nothing, dirty, filthy. Wherever you were sitting, if you needed to do it, you sat there and did it.

I had the baby with me on the train till we came to Auschwitz. We arrived early in the morning. It was still a little bit dark. The Nazis started to knock on the doors, "*Raus, raus, raus!*" We should get out of the train. In the ghetto they told us to take everything with us, so we did what they told us. In Auschwitz they took everything away. And as soon as I got out of the train my child was dragged from my arms. [Crying]

I left Lodz with my child in my arms; I saved her in the ghetto, and I still had her, till Auschwitz. The Nazis took the child away from me; a German woman stood beside them. The woman took the child from the German men. She disappeared, and I didn't know where. My child would be now *forty-four years old*. She was four years old when they took her from my arms. [Crying]

We saw what was happening. We couldn't fight back. We smelled a bad smell, burning flesh, but I didn't know who was burning there. We didn't know. They told us to take off our clothes, all of them, like the day you were born. They put us in lines, five in a line, five in a line, with no clothes.

I looked for my child all over. I asked whoever I could. Nobody knew. I don't know if I was lucky to survive; sometimes I say I shouldn't have survived because it's no life afterwards. I feel guilty lots of times for surviving. I know it was not my fault, but sometimes I suffer so much it's not worth living.

When I came to Auschwitz I had a picture of my little girl hidden in my shoe under the heel. I wanted to save it. I also had a little comb for the baby to comb her little hairs. I hid this picture and the comb under the heels of my shoes. When we came in they told us to give away everything. I had the shoes on my feet because I had the little comb and picture in the heels. At the *Entlousung* the lady said, "Take off the shoes." I begged her to give me those shoes. "Please let me have these shoes!" She said "No," and she took a rag full of solution[9] and slapped me with that rag right in my eyes, and I couldn't see. She was the strong one; I couldn't fight anymore with her. I just asked. And that's what it was.

Right after we came to Auschwitz I was put in barrack number 3. I remember it clearly. It was near the gate, near the tracks. For three days we sat there outside. It was thundering. It was in August. During the day you were hot; it was terrible. At night it was cold. We were thirsty. There was a puddle, a puddle of mud, from a stream of water. Mud. I felt thirsty, hungry, and from all the *tzores* we didn't know what we wanted. I bent down and grabbed the mud and put it in my mouth.

Then I was beaten up, made to kneel with my knees on the gravel because they caught me stealing a little bit of soup. A Nazi woman beat me up, and then she punished me because I was going to take a little soup. I didn't care; I saw the way life was going on there. I said, "We're not going to make it anyway, so what is the use of being hungry?" When people are hungry, you know you do anything. They made me kneel on that gravel for three hours. My knees were bleeding and cut in pieces. [Crying] That was the punishment so we wouldn't go get the soup by ourselves.

Brandla was sent with other women from Lodz to a labor camp in Christianstadt, Germany,[10] where they dug antitank trenches in the forest, and then she went to Parschnitz, Germany, where she worked in a linen-making factory.[11]

{ 89 }

In the back of the forest was a sandy place with big hills of sand. So tall! We used to dig the sand and put it on trailers, trucks. While we were loading up those trucks they took the sand to another place, and then after we were finished we had to go there, take the sand, and put it in another place. Just to make us work. Once I got buried in the sand up to here [points to a spot on her body]; they couldn't dig me out. The sand used to spill down when we dug holes. The more we dug, the more the sand spilled down. When you made a hole underneath, the hills spilled down lower. So once the big hills moved down, they covered us to here [points to a spot on her body]. Nobody died that time. We tried to help each other, to dig each other out with our shovels.

In Parschnitz in the factory there were a few older workers. They were good. They used to bring us a piece of bread. Before they threw this piece of bread to us, like to a dog, they looked around all over to check that the Nazis didn't see them. We were always hungry. We were nervous, sick, tired.

One girl was pregnant when they took her to the camp. She had a baby there. They killed the baby; they killed the lady in the camp. They didn't let her live. What would they do there with a baby? I didn't see it. We heard about it, we heard.

Brandla was liberated by the Russian army. She describes how some of the liberated women cut the hair of their German tormentors to embarrass them. Brandla felt numb at liberation, not happy. She went back to Lodz, which had become a center for Holocaust survivors.

We didn't know what we felt because we were disgusted, confused; we didn't know which way to go or if we'd find somebody or if we would have somebody left from this horror in our lives after such a terrible thing that happened. [Crying]

I came back to Lodz. I went there because I thought that maybe I would find someone. I found a brother! [Crying]

First I found some neighbors, three sisters. They recognized me, and I recognized them. They saw me; we were all crying. We sat there on the bare floors, slept there, sat for twenty-four hours, waiting for somebody; maybe we'd find somebody.

Some girls took me into their home; they were liberated earlier from Czestochowa. They threw the Nazis out of an apartment, and they had a home. I took a bath there and washed myself off; it was so beautiful to have a bath after so many years. They saw me sitting there in the refugee center, and they asked me, "Did you find somebody?" I said, "No, so far I haven't found anybody." "Where are you living?" I said, "Here, here's my place." A rucksack. A bag. I had a little bit of junk, whatever I could take from Germany. Whatever I found I put in the rucksack. After liberation I hardly could walk, but I found this Persian lamb coat, and I brought it to the barracks. One of the girls saw me with the coat, and she said, "Oh, you'd better not take this. If the Russians see it they'll kill you. They'll think you are rich, and they'll take it from you." I was stupid, and I listened to her, and she took it. She took it herself.

Every day I went to the refugee center in Lodz, and I saw husbands finding wives, sisters finding brothers, and children finding parents, and I said, "Do I have such bad luck? Not to find anybody of such a big family?" And my friend said, "Don't cry. We'll go so often that maybe we'll find somebody." I put up the names of who we were looking for on the walls, which were full of names. I was disgusted, and I said, "I'm not going there anymore." I was going down the steps, and my brother was going up. It was terrible. I walked by my brother, and I didn't recognize him. He hit my arm like this, and he said, "Brandla?" and I said, "Who is this?" He knows my name! I looked at him, and I said, "Carl . . . " [Crying very hard] We were laughing and crying, and we were so happy that we found each other. He was in a terrible state. He had rags on his legs, rags, not shoes. He was with the partisans in the Staszowa woods, and he was wounded. The A-Kovtses,[12] the Poles, shot him; he had a bullet in his chest, right here, and they cut him in his face. It was very close to the liberation.

Brandla met and married her second husband in Germany. He is also from Lodz. They arrived in the United States in 1949. They have two children and two grandsons.

I have a wonderful life. I have two wonderful kids. You saw my daughter; she makes my life a little worthwhile. If not for her I wouldn't be here.[13] I have a good daughter; my son is good too. That's what keeps me going. Sometimes God doesn't forget about us. I believe in God. I'm a believer, a big believer. Thank God.

How can we recover after that tragedy? We're never going to recover, honey. It doesn't matter how we look and how we try to push ourselves and work and laugh. Fun, laughs . . . It's not natural. How can we feel good after we went through such a tragedy? How can we? I don't like to talk too much about it. Happy? Not happy. Honey, we're never going to be happy.

—Interviewed by Ray Kaner, August 13, 1984

Sisters and Camp Sisters

The interviews in this section reflect the experiences of women who were siblings or who created sisterly relationships during the Holocaust. The interviews are arranged in order of their approximation of the progression of Holocaust history, beginning with those who found safe refuge, followed by those who hid in more or less protected circumstances, arranged in ascending order of the dangers they confronted, and ending with those who were caught in the ultimate Nazi trap, the concentration camp system designed to kill them.

Before World War II began, escape from Europe was a difficult, but sometimes viable, option for Jewish families with children. After September 1, 1939, however, almost all avenues of escape were closed, and Jewish children became particularly vulnerable. Escaping, hiding, living with false identities, or managing to survive ghettos, concentration camps, or death marches was especially difficult for children.

Estelle Alter's parents tried to protect their daughters in Belgium. Their father thought that obeying the notice to report for forced labor would keep the police, and further trouble, away from his family. After he was gone their mother realized that she could not protect them, as she could eventually not protect herself, and she made the desperate decision to place her little girls in a convent from where they were placed in various protected facilities for Jewish children that were run by the Belgian underground and funded by the Jewish community. The trauma of separation from their parents remains vivid in both Estelle's and her sister Regina's memories, but the constant presence of protective adults and a daily routine of meager but adequate food, clothing, and shelter did not traumatize them further. They instinctively depended on each other for emotional support, cementing a close prewar relationship into an almost symbiotic closeness that remains today.

Margie Nitzan and her siblings were left to fend for themselves in Italy, where, as German-Jewish refugees, they had been at an economic disadvantage from the moment they arrived. Their father was arrested in Milan, and their mother could not maintain an orderly household for her children. When Margie's mother sent her out of Milan for the relative safety of the country and the ostensible protection of the "Principessa," Margie at first thought herself fortunate. But her fortune soon soured, as the wealthy lady became abusive. Psychological and physical abuse broke Margie's hold on her Jewish identity and created new traumas that still trouble her. Like the majority of Jews in Italy during the Holocaust, Margie's family survived physically, but their emotional wounds were mortal. In a painful poem of self-assessment, Margie sees her baptism, performed out of loyalty to her sister, as the source of her ongoing trauma.

Edith Wachsman, eleven years old when Jewish life was threatened in Slovakia, was the oldest child in a family of eight children. When it became too dangerous for her bearded father, a rabbi, to leave the house, Edith, as the oldest sister, was delegated to do the shopping and other essential errands for her family. She helped her father grow vegetables when they could no longer be purchased, and it was she who hid her father's *tefillin* and retrieved them each day for his morning prayers. Edith was sent to meet her mother's train when her mother returned from Hungary just at the moment of German occupation, and it was Edith who returned empty-handed when her younger brother could not cross the Hungarian border to Slovakia and the relative safety of his family. She was able to cope with adult responsibilities because of the supportive presence of her family.

Eva Schonbrun was the younger of two sisters who were deported from Slovakia with their infant brother to the Bergen Belsen concentration camp. Protected by nineteen-year-old

Theresa, Eva, at five years old, also did what she could to share
the responsibility for their tiny brother. Theresa's devotion to her
younger siblings was tenacious and inventive, while Eva exploited
her position as a child, playing on the maternal sympathies of
older women to obtain extra food for their little family of three. Although their first priority was their own survival, Theresa was un-
selfish in her attention to other children in the camp. Their survival was no less miraculous than the reunification of their large
family after the war because of their mother's persistent search,
against all odds, for the children.

Sara Rigler, her sister Hannah, and her mother were another
family fragment, three vulnerable women in a harsh ghetto and
concentration camp universe. Without a male protector in the
Siauliai ghetto they were hungry. After they were deported to the
Stutthof concentration camp their loyalty to each other sustained
them, and Sara's final, desperate act of daring was but the last in a
series of risks they took for each other. In this risk Sara lost her sister and her mother. Although she was rescued from the Germans
by a group of British prisoners of war and nursed to better health
by them, she then faced a difficult ordeal. As a young woman
alone in the territory liberated by the Soviet army, she was in constant danger of rape by the liberators, escaping attack only by her
wits and by linking up with two other women who protected her
and each other. It is interesting to note the contrast between her
treatment by the British prisoners of war and the Russian soldiers.
By adding her sister's name, Hannah, to her original name of Sara,
she justifies her own survival as a vicarious continuation of her sister's life and perpetuates her sister's memory. In her work on behalf of the hungry and disadvantaged she perpetuates the values
that she learned from her mother.

Suffering and witnessing atrocities in the Lodz ghetto did not
prepare Rozalia Berke for Auschwitz. In the ghetto she did useful

work in the hospital, continued her education, and lived with her family even as their numbers diminished due to death and deportation. The "intake" process at Auschwitz, designed to dehumanize arriving prisoners, was a shock to body and soul. Rozalia got through it by literally holding onto her sister, not letting go of her hand. The two sisters then opened their hands to Dorka, an acquaintance from Lodz, who was despondent and suicidal after being torn from her family. Rozalia and Romana adopted Dorka, calling her their sister and behaving as if they were indeed blood relations. Throughout their experiences in Auschwitz, Stutthof, the death march, and the challenge of rebuilding their postwar lives, the three girls stayed together and have maintained a warm and loving relationship ever since.

Tilly Stimler was separated from her mother and older sister on the Auschwitz platform and from her remaining sister at a subsequent selection. Totally alone, without the support of family, she was adopted first by two other girls and then by a girl from her hometown with whom she stayed throughout her experiences. These camp sisters shared their food and plotted how to stay together until and after liberation.

Miriam Rosenthal was a young bride, naive enough to insist on getting married in Hungary in the spring of 1944 just when her real world was falling apart. In spite of the advice of her mother and sisters she left her family and acted on her adolescent idealism, marrying the young man she loved. Her illusions were shattered within weeks, as she was separated from her husband and deported to Auschwitz. At first she was with a sister-in-law. Later, on a transport to Plaszow, she found and bonded with cousins, one contemporary in age, one sixteen years old, and one a slightly retarded youngster. This combination of women characterizes the almost random nature of some camp sister relationships: "There are no discussions, no negotiations. They seem to trust each other in what they do with and for each other."[1] Throughout her pregnancy Miriam was the beneficiary of extraordinary gestures of support not only from her camp sisters and other women but also from men. One day Miriam was tempted by the offer of a double bread portion and left the roll call to stand with other pregnant women, but at the last minute she was drawn back to her camp sisters. "Even if I starve, I want to be with you," she said when they asked her why. In the Kaufering I camp at Landsberg, where the Germans assembled seven pregnant Jewish women as a *Schwanger Kommando* [pregnant commando] and allowed them to give birth and keep their babies, another bonding experience occurred as the seven women, randomly thrown together in an irrational, never-to-be-understood gesture, helped each other and formed a little family. The *Kapo* risked her position to obtain a stove for them and provided slivers of soap and rags for the babies, later suffering a beating for doing so. One SS man showed signs of humanity when he brought some supplies for the infants. Others jeered and insisted that the women continue their work routines. Boszi, the oldest of the seven women, nursed those babies whose mothers could not nurse. Miriam is still in touch with Boszi and with some of the other women, maintaining the special relationship that developed under unique circumstances. This group of camp sisters is an example of bonding that took place even when the women did not choose each other. Did their similar predicaments create the bond? Why did these women not destroy each other in conflict over scarce resources? There seems to be no other such instance with which to compare this episode.

The camp sister relationship is perhaps best exemplified in the clique of eight girls from Chrzanow described by Cesia Brandstatter. Sharing the same prewar Jewish background and values, they trusted and supported each other in the concentration camp. In retrospect, they wonder at this because it seems contrary to hu-

man nature. Several women in this book describe jealousies, rival-
ries, stealing, and other immoral behavior in concentration camps.
It is important to keep in mind that camp sister relationships, although they contributed to survival, did not insure survival. For
each example of love and trust between unrelated women, there
were many instances of hate, mistrust, and immoral behavior.
"Normal" standards of behavior were irrelevant in the dehumanized concentration camp environment. We can admire those who
overcame the dehumanization and draw inspiration from them.

The trait that best characterizes the relationship of sisters,
both blood relations and camp sisters, is trust. The love that siblings experience in a warm family setting engenders trust, which is
expressed in empathy and concern for the other's happiness and
physical well-being. The Nazi universe destroyed the families, community, and interpersonal relationships of its victims. When their
men were drafted to forced labor, families were left without bread-
winners and decision makers. Community leadership, usually all
male, was often executed by the Nazis soon after they occupied a
locality, leaving chaos and distress in the resulting vacuum. The ar-
bitrary, irrational nature of indiscriminate murder, witnessed by
children as well as adults, destroyed faith in civilized norms of behavior. There was no "correct" behavior that would ensure survival, only constant vigilance and a lot of luck.

Being able to trust another human being was a precious advantage in this system where prisoners were isolated by physical cir-
cumstance and by justified mistrust of authority. Most learned to
trust only themselves. Prewar friendships did not always survive the
test of the concentration camp. The bonding that occurred between women was not a rational act, but rather an instinctual
reaching out, sometimes but not necessarily based on prior acquaintance or relationship. Interviews with siblings and other
women demonstrate that some relationships did survive the dehu-

manization process. Like true siblings, camp sisters made a tremendous effort to remain together through the selection processes. This effort in itself gave purpose to their lives, and those who stayed together retained their trust and love for each other, sharing food and body warmth, protecting each other, and existing for each other as talismen of humanity. Sometimes this type of relationship was created on the spot between girls from the same hometown who found familiar faces in a sea of dehumanized strangers. Sometimes two sisters, like Rozalia and Romana, "adopted" another girl, including her in their tiny family relationship of trust and mutual responsibility and calling each other and referred to by others as *Lager Schwestern*, camp sisters. As prisoners were transported from one camp to another or marched endlessly and pointlessly through Germany at the end of the war, these relationships provided a measure of physical support, solace, and hope for the future. The trio of Sara Rigler, her mother, and her sister was joined by a similar threesome of Hannah's friend Ruthie with her mother and sister. Rachel Silberman, her mother, and her sister had a similar relationship with another family unit in the Stubhoi labor camp: "We were close together, and if anything happened to anybody, we would all help each other." Sometimes, tragically, they witnessed the death of one or more of their group. This closeness was a small, but sometimes valuable, advantage. "Their relationships . . . helped them to transform a world of death and inhumanity into one more act of human life."[2]

Many of these camp sister relationships are maintained today. These relationships are a substitute for the extended family of their own generation, which Holocaust survivors lack. The women still call each other sisters; their lack of blood relationship is often unknown to all but their immediate families.

Another reason why sisterly relationships were, and continue to be, such a source of strength to those who sustain them is that they allow the women to retain a sense of their prewar selves. All interviewees, even those who were too young to remember the specifics of prewar family life, have a definite sense of prewar family status and values. Margie Nitzan is proud of her father's Jewish erudition and appreciative of his efforts to support his family as a refugee in Italy. Edith Wachsman is knowledgeable and proud of the rabbinic lineage of her family and as a youngster had clearly absorbed the religious values she learned at home. Mutual love, respect, and responsibility for each other continued in her family even under the conditions of hiding in Czechoslovakia and withstood Edith's one childish moment of weakness. Miriam Rosenthal's value system was shaped by her participation in her mother's prewar charitable activities. Hannah Rigler refused assistance and other inducements by the Russians when she realized that the price was her personal dignity. Cesia Brandstatter's character and value system were shaped by her prewar education in *Bais Yakov*, which she shared with other girls from homes like hers.

This sense of social status and values was shared by camp sisters when they rebuilt their postwar lives. Most Holocaust survivors married other survivors, finding in partners who shared similar experiences instinctive understanding and empathy. The camp sisters continued to serve a similar role, sharing insights, as Hannah Rigler's friend did with advice about dating American men, and remaining loyal and trusted in a new, strange society where Holocaust survivors were disadvantaged refugees. These women spoke the same language and saw each other as worthy people with innate status and shared values.

Under the most adverse circumstances, young girls and women maintained or created stable familial relationships, which helped them preserve their humanity. Although these factors do not by themselves explain why these women survived, they certainly contributed to their survival.

Estelle Alter

Estelle was born in 1936 in Antwerp, the younger of two daughters in a traditional middle-class Jewish family. Both her parents worked in their grocery business; they lived in a comfortable apartment. When she was three and one-half years old Estelle had a tonsillectomy. She vividly remembers how jealous her older sister was of the attention she received and how her four and one-half year old sibling sharpened Estelle's new crayons "down to nothing." Nevertheless, Estelle was so attached to her sister that she started kindergarten a year early because she refused to be parted from her.

After the Germans occupied Antwerp[1] my father got a letter that said he had to show up at a certain time in a labor camp.[2] My father and his brother discussed the possibility that my father should take his family and run away into the mountains, but my father was afraid that if they caught him they would kill his family. So he became a scapegoat; he offered himself as a sacrifice: "Take me but leave my family alone."

At that point I was not going to school.[3] My parents were afraid to let us out during the day; they held us very close to home. I wasn't aware of the Germans actually being present at that point. All I knew was that my father had to be taken away, and it was such an emotional time that I don't think I saw much else. As young as I was, I knew that something terrible was taking place.

I remember the day my father went. He packed his little bag. My aunt and uncle came over with their children because they knew they might never see him again. There was such a tumult going on in the house. Everybody was so emotional. My father walked to the elevator, and I stood there in the doorway. I was screaming for him to come back, and he came back and he held me. Then he walked away, and he went into the elevator, and we never heard from him again. That was it. We never heard from him again.

We wrote to him, to the labor camp where we thought he went, but we never heard from him. After the war they found out that he eventually wound up in Auschwitz.[4]

My mother was left with the two of us. That night she was afraid to sleep in our own apartment in case the Germans came in the middle of the night to take us all away. So we slept in the attic, in our storage cubicle, on old-fashioned wooden beach chairs with multicolored canvas sling seats. If we heard someone walking we knew we had to hold our breath so we would not be heard.

We started walking the streets during the day. My mother had to wear the yellow *magen David* not only on her outer clothing but also on her blouses.[5] My sister was over five, so she had to wear it. I was too young. We walked the streets. My mother started looking for places where non-Jews would put us up for a night, two nights. If we stayed out after curfew[6] my mother and sister took off their jackets, folded them, and slung them over their shoulder to hide the *magen David* on the blouse. But we couldn't find a place. There was nowhere to hide. There was nowhere to run. After about a week desperation set in. My mother knew she had to do something drastic. That's when she went to the nuns and asked them to take us, only the two children.

She told us that in order for us to be saved she had to put us into a convent. We knew we were in danger. If you can't sleep in your own bed you sense there is something too terrible going on, that you have to take desperate measures.

I can't begin to tell you how we screamed and cried and begged to be with her. But she knew she had to be stronger than we were, so she just, you know, she *took* us. She didn't know where she was going to sleep that night, so by then the poor woman really couldn't do much else except to tell us, this is what's good for you, and this is where you have to be.

That first day is a blur. I remember mostly the days that my mother was able to come and visit us. I remember a room where they let us visit with her, and I remember the crying sessions when she had to leave because the visits could never be long. We cried for her to take us with her. Everything else is pretty blurred until later on.

I never suffered physically in the convent, so I must have been treated well. I had enough to eat, but what I ate is another story. We were served food that was strange to us, namely pork products, and we just couldn't get ourselves to eat them. As young as we were, we knew we weren't allowed to eat pork. We felt our Jewishness so strongly that we couldn't eat it. We skipped that part of the meal altogether, all the time. No one objected; they understood.

There were other Jewish children in this convent.[7] But the fact that my sister was with me and that she was a little older is what kept me sane. I firmly believe that because we were never separated we kept our sanity. That's why we have such a close relationship to this day. We comforted each other. I can't remember what we said to each other. Just being together was enough. Knowing that I could say to her, "Maybe today our mother will visit us," or she could say it to me, knowing that she was in exactly the same predicament and that she was my sister, just being with her was a comfort.

My mother's visits overshadowed everything. That's the only thing I lived for. When she visited she looked like she had cried all night. They literally had to pry us off her, that's how much we wanted to go with her. We didn't care who was in danger or not in danger. She was our mother! We had already lost our father. How could we not go with our mother? Here she is, standing in front of you, speaking to you. Why can't you leave with her? How do you tell that to a five-year-old?

The last time we saw my mother was in the convent, the few times she visited us. We never heard from her again, no. Just like my father was taken away and we never heard from him again. It was the same thing with my mother.[8]

Then the nuns arranged to put us into a home where there were many Jewish children, a Jewish orphanage, Wezembeek-Oppem,[9] near Brussels. I don't remember the trip to Brussels. All the personnel were Jewish. The orphanage was quite large. It had a large yard with fruit trees, and the building itself was large. It even had a room where we were able to hold assemblies, and it had a dining room. We slept in beds in dormitories. It was fairly good living in the middle of a war. We went to a public school. We walked to school in snow, rain, wind, mud, one hour to school and one hour back. I remember the days we had snow and we had no boots, and we walked in the snow. It was a long trek. There were adults who walked with us, people who took care of us from the orphanage.

It was a modern public school, beautiful. I liked going to school. I enjoyed the learning. I wrote, and we did a lot of coloring. We had sewing classes, everything. I don't remember boys in my class. I think the boys were on one side of the building and the girls on the other. I think the teacher was a woman. There was no discrimination against the Jewish children.

In the orphanage we had assemblies. We sang the usual children's songs, like *Alouette, gentille alouette.* In the back of my mind I seem to remember that I must have learned a few simple Hebrew songs, but I can't bring it to the surface. We played games, we played ball and hopscotch. We played checkers. We played a game that we created with pen and pencil, "Submarine," which children still play here. We had a few nursery-type books. At school I had a particular friend, a non-Jew. I remember her name, Nadine Gautier. She was in my class. I remember being invited to her house. I had permission to go, and I visited her several times.

We had very little clothing. For school they gave us aprons to keep our clothes clean. We wore the same dress for two weeks in a row, and the apron used to catch the dirt. They couldn't really provide individual wardrobes for so many children.

We used to see the Germans walking up and down the street, and I remember thinking, "How come they took my father away, and they're letting me walk the streets? How is that possible?" But it was. The adults did the talking if the Germans asked anything. We were never alone, always accompanied. We were never in the street at all unless we went to school in a group or returned from school. We just did not roam the streets. We were either in the orphanage or on the way to school.

We were in several places. We were taken away, and then we came back to the orphanage. We were thrown from pillar to post for a while. If things got bad in one area, they moved us en masse to another area, to another orphanage.

I remember somebody used to come in all the time to the dorm and say *"sheket bevakasha"* (quiet please). Who would say that if not a Jew to another Jew? Whoever was taking care of us at that time was Hebrew speaking.

Sometimes we got sick, and, yes, we got medical attention. If we had the measles or the chicken pox, people did come to help us. They must have called the doctor to examine us. But to this day, I don't know if it was measles or chicken pox. All I remember is having a rash with scabs. I remember they drew the shades to darken the room.

When the Germans were getting very, very close they moved us to another orphanage that wasn't Jewish, but en route they took a few of us and put us in a private home for a week or two. I was fortunate to be with my sister. There was a man and a woman and a daughter in her late teens. She had a mean streak in her a mile wide. She used to force us to drink vinegar.

That's right. Her parents didn't know. She frightened us so that we never told her parents. Her joy was to see us suffer. Fortunately, we were not there long, and they moved us to another orphanage where we were quite safe.

One day the Germans came and said they wanted to occupy the building and grounds. The people who were in charge took a few children who had the measles or chicken pox to the front gate and said, "Look, you are in a place where children are very sick. If you come in you will be sick." The Germans didn't care. They said, "Get them out of their beds," so they took us all and moved us to a stable so the Germans could occupy our beds. The stable was a circular concrete structure with a concrete floor. They threw some straw on it, and they laid us down, on our sides, one by one, like sardines in a can. You could not turn either way. We were fully clothed, and we had lice from head to toe because we couldn't bathe. We used the outhouse outside, and the Germans had our beds and the grounds.

At one point they decided that it was so dangerous that we couldn't keep our own names. They changed our family name to Felix. We used to go to pray in church, and they gave us rosary beads. I remember praying on rosary beads. We sensed the danger, and we knew that we'd better do what they told us. We realized that the people who were taking care of us really wanted to protect us, so we cooperated. We were taught the French prayers on the rosary beads. I used to take them to bed with me every night. I thought maybe this was going to help me and that this was going to save us if we were in such great danger. I said Hail Marys, and I used to cross myself and go to church like a good girl.

I knew that a war was taking place. We used to see the V2 rockets flying, and they had air raids, and we had to go into the ditches and cover ourselves with straw. We used to lie in bed at night and shake.

I remember liberation day vividly. They took the whole group of children to walk into the village of Wezembeek-Oppem. It was May 8, and we didn't know that anything had happened. When we got to the town, all of a sudden church bells started ringing, every bell in the whole area. Belgian flags were being unfurled from balconies. People started singing, screaming from joy, and crying and laughing. It's so hard to describe the joy. They told us what had happened. We were so excited that I don't even remember the trip back home, but I remember that when we got back to the orphanage there was a group from Palestine, from the Jewish Brigade.[10] One of these liberators put candy into a cannon and shot it into the orphanage.

Their reaction at seeing Jewish children was beyond description. They held us, they hugged us, they just made physical contact with us just to know that we were alive and well. They felt such joy at being part of a group that could save Jewish children. They couldn't stay very long; they were on their way somewhere. For me liberation was a great, great joy. It was as if someone had released all the tension. The fear was gone. At that point I couldn't even think about my parents yet. Not yet. But my next thought was that maybe, maybe my parents will come back. That's what everyone thought. That's what every child wanted. Some parents were found, fortunately. Every time someone was reunited with his family we used to beg them, "Did you hear from my mother? Did you hear from my father?"

Then something very, very wonderful happened. My uncle, my father's brother, who had hidden in the mountains during the war with his whole family, came back to Antwerp. He knew that we had been put in an orphanage because that had occurred before he went to the mountains. He got a bicycle and traveled from orphanage to orphanage throughout Belgium, not knowing where we were, hoping that he'd find us, and he did. He rode up on a bicycle, and he found us. He brought us chewing gum, I remember. We didn't even know what chewing gum was; we gave it away. The silly things you remember!

He wanted to take us, but he just couldn't. He didn't even have the means to feed his own family. He had three children. He knew we were being taken care of, so he left us in the orphanage. He explained things to us. They had almost starved to death in the mountains. The peasants didn't have enough to eat. They certainly weren't going to give food to the Jews. My uncle used to bribe his way through to buy food. Believe me, they didn't come back in great condition. They really didn't. By then I had lost my childhood, so I understood. My uncle used to take us for *Shabbos* to his house. We always went to him. He was a very religious man. That's when our Jewishness came into full bloom. I realized what we really were; the pieces started fitting together. I knew I was Jewish all along, but I became more aware of it after the war. All along I knew we were persecuted because we were Jewish. There was no doubt about it. Why else would nuns protect the Jews?

After liberation there was more religious observance in the orphanage, with candle lighting on Friday night. They taught us *brakhot*, but not reading the *siddur*.

I remember seeing American soldiers at liberation also. There was a parade. There was singing and soldiers marching with their rifles, and every-body was so happy, and you just got carried away with the joy of the day. It was an unbelievable feeling. I remember they captured Germans. The American soldiers and the Palestinian soldiers came to the orphanage and looked into every nook and cranny to make sure there weren't German soldiers hiding. They asked us if there were any German soldiers on the premises, and we told them no. But they double-checked. I saw German soldiers clearing the rubble, and the supervisors told us, "That's their punishment. Let them work."

My uncle contacted another brother who had left Europe when he was very young who lived in Pennsylvania. He told him that we were alive. That's when my uncle Sam came from the United States to bring us back with him. To this day, my aunt and uncle are sorry that they didn't keep us with them. But they were struggling. It was difficult enough with three children; they couldn't take care of five children. Sam came to Belgium, and he brought us back to the United States with a great deal of difficulty because it was not easy to acquire the immigration papers. It took quite a few months.

We were very excited because, as young as we were, we had heard that America was a great, wonderful place. The realization that our parents weren't coming back had hit us a long time before. Every time someone was reunited with their family we asked, "Why can't we have our mother and father?" We had constant disappointment. We were told by the officials who ran the orphanage that our parents were probably killed in a concentration camp. Later on my aunt and uncle in Belgium found out that most likely it was Auschwitz.

In August 1946 we went through Germany on a train. Germany was rubble from end to end. We stood most of the way because it was very crowded. We sailed from Sweden on a Swedish boat, the *Drottningholm*. It was a ten-day trip. On the first day we were seasick, but the other nine days were luxury incarnate. There was a lot of food. We were able to walk around freely; somebody made our beds. There was even a movie on the boat. To me it was like a luxury liner. It was an adventure. On that same boat was a couple, Scandinavians, who were returning to Minnesota. They approached my uncle and asked if they could help us. She acted like a mother to us. She made sure that we changed our clothes and that we washed properly. We kept in contact with them until just recently. We wrote to each other and brought each other up to date.

We landed in New York City and were met by my father's sister, who had a business in Brighton Beach.[11] We all piled into a taxi, and I remember driving through the dock area and asking, "Where is the gold?" My aunt lived under the El on Brighton Beach Avenue.[12] The noise was something I really wasn't accustomed to. I liked the ocean, but I wasn't impressed with Brighton Beach Avenue.

I started school in the fourth grade in Brighton Beach. I was very fortunate that they put me in a class where the teacher knew a smattering of French. We were, you could say, celebrities in that school. We were two of the first survivors to come to that school. As soon as we learned enough English the principal asked us to go from class to class and say a few words about our experiences. I remember how difficult it was for me. I thought my teeth would break in my mouth. We told them how we had been in the war and how we lost our parents and how we ran away from the Germans. We were the center of attention, and we ate it up. My teacher's name was Lieberman. She used to sit with me and teach me to read in English, individually. She gave me extra time during the day and after school.

My relatives spoke Yiddish, and I spoke fluent Yiddish, so I understood them. But I spoke to my sister in French. We had like our own little secret conversation because no one understood French. We were the only two. That way we were able to feel separate and special.

After four months we went to live with my uncle in Scranton, Pennsylvania. We went to a public school. There were a lot of Jews in our area, and we even had some Jewish teachers. I liked school very much because I felt very secure and safe there.

My uncle was a difficult man. He was a very bitter person because he had lost a wife in childbirth. We lived with him in a small, one-bedroom apartment. He made life very difficult for us. We were very, very unhappy. He used to yell at us constantly. I guess my sister and I comforted each other all the time. We also had good neighbors who were very kind to us. They used to take us in and feed us because they knew it was difficult for us to cook.

We kept house for my uncle. We had to cook. He worked in a place that made hats, caps, and he left for work very early, but he also did a certain amount of work in the house. He used to cook cereal for us every morning, but by the time we got up it was like a block of cement. We threw it out every day. He used to go out at night and come home late. One night, close to midnight, he woke us up out of bed because we forgot to scrub out the sink.

He used to harp and harp and harp until I thought I'd go crazy. He was unhappy, and he made us unhappy.

Estelle and her sister lived with their uncle for eight years. After four years the uncle married a widow with three sons who lived in a small town nearby, where Estelle graduated from high school. During the summers she worked in the Catskill Mountains to earn money and to have a social life. There she met the man whom she married at the age of nineteen.

My husband comes from a very religious background. We wanted our children to be raised in a religious atmosphere. When the children were born we decided not to play games. You have to be consistent. You can't say, "Do as I tell you and don't do as I do."

I have learned that you have to live and do *what* you can *when* you can because you just don't know what tomorrow will bring. You just don't. So I learned not to let opportunities go by. Take advantage of everything that you can.

—*Interviewed by Bonnie Gurewitsch, August 27, 1986*

The following conversation between Estelle Alter and her sister, Regina Glinzman, was videotaped at the Museum of Jewish Heritage on February 15, 1993. It clearly illustrates Estelle's assertion that "we have such a close relationship to this day."

Regina: After we got married we lived around the corner from each other. First we lived in East New York. When I moved to Crown Heights Estelle moved around the corner from me to Crown Heights, and we stayed there until we bought the house in New Jersey.

Estelle: This was a deliberate decision to live near each other.

Regina: There was just never any question about it. Our husbands just accept it; that's the way it is. They take it in stride. They like each other and are both easy to get along with.

Estelle: Since we've lived in the house we have an open-door policy. The only thing that's locked is the front door. The doors are literally open. I don't mean unlocked, they're *open*. The children always have access—

Regina: From one to the other—

Estelle: To Regina's refrigerator. [Laughs] Everybody just feels at home in both places. So it's an open-door policy, and yet you have the privacy of your own home. I mean, nobody walks in without giving a knock to say, "I'm here." But there's that closeness as if it's one big family.

Regina: We always considered it one household. The kids are always together. You know, you just go from one apartment to the other, upstairs or downstairs.

Estelle: You never feel like you have to make a decision by yourself. If something important happens, and you need that extra thought, somebody's input, there's always someone there to ask. And yet, because we never worked together, there are days that we don't even see each other. But we always know that somebody is there if we need it.

Regina: When my older daughter, the middle child, was very ill, Estelle was my lifesaver. My son was about six, seven years old, and he had to be watched and taken to school. I was pregnant at that time with my youngest. My daughter was sick for a year, and I used to go to the hospital every day, and Estelle was my lifesaver. After the baby was born my daughter was ill again and had to have a serious operation. If it wasn't for Estelle watching the baby, I could never have done it.

Estelle: Because we never had parents to depend on, it was always each other.

Regina: It was always each other. It was very important to me. There was always an aunt and uncle around.

Estelle: I can honestly say there were no moments of conflict.

Regina: Nothing that I remember. I know when Estelle used to go on vacation, she left Brian, the baby, with me, and she'd take my older daughter along. You know, we'd trade. We always managed somehow. We always helped each other out.

Estelle: We've lived in the house twenty-three years. I can honestly say it's been a peaceful, peaceful twenty-three years.

Regina: Right. When we decide we have to do a repair, we agree on it; we buy what we need. We share everything down the line. We don't ask who pays this much or that much. When the bills come, we cut them in half, and that's it.

Estelle: When we get the utility bills, the electric bills, we don't even look at the numbers; the only reason we look at it is because we have to add them up.

Regina: I add them up, divide it in two, and that's it. I think we have the same value system. I think that material things are not that important. We enjoy them, but it's not that we *have* to have anything. I know family is important, and our health is very important, and our children and our husbands are the most important. We know what's important.

Estelle: I always taught my children that, no matter what problems arise, if you can see there's a solution at the end, you can overcome the problems. Especially with health; if you know that you can get better, if there's a light at the end of the tunnel, you can overcome almost anything.

Regina: Jewish affiliation is very important to me, very. Since I went back to work full time, which is about twenty years now, I've worked for UJA [United Jewish Appeal]. It was always very important to me. I have a kinship with it. I'm helping fellow Jews. I've always been very active in the *shul* and with AMIT [religious women's Zionist organization] women; I know I don't have to worry about *yom tov*, I don't have to work on Jewish holidays. There's no pressure. I just love working in the Jewish community. It's very important to me.

Estelle: I work for the Yeshivah of New Jersey. I have worked for them for seventeen years. I love working with the children, and it's very important to me. I just enjoy the whole atmosphere. My children know that I work for the Yeshivah. I think there's a sense of pride in that, knowing that I'm working for Jewish children's education.

Regina: We have family in Israel that we're very close to, a surviving aunt and three first cousins. I've been there about four times, I think, Estelle about five times. Our cousins just called the other day. We keep in very close touch, write, call.

Estelle: Regina and I still confide in each other to a certain degree.

Regina: To a certain degree. We always talk our problems over; we always talk about it. Our husbands have no problem with that.

Estelle: It's good for them. They listen too. There are no secrets. We're not making world policy in our house!

Regina: My friends notice our close relationship. People at work do also. They can't believe we've been living next to each other all our married lives and that we're still doing it.

Estelle: Because we live in a peaceful way.

Regina: They tell us their stories. One friend told me she could never live with her sister. Her sister lives about three hours away, and she says that's about as close as she wants to get. People are amazed that we lasted so long.

Estelle: Really, I don't see what's so difficult about it. I really don't. You don't need a special formula. Like I said, just mind your own business and go about living. That's all.

Regina: We don't butt in. We know exactly—

Estelle: What our limits are—

Regina: What our limits are. And it's just been very easy. Really.

Margie Nitzan

Marga Levi was born in 1929 in Fulda, Germany. She was the third of four children of Orthodox parents. The older son died before Margie was born; the younger son was born in 1933. Margie's sister, Hannelore, was a year older than Margie. Mr. Levi was a paint salesman, whose job required him to travel to Switzerland and France. She remembers that in 1933 her father was told not to return home because the Nazis were looking for him. Mrs. Levi took the three children to Alsace Lorraine, where Mr. Levi joined them.

I remember in France we were looking inside a building, inside a hall where they had a party, and we were outside, we couldn't get in. I remember a song. My mother used to sing "Kikel, kokel, kakel . . . ," and my brother used to laugh. She had all three of us on her knees. It was a happy time for me in France except that we couldn't join the parties. But we had other friends, children of friends of the family, and we played with them on *Shabbos*.

My family was religious. My mother wore a *sheitl*. My father had no money; he was very poor, and Meyer Nussbaum took him in as his partner because he was an excellent salesman. He didn't have much [secular] education, but he knew a lot about Jewish things, the *gemara*. At first my father worked in France, but then they threw him out of France. They produced pictures that he was a Nazi in Germany, and they threw him and Meyer Nussbaum out of France. My father didn't know what to do anymore, so he went to Switzerland. There we lived very well. We lived in Basel, in a *pension*, but my father couldn't work.[1] We lived there for about a year, and then in 1935 we went to Italy, Milano.[2]

We lived in the Piazza Feravilla, Numero Tre, in Milano. I went to an Italian Jewish school, Instituto Israelitico Alessandro DaFano [Alessandro DaFano Jewish Institute]. I was all mixed up because we were hearing so many languages: German, French, Swiss, Italian. I was very bad in school; I had to repeat three classes, the first and the third. In the third grade I got a wonderful teacher by the name of Tina Levi, written the same as mine. She had black hair with a little gray; she was beautiful and good. She was my teacher for three years, and I learned many things from her. I remember I was afraid because I couldn't sing too well. I always had stomachaches because I wasn't such a good student in math. But I was very good in Italian. I could have been a writer. Every morning we had to say the *Sh'ma Yisrael* with the hand on the eyes.[3] Then we said the ten commandments. Professor Shauman taught us Hebrew. At home we studied Hebrew, too, with my mother. She taught us the *brokhos* for *bentching* after eating and washing the hands, for eating potatoes, for eating fruits.[4]

My father traveled to Switzerland as a salesman. That was his base. He sold his paint; he had a very good business. He found his own customers, and he spoke German to them. He never learned Italian, and my mother didn't either. They couldn't learn the language, but they loved living in Italy. They didn't want to go to America.

There was no anti-Semitism.[5] Even if they were Fascist, the people we lived with were not anti-Semitic. They respected us. We had people visiting all the time, Friday night, Saturday, people who had no homes or were without family. My father gave a lot of money to charity. We went to the synagogue of the Rothschilds, where all the refugees went.[6] We didn't have many Italian friends, only refugees like us. The Italians didn't bother with us.

The last day we were allowed to buy kosher meat my father and I went together to the Rothschilds and bought salami. Then came the law: no more salami and no more kosher salami for Italian Jews. It must have been before the war broke out.

Then they took away my father's passport,[7] and he couldn't travel to Switzerland anymore; he couldn't make a living anymore. So he started cleaning apartments of other Jewish people. And then the war broke out, and there he was cleaning, and the Fascists came in and arrested him.[8] He was hiding in the bathtub. They took him to San Vittorio prison.[9] My mother went to visit him with my sister and my brother. My brother was crying. It was cold, it was dark, it was horrible. My sister won't talk about it. They took my father to the south of Italy to a camp, Ferramonti di Tarsia, Provincia Calabria.[10]

We were still in Milano in the same apartment. My mother became very sick there. We children continued going to the Jewish school on the Via Eupili. All the Jewish children came there afterwards because they weren't allowed to go to school anymore.[11] We were all in one boat. No more money, no more books. The Italian Jews didn't take us in; we didn't feel welcome, even if we went to that school. My mother got assistance from Jewish organizations; we were starving.[12]

My father wrote to my mother, and my mother wrote to him in German. Beautiful handwriting. He used to write *"dein Vater, dein Mann"* (your father, your husband). My mother always read his letters to us.

My mother was very good to me. I didn't have to go to work. But she took my sister out of the fifth grade when she was twelve, and she had to go to work like a grown-up. She was no good to my sister. My sister worked for Mr. Bauer, wrapping napkins with two Jewish boys.

In 1943 Italian Jewish people didn't send their children to school anymore because of the bombardments by the Americans and because the German laws were getting worse and worse, anti-Semitism.[13] So I went to a class with friends in a private home. We had a science class. That's all I had in the sixth grade, nothing else. I ate there in a kindergarten class with another older girl like me. Maybe they took us in because we were so skinny and starved.[14] I had a marvelous time. My teacher, Tina Levi, was in charge there, and she made us work like in Israel. Work the ground to plant seeds like in Israel. Take showers, run, she made us do all those things. I remember the last year; we were in the fifth grade, she wanted to take us to a park, but then she didn't let us go. She was afraid because of the Germans. I still remember the Jewish holidays, like on *Sukkos* when we went into the *sukkah* and the teachers gave us candies. They knew that it was the end for the Jews.

My mother didn't give us any food. She only thought of eating herself. She sent us to the Committei[15] after school to eat. We had lousy food, soup. I don't remember anymore. On Saturday, on *Shabbos*, we went there, we had a little soup, and then they gave us an egg to eat on our way home. It was a long walk from the Committei to home. Then at night my mother didn't even give us a piece of bread, nothing. We just had that *egg*.

My mother had food for herself, chestnuts and pears and potatoes. Once I went to get ten kilos of potatoes, and I had to schlepp all that stuff home; I hardly made it. Some Italian people took me to get it somewhere out of Milano. We didn't eat ham. She sent me to buy the ham with our coupons, so I gave the ham to the baker, who gave me a hard piece of bread. I brought it to my mother, and she didn't give me a piece; she ate it.

On Sunday we used to go to the Zipels, Mr. Zipel and Anna Zipel, and she used to cook for my brother and me, and we would have a meal there. She was a friend of my mother's. She used to bring us food. She used to come on her bicycle, bring my mother some food. Then we would go downstairs to Frieslander, and we had pancakes, my brother and I, and we would go to the Milgroms, and they would give us food there. She used to say, "These poor little children . . . ," and then they would give us ten lire, and we would go home and give it to my mother. Once, the last time we went to the Milgroms, we used the ten lire and bought chestnuts. My brother made me. I didn't want to. But he was smarter than me.

I was in the center of Milano, and I saw a huge picture of *Jud Süss* counting the money. That was a film; I got scared. And the only other time I saw anti-Semitism was when I walked with my mother in the street. A woman started screaming, "Take off your *sheitl*, you Jew, you." So my mother started running with us.

She never told us *anything* about what was going on. *Never* my father or my mother. So we didn't understand everything that happened to us afterwards because they didn't talk to us. They should have talked to us. They didn't want to scare us, I guess.

She was better to us when we were small. She became rotten when we were bigger. I don't know why she changed, but she was rotten. She was mentally ill, I think. I don't know. I don't know what happened to her. When I saw her picture after the war, she was so serious, so starved.

In 1943 my father came home for three weeks because my mother had an operation on one of her feet. The Italian community saw to it that he came home because the children couldn't be home by themselves. He was released from the concentration camp for three weeks. At the end of the three weeks two Fascists came to take him back, and I told one of them, "How come you are so mean. How can you do such a mean job and watch people like that?" I didn't know what I was saying. He didn't say anything. He could have killed us for talking like that. But then at the end of the day, the two Fascists took my father, and the housekeeper saw us near the glass, my brother and I, and we were crying, and they took my father away again to the camp.

Then we had to go into hiding. They started arresting all the Jews.[16] We kept running; we ran and ran. Some Italian came after us and said, "Run away from here. They just arrested everybody." Mr. Bauer came to my mother and told her, "Mrs. Levi, we are fleeing to Switzerland. We cannot give you anymore money for the rent." My mother used to pawn her wedding band and her engagement ring every month because she had no money.

There was a French woman on the same floor I lived, and once we went to her and asked her, "Could your mother please give us some vitamins for my sister because she's so skinny and anemic?" She said, "I'm not the mother, I'm the wife." We became friendly with her. I started going into her apartment. She gave me delicious food, pasta with cheese and eggs, and cheese. She said to my mother, "I'm taking Marga with me." My mother said "All right." So she washed all my clothes, and then my mother said "No, Marga cannot go." But a year later when things got so bad, she said "Yes, you can take her now." Her name was Georgette Milanola. She was a French Catholic. She saved my life. I was with her two and one-half years.

She took me to Piemonte, in the mountains. The first month I didn't do anything there. I played around. But then after the month she sent away the maid, and I became her maid. She started hitting me and reading to me the Evangelists from the Bible and about how bad the Jews are, how dirty they are. How they're only interested in money. She started slapping me in the face, and she started praying with another Italian lady about the Ave Maria, saying the *rosario*. I used to cry. I used to think that religion wasn't true, my Jewish religion also. She made me read in *L'Osservatore Romano*[17] about the chief rabbi of Rome and how he became a Catholic.[18] I read that, and I started crying. The paper said that his whole family became Catholic. I didn't see a book, nothing except the Evangelists about Jesus Christ and the Temple and what he did with the Jews, with the money. All these things drove me crazy. I used to cry all the time there, and I didn't know when the war would end and I would see somebody again. We also had the Germans coming after us, looking for the partisans and the Fascists.

I had no contact with my mother and family for three years. I was only fourteen. She didn't give me enough to eat, but other people gave to me, and I learned how to steal. I was the only Jew in that town. Everybody knew I was Jewish, and there were some Fascists there too. But they didn't report me.

The Germans came to Piemonte once or twice. They asked for *partigiani*. Once she wasn't there when they came at five or six o'clock in the morning. They banged on the doors, and they ran in, and I got so scared. I had a picture of my father and my mother,[19] and I wanted to put the picture away, but I didn't. They didn't know I was Jewish. They liked me, but I didn't like them. I opened the window to see what was happening. They were there looking in so I pulled myself in on the bed, and I prayed. But then they ran away. They went to every house looking. There were a lot of *partigiani*. The Italians helped them.

Once, another girl from Piemonte took me down in the valley to have my hair done. There were some girls there, and they were talking about the Jews, about hiding and killing them. They were so happy that the Germans found them and killed them. Thank God I didn't say anything. All the girls were friendly with the partisans. They all had *partigiani* boyfriends. Once there was a big tragedy with the *partigiani*. The Germans came up and killed them and took their eyes out. People told me, and I couldn't believe it. They told me that they took the children of the Jewish women and shot them, and I couldn't believe it, and I didn't want them to know that I was Jewish. I didn't tell them, but they knew it because *she* told them. But I didn't believe all those things. I don't know what I was thinking.

She took me to church two or three times. There was no priest in Piemonte because the people were all Communists, and they didn't want the church to be there. The priest came to her and gave her communion and confession. She had a communion class of little children, and she would tell me to teach the Catholic religion to the children, and she made me go to midnight mass. At Easter I took her to church to take communion with the children. Little by little I forgot all the Jewish prayers. I learned all the Christian prayers, Catholic prayers.

I was very angry and very hurt about this. I never wanted to change my religion. I talked to the priests, I went to church, I made a mass once, *Festa la Madonna* (feast of the Madonna). I had a very good friend, a woman who was her maid. She ran away from her and married a man with two children because she couldn't take it any longer. She was a Catholic too. She gave me a beautiful paper to read with stories about young girls, about Catholic girls. I didn't mind; at least I could read something. But at night, when I was reading, I left the light on, and then la Georgetta came down, and I got so scared. She was so ugly, and she hit me, and it was awful.

Once I punched her, and she fell on the floor. I was older then, I was almost ready to leave, at the end of the war. She fell on the floor, and she got so scared. I asked her, "Why did your husband go with another woman?" Because he had a woman. Every night she would be in her apartment at eight o'clock preparing dinner for him, and I saw him. I used to bring her the milk, and he took this woman all over. Everybody knew about her except la Milanola.[20]

I was never mean; I never told her anything. Never. But this time I hit her. I hit her; I punched her in the belly. Every morning I used to get up at five o'clock to clean the house, and the priest used to watch me there from the window. She ate very well, but she didn't give me anything to eat. I brought her food up to her.

She was a very mean woman. All the maids used to cry when they would come out of her room. She was mean to everybody, not just to me. I had to pick up her stuff. There was no water in the house in Piemonte, so I used to carry the water up and bring it to her, and then she spit in it, and I had to wash all her things with her spit in there. I used to bring down her potty with the big stuff to throw away because she couldn't go to the bathroom with the other people, she was a *signiora*. Once she shit all over the floor. I used to read stories in a newspaper. Once I told a woman, "Oh, what a nice romance!" So she took away all the newspapers because she didn't want me to read the romance. So what if I read romance?

At the end she took me to Orta,[21] and I liked it much better there. It was near Lago Maggiore, in the north; it was a beautiful town. It had beautiful villas with roses. She had a garden with tomatoes. Then towards the end of the war she changed. She made me new clothes. She tried to send me to school a little bit, privately. But I couldn't learn anymore; I didn't want to learn anymore. She sent me to play with other children, but I couldn't play anymore. All this was to try to baptize me. She always, always said to the women that I was Jewish. "She's *Ebrea* [Jewish]." She said, "I'm taking you to the priest to be baptized." I didn't want to change. I didn't want to change my religion.

Six months after the war I was still living with her in Orta. Nobody came for me. I went back to Milano. My sister met me. My sister was coming to see me . . . My mother had fled to Switzerland. My sister and my brother were in a Catholic orphanage. My sister was scared because she was a Catholic already; she had already converted; I saw it on her face. I asked my sister, "Can I come to live with you?" "Yes, yes, yes." So I went, and that was the end for me. I got in with the nuns. I went to live with the nuns and the children in the Catholic orphanage. I wanted to be with children again. I was still young. I was not even sixteen.

My sister told me that the Germans came to look for her and our mother and brother. When they didn't find them they went away. Then my sister said to my mother, "It's your fault we almost got caught because you didn't want to go away on *Shabbat*. I'm glad I'm leaving you. Now you'd better go." My mother went to a Catholic old-age home near Milano, and my sister went to the orphanage with my brother.

> *Margie's sister told her of the difficult time their mother had in Milan and how she entered Switzerland illegally and lived in Lugano in a hotel for refugees. After they were reunited, Mrs. Levi told Margie that the Italian Jews had rejected her. "They didn't bother with her because they thought she left her children. They thought she had run away and that her children had been killed. So she was all alone and worried about us. She became very skinny and serious." The last contact Margie had with her father was in 1943, when he went back to the camp after her mother was sick.*

When the Americans came in they freed my father. He went to America, to Oswego.[22] Nobody came for us. Why didn't they? They were really selfish. A lot of things would have been different if they had come. Maybe I wouldn't have been baptized by the Catholic nuns.

I liked it in the Catholic orphanage, I loved it. The children and the nuns were nice. I was with my sister and my brother, and the nuns were very pretty. I believed in the religion. They made us study at night, but I didn't study. They said, "Marga doesn't have to study if she doesn't want. She's Jewish." So I didn't study. But I believed in all that junk.

I guess they were mad because I didn't become a Catholic, I didn't ask them to baptize me. So at the end, before I left Italy, the nun in my ward told me, "Marga, you have to become Catholic. Tomorrow, speak to the mother superior and tell her, 'Today I want to go with you to Como.'" She said I should become Catholic to help my sister remain Catholic when we went back to the Jewish people. She said my sister would not be able to resist the influence of the Jews all by herself to stay Catholic.

So they sent me with a nun and my sister to Como. I was afraid of the nun. The priest baptized me. I started shaking like a leaf, and I didn't know what the mother was doing. I didn't know how to confess. I had nothing to confess; I had no sins. And then three days later we went to Switzerland, to my mother in Lugano.

In Switzerland I had an awful time. I was scared to death of an old priest. I started shaking at confession. My sister went, but I didn't want to go. Thank God he said, "No, Marga doesn't have to." So I didn't have to confess. I was scared of him.

Just before we left Milano, my sister wrote to my mother that she had become a Catholic and that I wanted to. So my mother answered, "Don't do it because Jewish people don't pray in front of statues made of clay." It was just not the right answer. She should have run to us. The nuns understood she would never allow me to become a Catholic so they baptized me at the end. When the Jewish people found out about it they suddenly became so nice, coming to us, making us clothes. Mr. Bauer told my sister in front of me, "My daughter Ilse would never have done what you did." But the truth is that probably *any* Jew who had been in the orphanage would have done it. Three other children there did it. Three little girls. Their mother allowed them to become Catholic. After the war people said, "She did it to save her children."

> When Margie and her sister and brother got to Switzerland they stayed with their mother in Lugano in a pension. Their mother could not accept their Catholicism and tried to take away Margie's religious medals. After eight days Margie went to Basel, to German Jewish friends of Mr. Levi, who was in touch with his wife and the children. Mr. Levi "begged us to come [to America] and [said] that he would let us do whatever we want, to please come."

We all wrote to each other, and I saw my sister. My brother was in Vevey in Swiss France in an orphanage for Orthodox Jewish children. They were preparing him for bar mitzvah. My sister was working in the home of a woman who had six or seven children. She used to take care of them. She had a lot of work with the children.

In Basel I lived with a German Jewish woman, her husband, and her son. She had a house. She had a business. Their name was Sobol. They were very good to me. They gave me a coat. They sent me to the beauty parlor every week. But I wanted to go to church. I wasn't good to them. I'm ashamed.

Mrs. Sobol tried teaching me how to go shopping. I couldn't learn. [Laughs] I became scared of her because she reminded me of Milanola. She was a little fat, but she was much better than Milanola. She bought me beautiful clothes, very beautiful clothes. She did it because she knew my father. She didn't even know that I was scared. Maybe she saw it, but she didn't say anything. She went with me all the time. She took me to the beauty parlor. I didn't have to clean; she had maids to clean. The only thing I had to do was just nothing. I don't remember what I did. Eat and sleep. I started writing to the nuns, and I drove myself crazy. I went to the *shul* in Basel to the main synagogue every *Shabbos* with her and her son and her husband. I used to look down at the men all the time because I was interested in guys.[23] I *liked* it in the *shul*, but then I had conflicts with my sister. Every time I saw her, she wanted to go to church. The conflicts ruined my life.

My sister and I became so anti-Semitic. It was a shame what we did in Basel. We shamed all the Jewish people. We used to run. Every Saturday we used to go and live somewhere else because we didn't want to be with the Jewish girls. We made contact with Catholics, and they arranged all this for us. They arranged for us to go with them to church. On *Shabbos* we used to go to the *shul*, and we were there with the Catholics, and they could see the Jews walking into the *shul*. It was anti-Semitic. We were just *bad*. We started hating the Jews. You know what happens.

After the war, when I came back to Milano I thought all the Jewish people had converted, but it wasn't true. It was a big disappointment. It wasn't true at all. I thought that the Jews were no good and that the Jews were not nice and that the Jews were not handsome and not smart. We were so indoctrinated. In Basel we lived with Jewish people, and they paid for everything. The Catholics never paid for us. We went to the ORT school[24] and learned sewing. We learned everything about cutting and embroidery.

In December 1946 my brother, my sister, my mother, and I came to America. My father came to New York to pick us up. We lived in Williamsburgh. It was a slum. When I saw my brother again, he had changed, too. My father wanted us to live with them. My sister and I were working; we were bringing in the money. My brother was going to school, and my mother couldn't work, and my father had started his own business. He loved us so much, and we loved him so much, more than my mother. He tried to understand us. He wanted us to be Jewish again. We tried. Every Friday they prayed, and my mother *bentched licht* [lit Sabbath candles]. We lived with them, but we didn't follow the observances. We didn't *believe* in it anymore. We thought we knew better. We were anti-Semitic.

When we came together again, it was a terrible thing for my mother. We all ganged up on her. She didn't love us enough. She didn't love my father, and my father didn't love her. She had all her sisters, and she always complained about us, and she said we were no good because we became Catholic. She thought we were less than her. She was very Jewish; she was very proud of her religion. When we became Catholic, she couldn't take it because it happened to her and to my father. I couldn't take it either, to be honest.

On Sundays in Brooklyn we went to church just to hear the prayers, but we didn't take communion and we didn't go to confession. I didn't know what I would confess because I had no sins anyway. Even the priest said that. [Giggles]

In 1956, when we moved to Coney Island, we became Jewish again. We just stopped going to church, and we threw away all the Catholic things. And Jewish things too. Too bad I threw them away because we had beautiful things. Things that could have gone to museums. I had the teachers' report cards and Jewish books. When I was in second grade I got a book because I knew Hebrew so well, a beautiful book about Israel.

My father died in 1960. I lived at home until 1964, and then I got a job in a bank through a Jewish girlfriend. I left my brother and my mother, and I went to live with a girlfriend. I couldn't get along with her, so I went into the Catholic Y. There I had a nervous breakdown again, and I lived with my sister, and then I lived in a hotel in Manhattan Beach. Then, through an introduction, I met my husband; we got married. Then I became more and more Jewish because he's Israeli. We started talking about politics and all different things, and I believe what he believes. Now I'm Jewish. But once in a while I watch some of the "700 Club" on television; it's a Christian show at 6:30 on channel 9. I see Christians and what they do. But I wouldn't like it anymore for myself; I don't watch it anymore. Once in a while I go into a church just to look at a church. I don't kneel or anything. Just for curiosity. But I would like to find a synagogue where I could go in the morning instead of going to a church. I met Rabbi R. A woman from Pioneer Women[25] made me an appointment with him. I went to see him, and we started talking. He tried to help with problems I had with my husband, and later, much later, I told him that I lost my religion and what it did to me as a religious Jew. I asked him if I had to do something, and he said, "No."[26] He is a great rabbi, a handsome man. I studied Hebrew with him.

I'm still in touch with my brother and my sister. I call my sister too, but she doesn't want to see me. But if I would force her she would see me. She doesn't want to see me because she works. I don't work. She works at the state hospital as a nurse's aide, and she's very sick. She has diabetes, and she's very heavy, and now she has something wrong with her breast. I don't know. She had a gallbladder operation. She doesn't like religion. Her children are no good. They're not going to marry Jews. That's too bad. That's the sad part of it.

My brother is Jewish. He lives alone. He's not married. He's very sick, too. I see him, and I help him in any way and every way I can. But he makes me wait for him, and he doesn't cry, and I wait till 12:30 sometimes, and he doesn't come, and he doesn't call me. He sleeps. He takes one thousand milligrams of Thorazine . . . I know he's getting the proper care . . . They're giving me much less medication (ten milligrams), and they said I'm not paranoid, and I feel much better. Twice a week I go for group therapy, and maybe it's not the ideal thing, but it's better than where my brother goes, where I used to go.

I started reading the *Aufbau*,[27] and I ruined my head reading everything about the concentration camps. I used to think about it and hear screaming, and I just relive the whole thing. I went through it, and I was out of my mind completely. I had that syndrome: why was I living and the others died? What did they do wrong? I used to feel that I was a German and I killed the Jews. And that's really . . . I didn't do anything. I hope not.

I've been married twenty-one years. No children. I got married late. It was an introduction. I was afraid to get married, to have sex. But I wanted to get married, and the children didn't come. I went to a doctor and had other tests and had pain sometimes. I just had some teeth pulled, and I had a small operation and another operation. I went through a lot this year.

My mother died when Robert Kennedy and Martin Luther King died and [when] the Black Panthers and anti-Semitism [were going on]. My mother had a horrible death, too. She starved to death. She was in an old-age home. It was a terrible place to be. She always complained that she wanted to be with us. But we didn't realize . . . I went to see her every week, two, three times a week sometimes. At the end I didn't see her for a month or for three weeks; I don't remember. I blame myself for that too because she died then.

—*Interviewed by Bonnie Gurewitsch, March 26, 1986*

Margie has been in several psychiatric rehabilitation programs in New York. In April 1994 she added to her oral history file a group of poems that she wrote in a creative writing program sponsored by the Brooklyn Public Library Literacy Program. The following poem is dated March 4, 1994.

Margie Nitzan Autobiography

My
experience
with
religion
was
very
painful
It
almost
ruined
my
life
I
was
indoctrinated
and
I
changed
my
religion

I
became
a
Catholic
but,
I
didn't
understand
this
religion
I
naturally
became
an
antisemite

I was
very young
then
I did it
to help
my
sister
who
had
already
become
a
Catholic
It
was
a big
letdown
because
I
had
resisted
for two
and a
half years.
Until this day I regret it, It
almost cost me my
life.

In November 1994 Margie reported that she left her husband "in a moment of fear and anger." She is now living in a sheltered environment.

Edith Wachsman

Edith was born in 1931, the oldest child of Rabbi Abraham and Rosalie Klein. Rabbi Klein was a descendant of the Ḥatam Sofer,[1] and Edith's great-grandfather was Rabbi Moshe Shmuel Glasner.[2] Glasner was one of the founders of the religious Zionist Mizraḥi movement in Rumania and acted on his ideals by going to live in Palestine. Zionism, coupled with traditional, observant Judaism and an interest in secular studies, provided a rich cultural background in the Klein family.

Rabbi Klein was the district rabbi for an area of Czechoslovakia that bordered on Hungary. Edith remembers her childhood as simple and pleasant, with very warm personal relationships within her family and the close-knit Jewish community. The Kleins were expelled from Jelsava, Czechoslovakia,[3] when that area was annexed by Hungary after the Munich Pact in 1938. They reestablished their home in Revuca, twelve kilometers away, on the Slovakian side of the border.

Revuca was a very small community, about sixty or seventy families. Nobody was rich, but everybody had a business. There was only one poor person. He was a shoemaker, and on Purim he got the *matonos l'evyonim* from everyone! My mother made a beautiful Purim *seudah*; all the Jews came, and they all brought *shalaḥmonos*. My father was so proud of the beautiful food and my mother's *ḥallah*. He used to say, "All the husbands want to divorce their wives because your *ḥallah* is the best." My parents had a beautiful marriage. They adored each other.

Our house was right next to the *shul*, not far from the railroad station. I can still picture it. We had no running water, but no one did. There was a well in the yard, and there was an outhouse [laughter]. In the beginning we may have had two or three maids: a maid for the children, a maid to do the cleaning and washing. Another woman came on Monday to do the laundry, which was a big production. You had to cook the laundry in big pots and wash it in a tub, and then they took it to the river to rinse it out. Later on, when the anti-Jewish laws started,[4] Jews couldn't have any maids. They allowed us one old woman because of the young children, and I did the laundry myself.

I don't remember playing. I was too busy helping my mother. As a child, I never had a doll to play with. I had a jump rope, and we had a swing in the yard. We had a gate; we had an apple tree, a pear tree, and a walnut tree. I had very few dresses. I had a checked shirt and a navy blue skirt, called a *pepita* skirt, that were made for me. I had a few blouses for *Shabbos*. Every weekday we wore the same dress. My mother didn't knit, but she had somebody knit sweaters for us. The shoes were also made to order because you couldn't buy shoes. Every Thursday afternoon there was a big production. My mother used to brush my father's coat. She brushed and brushed until the spots came out. She didn't put water, God forbid, on the coat. There was no cleaning fluid, no appliances, nothing.

People didn't have radios, but there were posters in the post office and on the streets. They were posters with caricatures describing Jews, how they were vile and ignorant and dirty. I was always sent to the post office to pick up the mail; I used to have to wait there until I got it. I saw those pictures pasted there; it was so painful. They showed how they cut off the Jew's *payes* and ripped out his beard.

In the morning all the Jewish children went to a local public school. In the afternoon we all went to a *ḥeder* that my father organized. He hired a *boḥur* to teach us.

The principal of the public school was a miserable man, an anti-Semite. Tests in school were always given orally at the end of the year. Each child had to stand in front of the class and answer questions. [The number] 1 was the highest mark, then 2, 3, 4, and 5; 5 was failing. I remember my last semester in school; it must have been June 1940. I still remember that the sun was shining; it was pretty warm. I was standing there, and he was questioning me and questioning me. I gave him every answer, everything, and the guy couldn't stand it. I don't think he questioned any other child that long. Finally he asked me, "What is today?" That was something that you didn't read in books: What is today? I didn't know the answer. You know what that day was? The twenty-first of June, the first day of summer. For that answer he gave me a 2. I was in the third grade, and I didn't know that answer.

We had to go to school on *Shabbos*, too. But we were permitted not to write and not to carry books.[5] The schoolbooks had religious content. I was always chosen to read aloud about Jesus Christ or St. Mary. At a certain point before the deportations the few Jewish children in Revuca had to take school tests. They weren't given in our town. We had to go to a different city with different teachers. I had to study on my own. When my father would go to another town he would bring me books. I read old newspapers. That's how I learned Hungarian. I devoured anything I could get my hands on, reading, reading. But we didn't learn math, and I actually got a 3 on the test. The *goyim* were happy to see the Jews do poorly.

Every Christmas the Catholics would come and perform the nativity scene in our house just to antagonize us. They would come into the rabbi's house on purpose. We had to sit there and watch them perform. They were dressed in costumes; they were called "The Bethlehemtsis." How could you dare throw them out? How could you antagonize the *goyim?* I remember their processions during Easter. We wouldn't dare be seen on the street during Easter. They said, "The Jews killed Christ. You Jews killed Christ."

First they made us wear a yellow arm band.[6] Then that wasn't good enough; then it had to be a star.[7] Then there were differently sized yellow stars. I remember we even had to put a yellow star on the baby carriages. The people actually thought it was silly; they laughed. You were not allowed to go from one town to the next. There were curfews. You were not allowed to leave your house before ten [in the morning] and after seven [in the evening]. Once when one of my brothers was sick they sent me to the drugstore. I was frightened out of my wits. Even when he was allowed, my father never walked in the streets. He was afraid; he would walk behind the houses.[8] *Borukh HaShem,* the *shul,* was nearby, so he didn't have to go too far.

I was the one who did the shopping. The farmers would sell the fruit and vegetables in the morning. After 10 A.M. there were no more vegetables, so what did we do? We rented a piece of land behind our house, and we grew our own vegetables. We were so happy; we were so proud! My father and I dug up the ground. We ordered fertilizer; it smelled! Then we planted everything: carrots and peas, beans, radishes, scallions, tomatoes, lettuce, potatoes, and corn. Just wonderful!

Anytime of the day or night the police could come and search the house. We were terrified of policemen. We were not allowed to have anything valuable. The police went into the cabinets; they searched everywhere. If they found something made of silver, like a silver *bekher,* they took it away. Most Jews got rid of their valuables; they exchanged them for token things. We got rid of my mother's ring; we sold it or something.

My father learned *shehita* then, and soon they forbade that, too. He learned *shehita* because he was afraid we wouldn't be able to have any meat, and later on the *shohet* was deported. One day a policeman came in: "Rabbi, your *halef!*" He wanted the knife. My father took the knife from the top of the bookcase and gave it to the policeman. My father was so happy. Why? Because that was the bad knife; he had hidden the good one. He was so happy that he had outsmarted them. It wasn't the intrinsic value of the knife. That didn't matter to us as much as being able to keep *Yiddishkeit*. I remember that.

Then they rationed the food. The *goyim* got about three kilos of flour a week; the Jews only got half. We had our own chickens, and they laid eggs, which we ate. Then, one *Shabbos*, I'll never forget it; there was no chicken. They sent me to the next village to try to get a chicken for *Shabbos*. The *goya* said, "If you want to get a chicken, go chase after her." The chicken climbed up a tree. I was afraid. I said that I didn't want to go up after her, so I came home without a chicken. *Lekovod Shabbos* my father *shehted* our hen that laid eggs. We were so devastated, like she was part of the family. My sister Zissi absolutely refused to eat it. But *lekovod Shabbos* we *had* to have chicken.

Still, it wasn't that bad. Later on, when we were hiding, things were much worse. I don't remember being hungry because we managed somehow. My mother made noodles; we ate a lot of noodles, and later on we remembered how good they were.

My father traveled very often because there were Jews in a lot of little villages in the area. He was a *mohel* too, and he was called everywhere. On *Yom Kippur* I tried to fast all day, although I didn't have to. One woman said, "I would fast three days if I knew that the *tzores* would stop."

First they deported the men.[9] I remember it was on a Thursday. We were in the middle of *matzah* baking. In 1942 there was no *matzah* factory anymore, so we had to bake our own. They made a *matzah* bakery in an inn, where people came to drink. In the middle of the baking they came to say that all the young men had to go. They organized special *tefillos*; everyone had to say *Ovinu Malkeinu* every single day.[10] That's when I really started to *daven* every day. Until then I *davened* only on *Shabbos*. Special prayers were ordered and fasting on Monday and Thursday.[11] I was so sure that these special prayers would help. I thought if I prayed, everything would be good.

Then, on *Shabbos Hagadol*, they took all the unmarried girls, sixteen years old and up. I was a child; I watched them march. That picture will never leave my eyes. It was on a *Shabbos* morning, noontime, I think. I don't think they were crying; they were walking proudly. They weren't beaten or anything, but they went, they went. By that time we were "softened up" with the Jewish Laws. You understand. First they took away the boys, then they took the girls, in April.

So when the order came on a *Shabbos* that all the rest of the Jews had to go,[12] they thought, "Good, we're going to see our children again." They were told, "You're going to be together." I remember that *Shabbos*. We tried to get as many chickens as we could, and my father *shehted* them.[13] I remember I helped with the flicking of the feathers, and I remember my father said we didn't have to soak and salt the meat for too long.[14] Five minutes and ten minutes, it was enough. Just so you would be able to cook it. We took some food over to the public school for the Jews who were gathered there because they had nothing to eat.

In the morning they were also marched through the town. I saw them marching early in the morning, and they were put on the regular train. They were not put on any wagons.[15] Later on, we heard they were switched to cattle cars near the Polish border. I understand that they were taken to Lublin, where they put them in trucks and killed them with gas.[16] Hardly anyone came back from these transports.

The Kleins were among the last Jews remaining in Revuca. They lived in constant fear of deportation and were prepared to leave at anytime, their knapsacks packed with a three-day supply of food.

My father ran an "underground railway." He smuggled Jews over the border,[17] and my mother smuggled children through to Hungary. She would take the children who were our age with our passport,[18] always going through a different crossing. Polish Jewish parents who wanted to save their children would send them to Hungary. My father used to send letters so that people would know to come to us. My mother would give them a little piece of *shmurah matzah* from the *afikomen matzah*. That was the *segulah*.

In March 1944 my mother went to Hungary, probably to take children over, or maybe she just went to visit her parents. My father heard that the Germans had occupied Hungary.[19] The first thing they did was close the border. How was Mommy going to come back? You cannot imagine how scared, how worried we were. When she was supposed to come back, my father told me to go to the train at the point on the Hungarian border where she would change trains, where she would be coming in. In 1944 I was twelve. I waited for the train. I was sure she would bring my brother Yehudah.[20] Then I saw her. You cannot imagine my happiness when I saw her waving to me from the train, from the window. But where was the child? He didn't come because she found out about the closed border at the last minute. She would have missed the train if she had gone back for him. She sent a telegram to her family to send him to Jelsava, and she stopped in Jelsava to wait for an answer. The family said, "Don't worry about him," so she returned without him. Our happiness at seeing her was mixed with sadness because the child wasn't there. They sent me toward the border again to see the *goya* who was supposed to bring the child to take him across to us. I was waiting and waiting and waiting, and nothing came. I can picture him, *nebekh*, in the gas chamber . . . [Crying]

From August till October 1944, there was a *powstanie*, a partisan rebellion in Slovakia.[21] It was such a wonderful, exhilarating feeling. We didn't have to be afraid anymore. We felt we were going to be liberated soon, and we waited for those Russians like you wait for *moshiaḥ*. Then we realized that the Germans were going to fight; they were not going to give up till the last man. On *Sukkos* the partisans wanted everybody to go dig trenches, and they wanted to call my father. My father said, "It's *yom tov*, you know I can't," and somehow he got away with it. Later they apologized for asking him to do it.

We remained in Revuca till October 1944, when we saw that the German army was coming. My father got false papers.[22] He filled out forms that said we were from Humenne, part of eastern Czechoslovakia, near the Polish border. Humenne would be one of the first parts of the country to be occupied by the Russians, so the Germans wouldn't be able to check the information. On the false papers our family name was Klimo instead of Klein, but our first names were the same: my name was Edita, my sister was Eva. My brother Moishie was called Martin, my brother Shloimie was Stefan, and my brother Yankie's *goyisher* name was Josef. I understood what was involved, but for the little children it was very hard. My brother Moishie was born in 1938; he understood. Shloimie was two and one-half, but he didn't talk at all, and who had time to worry about why the child didn't speak? We told him, "Your name is Stefka, Stefan," and that was it. In the house we spoke German or Yiddish. When Shloimie started to speak, he spoke in Slovak. Until then we just didn't remember him speaking at all. Little Yankie was a year and one-half. He was no problem, and Chanie was only four months old. The only problem, which terrified us, was what would happen when the boys would relieve themselves. There were no indoor toilets; what do you do with the kids? We tried to keep them in the house, in the room, but how much can you sit in one room? We were terrified because only Jews were circumcised.

We stayed in Revuca until we heard the bombing. It may have been October 19, 1944; I don't remember exactly. We threw our *klei kodesh* in the well and left the soup on the table. We loaded up two or three baby carriages. We started to leave town, walking, and then somebody gave us a ride. Oh, the officials were very upset that the rabbi was leaving. They were very angry that we panicked, that we left. But my father saw the officials coming back from the German front, and their faces were very down. He noticed that they were leaving town, and he said, *"Lomer gayen."* Three hours later they ordered the evacuation of the whole town. We spent the night with friends in a little village nearby, Murany,[23] and then we continued on. Eventually we spent *Shabbos* in a house with Jews in Polhora. We slept on the floor. We stayed only overnight, and then we moved on. We had to be *mehallel Shabbos.* We took the train and arrived in Banska Bystrica, which was full of Jews. There people knew us. They took us in, gave us food; they shared with us whatever they had.

Suddenly, one day, I saw a man and didn't recognize him. It was my father. He had taken off his beard. It was such a shock. He looked so different. A friend who had an apartment in a little village, Riecka,[24] offered it to us. He gave us blankets; he gave us gold. Nobody wanted to go with us because of the children.

In Riecka we lived on beans and potatoes. My mother found different ways of preparing them. It was very, very hard without bread, but we just couldn't get it. In Revuca my mother used to bake bread once a week. There were no refrigerators, so towards the end of the week the bread was dry, and we didn't want to eat the rind. But now, in Riecka, I cried for that rind. When I stole a piece of bread, oh boy! Did I get it! It was the middle of the night. I feel very guilty about that. But I felt deprived of so much; I was doing so much; I felt I deserved it. Maybe at a certain point you just become selfish . . . My mother was totally self-sacrificing, and my father was a lost soul. He sat and cried and said *Tehillim*; he never moved out of the room.

One day the Germans came to the village. They were searching for partisans. My father hid: in the outhouse, in the attic, everywhere. He didn't put on *tefillin* that day. It was the only day in his life that he didn't put them on. The *tefillin* were hidden in the woodshed, and either my sister or I went to get them each morning. We always took care of the wood for the wood stove. It was our job. We had to go chop the trees in the woods to get wood. Sometimes we couldn't find dry wood, and we had to chop down young trees. But the young trees' wood was very wet; it smoldered and didn't burn well.

The townspeople of Riecka had a sort of tacit agreement among themselves. They protected each other. They didn't give up the partisans. The *goyim* thought that my mother was truly *goyish* because she had red hair. Of course she always had her hair covered with a kerchief.[25] They thought that she was a *goya* and that my father was Jewish.

Later, when the Russians came, nobody reported on the people who had cooperated with the Germans. I don't remember any animosity, any hatred. The mayor's wife used to drop food in front of our door during the night every time they killed a pig or a cow. She wouldn't do it openly. When they would kill a cow and the whole village had meat they said, "Why don't you come?" We'd say, "We don't have the money." Once my mother decided to cook some of the meat. She borrowed a pot from the *goya*[26] and cooked the meat and was going to give it to the little children. Shloimie was two and one-half. He refused to eat it; I don't know why. My father said, "If this child will not eat nonkosher meat, nobody will." So we never, never ate nonkosher food. Never. Nothing.

Riecka means "little river." There was a little stream where we were able to throw the nonkosher meat that people gave us. For *Pesah* my mother was able to *kasher* the few little pots that we had. There was a bombing at the time, and nobody else was out; everybody was hiding.

In Riecka the miracle happened, the skipping of our door. They sent me to the next village, Podlavice,[27] to a bakery to try to get some bread. It was in the winter, November or the beginning of December, 1944. At these bakeries you brought your dough, and they baked it. But I was hoping that maybe, maybe they would have some extra for me. Maybe someone would sell me some bread. Of course there was no bread, so I started to walk back to Riecka. On the way, in front of me, I saw a company of German soldiers.[28] Now, I knew only one *tefillah* by heart, the first *parsha* of *Sh'ma*, and I kept repeating it and repeating it, again and again. As they were marching in front of me, eventually we came to a fork in the road. The left road led to another village. To the right was Riecka, our village. I saw that they were going towards the other village when all of a sudden the German commander said, "*Halt! Recht!*" I knew this was *it*. I walked past them, and the commander stopped me and asked me in Slovak, "Could you tell me, is this the right road to Riecka?" I said yes (I didn't think I had a choice), and I actually led them to the village.

At the beginning of the village the commander stopped them and gave them their orders in German. Of course I understood: *"Juden, Partisannen un Waffe"*—Jews, partisans, and weapons, that's what they had to look for. He pointed to a hill. "That's where you take the *Juden* to shoot them," he said. They went into the village. They were looking for the mayor or somebody important. I went home and told this to my parents. You can imagine their reaction. The next thing we heard was the village crier. They started drumming, and all the people came out and listened to the announcement: anybody who harbored Jews would be shot if they did not give them up. The people whose house we were in had seen our false papers. They didn't know who we really were; they could say they *thought* we were not Jews. The Germans searched from house to house, from room to room. There were maybe forty Germans at most. They didn't come with armored vehicles. They all had guns. They wore gray German *Wehrmacht* uniforms.

The Germans were searching, and I was standing there, watching, outside our house. There were three doors on the house to three apartments. We lived in the middle apartment. One *goya*, to the right, was talking to them, so they searched the apartment to the left, and on the right the woman kept them busy, talking. Another soldier went to our door, in the middle, and started to open the door, and the *goya* yelled something like, "You were there already!" and he walked away. We were the only Jews there in Riecka. They searched but didn't find anybody. I think if they would have found guns, they would have shot people. They didn't find guns either. There was nothing. They left. My father always told this story to his grandchildren on *seder* nights.

Once I had to go to a funeral of an old woman in the Catholic church. I looked to see what others were doing. I kneeled and I crossed myself. After the funeral one of the women gave me a few crusts of bread, which I ate. It seemed to me that she gave me the crusts because she didn't have any teeth. She must have chewed around the edges first, and then she said to me, "Take it home." I think it was that woman who said to the German soldiers, "You were there already," and they skipped our door.

In Riecka we had no *Shabbos* candles. My mother put on the electric light instead. Friday nights my father talked to us about *Eretz Yisrael*. We would all sit at the table, and there was a little bit of relaxation. On *Hanuk-*

kah my father lit candles in one of the valises. If somebody knocked on the door he would slam the valise closed. My sister and I sawed some wood on *Shabbos*. Somehow it didn't bother me. Some things just had to be done. My father didn't tell us to do it, but he didn't tell us not to do it. We just went and did it on our own.

Some of the children slept in the baby carriages. My sister and I slept on the floor on a straw mattress. Our family had our own separate kitchen, so we didn't have to cook with the *goyim*. The *shiksa* played with the little children. She was so crazy about those little boys. She said, "I don't care. Even if you're Jews, you're human beings."

Pesah, 1945, came in the middle of bombardment. We saw the flames. We were sure we were going to be freed. At night the sky was lit up, flaming. It was gorgeous, gorgeous, like the most beautiful painting. People were afraid of being shot. Everyone stayed in the house. My father was afraid to take out his *siddur*; he said the *Haggadah* from memory. We had five *matzos* that we had baked, using a rolling pin that one of the German soldiers had given me as a present. He must have looted it from somewhere. We had an egg.[29] I think we did have a potato for *karpas*. My father was trying to remember the *Haggadah* by heart, and my mother sat by candlelight repeating after him. We kids were just frightened out of our wits by the shooting.

The next day different soldiers walked into the village. They were Rumanians. They asked everybody to come to the front of the village, and we were told, "You are free." Anybody who had Germans in his house was told to please give them up. That was it. My father spoke a little Rumanian because he was born in Rumania. He spoke to the soldiers, and he told them that he was Jewish. The officer said, "You'd better leave." My father said we must go even though it was *yom tov*. We packed up our belongings and our baby carriages. The Rumanians told us to be careful because there were still snipers.

We left on the first day of *Pesah*.[30] We heard later that our house was bombed that Sunday and that three Rumanian soldiers who were billeted in our room got killed. When we got to the next village, Podlavice, we were so hungry. A woman gave us bread, and we ate it up. My father allowed the bread for the children.[31] He was disappointed in me; he thought I would not eat the bread. I think we left Podlavice on *yom tov* again,[32] and we arrived Friday morning in Banska Bystrica.

Soon we left Banska Bystrica. We trudged on again, on foot. Eventually we came back to Revuca. Dr. Tomaschoff, the only Jew left in Revuca, took us in. My father used the *halef* that had been hidden,[33] and he *shehted* a chicken. It was a real *yom tov*. Our house had been used as a stable for horses. All the *seforim* were piled up in the yard. I don't think we stayed there for more than two or three weeks.

We finally settled in a town called Tornalja.[34] There my father became the *Rav*. There was such devastation among the people who came back. There were young girls who survived and older men who lost their wives. They married each other, but many of these marriages didn't work out. We also didn't feel comfortable there. There was such resentment against children. My uncle survived; he lost his wife and five children. He couldn't look at the non-Jewish children. He would say, "I feel like taking the child and ripping it into pieces, just ripping it into pieces."

Rabbi Klein was instrumental in the reburial of Jews who were buried by the Germans in shallow mass graves. Edith was sent to a public high school because there was no Jewish school. There she had to learn Russian. In the election of 1946 Rabbi Klein, in spite of his Slovak citizenship, was disqualified as a voter because he was not a Communist. At that point he decided to immigrate to the United States, where he was able to serve the Jewish community as a rabbi. Edith attended Seward Park High School on New York's Lower East Side and then the Bais Yakov *High School in Williamsburgh, Brooklyn, where she graduated.*

I never went to college. My father wanted me to go, but I felt I had to help my mother because I was the oldest. I knew that my father wouldn't demand that I go to college. I never was good in math because I actually never went beyond the third grade in arithmetic, so I felt very inadequate. I had no confidence. I never learned fractions or percentages. I have a good memory. I was very good in history, English, and biology. I don't know how I got 80 or 85 percent in algebra, but I think I never deserved it. I was just lucky. I really think I didn't deserve to graduate because of my poor math; I didn't have a good background in it.

I got married in May 1953. I have three boys. They went to *yeshivas*. I never anticipated that they would be so very *frum*. Maybe this is why I was saved: so that my children should devote their time to *Torah*.

On the second night of *Pesah* my father always told the story of how we survived. He would always show us his documents and talk about it and say how grateful we should be to *HaKadosh Barukh Hu*. We really relived it there at the *seder* table. He would insist on telling the entire story because he wanted it to be remembered.

What helped us to survive? I don't know. We just had faith. When I saw that business with skipping our door, I said, "I saw *HaKadosh Barukh Hu.*" I believed so much. I wish I would have such *emunah* now as I had then.

—*Interviewed by Bonnie Gurewitsch, February 8, 1987*

Eva Schonbrun

When the Germans occupied Bratislava, Czechoslovakia, in the summer
of 1944, Eva's father made arrangements for nine of his children to be
hidden with Czechs in Bratislava and neighboring villages. Eva was
then five years old. An older daughter, Theresa, nineteen years old, had
Aryan identification papers provided for her by the non-Jewish manager
who had taken over her father's business when it was "Aryanized" in
1941. This righteous man, Mr. Walaszek, also allowed Eva's father to remain a silent partner in the business, enabling him to retain a source of
income that paid for the children's upkeep and for the rent on Theresa's
room. Theresa made the rounds of all the children's hiding places once
a week, checking on their welfare and paying their protectors.[1]

   Yom Kippur, the holiest day of the Jewish calendar year, was on September 27, 1944. In honor of the holiday, the entire family gathered from
their hiding places at the apartment where their parents were living with
the oldest daughter. The day, spent in prayer, passed uneventfully. In
the evening, as Theresa accompanied a brother back to his hiding place
in Bratislava, she became aware of suspicious activity on the streets,
which aroused her fears of an Aktion. She returned to her parents' apartment, but the broken door, smashed by a German bayonet, was evidence
that a raid had already occurred. Hearing noises from inside she entered
the apartment and found only her nine-month-old baby brother in his
cradle, which her father had shoved between two beds and covered with
bedding during the raid. The sounds were the baby's gasps for air. Her
parents and two children and her married sister and her two children
had been arrested and taken to the camp at Novacky.[2]

I was at the place of a non-Jewish woman. One evening the Germans
came and checked all the houses to see if anyone was hidden. The
woman was getting money for hiding me, so she quickly pushed me into
her bed, which was very tall, full of quilts and eiderdown pillows, and cov-

ered with a lace cover. She pushed me in between the bedding, and I heard the thump! thump! of the Germans coming through. I lay there, not breathing, until I heard the boots going out of the house. Then I knew it was all clear, and I could be taken out.

This woman's husband had been taken to jail for some sort of misdemeanor. He was told that if he turned in a certain number of Jews he would be released. So, without any scruples, they just turned me in. His wife told them that not only did she have me but she knew where my older sister and baby brother were hidden. That's how one night we were all rounded up and taken to the police station.[3]

When we were taken away I remember my sister said, "Take as many clothes as you can." When we came to the police station everyone said you couldn't take anything. So my sister dressed me in all my dresses, about five or six dresses, one on top of the other. We were allowed one valise and a little chamber pot.

We were herded into an open cattle car, and we were taken to Sered.[4] I remember that ride vividly. My sister was nineteen years old, and my little brother was nine months old. We were standing up like cattle in the *Waggon*, and it was raining.

Theresa tells of a strange incident that occurred while they were being deported. Standing up in the rain in an open cattle car, cradling her baby brother on her arm with five-year-old Eva next to her, Theresa, after her ordeal at the hands of the Gestapo, was crying. A German soldier took out his handkerchief and wiped her face, saying to her, "Be strong; it cannot last too long." This gave her strength and a "strong belief" that she would be reunited with her family.

From Sered we were taken to Bergen Belsen.[5] I remember the big, big barrack where we lived. We slept one on top of the other like on bunk beds. My sister, my little brother, and I slept in one bunk. My sister kept him, and everyone kept telling her, "Drop the child. He'll never survive, and you'll only be hampered by him because he will get you killed." Anyone who had children was executed right away because children were just too much trouble. My sister wouldn't let go of the child. I slept on one end of the bunk, and she slept with the baby on the other end. I was considered very well-off in camp because I had all those dresses on myself, one on top of the other. I used the chamber pot as a pillow, and my sister used the little valise.

We didn't do any work. It wasn't a labor camp. I did a lot of walking around. I was left pretty much on my own.[6] I wasn't bothered too much. The baby was always there. The way the baby survived was a miracle.[7] With the morning coffee we were given a small ration of black bread, and we would nibble on that the rest of the day. We got a little bread at night. That's all we had.

There was a camp nearby that was worse than our camp. It was only for women; no men, no children, only women. One day I walked over there, and I passed a tall pile of rutabagas. They gave it to horses, to animals, to eat. That was our food besides the dry bread. I walked into the women's camp because a *Blockalteste* there liked me very much,[8] I suppose because I was a child and no children were allowed there. She used to beg me to come and visit her. She promised me food, so of course I went.

I walked in there and saw this large, large room. Oh God! The women were all lying on the floor. They were worse off than we were. We had wooden bunk beds; they had nothing. They had a blanket each, and they were lined up on the floor one near the other. It looked like they had even less to eat than we had because they were just lying there. They couldn't walk. They were too weak. When I walked in they got hysterical. They stretched out their hands and cried, "Oh! A child! A child! A child!" I'll always remember that. They were grabbing me. They all just wanted to hold me.

The *Blockalteste* had her own little cubby. She had a bed surrounded with mustard-colored satin curtains. Satin curtains. She hung them on a rope. I remember that so vividly. It was just a little corner. She had a lot of food staples in there. She had cookies; she had ham. She gave me a piece of ham and some cookies, and I tasted that ham, and it was delicious. It was good.[9] I remember bringing those cookies back with me for my brother, and my sister melted the cookies in water and pushed it into the baby's mouth.[10] I kept going back. Always, whenever I went there, I got something to take back with me, so I used to make my trips over there often.

Another thing I remember was the house where they threw all the dead people.[11] It was a big bungalow, a wooden house. The dead were thrown in there, one on top of the other, naked. The pile reached the ceiling. You could see those dead bodies thrown into a tall, tall mountain until they would come and take them away. The prisoners of the concentration camp had to handle them. One time a load of bodies was being taken away on an open cattle truck. One very old and exhausted Jewish man was supposed to

EVA SCHONBRUN

load the dead ones from that tall mass of bodies onto the truck. He couldn't anymore, and he dropped a body, and a German took a whip and started hitting him with it, and the blood started pouring down. I remember that so vividly. That was the one German I took my vengeance on. When we were liberated the first thing they did was to get the bodies out of the way because of sanitation, but this time it was German soldiers who were loading the truck. I recognized the German who beat that old man, and I so vividly remember taking a stick and stones and throwing them at that German. This was the big vengeance I took as a child.

I always wonder what happened to the girl who used to make up songs and sing at night when the lights were out. She sang songs about Israel, that this was our promised land. This was our hope after all these years of suffering. It used to be quiet and dark, and she would sing and sing. She wasn't scared to sing.

We didn't know we were being liberated.[12] We didn't know anything. All at once we were awakened early in the morning, and the British started to spray us with DDT powder. All of us were sprayed; we were full of lice. Then we were given this soup to eat. Soup! No one had had soup for years, for months. To us it seemed so greasy. It was supposed to be so delicious. Everyone grabbed it, and everyone got sick: diarrhea, vomiting. What was this sudden thing? Treated like royalty: soups and bread, and we didn't know why. All at once we saw English soldiers marching in, telling us we were liberated. We were free, and we'd be taken care of. That's when we realized what was happening. Everyone was so sick, vomiting. That was the big liberation.

After the liberation we didn't know if anyone in our family was still alive. I was taken away to the sanatorium,[13] and I was very well taken care of. The English were managing it. My sister wasn't supposed to come along with my brother and me to the sanatorium,[14] but she managed to come, to work in the kitchen just so she could be with us. My little brother was terribly, terribly sick. They didn't think he was going to live. An English doctor donated his own blood to my brother. He got transfusions in the leg; he still has a mark there.[15]

Then we found out that our parents were still alive.[16] It was very interesting. We were all ready to go to Switzerland.[17] We were already on the *Waggon*, and a telegram arrived that our parents were alive and that they knew we were alive. We were told to come home. We got off the *Waggon*, and we went to Prague, and my parents met us. My mother used to go to the train that brought people home every day. She stopped everybody: "Have you seen

{ 143 }

my children? Have you seen my children? Did you see children?" And they all said to her, "Don't bother standing here. No child will come back." They said, "A child? How do you expect a child to come back?" But she didn't give up. She kept coming, day after day, to ask.[18]

My little sister had been on a farm. She didn't know anything about the war. She was taken care of marvelously by some Catholics, wonderful, wonderful people whom we correspond with even today. They sent her presents when she got married. After the war she would tell my mother, "Let's go into a church and pray to Jesus. I'm sure he will listen to us and send back our sisters and brother."

One day my mother met someone. She asked, "Did you see my children?" He said, "Yes, I did; I was with them. They are all right." That's how we met again. My mother kept the little bunting my brother was dressed in. We still have it. My mother claims that her child was born twice. He was so terribly sick. The doctors told her to give up hope.[19] He couldn't hold food down. As soon as food was put into him it shot out of his body with such force that it went up to the ceiling. But my mother persisted till a little bit of food stayed in. He has a bad stomach even today, but my brother is all right.

I was very sick afterwards, too. For a whole year I was in bed, getting needles every single day. Pneumonia, the liver, you name it, I had it. But I'm alive.

—Interviewed by Sarah Freund, January 7, 1977

Hannah Sara Rigler

Sara Matuson's parents were Zionists and traveled to Palestine on their honeymoon. They bought a house in Tel Aviv, and Sara's older sister, Hannaleh, was born in Tel Aviv on November 13, 1925. The family returned to Lithuania in March 1926 because of family loyalties and Mr. Matuson's illness, but they hoped to return to live in Palestine so their daughter could study at Hebrew University in Jerusalem. Mrs. Matuson spoke fluent Hebrew, and the well-known Hebrew poet, Hayyim Naḥman Bialik, was a close friend.

Sara's father was an ordained rabbi who supported his family as a successful businessman. Her mother graduated from the university in St. Petersburg with degrees in languages and history. Sara remembers people calling her a "walking encyclopedia." She was also an excellent cook and baker.

Sara Matuson was born on November 21, 1928, in Siauliai, Lithuania. As a child, she was a tomboy. She was good in gymnastics, grew sunflowers in the garden of the apartment house, and took piano lessons. She and her sister, Hannah, attended a private Hebrew school called Gymnasia Ivrit Bialik. On the Sabbath Sara sat with her father in the men's section of their Orthodox synagogue, and in the afternoons the two would walk and talk and play mathematical games.

When the Russians occupied Siauliai in June 1940, Mr. Matuson's factory was nationalized, and he was imprisoned for six months. A Russian family was billeted in the Matuson's apartment. Soon after the Germans occupied Siauliai in June 1941, Mr. Matuson was arrested again. He was one of the one thousand leaders and prominent Jews who were shot within two weeks of the German occupation.[1]

They started taking people to the ghetto.[2] We were waiting for my father to get out of prison, so we didn't go to the ghetto, and then the ghetto was closed. No more people were allowed to get into the ghetto. But my sister had a friend, Sonia Berelowitz, whose father (Herzl Berelowitz) was in charge of food distribution in the Kaukazas ghetto. They vouched for us, and they gave us a bed, so we went into the ghetto.

We lived in a little house without running water, without bathrooms. There were outhouses. It was close to the cemetery, out of town. In that house there were, I think, six or seven rooms. There was one family in one room and another family in another room, and the man who was the head of the ghetto, his name was Lejbowich,[3] had two rooms. He lived with his wife in the kitchen, and we used to cook in there. The other room had three beds. My mother and sister had one bed, and Sonia and her grandfather had the other two beds. I used to go to a friend of mine, Mara Edelstein, who lived in another house, and I used to sleep with her because there was no room for me.

I don't think my mother or I worked. I think my sister was sent away for a short period of time to a camp to work cutting turf (peat).[4] They used to use it for heating. My father wasn't there, and without the man you were really nothing. My mother was educated, but she had never worked. In the ghetto a man could fight for you. We had to rely on the rations that they gave, and I suppose the rations were small. I know we had very little to eat. My mother used to make something from flour, and she'd say it was liver, but it was all flour. A woman who worked outside taught me how to knit. I knitted a whole dress with a design of fir trees, and she gave me a bread for that.

Then they closed the ghetto of Kaukazas.[5] We moved to Trakai, and there we had two beds and lived together. We lived right near the gate. There we had it better because the man in charge of Trakai ghetto was Mr. Pariser.[6] He was Jewish with a German wife, and I believe one of his parents was a German. He became the head of the ghetto. My mother knew Mr. Pariser very well because when the Russians lived with us in 1941 she gave him work. He used to teach German to the Russians. So he got work for my mother and my sister in a brush factory, and I worked for the head German of the ghetto.[7] I cleaned his rooms. He used to come every morning and pick me up, and I went to his apartment and cleaned it. He taught me how to clean, a very valuable skill. So we had something to eat, and we had it better. We were there in Trakai until July 1944.

We had one *Aktion* that I remember clearly. The man I worked for took me to the place where I lived, and he closed me up in the attic, and he said, "I want you to look towards the ghetto; you'll see something very beautiful today." This was the children's *Aktion*. They came and they took out all the old people and all the children, and the only thing you could hear was the screaming and the yelling because it was so close [crying].[8] All the elderly people, people who didn't work, and the children were taken. Some children were hidden and remained, but you didn't see them anymore in the ghetto because children were not allowed anymore in the ghetto. So we came back to such a stillness. Before that you had the children running around and screaming and playing. You didn't hear anything anymore.

We used to hear the bombs falling all the time, and so we knew that the Russians were close by. Then in July 1944 they told us we had to be ready, we were being evacuated.[9] We were going to a safe place, away from the bombing. So my mother packed, and we packed. We packed our bedding, and we put on three or four dresses and boots. I had navy leather boots with a red lining that my father made for me, and I had a leather coat with a lining, a winter coat. We all got ready for the evacuation. The evacuation started in July, and everybody was ready, and we walked to the airport. That's where the trains were waiting for us. It was very hot. We were carrying bundles with us, and the thirst was so bad that we started drinking the puddle water. I think that was the beginning of being dehumanized. We came to the airport, and I went looking for water; my mother fainted. There was no water to be had, and the Germans were laughing that not one person was missing. We waited there overnight, and then they put us into the trains, the cattle trains [crying].

It was really standing room only. I remember hearing the closing of the doors and then putting on the metal bar. There was no water. Everybody was thirsty. I don't know whether there were forty or fifty people in one cattle car. There were no windows, there was nothing. We didn't know where we were going; we were just moving. I think once or twice the train stopped, and they opened the doors, and they let us out to relieve ourselves. I don't remember whether we were given something to eat. I don't know whether we traveled four, five, or six days. We came to a place near Danzig, and there we saw a sign, Tiegenhof. They told us to take all our packages and luggage, and we were put into a train without even a top: open wagons. We were taken again for a very short ride, maybe a half an hour, and when we came into the next location, we found ourselves in a forest. This was Stutthof.[10] We saw barbed wire and trees, and they told us to leave all the clothing there, that they would deliver it to us, that we wouldn't need it. That was when they separated the men from the women, but we were all women so we were together. The ground was sandy; we were sitting outside. I don't know what we were waiting for. We sat there the whole night.

My mother had a beautiful diamond watch that my father gave her for her engagement. It was covered with diamonds. I remember she wound thread around the watch, and she buried it in Stutthof. She still had some loose diamonds on her, and she hid one of them; I didn't know where at the time. In the morning, they told us that we were going to take a shower. So we had to undress, naked, and we went into the shower room, which they called *Entlousung*, although at that time we didn't have lice yet. We were examined. I don't quite remember that; I sort of forgot for my own sanity. We had this cold shower, and we were given a pair of clogs and a dress, and that was it. At that point we got numbers. I remember my number was 54,386. When I came out I had a dress that had stripes; it was red, white, blue, a thin dress, like rayon, with a very big *magen David* in the back, big, about this size, in red, and a pair of clogs, and the hair was all stringy and wet, and we almost didn't recognize each other.

Then we were sent into a barrack, and they said that was where we would live. I remember a wooden barrack and straw on the floor. We had to be in line for food, for soup. They dished out the soup from a very big wooden barrel; it was tremendous. You stood in line, and somebody would ladle it out. It was actually water and cabbage leaves, and we got one bowl for three people. So we had to share one bowl, and then when we finished the bowl, we had to hand it in. A German stood in a room, and he used to throw the bowls at you to hit you. Then we stood on *Appell* for hours. We were in Stutthof for two or three weeks. We were all working, and there was a selection. They asked me how old I was, and I think I said fifteen. I was a very skinny kid, and my sister was eighteen. My mother and we all went to one side. So that must have been to the life side. Now at that time I wasn't aware of gas chambers.[11] I didn't know anything. We saw the buildings with chimneys[12]; we did not know what they were. All I remember is mountains of shoes as big as buildings, baby shoes and adult shoes and old shoes.

Stutthof was not a work camp.[13] It was only for destroying people. But the Red Cross was coming to check the camp, and the Germans needed live bodies, so we were the bodies that were alive. I was so content just to be together with my mother and my sister that I didn't look at anything else. We were there about two or three weeks, and then they started sending us out to work camps.

We lined up, and they took us to work in little boats, ten to a boat. That's when we came to the first camp, Baumgarten. We lived in tents, ten people to a little tent. That was July, August. We were given a blanket. I remember we used to divide the bread, and also eventually we got a coat. At that time we didn't realize that your coat was going to determine your life. How important it was. I think had I realized, I would have fought harder. I got a thin, green coat, and my sister got a coat with no lining, a thin coat with a fur collar, and my mother got an *aibervuf*, which is like a cloak with no lining that you wear only over a dress.

I don't know how long we were in Baumgarten. We dug two kinds of ditches for the Germans. One ditch was in a cone shape. Another type of ditch was dug straight down, six or eight feet, trenches, I suppose, for the soldiers. My sister and I used the pick and the shovel because the ground was frozen and we had to dig about eight feet deep, and my mother used to be on top, shoveling away the earth. I don't know how I did it. Our tent camp was surrounded by barbed wire. In the morning, they used to take us out to work, and they would bring us back at night. When we finished working in that camp we went to the next camp. I think I was in about four or five camps like that.

Then the winter was upon us. We didn't get any winter clothing. This was when you realized how important your coat was, and the blanket became everything to you. It became your cover and a cover for your feet because you still had only clogs. It's hard to think how we survived all this; after all, it was winter in Poland. We got very little bread, and we got coffee in the morning. I think we used to use the coffee to wash ourselves and to drink.

In the last camp, we were in a wooden barrack that was round. It had straw on the floor. There were about seventy people in one barrack. I remember that we used to try to be so close together for warmth, body warmth. We had a lot of body lice, and they were so big they were eating us alive. I think we got soup and a piece of bread during lunch time. We used to fight to be at the end of the line; maybe the soup would be thicker. And the person who used to cut the bread . . . I don't know if you can visualize ten people watching one person cut the bread into ten slices so, God forbid, one slice wouldn't be a little thicker than the next. You became so preoccupied with food, with just bread and nothing else. It was your survival.

Then, in December, they said that the Russian army was very close and that the Germans were going to save us.[14] They took us deeper into Germany. That's when we were taken on what was subsequently called the death march. When we set out we were about thirteen hundred women. When we came to Gross Golemkau[15] we were about three hundred. So they marched us, and we dragged our feet.[16] The routine was that we walked the whole day, and at night we were let into a barn if a farmer had a barn available. You were led in standing, and then subsequently you sat and you peed on each other. If the farmer had some food, we would get something to eat. We got fed very seldom. We were so hungry we ate the snow on the ground. I know people ran to dig up raw potatoes and turnips that were left in the ground. They were shot on the spot. I remember once a farmer cooked potato peelings for his pigs; we were given that [crying]. We were really most preoccupied with food. My girlfriend, Pulia Zilberstein,[17] froze to death, hungry. I was given a piece of bread for burying her. Another girl, Ruthie, and her sister and mother and my mother, my sister, and I were somehow always together at the end of the *Kolonne*. And, oh God, about halfway through the march, a little later, her mother was shot; she couldn't walk anymore.

There was one German with us who was very nice. He had smiling eyes, and he had a mustache. When we passed through a certain town he said to me, "You know, my family lives in this town. If you want, I'll take you to them, and they will hide you." I said, "I have a mother and a sister." He said, "I can't take three; I can only take one. I'm willing to take you." I don't know why I was singled out.

But he gave me a bread. We ate a little piece. My mother slept on the bread and somebody stole it [crying]. That night there was a fire in the barn. So I said to my mother, "Let's run!" "Where are you running?" My mother had a favorite expression: whatever happens with all the Jews will happen with us. She was a fatalist. I kept urging her, "Let's run; let's try to do something," because they didn't even count us in the morning. They just used to check the barracks to see if anybody was left, but they didn't count. I know one girl ran with somebody else. They survived, but they said some other people were shot. But my mother didn't believe in that.

When we came to Gross Golemkau, my mother still had the diamond ring that she had hidden when we arrived in Stutthof. You know, it is very hard today to think what hunger is like. I used to think that if I ever had a piece of bread [crying], I'd never want anything else. I said, "Give me the ring. I'm going to get us bread." I didn't think how or what. I was so desperate. So my mother gave me the ring . . . My intent was to get the bread and get back. I didn't think how I was going to do it.

So I took the ring, I slipped out of the line, and I went into a barn. In the barn were a couple of horses. I waited for somebody to come in, and a fellow came in, and I said to him, "Here's a diamond ring. Bring me a bread," and he said, "OK." He went out, and he came back with the police. I was in the police station! So the policemen said, "What are you doing here?" I said, "I came to get bread." "Where are you from?" I said, "From there, from the *Kolonne.*" You could still see the death marchers; they weren't that far away. Then the police said, "Do you know you're dirtying our *Judenfrei* town?" And they started chasing me, and before I knew it there was a whole posse, people with pitchforks, with guns, chasing me. I don't remember thinking or anything. All I knew was they were going to kill me. I knew that, but they were not going to kill me in front of my mother because I didn't want her to know what happened to me. So I was running . . .

I think my father must have carried me because my feet were frozen in my clogs. I ran so fast. People were still lined up on the sidewalks because they were watching the death march, so there were people on the sidewalk watching us. I turned to the right, and there were people in uniform. I didn't know who they were. But I separated them, and I went behind them. I figured they'd follow me and kill me behind them. So I went into another barn, and I lay down in a trough. They looked for me for about two hours, and they didn't find me. I didn't think about it at the time, but now I believe my father carried me and ran with me, and he must have protected me because there's no way . . . I can't actually account for . . .

After a couple of hours a man came in, and I assumed he was Polish. I said to him, "Are you Polish?" and he said, "No." We spoke German. He said, "I'm British."[18] I told him who I was, and he said, "Oh. They gave up. They're not looking for you anymore." Right away he brought me soup and bread, and of course, I devoured it. A Russian girl, Zoya, was with him. Later I found out his name was Stan Wells. After they gave me the food he said, "Zoya is going to go to her compound. She lives with Russian people. They have brought Russian people from Russia to work in Germany. She will find out if they will take you; or we are ten men, all together. I'll discuss your problem with them tonight, and whatever will happen, we will decide tomorrow morning what to do with you." It was a very small barn, and I remember every detail. The door was to the right, and there were chickens on one side, and there were two or three cows standing there. The cow was eating my scarf. I had a scarf made from the inside of my coat, and she was like nibbling on me. Stan said, "Mrs. Muller, the woman who owns the barn, doesn't believe that I feed the cows. She comes to check every night to see whether there is food in the trough, so she'll come to check." The only thing that could protect me was if he took away the gasoline lamp so she couldn't find it. Stan said, "God be with you. I'll see you tomorrow morning." When I was lying in that trough I realized what my mother meant when she said, "Whatever happens to all the Jews will happen to us." I was so alone.

I must have fallen asleep. I don't remember. But late at night somebody came into the barn, and she yelled, "Where is the *Lampe?* Where is the *Lampe?*" She went to the trough, and she felt around. She touched my leg (I had clogs on), and she said, "Who is there? Who is there?" Of course I wasn't even breathing or anything. She never felt further than the clogs, and then she left. Why didn't I get up from the trough and hide in another corner? I think at that point I thought: let fate take its course. I remembered my mother's warning . . . [Crying] I think I didn't care because I was alone.

She never came back. In the morning Stan came in, and I told him what happened. He went into the house, and she asked him where the lamp was, and he said, "It was there." She said, "You know, a soldier slept in the trough. I couldn't wake him up. I wanted to bring him into the house." So Stan came to tell me that I was safe. Zoya came and said the Russians didn't want any part of a Jewish girl. Stan said that he discussed it with the other British fellows, and they all decided that somehow or other they'd hide me. They were Stalag 20B.[19] They were in a room, and above them was straw, and there was a chimney going up from their room. They would make a hole in the straw and put me in the straw. In the morning when they hung out their clothes they would bring up food for me, and when they came at night to pick up the clothes they would bring food again.

They all met the night before, and they decided they were going to try to save me. At night somebody was going to come and pick me up. At night a man came. His name was Willie Fisher. He told me to put on an army coat that he brought. I didn't comprehend what he was telling me. He told me to walk on the other side of the road and not to talk to anybody because he was going to take me through the town. He took me to this place, and he took me upstairs to the straw, and he showed me where I'd be. Somebody came in and brought me medicine for my legs. I had big holes in my legs. They were full of pus. Somebody else brought paraffin for my hair because I was full of lice, and they took away my clothes to disinfect them. They brought up some clothing for me, and they bathed me. They gave me a lot of food to eat, and I was so famished I ate I don't know how many plates of soup and bread, and then I had diarrhea.[20]

I lived in this barn for two or three weeks. In the barn there were horses. There was a Polish man who used to come to take care of the horses. He would go upstairs to take the hay and bring it down for the horses. Sometimes I used to prepare the hay for him so he wouldn't dig so deep with his fork. Kids used to play hide-and-seek in the barn. I would be lying down in this hole, and of course I had to relieve myself. So I went where the horses went. It's hard to comprehend how one sort of managed. After about a week or so one of the fellows came up to see me. His name was Allan Edwards. Allan stole a sweater for me from a wagon of refugees and a pair of shoes and stockings and maroon coat, so I had something to wear. Allan would remove the gates on the barn at night and slip out and go to girlfriends or whatever and then come back to the barn at night. Sometimes he used to come and stay with me the whole night. I told him how lonesome I was, and he told me about his family; that they had a bakery and they made bread and that after the war we would meet again. You know, like talk. At that time, I thought he was the handsomest man I had ever seen in my life because he was so good to me.

Then they decided that I was going to meet all the fellows.[21] One night they came, and one fellow went behind us with the broom sweeping the snow so that nobody would see footsteps. They shoved me into their room through the window, and I met all the ten guys. We sat and we talked, and each one had a little present for me, thread, or a needle, or something, and they all said that they would do whatever they could to help me. They told me that the Germans were taking away the horses, so I would have no place to stay, but they said, "Don't worry. We will build a double wall in our room." When they went to work they would leave me there. Then, one morning, Allan came up, and he said, "We are leaving tonight. We are being evacuated.[22] They're taking out all the prisoners of war, and the straw is being taken out the next day too. I don't know what's going to happen to you. Where I work there is a Polish fellow. I told him that I have a Lithuanian girlfriend, and I asked him to come and pick you up at night. So he said he would come in the middle of the night to take you to his room because he has an extra bed." Or there was another alternative. Stan Wells was not going. He was staying here with his girlfriend in camp. So Allan said, "We can shave your head, put a cap on you, and you'll be another man." He said, "What do you want to do? What's your choice?" I said, "How can I go as a man? If they take me into the showers they'll see I'm not a man." He said, "The fellow will come to pick you up. He'll think you're a Lithuanian girl. He'll come in the middle of the night." I said, "Well, I'll stay and wait for the fellow." They left, and I waited for the fellow to come. I waited and waited, and there was no fellow.

This was the second time that I felt so alone. I wasn't thinking of suicide. But I said, "I wish myself dead." So I lay down, and I said, "I'm going to die." But I didn't die. I pinched myself, and I said, "You're still alive," and I started crying so bitterly. What was I going to do? I didn't know what to do. I couldn't stay where I was. It was getting light, and I was afraid. I left the barn, and I walked in the street, and I found my way to the first barn, where I first met Stan. I don't know how. Again, I think that my father must have led me there because I went from one side of the town to the other. On my way, I met a Polish man. He didn't know me. He asked me for papers.[23] I spoke perfect German. I told him that I was rushing to work, that I was very late.

I came back to the same barn, and I found Zoya. It was only two or three weeks later, but she didn't recognize me. In Russian, I told her who I was; I gave myself the name Sonia. I figured the name Sonia was Polish, Lithuanian, anything. I told her who I was. She said, "Now I can take you to our compound. Nobody would know." While I was waiting for her to finish her work I looked out, and I saw a few big houses. I thought I'd go look for work, so I told Zoya I'd be back. I went into the first house and said I was looking for work. The man, whose name was Heinrich Binder, said to me, "What can you do?" I said, "I can do anything. I can milk cows, I can feed the pigs." He said, "Yes, I do need help, but I have no place for you to sleep." I said, "Oh, I can sleep anyplace." So he took me up to a room, and he said, "There is somebody sleeping there, but there are two beds. Would you like to sleep there?" I said, "It's fine." He introduced me to a girl who worked there, Annie. The first job he gave me was to sort out the rotten potatoes from the winter in the potato cellar. He followed me to the cellar, and he said to me, "Sonia, you are not Lithuanian. You are the Jewish girl we lost in town three weeks ago." And I said, "Mr. Binder, how can you say something like that? It's a death sentence! I'm not Jewish, I'm Lithuanian." He said, "Lithuanians don't speak such German. You are the Jewish girl we lost." I looked around the cellar. The potatoes were on one side, and he was standing there, and I figured, what's he going to do—kill me? So I said, "Mr. Binder, you're right. I am." He was the head SS man in town. He said, "Any other time I would kill you, but today you are going to be my passport to life. Write a card in Yiddish that I saved you. My wife is already in Koln, which was liberated, and I'm going to follow her. Only you and I will know that you're Jewish." So I wrote him a postcard in Yiddish that he saved my life.

Mr. Binder told me that it would be a secret between him and me. All the time he used to make eyes at me as if we had a secret together. He told me that I should watch out for Annie, who was an ardent Nazi; I should be careful of her. He said he'd teach me to milk the cows or whatever I needed to know. I proceeded to do the potato cellar, and then I went over to Zoya to tell her that I wouldn't be going with her to the Russian compound because I got a job with Heinrich Binder. Then I ate and returned to the house. When I went up to sleep there was a Polish fellow there, and I told him my name was Sonia and that I was Lithuanian, and he said, "Oh, my God." I said, "What's the matter?" "I was supposed to pick up a girl last night in a barn. I promised Allan that I would pick her up." I said, "Why didn't you pick her up?" He said, "I overslept." I said, "That girl is me. You were supposed to pick me up." I stayed in that room. I didn't know how to milk cows. They taught me how to milk the cows and feed the pigs and so on, and Annie and I got on pretty well. Annie used to say, "Sonia, we lost the war. But we won the war against the Jews. We killed all the Jews in town." She must have been twelve or thirteen, young, thick blond hair, braids.

Since Binder was the head SS man, everybody came to his house to eat on Sunday. He had an old father who used to chase me all the time in a wheelchair. I used to wait on the table, and they used to sit down and give compliments. Annie slept with everybody. I used to "milk the cows" every ten minutes. Every ten minutes I said they had to be milked, and it was really sort of a difficult situation. I used to sleep with the cows a lot too. Annie used to say that I screamed during the night and that I had nightmares and that I talked in some language that she couldn't make out.

After a couple of weeks, Mr. Binder said that he was leaving to go to Koln; he didn't want to wait for the Russians. He left the farm to me. He said, "You watch the farm, and when I come back after the war, you'll give me back the farm." He gave me Annie's passport. He took out her picture, and he gave me her passport. He said, "While you're here, you'll be German. Nobody will touch you." Then he left, and I was left on the farm.

When the Russians came and finally took the town, I said, "Ha, the Russians are here. That's nice. I'm going, and I'm looking for the commandant." Now remember, I spoke perfect Russian. I looked for the commandant. I said to him, "Are there any Jews there?" He said that all the Jews were behind the front; Jews didn't fight. So I told him that I was Jewish. "Come in, let's discuss it." He took me into a very big room. The room was filled with tables and chairs, like a storage room. The next thing was that he was grabbing for me. Now, here the war was won. And they knocked on the door, and they yelled, "*Natchalnik!* What should we do?" He yelled, "Fire!" I ran, and he ran after me, and I jumped on a table and a chair, and I said to him, "This is crazy." So he said to me, "But don't you understand? I want to marry you." So I said, "Do you love me?" And he said, "Ask me anything." I said, "Don't touch me." So he said, "OK," and he didn't. I really feel that there was somebody watching over me.

He wrote three letters: a letter to his mother, a letter to his sister, and a letter to anybody who would find me in which he said not to touch me because I was the bride of *Natchalnik* Palkovnik and that he was sending me away from the front with his attaché. He said, "Go deeper into Russian-held territory." I went, and the bombs were falling; there was crossfire. I ran with the attaché, and the guy kept yelling, "Dive! Go on the ground!" He died right near me. I kept running on.

I came to the next town. I looked for an official place. I went in, and I introduced myself, saying I was Jewish and I was the bride of *Natchalnik*, and I showed them the letter. They said, "My God, he took up with a Jewish person. He must be a spy." So they took away all my letters. I was arrested as a German spy, and they said they'd prosecute him because he'd taken up with a spy. At night they interrogated me. I spoke perfect Russian. My experiences were so fresh in my mind; it had just happened. I told them my story. The commandant said to me that he had witnesses coming in who worked with me in Germany and that they spied with me. Witnesses! I said, "I should cut out my heart and show you I'm not a spy." I said, "You know, I'm almost sorry I stayed alive. These are my friends, the Russians." So he said, "For that I should shoot you. But you know, your imagination is so vivid. What you tell me nobody can go through. Nobody can go through it and live. I think when you survive all this, you should write books because you have such an imagination."

They decided that I wasn't a spy. They released me at night, and they told me that I should stay on as a *Dolmetscher*, a translator. I can still see the room where I was supposed to sleep. There was a double bed, there was a couch in one corner, and there was a cot on the side. I lay myself down on the cot, and then somebody came and started waking me up. He said, "You don't have to sleep on the cot. Go into the double bed." I told him I had a stomachache. So he said, "Go to the bathroom." The bathroom was an outhouse. So I stayed the whole night in the outhouse. In the morning I came back in. The old cook said to me, "*Devushka*, how are you? Those people are animals. Are you all right?" I said, "Yes." He said, "I'm ashamed of what my country-men became." They used to line up in a barn where a girl was, and they used to rape her until she was dead. They told me to clean their houses. I went to clean the room, and one of the guys said to me, "Come in." I said, "I don't go into the room if anybody is there." So he said, "Well, I want to marry you." I said, "Give me a half an hour; I have to think about it." Then I left, and I started walking by myself and crying.

I don't know if I was speaking Yiddish to myself, but a Russian Jewish guy picked me up. He said he'd send me with the mail truck five hundred miles. He took me to the canteen, and I had tea with milk and bread and butter, a luxury. Then we went to his house. It was one room remaining from a bombed-out house. I went to sleep, and he came into bed too, and the whole night we fought. I slept in pants. I still had my concentration camp pants. He told me that I was not going with the truck, that I was not going anywhere because I was so bad. But in the next bed, a man and a woman got along very nicely. I teamed up with her, and I traveled with her. I was making my way back to Lithuania to meet my mother and my sister and my father; I didn't know yet what had happened to anybody. In one town the stationmaster showed me a big map and explained how you could go here and you could go there, and the next thing he was ripping my coat. So I pushed him away, and I jumped out the window, and I went back to the station, and I sat with a young fellow the whole night waiting for the train to come. He said to me, "*Devushka*, they tried with you too?" They were like animals. I can talk about it now and almost laugh because I was very, very lucky. What I saw there was unbelievable.

Finally, I met a Jewish girl, Sonia, from Kovno, and she was with a Polish girl. The three of us teamed up and said we would stick together. We went wherever the train went; we just used to sleep at the station, wait, and take the train as long as it was going deeper in Poland towards Lithuania. Sonia was five or six years older than I was. She said to me, "Look, Soreleh, I was already married before the war, so if anything happens, it's so important to be a whole . . ."

We came to one place where we were the only three girls in town. There were about ninety or one hundred men in town. There were two seventy-year-old German ladies, spinsters, and they were constantly being raped. We couldn't get food. We were starving. We kept changing the place where we slept. In another town we were waiting in the station in the train, and they came to check passports. Now, we didn't have passports. We didn't have anything. So Sonia said to me in Lithuanian, "Soreleh, if we have to, I'll go." We knew what it meant, to be raped. One man lying on the floor understood Lithuanian, and he said, "Oh, no, I'm going to say you're my wife." So when they came for passports he said, "Don't you touch her. That's my wife." When they came to Sonia, somebody else said, "That's my wife." They took a German woman with a baby. They left the baby, and the baby cried the whole night. We were so petrified that not one of us moved all night. In the morning, they threw the woman in. I don't know whether she was alive or not.

That same day they took us into a school to check for passports again. Sonia went first. When she came out she said to me in Yiddish, "Don't ask." Then I went in, and he said, "Where do you want to go?" I said, "To Lithuania." He started feeling me up and down, and he said, "If you're good you'll go to Lithuania, and if not you'll go to Siberia." I pushed him away, and I ran out. Then the Polish girl went in, and we didn't see her for two hours. He raped her on the table. Then we got a note that we could go wherever we wanted, and we got bread. The three of us got into the train that was transporting horses, and we lay down on the straw. We were holding hands, and the train was going, and the next thing we knew, the train stopped. Somebody stole cigarettes. They were checking where the cigarettes were, and they found us. We showed them the note. And they said, "How many nights did you pay for that note?" The Polish girl became pregnant, she told us. I never saw her again.

It took me two months to get to Bialystok.[24] There I found a Jewish community, and I saw that there were more survivors. I found people who were together with my mother and my sister, and they told me that my mother died two weeks before liberation from hunger and that my sister died the day of liberation. [Crying] They told me not to go to Lithuania, to stay in Bialystok. I started working for a barber.

After the barber left Bialystok Hannah went to Sosnowiec, where she joined a Zionist group that was planning to immigrate to Palestine. They traveled to the American zone in Germany, where Hannah spent a few months recuperating at the St. Ottilien convalescent hospital. There she took a nursing course created as part of an effort to employ Jewish

*nurses for the Jewish patients, who mistrusted German medical person-
nel. At St. Ottilien Hannah made contact with an uncle in the United
States, who urged her to come to America. A friend of her father's who
worked for the* Vaad Hatzalah[25] *arranged a marriage of convenience between Hannah and a rabbi to facilitate their immigration to the United
States.*

The rabbi wanted money for the arrangements, so I wrote to my uncle.
My uncle said, "Anything. Just come." That's when I gave myself my sister's
name, Hannah. And so I came to America. It was August 3, 1947. I came on
the SS *Marine Fletcher.*[26] I came with this rabbi. I was seasick. My uncle
was waiting for me. I went right away to school, and I didn't realize what
I was getting into, how difficult it was to get a divorce in America. I had a
lot of complications with that. I started school right away in September at
Midwood High School in Brooklyn. My uncle was a farmer, and he lived in
Bushkill, Pennsylvania, so they rented a room for me. I had a very hard time.
The people I lived with weren't very nice. I had promised the rabbi money,
but my uncle was a very poor man, so I went to work as a waitress in a small
hotel to try to make up the money. The *Vaad Hatzalah* took $1,500 from my
uncle. The man *lived* on $1,000 a year. This was my encounter with *Vaad
Hatzalah* and with religious people. My father had *s'mikhah*, and I believed
in religion, but in America it was quite different from in Europe, as I found
out. It took a long time to get a divorce. The rabbi refused to give me a
divorce. He decided he was in love with me, so I had difficulty there [laugh-
ing]. It took a few years. I got it in Reno, Nevada. It was very complicated to
go out of town. For a long time I didn't talk. I was afraid I would be deported.
At that time no one in high school was married. It's different today.

They were *very* nice to me in high school. The teachers were just wonderful. They gave me three and four classes in English, and I had a Mr.
Blake, who taught me math in Hebrew, and I finished the whole high school
in three terms. I hadn't gone to school since 1941, and this was 1947. I missed
the formative years, six years, the best years. I took my Hebrew Regents and
the German Regents,[27] and I passed and got a scholarship to go to medical
school. I started college, and after one term I went to nursing school. But in
nursing school you weren't supposed to be married, and they found out I was
married, so I had difficulty with that. Nothing went smoothly. I finished nursing school in 1952, and I got married the next day.[28]

I met my husband on a blind date. I finally became a nurse, and I worked.

We had a good life. My husband is a wonderful human being. Really understanding. When I dated him, I was very close with a Hungarian girl. She told her American boyfriend what she went through, and he said, "I don't think you can be normal," and he wouldn't go with her anymore. So she said to me, "Before you go with Bill you must tell him what you went through." So I told him what I went through, and I said, "So what do you think?" He said, "I'll just have to be extra nice to you to make up for all the things you went through." We've been married now almost forty years.

Hannah speaks with pride of her two children, who are named in memory of her parents. She describes her work in politics as a state committeewoman and in civic groups. She returned to Brooklyn College and earned bachelor's and master's degrees and worked for the New York City Board of Education, Division of Food and Nutrition, supervising meal programs for senior citizens and the homeless until her retirement. She now has two grandchildren.

After she married, Hannah attempted to locate the British prisoners of war who saved her life. A friend of hers living in London contacted a reporter who wrote the story in the Sunday newspaper The People, *which elicited the following letter from William Fisher: "My Dear Sarah: The result of my reading [the article] was . . . to make the miserable cold day into perhaps what was the sunniest and certainly one of the happiest of my life. I'm by nature pretty hard and insensitive, but I must confess I do know now what tears of happiness mean. My joy of you being alive and well and being transformed from that tragic waif I once met into what your photograph shows, a very beautiful and obviously happy woman, in some measure made up for all the guilt I felt at being unable or perhaps too cowardly to do and risk more for you than we did. For I have never got over that feeling and we perhaps should have taken you with us."*

In the course of her correspondence with William Fisher he sent her the diary that he had reconstructed in pencil while traveling on a Russian train between Brest Litovsk and Odessa. It was based on his original notes written on scraps of paper and backs of photographs that were confiscated by the Russians.

In 1973 Hannah traveled to England for the first of several reunions with the ten former prisoners of war and their families. In 1989 Yad Vashem, the Israeli Remembrance Authority, designated the men as

Righteous Among the Nations, and Hannah planted a tree in their honor on the Avenue of the Righteous.

If somebody would ask me, "To what do you attribute your survival?" I would say, "Luck. You had to be lucky." I feel in my case that there must have been some divine person or spirit that really guided me or watched over me because I had so many close calls and I survived so many different situations, even not being raped by the Russians. I really feel that my father must have saved me because I was the only person who survived from my family [crying].

—*Interviewed by Joni Sue Blinderman, August 3, 1992, for the Museum of Jewish Heritage*

Estelle Feld Alter, passport photo, Belgium, 1946. *(Gift of Estelle Alter, Museum of Jewish Heritage, New York)*

Right, Estelle Feld Alter and her sister, Regina Feld Glinzman, aboard the SS *Drottningholm,* with two women who befriended them, en route to the United States, August 1946. *(Gift of Estelle Alter, Museum of Jewish Heritage, New York)*

Left, Margie [Marga] Levi Nitzan and her sister, Hannelore, Fulda, Germany, ca. 1933. *(Gift of Margie Nitzan, Museum of Jewish Heritage, New York)*

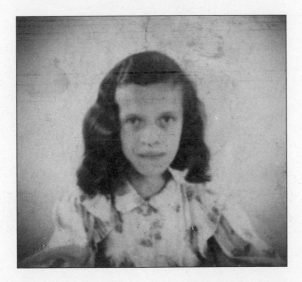

Margie [Marga] Levi Nitzan, Milan, Italy, ca. 1943. *(Gift of Margie Nitzan, Museum of Jewish Heritage, New York)*

Edith Klein Wachsman and her siblings. *Seated in front, left to right:* Shloimie, Yanky, Chanie, Moishe. *Standing, left to right:* Eva (holding baby, Esther) and Edith. Tornalja, Czechoslovakia, 1946. *(Courtesy Edith Wachsman)*

Edith Wachsman, Brooklyn, New York, 1998. *(Courtesy Edith Wachsman)*

The Matuson family. *Front row, left to right:* Hannaleh, Sara Rigler, cousin Luba. *Back row:* mother, Gita, and father, Shmuel Leib Matuson. Siauliai, Lithuania, 1938. *(Hannah Rigler File, Yaffa Eliach Collection, donated by the Center for Holocaust Studies, Museum of Jewish Heritage, New York)*

Hannah Sara Rigler, recuperating at St. Ottilien sanatorium near Munich, Germany, ca. 1946–47. *(Gift of Hannah Rigler, Museum of Jewish Heritage, New York)*

Rozalia Berke *(front, right)* with her sister, Romana *(front, far left)*, camp sister Dorka *(behind Rozalia)*, a cousin, Emil Nowak, and friend Hania Korn *(directly left of Rozalia)*, Lodz, Poland, 1945. *(Courtesy Rozalia Berke)*

Rozalia Berke at the American Gathering of Jewish Holocaust Survivors, Washington, D.C., April 1983. *(Rozalia Berke File, Yaffa Eliach Collection, donated by the Center for Holocaust Studies, Museum of Jewish Heritage, New York)*

Tilly Fried Stimler, London, England, 1946. *(Courtesy Tilly Stimler)*

Right, Tilly Stimler, with her camp sister Ika Steinmetz Klein, visiting Washington, D.C., 1983. *(Courtesy Tilly Stimler)*

Five of Miriam Rosenthal's camp sisters and their babies who were born in the Kaufering I camp, recuperating in the St. Ottilien sanatorium near Munich, Germany, June/ July 1945. *Left to right*: Boszi Leggman, Ibolya Kovacs, Suri Green, Magda Fenvesi, Dora Loewy. Magda's mother is standing behind her; the nun is unidentified. *(Miriam Rosenthal File, Yaffa Eliach Collection, donated by the Center for Holocaust Studies, Museum of Jewish Heritage, New York)*

Miriam Rosenthal *(standing)* and her husband, Bela *(seated at the head of the table)*, at the Passover seder table with their grandchildren, Toronto, Canada, April 1997. *(P. Gower/Toronto Star)*

Cesia Geldworth Brandstatter's Bais Yakov graduation class, Chrzanow, Poland, August 1934. Cesia Geldworth is seated in front row, third from left. Dora Zeltenreich, Cesia's camp sister, is seated third from right, and Frieda Elbaum, another camp sister, is standing at far left. (*Cesia Brandstatter File, Yaffa Eliach Collection, donated by the Center for Holocaust Studies, Museum of Jewish Heritage, New York*)

Cesia Geldworth Brandstatter as she appeared on her ghetto work card issued in her Yiddish name, Czarna Laja; Sara was added as a middle name by the Nazis. Poland, May 1942. (*Gift of Cesia Brandstatter, Museum of Jewish Heritage, New York*)

Rozalia Berke

Rozalia Berke was born in 1926 into a traditionally observant family in Lodz, Poland. She had three brothers and one sister, Romana. Her father was a successful businessman, and the family lived comfortably. In 1939 Rozalia had completed a year of Gymnasium studies and was planning to go to the university.

On September 1, 1939, I woke up to go to school, and my mother said, "No school today. You are not going to school." We heard a big noise of marching boots as the Germans marched into Lodz.[1]

Our lifestyle was immediately interrupted. After a few weeks two SS officers came up.[2] They looked at our home, and they said they were from Berlin. Berlin was being bombed, and they needed to take out their families, and they liked our home. So we would have to be resettled, evacuated.[3] In the attic my mother made homemade wines from raspberries and blueberries and plums and apples. Those two men sampled the wine, and they said, "Oh, how good it is!" The SS man said, "My wife will love it, I like it too. So don't you move it with you. Leave it here." They told my mother what she could take and what she couldn't. My mother was preparing the wine for the *bar mitzvah* of her three boys because it wasn't customary to buy wine. I felt so robbed. How could they take away the wine that my mother made for my brothers? It was repulsive. I couldn't understand why they did it.

By the beginning of October we were already resettled in an apartment on Drewnowska Street.[4] At first we could get out of the ghetto[5] and get into town, but when they built the bridges[6] and closed the ghetto our troubles really began. Food was rationed.[7] My mother couldn't get a loaf of bread for us. My mother had lots of precious family jewelry, gold and diamonds. She tried to give it to the SS man for a loaf of bread so we could be fed. She denied herself her slice of bread so she would have food for us five growing children. I also learned to do it and give it to my brothers. It became progressively worse when they closed the ghetto and they gave us the yellow stars to wear.[8] When bread was scarce and I saw that Mother was not eating her slice of bread or her one potato, I said, "I'm going to town to buy bread." I didn't have a Jewish "look" or a Jewish name. I took some money from Mother. With my yellow Jewish star, I went to the bridge, and I climbed up, and the SS man said, "Where do you think you are going?" And I said, "I'm going to Litzmannstadt." He said, "Why are you going to Litzmannstadt?" and I said, "We are hungry." He didn't see my star because it was in the back. He said, "Well, OK." And then I said to him, "I'm Jewish," and he answered "Oh, you stupid girl, you can't go out." He wouldn't let me out with the Star of David. So I came home crying. I was wearing my school uniform; if I had gone without that star, he would have let me through. So again I cried my eyes and my heart out.

Then came the order that everybody had to work[9] in order to get food rations. My oldest brother, Shimon, got a job under Neftalin[10] in the office of Vital Statistics. My younger brother worked in a [food] co-op on Drewnowska Street, and Shimon arranged that I would go to work at the Lagiewnicka Street hospital.[11] He arranged for my sister to continue her education in Marysin, where Rumkowski picked the cream of the crop of the children to continue their education.[12]

The chief of the maternity department where I worked was Dr. Tiktin, and under him there was an RN, Mrs. Lolarh, and nurse-midwives. Dr. Ser was the head of the outpatient department. At fourteen years old I couldn't do much work in the hospital, but Mrs. Lolarh said to me, "Well, you can feed the babies, can't you?" And I said, "Oh, yes." She showed me how to hold an infant so I wouldn't drop the baby, how to support the baby's head, and how to bring the bottle and feed the baby. There were very few infants, usually two, three . . . At one time we had five. It was a beautiful white nursery with white walls. It was kept immaculately clean, and from time to time the SS, a doctor, and some medical staff came up to check whether it was clean or not because they wanted to close that hospital anyhow.[13] There was no treatment there, so they just checked it for cleanliness. They would put a finger on the wall to see how clean it was. I remember vividly that after every baby change, after every baby feeding, the floors were mopped with disinfectant, and it was kept up well. The SS men made spot-checks, inspections, on the hospital. They dropped in to see how many patients there were and who they were. Sometimes they dragged out some patients.

One day, three SS men came up to the nursery, and I was just coming in to feed one of the babies. One SS man went to the crib where that baby was. The baby didn't have much hair, just a few little hairs on top of the skull. The SS man picked up that baby by those few hairs and literally threw it against the wall. The skull was crushed, and little drops of blood were trickling down the wall. The other two SS men went to the two other cribs and picked up those two infants and did the very same, just dumped them against the wall. [Crying] And the blood was just trickling down over that white wall. We were told to tell the mothers that the babies died in a bacterial epidemic. I can still see the blood trickling over those white walls. I will never forget it. [Crying] I really want it to be recorded into history that it happened. I saw it with my own eyes. We were told by Mrs. Lolarh to hush it up, not to talk about it. We didn't know anything. We didn't see anything. But I was in that room with the doctor.

I did what the doctor and Mrs. Lolarh told me. I didn't even tell my own mother because I was afraid and they were afraid. What good would it do? The infants were killed. I have to live with this memory. I dream about it. It's in me, and I really want history to know about it.

In 1942 Rozalia's mother died of starvation. Her father also died, and her youngest brother, Juda, was deported in the infamous children's Aktion *called the* Szpera, *in which children were rounded up and taken away to be gassed in Chelmno.*[14]

In 1944, the ghetto became very restless. Rumkowski and the ghetto administration assured us that we had nothing to fear because there were factory orders for two more years.[15] Our labor forces were needed. We were safe and secure. However, in the summer of '44 there was discontent and rebelling, and everybody was thinking how to dig a bunker, how to build a bunker, where to hide, how to hide, and survival was really on everybody's mind. When the last transports left, I remember it was summer. We didn't know what to do, where we were going to hide.[16] People who were suspicious decided, "We won't leave. We will find a place, and we will hide because the Russians are approaching." But my brother who worked in Vital Statistics was a very loyal and obedient type. Word came that everybody had to leave. If we hid and the Poles found us, they would turn us over to the Germans immediately, and we would be shot. So why hide and get shot, whereas if they took us away, they might need us for work. So my brother decided that we would all go wherever they took us.

We didn't know we were going to Auschwitz. We knew that we were going to be deported somewhere for work. We packed all our family jewelry. We distributed all the rings, necklaces, gold watches, and earrings into our four knapsacks. My two brothers and my sister and I were together. My oldest brother said, "You hold hands all the time so you don't get separated or lost. *Stay together!*" I remember vividly that he said to me, "You have a good mind. Stay alive to tell the world what happened. Take care of yourself and your sister. You have a good chance!"

The transport was beyond human dignity. They closed us into that cattle car. No drink, no water, and nothing for evacuation. When we arrived at Auschwitz and they let us out, we sighed with relief; at least we went into the open air. But then we looked at the barbed wires, and we saw some people who knew us; they were using silent language, telling us that we had come to hell. Tears were dropping from our eyes. Immediately we were separated from my brothers, but I was still holding hands with my sister. Even when they had the segregation, we went together. We went into those little delousing rooms as they called it.

We didn't dare take any of the jewelry and valuables out of our knapsacks. Everything was left with the knapsack. There were some girls who shaved our heads, put us under the shower, and said, "You will go to work, so you must be clean." We were stripped of everything and put into a sort of bunk bed for about twelve of us. This was for sitting and sleeping and eating and everything. Dorka Joskowicz, our friend from Marysin, came with her mother and sister, and she was immediately separated from them. She was crying, and she wanted to go to the barbed wire.[17] She said, "I don't want to be left alone, all alone." So my sister and I went to her and said, "Come, come with us." She said, "But will you adopt me as your sister?" And we said, "Yes." So she came with us and sat in the same bunk.

The following day they called us out, counted us, and said there was no room here; they were going to transport us for work. But before we were transported, we had to have numbers. So we stood in line, hundreds of thousands of people. Each time we came to that table to be stamped, with one hand I held on to my sister and with one hand I held Dorka. I said, "Back, back," and Dorka cried, "Are you crazy? They will kill us. They won't send us to work." I said, "Look, the number won't make us go or not go to work." I didn't know; this was an instinct. There was no rationale for it, but I dreaded being numbered. Everything was so appalling to me. How they could tattoo us, put on numbers? I said, "I can never live or reconcile with it. Let's go to the end." So three times when it was our turn in line we went to the end. All the other girls said, "Thank you, thank you." They were so grateful because the general belief was that if you didn't have a number, you wouldn't get work and you would get killed if you stayed in Auschwitz.

The following day they started again after they gave us a little watery soup, which everybody ate with the same spoon. As we were in the line for the numbers, some SS men came in, and they were picking people out, and we were picked to stand on one side. So after three times when we ran away from that table where they tattooed people, we were picked to go away to work somewhere.

Dorka Joskowicz was a beautiful girl. She looked very Semitic; she had beautiful black hair, and she had a typical Jewish long, narrow nose. I was shorter than she, and my sister was taller than I am. When they made the *Selektions* Dorka always walked with her shoulders down so she wouldn't be outstanding and the Germans wouldn't separate her from us. We were always holding hands, the three of us, staying together, not separating, since Auschwitz. In fact, we were called "the three sisters," but Romana and I are not blood relations of Dorka.

When we came to Stutthof they asked us what work we could do. I told them I worked in the hospital, so I immediately was placed into the Red Cross building, and my sister and Dorka Joskowicz were placed to sew fur linings for the army because it was a labor camp.

Conditions in Stutthof were a little better, but it wasn't good, far from good. We went to sleep hungry, we woke up hungry, and the nights were occupied with how to get a potato, a slice of bread, to survive. When we marched to be counted some people couldn't even march.

There were very good relations between the Jews from Poland and Jews from other countries. If there was a Jewish *Kapo*, and someone couldn't go out to work, she tried not to have them immediately taken away. She would give them a broom or something so that it looked as if they were working, even if they could hardly stand on their feet. Dorka was just terrific. She said, "I can do business." I said, "What are you, crazy?" She said, "You know, my father had a factory in Poland, so I know how to do it." She was so beautiful. When she went close to the barbed wires, the men always threw her a potato or a carrot or a slice of bread; one time they threw her some kind of bacon. She shared it with us, especially with me and my sister. When I didn't want to eat, she said, "You are going to swallow it. I'll see to it. Don't you save it for us. We will make it up." And so the relations were good. It was winter, and we were cold; when Dorka and Romana were sewing in that factory, they managed to get out little fur pieces, which we put inside our coats to keep us warmer.

I worked in what they called the infirmary. I wore a Red Cross arm band. When a sick person came into the infirmary they took them away.[18] If someone was bleeding, first aid consisted of a piece of gauze, a little iodine, something like that. When we marched to work, they always wanted someone to go as an aide and bring the person who couldn't march to the infirmary. I never did this. I picked up a little snow and put it on their tongue so they would have a little water to stop the dehydration. The German who was watching us hit me in the shoulder with his rifle, and he said to me, "If you do it once more, I will kill you. You are not to bend down and pick up snow and give it to people." When I got clobbered, I whispered to the next one, "Give her a hand, lift her, help her, and get her through." This was what they called "first aid." In Stutthof the administration building, where the German officers were, also had a Red Cross on the roof for foreign planes to see so it would not be bombed. It was a shelter, really.

The Germans always had mistresses. All we heard was laughter and drinking and giggling and moving at night. They were not Jewish women. I did see one or two times that men prisoners managed to get into the Jewish women's barracks under a pretext of doing some work, which was unusual, you know. It was horrifying to me. Once, inside, I saw some kind of a relation with a man who managed to come in with the women. Of course, then she had enough food left because he brought in some food. But the commandant and every *Aufseher* or *Aufseherin* had a Nazi in the office.[19]

At the end of '44 they started taking transports from Stutthof to work. I don't know how it came to me; it was instinctive; I knew that we should not go on any transport. The Russians were bombing the area. The Nazis began marching all the prisoners out. Civilians had to leave their homes because they were bombed out. Since I didn't do physical work like my sisters I had more time to meditate and to think. One evening, in the bunk we shared, before other people came in because we were afraid the word would spread, I said, "Look, girls, we have to get out of here and get out alive." They said, "How?" How? Well, I myself didn't know how. I said, "We have to find some way." I said, "When you hear bombing, when there is panic in the German administration, it will be easier to get out of here." There was snow on the ground, very cold. But we had those pieces of fur in our coats. I said, "We won't freeze. Let's get out of here at the first opportunity." And then before even we planned it, the Germans evacuated Stutthof because the Russians were close.

They took us on a death march. They said they were taking us into Germany to *Arbeitslager*. I said to the girls, "At the first opportunity we are getting out of here, all three of us. Let's hold hands." It was at night, it was dark, and we saw people marching by the thousands: horses, belongings on wagons, and people on foot and children and nuns. All of a sudden, there was that sound of the $V2^{20}$ and their airplanes, and they made such a dreadful noise, Wooooo. The skies lightened up. I said, "Now is the time. Let's go, let's go." I pulled both of them, and we went out of the line of march. The German didn't even watch us anymore because he didn't know whether he should leave or whatever. We left the columns and rolled into a ditch. We didn't know where we were, but there were some trees, and we waited and waited and waited. We were very cold, so we stood very close to each other so one would keep the other one warm, and we waited until the marching people passed us.

I felt sparks in my eyes; I was very hot. Dorka and Romana were cold, and I was warming them up with my heat. I had a temperature of 104. I had pneumonia and typhoid fever. I couldn't stand on my feet. I sat down. I almost fell down. They said, "What's the matter?" I said, "Nothing." Then I said, "Look, please, do me a favor. You run; leave me please here. I can't go. I can't stand on my feet. Please run!" And they said, "Are you crazy? We won't leave you. Even if they shoot us here, we won't leave you. You have to come." "But I can't walk, I can't stand up. You see, that's why I'm on the ground. I can't walk with you." So they lifted me up one on one side, the other on the other side. They took my hands, and they literally dragged me. So we walked; I don't know how long because all I had were sparks under my eyes, and when their hands were cold, mine were boiling. They said it felt so good that I was warming them up.

We saw a house with some light inside, and I said, "Look, please leave me here and run away. Run, run, run for your lives." They wouldn't hear of it. They said, "There is a light, there is a house. Let's go in. They will let you sit down." I said, "Yes, but we have the stars on our backs, and we can't go in with the stars on our backs." So Romana and Dorka took off our tops and with their teeth they pulled off the Stars of David, and then we turned those little fur-lined coats with the fur on top, and we knocked on the door of this house. A woman opened the door. During the year we had all learned German. The people said, "Who are you?" And we said, "Well, we are Polish, and our homes were bombed, and we are going to find some shelter on the way. And I am ill." So she said, "Oh, I'll let you sleep overnight. I will give you my bedroom." She gave the three of us her bedroom, which was delightful. We went into the bedroom, and I dropped into that big bed. We closed the door.

A few hours later we heard the noises of boots coming in. It was the *Burgermeister* of the town. SS men were coming in and reporting to him. While I had the high fever I could have water, and every half hour we heard different reports coming in: "*Die Russien kommen, die Russien Kommen*" (The Russians are coming, the Russians are coming). At 4:00 A.M., we heard the chickens and the roosters waking up. All of a sudden we heard a pair of boots and "*Alle raus fun hier, die Russien kommen, die Russien kommen, alle raus*" (Everyone out of here, the Russians are coming). The woman knocked at our door, and she said, "Get ready, quickly. The Russians are coming." And that man said to her, "Don't you care about others. You come out, quick, quick." He took her, and they ran away and left us in their home. When Dorka and my sister went to the refrigerator in the kitchen, their eyes popped out. There was bread, there was cheese, there was butter, there was ham, so much food that we hadn't seen since 1939. They said, "Now, you won't be starving. See, I'm eating." They could eat. But when they gave me a little piece of bread, I couldn't even swallow it. I couldn't eat; I vomited. We stayed in that home because there was enough food to eat. I rested up, and I became better, and then the Russians came.

We were afraid of the Russians, too! We left there and walked to Putzig, where the closest hospital was. By that time I didn't have a fever anymore, and I recuperated. The hospital was run by nuns from a nearby convent. The Reverend Mother said to me, "With your first aid experience and hospital experience I need you here because we have an epidemic of typhus." The Germans were still in Putzig, and the chief doctor was a German SS man. We all said we were Catholic, bombed out of a little country place, and we didn't know where anybody else was.

Then Dorka took sick with typhus fever, and she went to bed. My sister and I said she was our next-door neighbor. Dorka was in bed, and I was already wearing a white uniform to help the nun with people who had typhoid. I could take temperatures, and I could give them liquids. Very many had diarrhea; they needed to be given a sponge bath, which I could do. When the German SS doctor came in in the morning I always stood behind because they always needed something so I brought it in. He said to the Polish doctor, "*Sie zehst doch eine Jüdin*" (she looks Jewish) when he looked at Dorka in bed. And I said, "*Herr Artz*, she isn't Jewish; she is Italian." And the SS man said to me, "Italian? What is her name?" And I said, "Danuta Jaszembiska." I honestly don't know where it came from. I knew to give her the same initials, DJ. He already had his hand on his gun, and if he didn't believe me, he would have shot her in bed and my sister and me for lying. God was with us because after twenty-four hours the Russians were in and the Germans escaped.

We were liberated at the end of February in 1945—or was it March of '45? I don't remember. I didn't cry. I tried for all the years to put it out of my mind and hide it very deep inside. I didn't talk about the Holocaust until 1980 when I was asked by the Anti-Defamation League in Columbus to go to the educators and give them firsthand information to incorporate into the school curriculum.

We went back to Poland. I hoped that my brothers Shimon and Chuna had survived. The caretakers gave us the keys to our apartment, where the SS men had lived, so we immediately had somewhere to live. All three of us enrolled at the University of Lodz. Then people who came back told me that Shimon died in Auschwitz, the day of liberation when the Russians came in. He had dysentery, and he died in the infirmary in Auschwitz. Chuna tried to run away two days before the liberation, and the SS men shot him on the spot. We didn't have any hope for Juda. So we started making arrangements to leave Poland. Dorka found her first cousin, who returned to Poland from Russia. We all lived together in Poland, and we really were known as the three sisters.

Dorka had relatives in London and made contact with Rabbi Dr. Solomon Schonfeld, a prominent British rabbi. Schonfeld had come into Poland to take out Jewish survivors with English relatives and also Jewish children who had been hidden by Christians.[21] Because they were under twenty-one years of age, Dorka and Romana were able to leave Poland on the last of several children's transports organized by Dr. Schonfeld. Rozalia was twenty-one and had a Polish passport. Between 1945 and 1947 she worked closely with Dr. Schonfeld in Poland, identifying Jewish children and facilitating their immigration to England. She finally left Poland in 1947 with twenty-eight or twenty-nine Jewish children who were listed on her passport. In England she studied nursing in a hospital and married a Polish Jew who had fought with General Anders's Polish army at Monte Cassino, Italy. They immigrated to the United States in 1955. Rozalia attended the University of Cincinnati, earning bachelor of arts and master of arts degrees. She worked as an obstetrical nurse and as a midwife. She and Romana both live in Cincinnati, where Rozalia is active in Jewish community affairs. Both sisters remain in close touch with Dorka, who lives in England and Israel. Dorka visits them often in the United States.

—Interviewed by Aviva Segall, August 15, 1984

Tilly Stimler

Tilly Stimler was the youngest of nine children in an Orthodox family in Ruscova, Rumania.[1] Her schooling was interrupted at the age of fourteen when the Germans occupied Ruscova in 1944. Her parents had heard news from Budapest that "Jews were killed in Poland." They did not believe that they would be harmed but arranged to hide their two youngest children, Tilly and a sister. This arrangement ended when Tilly's father was arrested with the leadership of the Jewish community. His farewell kiss was "the most painful thing," and he was never seen again. The Passover holiday passed uneventfully. After Passover the Jews of Ruscova were taken to a ghetto in Visou Maro[2] for four weeks and then were deported to Auschwitz.

We arrived in Auschwitz on *Shabbos*. It was between day and night. You could see the smoke from the chimneys. You saw Germans with those leather coats. To this day I get petrified when I see a man with a leather coat. They said, "*Schnell, schnell!*" Forward, march, march.

As we were shoved out of the train, we were told to leave all our things right there and they would be sent after us. We wanted to take as much with us as possible, so I remember I wore a few dresses. Maybe, in a way, those dresses saved my life because I looked older. Then my mother said, "Oh, I'd better go back and take some of the cookies that I baked, so I have something to give to the children till they send the things." My older sister[3] said, "Wait, I'll go with you," and my brother[4] was shoved away immediately; we didn't see him anymore. I remember my mother saying to me and my sister,[5] "Stay here and wait for me." But meanwhile the Germans kept pushing us, "*Schnell*," go, go. So we kept walking, and then, after walking quite a few steps, they said, "*Funf in Reihe*" [five in a row].[6] My sister happened to be in the same row as I. I didn't even know how; I was just walking. We were taken to this barrack, and we were told to take off all our clothes, and I never saw my mother and my older sister again.

We were told to take off all our clothes, and we had to take a shower. They cut off our hair. They gave us gray clothes, and as we stood there in the assembly line with the gray clothes, I saw the men come out, and I did see my brother. I didn't have time to call out his name because right away they were pushed out the other way. I saw him for only a split second. It was the last time I saw him.

With our hair chopped off we all looked like boys; nobody recognized anyone else. We were told that this was a camp; we had to take orders, and we had to be disciplined and very strong. We could never open our mouth to talk unless we were addressed, and even then we had to watch what we said because for any little thing we could be shot. Then they told us that we should go to sleep. I don't know if they gave us anything to eat at night or not. We were hungry and tired. It was very hard to sleep, especially the first night, not knowing what was awaiting us. We were eight or ten on one bunk. If one turned over, the others had to turn. Some young kid started to scream for her mother. You have to understand; we were never sent away. It's not like here, where kids go away to camp, to school. We were always home, always with the family. There were so many screams. Young girls were screaming for their mothers, and that kept us up most of the night.

There was a *blockhova* who was in charge [of the barrack], and she had other helpers who were called *shtubhovas*. They would hit us for any little thing to keep the discipline. At three or four in the morning we were called to roll call outside. We had to stand *Appell*, and we were told just to keep quiet and stand, and it was raining. Day after day it was raining. I remember my deepest impression was, how could they leave us in the rain; I'm going to catch a cold! I remember my mother used to say, "Don't go out in the rain; you'll catch cold." I was the last in line. Not far from the *Appellplatz* there was a roof overhang, and one woman let me stand under the roof. But the notorious Nazi woman Irma Grese,[7] who was executed after the war, came over and gave me one big push to get back to stand in the line. Later I realized that I was very lucky that she just gave me a push because she could have just as well shot me or hit me or beat me to death.

Then they started to make selections for transports. We had to stand naked in front of Dr. Mengele.[8] He was referred to as the Angel of Death. I was rejected. My sister was accepted [for transport to another camp], and I had to stay back. I was really happy in a way for her, that she was able to go.

Then they moved us into another camp.[9] I was still lucky that I knew a few girls from the other camp. You tried to stay together with your own. There two girls said that when the next transport went, I should stay between them so maybe the SS wouldn't notice my being so skinny and frail looking. But again I was rejected. I really thought that the only way to get out of Auschwitz was with a transport or through the chimney.

One time when we were taken to be tattooed some of the older girls remembered parts of *Tehillim*, and we kept repeating them over and over again, and I wasn't tattooed. I really believe *HaShem* watched over us even there in Auschwitz. There's no doubt in my mind. Otherwise, I would never have survived.

One girl went to the hospital. She was from my hometown, and when she came back I was really very happy to see her because most of the others had left already and I was kind of left alone. I told her, "Two transports went, and twice I was rejected." She said, "Oh, I wish I had come out earlier. I'm sure I would have been able to go out." Deep in my heart I was glad that she was there too. Then they said that they needed some more people. Of course, she volunteered to go. I didn't volunteer; I knew I wouldn't be accepted. I was sad to see her go, but she came back. Lucky for me. They probably had more than enough people. I was happy that I had somebody. The next time there was a selection, again she said, "Keep close to me." There was another woman who was also little, but healthier. She said, "Maybe he won't notice you, and you'll be able to go with us." So, as I was trying to go through, Mengele said, "How old are you?" And you know, I really feel that an angel told me what to say. The Germans always said that you had to tell the truth because they were very precise and that if they caught you in a lie you were sure to be killed. I was fourteen, but I said eighteen because I was tall, and they said, "OK, go."

My friend was so happy to see that I passed. We were really very lucky because we were sent to a good camp in Breslau.[10] We were each given a bed, which was really a big luxury, like the Waldorf Astoria. It was really clean, and we were each given a sheet and a blanket. There were only about twenty-five of us in a room. Everybody kept saying, "I wish my mother was with me. How good it would be here for her. I wish my older sister was here, I wish . . ."

We were really treated humanely. We were able to take cold showers on the premises, and they even gave us a few days' rest before we started work.

I know they gave us new clothes a few weeks later. We went to work every day, of course, at 7:30, and we came back 7:00, so we worked the whole day, about twelve hours. My friend, who was about eight years older than I, said to me, "Oh, Zivialeh (that's my Jewish name), if I could get into the kitchen, it would be so good for you. I'd be able to help you." I didn't feel she had a chance because there were other girls already. But she said "Zivia, by God everything is possible." Just like that. And that same day, or the next day, the German woman called out that she needed more people for the kitchen, and sure enough my friend went in for the job. I feel this saved my life for later because, with *HaShem*'s help of course, she was able, through her work, to sneak out food for me. There was more food there in general, and it was better than in Auschwitz.

Tilly describes being treated decently. Prisoners were not afraid of being gassed, as in Auschwitz. She mentions that two women gave birth in Breslau and were allowed to keep their babies. In January 1945, as the Germans retreated westward from the advancing Soviet armies, the prisoners in Tilly's camp were marched out.

We had to leave on foot because they said they didn't have trains, and as a matter of fact, the German woman who was in charge went so far as to apologize: "We don't have enough food. We have to make do with what we have because we didn't have time to prepare for evacuation." So, we just got our meager rations. Maybe someone got an extra potato. So in January we had to start walking in the snow. I had shoes and a coat because they had given us some warm clothes for the winter.

At night we stopped and just spent the night in the snow. I remember the older girls telling me not to fall asleep because if you fell asleep you got frost-bite and you might even freeze to death. I remember always being watched not to fall asleep. One night we were lucky. We did sleep over in a barn. So at least we had that. But then we walked for quite a few days until by the time we arrived at Gross Rosen camp,[11] hungry and thirsty, the only way we could quench our thirst was with a little snow, or we would revive ourselves by washing our face with snow.

They stayed in Gross Rosen for two weeks without working and with very little food.

That German SS woman from Breslau was decent. She came one time to visit Gross Rosen. She saw that the *blockhova* had kept us outside a very long time in the freezing cold, and she hollered at her and said, "Why do you keep my children out for long?" The *blockhova* said, "Look, I have to count them." So she said, "If you can't count them in a half an hour you shouldn't be a *blockhova*." That shows how she felt sorry for us. She asked us, "How are you doing? I'm sorry there's not much I can do to help you."

From Gross Rosen they were transported to Mauthausen[12] by cattle car. The two babies who were born in Breslau suffocated in the crush of people on that trip. The sight of crematorium chimneys in Mauthausen frightened Tilly, and she reports hearing shooting "all the time." From Mauthausen the women were transported to Bergen Belsen.[13]

In Bergen Belsen people were dying like flies of typhus. There wasn't a barrack without sickness and disease, and even the air was contaminated. When they came to choose the weak people and they wanted to take me, the *blockhova* said, "Yeah, take her. She's always sick. She doesn't go to work." I couldn't go to work. How could I go to work? But although we were taught never to talk back to a German, I said, "No, no, I'm strong already. Tomorrow I'm going to go to work." I dared to talk back! When I think about it, I just can't believe I did it. I guess my instinct told me that it wasn't good to be taken with the weaker ones.

I remember one night I couldn't sleep. I was so hungry, and I knew there was food in that big kettle. So I made up my mind that that night I'd go down and risk my life to get a little extra soup. I did, and thank God I wasn't caught.

During the last few days the situation was getting worse and worse, and they kept bringing new people. I remember one of the girls saying how lucky our parents were. I think it was the first time I came face to face with the reality that they had killed our parents.

I remember a woman saying to me, "Here, have my piece of bread. It's *Pesaḥ*. I'm not going to eat it." So I said to her, "Well, I don't know. If *you're* not going to eat it, I shouldn't eat it either." She said, "You're a young child. You need to survive. Eat it, I'm telling you. I don't think I'll survive anyway." In fact, she didn't. But she said, "You're a young child; maybe that piece of bread will help you survive."

The situation got so very, very bad that you didn't even have room to stand in the camp because so many more people were brought in. Then, a miracle happened. Three girls walked by, and I recognized them. They were from my hometown. I called out their names, and they looked at me, and they said, "Who are you?" I told them my name. "Oh, my God, is that you?" one said. "You're not recognizable. Get up; come on, walk!" I said, "No! I don't have the strength to walk anymore. And besides, if I get up, I'm not going to have a space"—there was no place to sit. But she said, "Come on, you know it's only a matter of a day. Maybe if you walk . . . Don't you hear the shooting? The Allies are coming closer every day. Any minute, it could be tonight, it could be tomorrow, we could be liberated. Just hold on. Just don't let yourself go." So all three of them picked me up, and I guess seeing three familiar faces must have given me some moral support, and they did take me out. The air outside wasn't much better than inside, but maybe that made me want to live and helped me survive. And sure enough, overnight there was a lot of shooting, and when we got up in the morning we heard that the English had come in, that all the Germans had left.

At liberation Tilly was so sick and weak that she could not eat the food provided by the British troops. This was actually a blessing because the food they distributed initially was inappropriate for starving people. After a few days of vitamin therapy for her loose teeth and infected gums, Tilly gradually improved.

Because Tilly had a brother in England she was evacuated there on a children's transport. After further recuperation she attended school for a year and then got a job. She stresses that, in spite of what she went through, "we didn't think anyone owes us anything." On a vacation in Belgium she met her husband. They married, eventually came to the United States, and had two children.

I was lucky I was with the religious girls. I feel, as you walk, *HaShem* leads you. I was led with these very nice girls who looked out for me. I was also nice to them. One time, I remember I went to bring the food for them while they were still sick. They took me in like I was their protégé. Some of them were sisters; some of them were cousins. But I was really all alone.

I thank *HaShem* that my husband and I survived. Many children my age didn't survive. I really consider myself lucky that there was a purpose in my life, that I did achieve something. I was able to have two children. Since he married, my son continues learning.[14] He has, *kein ayin harah*, four children. My daughter is married, and her husband is in business, but still he learns in the free time that he has. My daughter does a lot of *ḥesed*.[15] I'm really proud. I feel I raised two very nice children. So I really feel that there *is* a *reason* why I was saved. I made my contribution towards the Jewish nation continuing. That's how I look at life.

—*Interviewed by Aviva Witkin, March 1, 1986*

Miriam Rosenthal

Miriam was the youngest of eight brothers and six sisters of the Schwarcz family in Komarno, Czechoslovakia. Her parents, wealthy Orthodox Jews, set an example of frequent and generous acts of charity and hospitality. Every Friday Miriam accompanied her mother when she distributed Sabbath food to poor people, and the Schwarcz home always accommodated visitors and poor students who studied in the yeshivah *that her family supported. Mrs. Schwarcz saw to it that poor girls had the skills and trousseau they needed to get married. By 1938 most of Miriam's older siblings were married. Jewish holidays became occasions for huge family reunions, as children and as many as thirty-five grandchildren assembled in the Schwarcz home, making the celebrations festive and memorable.*

When Germany annexed Austria in March 1938, Mr. Schwarcz bribed government officials to allow his Viennese family to come to Komarno, where they were accommodated on the Schwarcz farm, living quietly and unobtrusively. Reports of the cruelties of life under German occupation did not influence the Schwarcz family. "It won't happen here in Czechoslovakia," they said. After Hungary occupied their area of Czechoslovakia, Miriam's brothers were taken to forced labor.[1] Miriam would use her bicycle to take food, money, or cigarettes to her youngest brother, who worked in their city.

In the summer of 1944 Mr. Schwarcz died of a heart attack. Miriam, her mother, and her brother lived alone in their large city house until word came of the German occupation and the arrest of their rabbi. They quickly escaped from the city to their farm, joining the refugees from Vienna and Miriam's married sisters. The local gendarmes said to them, "You are such good Jews, we will look after you."

Meanwhile, Miriam, who was engaged to marry a young man

who lived in Miskolc, Hungary, sent her fiancé a telegram. "The wheat is ready for transport," read the coded message. "It will get rotten if we keep it much longer." Her fiancé, Bela, understood this to mean that Miriam was in danger.[2] One day a messenger arrived with false papers for Miriam and waited to escort her to Miskolc.[3]

My mother and my sisters carried on, crying. "You are not going to leave us. What will happen?" I was twenty, a young girl. First of all I was thinking about myself and my fiancé, whom I was in love with, and all my beautiful dreams. My mother said, "Don't leave me and your sisters." I said, "But I have a chance to go!" "But we don't know what will happen to you! Don't get married! Don't get married!" my mother kept saying. It was a terrible departure from my mother and the family. [Crying]

I said goodbye to them, and a *gendarme* came with me in our carriage. I don't know how much money he got from my mother. We went to the city, to our house. In the house I started to pack like a fool. I had these huge suitcases, and I was thinking, very naively, which dress should I take and which lingerie and which shoes? How could I know what was in store for me? Then the Gentile man said to me, "That's enough. How are we going to bring all this?" I said, "I have to take this." I was so brave. I locked the house. I was dressed up like his daughter with a black kerchief and a black coat and the cross.

We arrived at the Grand Central Station of Budapest. Germans, Germans, Germans . . . We took a taxi to my sister's house. She opened the door. "Miriam!" she screamed. She didn't know anything. There had been no communication, no telephone, nothing. I said, "Quickly, give him food. He's very hungry, this man." I asked, "Where is your husband?" "They took him away. I don't know where he is. Where are you going?" So I started to tell her the story. "Please, Miriam, stay with me. Please don't leave me here alone with the two children." Crying, crying, crying, the whole night we sat together. I said I couldn't stay. My fiancé was waiting for me. That man came all the way to the farm to take me to him. "But you don't know what will happen. They are taking the Jews away. If you stay here, at least we will be together." Again, something in me said I had to go. Many times I have had these guilty feelings that I should have stayed home with my mother, with my sister. She had the two children. I should have done this. How selfish I was. All this guilt, guilt, guilt in me. I said, "Don't ask me to stay. I have to go." She said, "Okay, go. *Zoll zein mit mazel*" (May it be with good luck).

So I went on the train again to Miskolc. This was before *Pesaḥ*, 1944. We arrived and went directly to my fiancé's home, and I saw all those faces: my mother-in-law, everybody, crying. "The Germans are in the city!" I said to myself, "What did I do? Why did I come? I should have stayed with my mother." But we asked the rabbi, and he said the marriage had to take place. "You came, and you are engaged; we have to make a wedding. It will be here, at night." Only the rabbi would be there, and the family. Nobody was supposed to know.

I had this young, young girl in me still, you know, who was dreaming about wedding gowns and all that. Of course I didn't have a gown, but I took my beautiful black suit and my big black hat out of the suitcase. As I look back on it now, how stupid I was! How did I ever . . . ? The rabbi came, and there was the ḥuppah, and I remember walking around the groom under the ḥuppah,[4] and the yellow star was on me under the ḥuppah.[5] It dawned on me that I didn't have anyone from home. My family was not here with me, not my sister, not my mother. In my mind, very, very clear, I heard the voice of my mother. How could I do it? Why did I do it? It was terribly confusing. There was nothing I could do.

> *The newlyweds lived with the groom's parents for two or three months. Miriam's husband would return occasionally from his work camp and stay with her for a week or a few days. In mid-April 1944 Miriam's father-in-law was brutally beaten in front of his sons by two Hungarian gendarmes who were looking for money and jewelry. Then the Jews of Miskolc were forced into a ghetto, crowded into the open yard of a brick factory. At the beginning of June 1944 Miriam's husband was sent to a distant labor camp, and she was deported to Auschwitz with all the Jews of Miskolc.*

Before the transport to Auschwitz my husband and I agreed that if we came back, I should go back to Komarno. That was our arrangement. And somehow we said goodbye, and he was taken for forced labor. Then the deportation. Everybody had to take their things down to the station. There were wagons, box cars, thousands and thousands of people going into the wagons. The Hungarian *gendarmes* and the Germans, like animals, shouting, hitting with sticks and leather straps, pushing and yelling and screaming. Still, people were hoarding, trying to hold onto their little belongings, whatever you had in your hand. I remember that, until the last minute, I held my father's picture. Don't ask me why.

I was with my sister-in-law and her two children, a two-year-old little girl and a six-week-old baby. My sister-in-law came straight from the hospital. They let her stay in the hospital for a while as a nurse, but then she had to come on the transport. I don't even know how to describe the cattle car. It had a huge door and tiny little windows with wires. We were packed in like sardines, old people, young people, children, sick people. No toilet, nothing. Locked, this heavy door was locked, and that was all. Even now when I'm on a train the memory of that trip comes back [crying]. You went, and you went, and you didn't know where you were going [crying] . . . And the people were yelling and crying and hungry, screaming, hitting each other. I have to go to the bathroom. There's no bathroom. A pail in the corner. To see my mother, father, the babies there . . . How do you change a diaper? How do you put a baby down to change? [Heavy sighs]

Sometimes the train stopped. We would yell for water. Sometimes they opened the wagon and put in a pail of water. We asked, "Where are we going? Why do we see only pine trees? Always trees and forest. No station? No people? Where are we going?" We were guessing. Maybe they were taking us for work. Who thought they were taking us to death?

After three days in the wagon we arrived at Auschwitz. How happy we were that the doors were open. Finally, air! We could breathe! When they opened the door we saw hundreds of Jewish prisoners in those striped clothes with a cap, with a yellow star, and Germans, SS, dogs. They were out there waiting for us, running back and forth, and they were talking to us. Everything happened so fast, you didn't know what was happening. All of a sudden we heard in Yiddish, "*Gibt die kinder zum Mame. Trug nisht, trug nisht*" (Give the children to the mothers. Don't carry them). Why? Don't ask. I could hardly understand Yiddish because in my parents' home we spoke German and Hungarian. Everything had to go so fast: *Schneller, schneller, schneller!* Right, left, was what we heard. My sister-in-law said, "If that's what they say, then we have to do it." So she gave the two children to her mother-in-law. There was no time to ask a question; everything went so fast. The Germans in their black boots with the whips and the dogs. All of a sudden, a few minutes later, we were alone. Where were the children? My sister-in-law asked, "When am I going to see the baby?" So naive.

We came to this place where we were stripped naked. We were shaved, underarms, everything shaved. The black hair was put separate, the blond hair separate. We thought they did it so we would be clean, so we wouldn't have any lice. Everybody got this striped dress, no underpants, nothing. We got big wooden shoes. We didn't have any mirror. We looked in each others' eyes to see. We didn't have any hair. Oh, my God. We looked terrible, like monkeys. Some of the girls laughed because it was hysterical. "I don't recognize you. You look like a monkey!" We all looked the same. But everything went so fast. There was very little conversation. No belongings left with you, stripped naked, not a handkerchief, not a pill, not a mirror, nothing! Absolutely nothing. You were dehumanized completely. Then we got the numbers. We had to stay in line, and then, from then on, that was what you were. No name, nothing, that was your number.

We went into C *Lager*,[6] and we had a *Lageralteste*. Her name was Elsa. She was Jewish, and all the *Kapos* were Jewish. She came in at five o'clock in the morning. She said, "You just came from Hungary. Look how healthy you are. We have been here four years already, and you don't know what we suffered here.[7] Hardly any of us are left. What do you think is waiting for you here? Every day there is a selection." She told us what happened every day. Then we knew what was waiting for us.

There were Polish Jewish girls there who had been in that camp four years already. They were so hard; they had no more feelings. Can you blame them? They were not human anymore. Elsa said, "Children? What are you talking about? You're not going to see your children. You're not going to see anybody. Look at the smoke. That's where your parents are. You won't see your children anymore." We thought she was crazy. We didn't believe her.

The *Zahlappell* was at five o'clock in the morning. Elsa came in with a stick. "Get up!" She had to do it because she was under the SS. She had to show that she was a good *Kapo*. So we had to get up for *Zahlappell* in the cold, in winter, in the wooden shoes. No stockings, no underpants, no blanket, nothing. We had to stay out in the freezing cold until they counted. Then she would say, "Twenty to work, twenty there, fifteen there."

The one who slept at the very end of the *pritch* always had the worst of it because she got the whip in the morning to wake up, so every night another girl slept at the edge. We slept so tight to warm each other with our body heat. When we turned around everybody woke up, and we all turned to the other side. One day I was sleeping at the end. Elsa came and said to me, "You with the other five girls." We had to carry dead bodies to the crematorium on a stretcher, and that was when I knew about the crematorium.

There were always transports. Always going, always going. Get up! Where are we going? There was a transport going to Plaszow. The transport was going out of the camp. Rumor said that if there was a transport, go. As long as you can get out of Auschwitz, go! So I got into the transport, and I met my first cousin Hilda from Komarno. We were the same age, and we grew up together and were always the very best friends. Hilda had her sister Ilie with her, who was a slow child. I also met Ernushka, a young girl, my sister-in-law's sister, who was like an adopted child in our home.[8] She was only eight years old when she came to our house, and she grew up in our family. My mother brought her up. I asked them, "Tell me what happened. What happened to my mother? Where is she?" She told me how brave my mother was. She was so religious; even in the *Waggon* she said, "This is God's will. We shouldn't complain." She was the one who was encouraging the other people. She was that kind of woman.

Hilda, Ilie, Ernushka, and I went with this transport. Again a *Waggon*, again the same procedure, the pushing, the yelling, but somehow we started to get used to these things. We had to. We arrived at Plaszow.[9] The camp was built on the Jewish cemetery in Cracow. It was like a huge football field filled with people and people and people as far as your eyes could see. People and SS and *Kapos* and German dogs and huge watchtowers. Barbed wire fences all around you and all these thousands of young girls in line, five in a row. There was a Polish *Kapo*; he was wearing leather boots, and he carried a leather whip. But he was talking Yiddish, and I could hardly understand what he was saying. Other women told me what he said. He looked at me and asked, "A Jewish girl who doesn't speak Yiddish? What do you speak?" German. *Oy vey!* "You come with me. You look like my daughter." His wife and daughter were killed in this camp. He was about forty years old; he had gold teeth. His name was Heinrich Reichsfeld. He took twenty of us to a *magasin*, a big room filled with featherbeds and down pillows that had been taken away from Jews. Our job was to open up each piece and see if there was any jewelry inside. I asked him why he picked us to work there, and he kept telling me I looked like his daughter. He saved our lives in there because the others had to work on the mountain carrying stones. People who knew me begged me, "Miriam, please tell him to take me in." I said I couldn't; I was not the boss. The Germans said he could only take twenty; that was all.

One day I felt something like, you know, kicking or moving inside me. I think I was in my third month, but I didn't know I was pregnant. What did I know? Nobody had their period because the Germans put bromine in the food.[10] Everybody was swollen from hunger, had a big stomach. I said, "Oh, my God, what's that?" There were older women in the camp and my sister-in-law. They said, "You're probably pregnant." I said, "What?!" One of the women told this Heinrich Reisfeld that I was pregnant. Don't ask what he did. Every day he brought me a piece of cheese, a piece of bread, a piece of this. "You have to eat well. You're going to have a baby, and you have to eat." Some of the men who were in that camp four years by then were terrible. But he was a very good person, and he wanted to help me.

He said to me, "If there is a transport, you stay here, and I will save your life, and we will be liberated." I said, "I can't do that. I'm going with my cousin." I didn't want to be parted from the others. He kept bringing things for me. Can you imagine a hard-boiled egg! One day we saw from the window of the barrack where we slept that they were shooting Jews. They were put by the wall. It was terrible. That day there was a transport. We thought, let's get out of here. Even if we had to go back to Auschwitz, it would be better than here. I said goodbye to Heinrich Reisfeld and thanked him for helping me. "If we survive," he said, "and you don't have your husband back, I want to marry you." To me he was an old man. He had gold teeth, and he was losing his hair! Anyway, we went back again in the *Waggon*, back to Auschwitz and the selections.

When we arrived Mengele[11] was standing there, a beautiful, tall soldier with white gloves. Everybody knew Mengele. He had a whip in his hand and the German dogs beside him and the SS. And left, right, *links*, left, *links*, left. Everything went fast, no walking, fast. In front of me was Ilie, one of the cousins, the slow-witted girl. Even her walking was slow. He noticed, and he sent her to the left. We looked after her; in two seconds she disappeared. No more. We didn't see her.

We went back again to have the disinfection and back again to the barracks. I was still with my other cousin. I told Elsa, the *Kapo*, that I was pregnant. When she heard that I was pregnant, I thought she would pass out because she knew what was waiting for me. She knew that they looked for pregnant women at the selection. They said that pregnant women would get double rations, so they should step forward, but they went to the gas. Sometimes Elsa sneaked a piece of bread for me. Ernushka, my cousin, was a *malekh*. She gave me half her portion. The hunger was terrible to take and so was the fear every day that I would go to the gas. One day they said everybody who was pregnant should step forward to get a double portion. There were about fifty women in line. I thought, "You're pregnant too. Oh, it's going to be terrific. We won't be hungry anymore." I was the last in the line.

I don't know why, but somehow I turned around and ran back to the rest of the group. I don't know why. I felt my parents looking down on me [crying], watching over me. I don't know what it was. God was good to me. I can't explain it. I went back to the rest of them. They asked me, "Why did you come back? You are so silly!" I said, "I don't want to go. I don't care. Even if I starve, I want to be with you."

The months passed, and I got bigger and bigger. I called Ernushka my sister because she was like a sister. She grew up in our family. How good she was to me! She was a child of sixteen. She tore off a piece of that gray blanket that we got, like what they used to cover horses. If they found out that you tore a piece off you would be shot the minute they saw it. She risked her life so I would be able to put it around me in the *Zahlappell*, so I wouldn't be cold. She gave me her bread. "Miriam, you have to eat. Miriam, you have a baby. You have to eat. For us it doesn't matter." How can you forget that? In a place like that you really found out who was a good person. To give away your portion . . .

All of a sudden there was a transport again. We said, "Let us go out of Auschwitz again." Where we were going, nobody knew. "Let's go. It doesn't matter. Let's go." Ernushka came with me. Hilda came with me. Again there was a selection to see who was strong, and so, one, two, three, we were in the *Waggon* again, again for a trip.

We arrived at Augsburg, in Germany. We came into a factory,[12] a Messerschmidt factory where they made parts of airplanes. We saw civilization, and we saw people. We saw other *Häftlings* from different countries, not Jews. They were political prisoners. They were working in this factory. They were wearing civilian clothes, and some of them were allowed to go out at night. We had to stay in the factory, but this was a palace compared to Auschwitz, and we were happy. We got two blankets. Can you imagine it? Two blankets! The soup was better, and the rations were better. One of those political prisoners, a German, was working on the same machine with me. The window near the machine where I was working looked out on an apple tree, and I saw the apples. How I craved an apple! If I could only have an apple! The next day this German guy brought me an apple. He left it by the toilet.

Of course, you could see that I was pregnant, but nobody paid attention.[13] Nobody said anything. The girls were so happy. They said, "Miriam, you are going to have the baby. Maybe we'll be free." We were so happy that the Americans were coming; they were bombing. The Germans were scared. They ran down to the bomb shelter. We were happy that the bombs were falling. The political prisoners brought news for us. We heard what was happening: Americans were here, and Russians were there, and the Germans were going to lose the war for sure. Everything was fine.

One day, when I was in my seventh month, two SS came to look over the *Häftlings* to see how they were working, and they stopped by my machine. "Ah, *du bist schwanger. Du bist schwanger, du schwein*" (Oh, you are pregnant. You are pregnant, you pig). "What are you doing here? How did you come here?" Of course, you were not allowed to answer anything. They took me away right then and there. It couldn't wait till tomorrow or till the afternoon. I couldn't even say goodbye.

I went with the two SS to the station. I was wearing my striped uniform with *Ka Tzet* (KZ) in big red letters on the back, and my wooden shoes, and we went to the Augsburg station on a normal passenger train. Can you imagine? I was traveling on a passenger train with these two SS. They were quite decent to me. They told me that they were supposed to take me to Auschwitz but that the Russians were bombing, so they would take me to a *Straflager* (punishment camp). I would be better off there than in Auschwitz, where I would go in the gas. These two SS men went out to the corridor to smoke and talk, and they left me alone with normal people dressed in normal clothes. It was winter, and I was shivering. The people looked at me like I was absolutely crazy. One German woman spoke to me. "*Frau,*" she said to me, "*was ist passiert mit Ihnen?* (what happened to you?) Why do you look so strange? Why don't you have hair?"[14] I said, "Don't you know? I'm a Jew, and they're going to kill me. Don't you know what happened to the Jewish people, what's going on?" They all looked at me like I was crazy. She opened her purse, and she took out a piece of bread or cake, I don't remember what it was. She gave it to me. "Sure," I said, "I'm going to die. All the Jews are going to die. Don't you know there are gas chambers?" She just—she didn't know what I was talking about. It was hard to believe, *Ja?*

The SS came back. We got off the train at the Landsberg station. One of them said to me, "*Adieu,*" goodbye. The SS left me at the door at Kaufering.[15] They signed some papers, and I went into the camp. A German *Kapo* took me into a room, and you can imagine my surprise. Six pregnant women were standing there. I thought I'd die of shock. They were all Hungarians. Right away, of course, came the questions. Where were you? Where did they bring you from? What happened? They said they had just come yesterday. The SS found each one individually, in a camp, in a factory, just like they found me. They brought them together, and we became the *Schwanger Kommando* (pregnant commando). We were kept separately in a little wooden hut.

Our job was in the laundry, washing the prisoners' clothes with millions of lice on them. It was very cold. It was in December. The men were separated from us by a fence. You could see them. There was just a wire in between.[16] It was a work camp. The men were like skeletons; they looked like *Musselmanner*. Most of them were Hungarians. They were in terrible shape. They suffered terribly from disease, the cold, no food. All together, the women and the men, at the same time, went out looking for food. We had a wooden platter, or some had some other container for food. It was icy. I had no stockings, nothing. Just that dress. It was icy, and I was carrying my soup, and I slipped on the ice. I fell on my back, and my soup fell out. Nothing happened to me. I got up. I lost my soup.

We had to go to work every day like the other prisoners. There was no consideration because we were pregnant. We had no extra clothes. We wore whatever we had. Our food was just like everybody else's. We were hungry. One day an SS came into our little hut, and he said, "Here is a man; he is going to be your doctor. You're going to have your babies." Imagine that man. His name was Dr. Vadasz, from Hungary. He had been a gynecologist. But he was a skeleton, skin and bones. He could hardly speak anymore. He was crying to us, "Children, how can I help you? With what? I don't have anything, and I don't have strength. Only God can help you, nobody else." But miracle after miracle happened.

There was a little room set up like a hospital, the *revier*. They used to show it to the Red Cross, pretending that that was where they treated the sick people. Luba was a Jewish *Kapo*. She said, "I'm going to put a stove for you in this little hut, but I am not responsible. I have to do it because otherwise you and your babies are going to freeze. So you have to look after this stove." Every night we took turns putting in pieces of coal so the fire wouldn't go out.

We had the babies one after the other. We helped each other. Dr. Vadasz had a *tallis* wrapped around himself as an apron. We had a little bowl of water that we warmed on top of the little stove. And one baby was born, and another was born. Luba always sneaked in some *shmattes* for us to use as a diaper, for a cover, and a little piece of soap. One SS man came into our little hut, and he said to us, "In real life I am a teacher. I'm a human being.

Here I'm an SS, but I want to help you." So under his cape he sneaked in a piece of cloth for the children. He always brought something. He said, "I know I will be killed before the war will be over. But something in my conscience will feel better that I helped you." So he brought this stuff.

Meanwhile, other SS came in and looked at us to see what was going on, to see how many babies we had already. Some of them were joking, very sarcastic. "You Jews, do you think you're going to have a sanatorium here? You should be happy that we let you have the babies." They were making fun of us. One of the women was in labor, and he was just standing there and making fun. If one was having her baby the others had to go out to work. One woman who had already given birth stayed with the other babies. We took turns. We had to go outside to the toilet in those wooden shoes. It wasn't a bathroom. It was a latrine. A deep hole was dug, and there was one rod to sit on. In that freezing cold you had to go, and it was terrible.

Mine was the last to be born. I had problems. I had labor for forty-eight hours. Dr. Vadasz didn't have anything to help me with. No needles, nothing. He said, "Look, my child, what can I do? You have to do what I say." From the men's camp I heard that the men were *davenning*. The woman who was with me said, "Do you hear? Do you hear how the men are praying for you? They are saying *Tehillim* for you."[17] The men were standing there in the night, in the cold. They knew that I was giving birth, and they said to tell me that it was Purim day and that they were praying for me.[18] It was Purim day. Purim day. Leslie was born on Purim day. He was a beautiful baby.

David, a Polish Jewish *Kapo* who worked in the kitchen, bundled him up in a rag and took him to the kitchen to weigh him. He was five kilos. That's ten pounds, yes? He was fat. He had blond hair, blue eyes. The German SS came in and said, "Ah. He's a German. He has blue eyes, and how lucky you are that you had the baby here." A few days later I developed a very high fever. Dr. Vadasz didn't know what it was. I was unconscious. I didn't know what was happening. Everybody told me later what happened. The SS came in and said they had to evacuate the room. They had to take me out. Luba said, "Look, she's dying. What are you going to do? We'll take her to the *revier*." So they lifted up my "bed," the wooden pallet. While they were walking, I started to bleed. You see, the placenta was left in, the afterbirth, and I started to hemorrhage. Everybody knew that I would die. There was no hope. Dr. Vadasz came in and made a scraping, a cleaning, with his bare hand. He had no rubber glove or anything. They raised my pallet on bricks so I would be slanted in order to stop the bleeding. There was no blood transfusion. I was unconscious and so weak I didn't know anything, absolutely nothing.

When I came to myself Dr. Vadasz told me what happened, and I said, "Where is the baby?" The baby was with Boszi, one of my friends who now lives in Brazil. She had so much milk, I can't imagine from what. She nursed Leslie for four weeks. It just shows you again. God's miracle. Boszi had her own baby, and she was also nursing babies of the women who didn't have enough milk. She was nursing, nursing all the time. She was the oldest, ten years older than I. She was like a mother to us. She told us what to do. We were her children. David kept bringing soup from the kitchen. He was not afraid anymore. He said, "You have to eat, and you have to be strong, and you're going to take the baby home." And he brought in an old watch. I'll never forget. He hung it on the wooden walls so we would know the time when we were feeding the babies.

The Germans probably knew something was happening. The Russians were very close on one side. The Americans were closing in on the other side. There was chaos in the camp. People were coming and going. The women told me that while I was in the *revier* an SS man came into their hut and saw the stove and kicked the stove out and turned the hut upside down. He demanded, "Who gave you permission to have the stove in here?" The women didn't say anything. He said, "If you don't tell me, all your children will be shot and you will be shot." So the women said it was Luba, and she was beaten up in front of them. That poor woman. She was bleeding. She stood there like a rock. Not a tear was coming out of her eyes. The women told her, "Luba, we did what we had to do. We are so sorry, but we had to tell." She said, "Never mind. They didn't shoot me. I'm still alive; I'm still here. So I got a beating. So what? It's not the first. It's not the last." Sure enough, we got the stove back again, we got coal again, we made a fire again. We still had to go out to work in the laundry. Once we had to push a wagon full of dead people and dump it in a big, big pit. They threw lime on it.

One day an SS came and said the camp had to be evacuated.[19] Where were we going? Nobody knew. Everybody was in line. There was yelling, shouting. "Everybody in line!" We were marching. We were all holding our babies. I put Leslie in a rag, and I tied him around my neck so it was easier to carry him. There were SS on one side and SS on the other side and lines of people, people, walking, walking. It was muddy; the snow was melting. The sun came up; it was muggy. And we were marching. Where? Nobody knew. All of a sudden we came to *Waggons* again, open *Waggons*. "Everybody on the *Waggons!*" I don't know how many people were jammed in. The train started to go. All of a sudden we saw airplanes, and they started to bomb the train. The screaming, the yelling that went on, the injured, the dead . . . The train stopped. We jumped out. Everybody was running like crazy to the forest. Some people went into the houses of the little German villages to ask for food. I was running, too. I lay down under a tree, and I covered Leslie up with the leaves, and we were just quiet. I looked in his eyes to see if that baby could understand what was happening. He looked at me, and I was praying and praying, "Please, God . . . " I was just praying all the time.

But they brought new *Waggons* and a new engine, and we had to go on. They started to shoot to gather all the prisoners. Some were shot; some ran. So we all went back to the *Waggons*. Where were we going? Nobody knew. All of a sudden we arrived in the middle of a city. The train tracks were in the middle of the city of Dachau.[20] We already knew what was happening in Dachau. Everybody knew this was the end. But this time we didn't care. Somehow, you didn't have any more strength to fight on. We were in God's hands; what would happen, would happen. But I kept saying, if I could just bring Leslie home. I wanted to bring him home. I wanted to bring him home. I kept saying that I had to be strong.

The SS man opened the *Waggons* and didn't say anything. He walked away. We had to wait. I jumped out and ran into a house. I left Leslie in the *Waggon*. Can you imagine, I left the baby there! I said, "I must have bread. I must have milk." We were starving. I didn't care if they shot me, I *had* to go. When I went into the house the first thing I noticed was a mirror. That was the first time I saw myself in a mirror. I wondered, is that me? I was skin and bones, and I looked old, terrible. There was black under my eyes. The woman came out and said, *"Was wollen sie? Was wollen sie hier?"* (What do you want? What do you want here?) I told her in German, "I'm hungry. They are going to take us to the gas. We are Jews. Don't tell me you don't know. The train is in front of you. You can see what's happening here." She said, *"Ja, ja, Frau"* (Yes, yes, madame). She brought me milk and a piece of bread. I knew I had to go. I ran back to the train, and the German was just walking there. He didn't say one thing.

When I came back to the *Waggon* the people were behaving like animals. I held this bread, and everybody jumped on me. I didn't even have anything left because everybody was grabbing. One of the men recognized me, Dr. Bandler. He was a *Musselmann*. He was crying, "Miriam, I'm starving. Miriam, please help me." I said, "Who are you?" I didn't recognize him.

"Don't you recognize me? Dr. Bandler, from Komarno." I said, "Doctor, Herr Doctor, how can I help you? I can't. I have nothing." So I went back into the *Waggon*, and the train started to move again.

We arrived in Dachau (the camp). It was night. We heard shooting, shooting, shooting. It was about three o'clock. Then it started to get light. Suddenly, screaming: "We are free! We are free! We are free! Americans! Americans!"[21] Everybody jumped out. We didn't know what was happening. The Americans were shooting the SS; the SS were shooting. People went crazy because they didn't know what to do. All we knew was, free, free! Americans!

Then the American soldiers told us to be quiet and not to worry, that we were free and that they were taking us to a big place. It was prepared with clean blankets and wooden beds, and there was food and chocolates and cigarettes. I saw a black American soldier for the first time. Some of the Americans said they were Jewish,[22] and they gave us prayer books. I remember a high-ranking officer, American, saw the baby, and he started to cry. He said, "We have seen only the dead, dead bodies in the crematorium, and now I see a live baby." He started to cry. They took movies of us. We settled down, and they wanted to make sure that we got stronger. They took Leslie and the other babies away to a hospital. There were tents set up as hospitals.[23] Leslie was full of lice, and he was very undernourished because I had no food for him. They told me they would call me in and explain everything, tell me what I should give the baby, what kind of formula. They didn't want us to leave until he got a little bit stronger, until he gained weight. Although he was so fat when he was born he lost all that. He got very, very skinny. The nurses said they would like to take the seven babies away to a place where they would rest with the mothers, and they would have taken me, but I said I didn't want to go anywhere. I just wanted to go home.[24]

They gave me diapers, bottles and nipples, and Carnation milk,[25] whatever I needed. They put me in a jeep with a nurse, and they took me to Prague. In Prague they had a Jewish agency waiting for the refugees, with warm food and beds. They were very well organized. I stayed there for two or three days, waiting for the train. I sat on top of the coal wagon full of coal. I think that trip took me a week. Every time the train stopped I went to the engine man for hot water for the baby's formula. The Russians on the train did terrible things to the Jewish girls. There was no use telling them that you were a *Häftling*, you were Jewish, you just came from a *Lager*.

Finally, we arrived at Bratislava, not far from Komarno. Again, there was a Jewish agency that was well organized. They asked me what city I was from, what kind of help I needed, if I had money, if someone was waiting for me. I said, "Of course, I want to go to Komarno." "How are you going to go? The bridges are all bombed." I had to wait. Finally, I got on a passenger train. I didn't know who would be there, if they were all dead. You always hoped, until the last minute, that maybe somebody would be home, with a big family like mine. It was an impossible hope, but still, inside me I was always hoping, hoping.

I came home to Komarno, and who was at the station but my brother! He didn't recognize me. You can imagine how I looked to my own brother. I recognized him because he had arrived home earlier and he had gotten back to his normal weight. I was yelling at him, "Sanyi! Sanyi!" He looked at me. I was holding a baby. He couldn't understand. Where had I picked up this baby? You can imagine our reunion.

We went back to our house. The house was empty, no furniture, nothing. It was totally empty. [Crying bitterly] I walked around in the rooms, and my brother said, "Nobody's here. Only I'm home. Don't worry. I will look after the baby, and we will have everything. The Russians are here. They are living in our house. One room is for us, for you and for me. I'll get the girl from the farm who used to be our maid, and she will look after the baby. You are going to be strong, and I will look after you." He bathed Leslie. He got a doctor to check Leslie, but we didn't know where we were going to find a *mohel*. What were we going to do? Leslie would be four months old, and we had to have a *mohel*.[26] He brought in everything that he could from the farm. The girl looked after Leslie, and I got stronger and stronger.

In Komarno in the *shul* there was a kitchen for the refugees. In the yard there was a big stove where they cooked soup. My husband's cousin was also there as a refugee. Leslie was in the carriage, and I was helping in the kitchen giving out food to the refugees, and this woman said, "Miriam, how nice that you are home. Whose is the baby?" I said, "That's my baby." She said, "I'm going back to Miskolc, where your husband lived. Maybe he's home." She got home, and my husband was home! Can you imagine? He was looking for me, but there was no communication. No telephone or mail or anything. She took the message to my husband. He had been in forced labor in Hungary. He said that when he heard the news about me and Leslie he couldn't understand. He knew we were married for three months before we were separated, but somehow he didn't connect it with my pregnancy. He said he thought maybe it was one of the SS because he had heard these stories. Anyway, when he heard the news he packed himself up with a piece of bread (he didn't even have shoes to wear; I think he had a pair of galoshes). There were no trains. He went on a little ferry boat, God knows how.

He came into the house, and somehow I didn't recognize him. He also was so skinny, and somehow the image of him was so different. I just couldn't remember how he looked before. But then he took one look at the baby and said, "He's surely a Rosenthal! He looks just like my father!" I don't have to tell you about our reunion. The crying. We were so happy. I said, "You don't have shoes on," and he said, "Never mind the shoes. I have blisters from walking."

Then my other brother also came home, also from forced labor. My sister-in-law came home and stayed with us. Little Ernushka, the one we adopted, also came back, and so did my cousin Hilda. We were all under one roof because our house was big. Gradually the Russians left, and we got some furniture back into the house. Then my husband and I decided that we would go back to his hometown, to Miskolc. We took Leslie, and we stayed with his brother and his wife. People came from all over to ask me if I had met their wives because they were also pregnant. What could I answer? I always had this terrible guilt. Why did it happen that I could bring home a child and everybody else lost their children? Why me? Why me? Why not my sister? Where are my sister's children? This terrible guilt haunted me.

Miriam corresponded with her sister in Toronto, Canada, about immigrating. The odyssey of her immigration took her, with her husband and child, back and forth twice from Miskolc to Komarno and then to Paris; Ellis Island in New York; Havana, Cuba; back to New York via Miami; and finally, in June 1947, to Toronto.

They stayed for a while with Miriam's sister in Toronto. Miriam's husband got a job stuffing mattresses in a factory. Miriam worked picking up the runs in nylon stockings in a factory. Although they had very little, Miriam describes herself as very happy because she was with her sister, whom she looked up to like to her mother. Miriam's husband was offered a position in a small town as a Jewish studies teacher, and although it meant separating from her beloved sister, it meant a secure livelihood for their family.

Miriam and her husband had two other children, and she now lives in Toronto, where she has her own business. She still corresponds with

Boszi, who saved Leslie's life when she nursed him in Kaufering. Boszi came to Canada from Brazil to attend Leslie's wedding. Miriam is in close touch with her cousins Hilda and Ernushka and maintains contact with some of her six camp sisters from Kaufering.

—*Interviewed by Esther Sacknowitz, December 21, 1983*

Cesia Brandstatter

Cesia Brandstatter was born in 1920 into an Orthodox family in Chrzanow, Poland. About one third of the town's population was Jewish. Cesia's family lived comfortably in a large house on a main street. She has very sweet memories of a large, close-knit family, and she still has beautiful memories of her prewar life in Poland.

I t was a better life than here. It was a more structured, meaningful life. All Jews belonged to organizations. Whether right wing or left, *frum* or not *frum*, they belonged somewhere. They were not brought up in the streets as they are here. There was school, there was homework in the afternoon, preparing for the next day, there was organization life in the evening. Since I was six years old I was in *Bais Yakov*.[1] When I was thirteen years old, I became a leader of a group of girls in *Bnos*.[2] We had discussions on various topics, books, and reviews. We studied the *sedrah* of the week, read political reports every Thursday, sang, and went on hikes. There was really not one wasted minute.

First we attended the Polish school. Then, from three o'clock until five or six o'clock we went to *Bais Yakov*. This was our entertainment. We liked to go there; we were at home there. We learned so much there. The language of instruction was Yiddish. We had only Jewish subjects. We were taught how to read Hebrew. We learned Jewish history, *Tanakh, ḥumash, Navi, Kohelet,* and *Kesuvim.*[3] On *Shabbos* afternoon we would sit and sing. We had lectures, and we read the letters of Shimshon Raphael Hirsch.[4] We had political discussions. We read the newspapers, and we had book reports. We read the classics of world literature.

The only thing that I regret very, very much is that they didn't teach us to speak the Hebrew language. It was not allowed.[5] We were brought up to love Israel. But at that time Zionism had nothing to do with religion. That was the reason we were not allowed to learn *ivrit.* I will tell you a secret.

Cesia, a friend of mine; another girlfriend, Hinda Wincelberg, who unfortunately perished in a concentration camp; and I (we were a trio) took Hebrew lessons secretly in an attic. We paid for the lessons. Our teacher was a girl who came from Lodz, from the *Agudah*. But, God forbid, nobody should know about this.

We were always very active in helping needy people. We used to go to the jail to bring kosher food to imprisoned Jews. We used to visit sick people in the hospital. It was part of our organized activities. Each group had a different day to go to the hospital with food, with books to entertain the patients, with a good word to lift their spirits.[6]

There was anti-Semitism. But my family and I, personally, had very good relations with everybody. As a matter of fact, after liberation, when I returned from the concentration camp, I met a Polish neighbor whose name was Stanislaw Palka. He saw me walking on the avenue on one side of the street, and he was walking on the other side in the opposite direction. He noticed me, he looked around, and he pointed with his finger, you come with me! Not talking, just pointing. He motioned to me that he had a card for me, and I understood that it was from Russia from my brother and sister. Of course I came with him. His family accepted me very warmly. They brought me a glass of fresh goat's milk, and they told me, "Before you talk, before you eat, drink this because you need it. You didn't have it for a long time."

When we came back from the concentration camp there were Polish people standing near the tracks, and they said in Polish, "Oh my, more of you came back than went." This was the usual greeting.

Before the occupation we helped those people who arrived from Zbaszyn.[7] The refugees from Germany came only with very small packages. Their lifestyle, their standard of living, was much higher in Germany compared to Poland, but we did what we could. They were our brothers, they were our sisters, and we were afraid that our fate would be next.[8] We were near Katowice, near the border. So we were very, very concerned.[9]

Cesia's sister married in August 1939. Cesia and other members of her family went to Stary Sacz to bring her sister's belongings to her. By the time Cesia returned to Chrzanow, the Germans had occupied the town.[10] Her sister, brother, and brother-in-law made their way east and ended up in Russia.[11] Cesia's parents sent some of their belongings to another town, hoping that they could escape there, but to no avail.

I don't remember exactly when we had to put on the yellow *mogen Dovid*, but it was soon after the occupation.[12] The Germans started to evacuate people to different streets. They started rationing food. A *Judenrat* was formed.[13] Mr. Cuker and Mr. Teichler[14] were involved. One beautiful day they captured them, took them to Auschwitz, and very shortly, I don't recall how long it took, two boxes of ashes arrived in Chrzanow, to the *Judenrat*.[15]

There were shortages of food, standing in line for a piece of bread.[16] This I remember as if I was standing in line right now. If you reached the bakery at 5 A.M., you stood in line until they closed the bakery at 3 P.M.; no more bread. It was a daily routine. I was working in Rosner's *Schneidersammelwerk-stätte*[17] in order not to be sent away to a concentration camp. Of course I had to work on *Shabbos* and *yom tov*. There was no way out of it, but it was better than going to a concentration camp.

At various times during the war we lived at four different addresses. At first, we lived on the main street; it was like a boulevard, a very nice street. The Germans took it over.[18] We had to move to a second place. The Germans made this section *Judenrein* too. Then we moved in with my mother's brother near the marketplace. We had a room, they had a room, and we shared a kitchen. And God willed for us that this became *Judenrein* too. So we went to live in my mother's parents' little house where my aunt used to live. Two aunts were there already.

My friends and I were not in a close touch with each other because we did not have time for socializing. All the girls were working in order not to be taken to a concentration camp. This kept us home until the Final Solution in Chrzanow, the liquidation of my city.

One day in 1942, *Shavuos* time, at four o'clock in the morning, there was an *Aktion*.[19] They started to knock on the doors with rifles. They broke open the door: "*Juden raus, Juden raus*." We could hardly get dressed. They took us to a section of town where there were *Batei Midrash* and synagogues and all the Jewish institutions.[20] Merin made the selection.[21] He was a Polish Jew from Sosnowiec. Wearing white gloves, he pointed at us to go to the right or to the left, and he took me also. All the people Merin selected were gathered together in the old people's home.

I was with my parents and my aunts. I ran away. I tried to get to my workplace in order to find help at least to free my parents. My workplace was located in a synagogue right across from the old people's home. It was very dangerous because we were very carefully guarded like dangerous criminals and murderers.

There was a big arch. SS men were standing on both sides, tall guys, 6 feet, 6 inches, or 6 feet, 5 inches. I am not tall, so luckily I just sneaked through without being noticed. I don't know how it happened. I didn't care if they caught me and shot me; I had to try to do something. My luck was that they didn't catch me.

I went into the office. Benji Meltzer was working in his office. He said, "What are you doing here? We have you on the list of people we are going to try to rescue." I said, "I ran away. I came to make sure that you know about me and that first of all you will try to rescue my parents." He said, "Look at the list. You are the first one on the list." And I said, "OK. I did what I had to do, and now I'm going back." He told me, "No, you are not going back. You are staying right here." I was very aware of what was going on. So I said to him, "What will I say when my sister and brother return from Russia, and I am alive? What will I say? What will be my excuse that I am alive, and I didn't go with my parents?"

The caretaker, Mr. Lapka, was a very nice man. Because of his position he was free to move around in the whole section. I offered to give him whatever I had, which was not much, if he would help my parents escape. He went and told them where I was and gave them advice on how to escape. My mother convinced my father to escape first and promised to follow him.

Mr. Lapka took care of me. On a long table near the wall in the workshop where I had been working he piled a mountain of colorful raincoats that we were manufacturing at that time. I laid down on a bench, which he put behind the table, near the wall. I was covered by the mountain of raincoats, and that was how I spent the night.

Eventually, I went home. My father came home; my mother I never saw again. They told us at the Jewish Community Center to prepare a suitcase for people who were to be deported and bring it to a certain place. Mr. Weiss, a good friend of ours, who was working for the Jewish Community Center,[22] brought me a little note from my mother. It was written on a little piece of cloth. It's more precious to me now than anything I own. The note is written in Polish to my father and me: "Please, don't cry. It will be much harder on me if you cry. I will try to register to go to Tarnow. Please send me some slippers because my feet are aching." She was young . . . in her 50s. She thought that she might have a better chance of being rescued from Tarnow, where my father came from, because it was farther from the German border.

The people who were not deported in that selection were given blue stamps[23] on their identification papers. Another time there was a red stamp.

My father didn't have any stamp, and I knew that I had to do something about it because I understood that some day the Germans would come up with another trap, another way to catch Jews. A friend of mine told me that someone was making fake stamps. "Go to him, tell him that you are Srulek Geldwerth's sister, and he will do it for your father." I approached him, and I said, "Whatever I have I will give you; you have to do it for my father." I got my own blue stamp from the place where I was working, and he made the fake stamp for my father. He didn't want to accept any money.

Shortly after this, in July or August 1942, there was an *Appell*. All Jews had to come to the hanging place where they had previously hanged seven Jews.[24] They called everybody to appear and to bring their identification books with those blue stamps.[25] My father and I passed because we had them. There were some difficulties; they wanted to keep my father again. But Mr. Weiss vouched for my father. He told the Germans that my father worked for him. It was a miracle that they let him go.

On February 18, 1943, I was all alone in the house. I had just come from work. My father worked a different shift. Again, banging on the doors. I met my cousin and my aunt with her two little girls. There was a selection. They took me.[26] I was on the side to go to concentration camp. All of us, the young people, wanted to go to Auschwitz. Our attitude was, it was our parents' fate; it should be our fate also.

They sent us to Sosnowiec. We were in a transit camp there for three weeks. It was much worse than hell.

Cesia found seven friends in the group with which she was deported. These were girls she knew from Bais Yakov *and from public school.*

The room where they brought us had a very high ceiling; it was divided horizontally. In the middle they made steps and another ceiling and a floor. We went up the steps to the second floor, and in that place where we were standing in our coats we laid down and we slept. In the morning they took us down to the basement, a huge basement. There were so-called washing basins. A pipe with the diameter of an inch, no more, ran the whole length of the basin. In that pipe there were little holes, like the diameter of a thick needle, on two sides. One girl could stand on each side. On the floor, they put some wood so we were not standing on the bare cement. That was how we washed ourselves. I don't know from where, but we got a piece of soap; it was like a piece of stone. We washed ourselves because we were very, very afraid of getting lice. I took off my bra, and I washed it under this drip of water with this soap, and I put it back on, wet. I did the same with my panties, to keep clean. How did we dry ourselves? Reva Unger happened to have a towel. This towel was used by all eight of us. You can imagine how dry or how wet it was. And as if this was not enough, in case we had to wash our hands[27] and we were upstairs where we were sleeping or standing, we flushed the toilet and washed our hands in the toilet bowl. I just have to describe to you the circumstances, the conditions, in which we lived.

I will tell you something else from this transit *Lager* that is very important, and the world should know and should listen to it. We were called for *Appells* every morning. We stood in a big field, and of course it had barbed wire all around. I was standing in the first row holding hands with my friends. In front of us, fifteen, twenty feet away, was a two- or three-story building. I was holding hands with Recha Zussman. We looked up at that building, and in a window we saw a face, a boy's face, a red-haired, freckled-faced boy seven or eight years old, and the boy was knocking with both his fists against the glass and yelling, "Mommy, where are you leaving me?" That was Recha Zussman's child. She was squeezing my right hand and squeezing my friend's hand on the other side, asking, "Girls, what shall I do? What shall I do?" What could we tell her to do?

The other episode also happened during the three weeks we were in this transit *Lager*. A van arrived, completely black and closed up. No windows. We found out that this van had arrived from Chrzanow. It was filled with people, including children. The cousin of Dora Halberstam, one of my friends, said, "I am going to check whether my child is there." We begged her not to go because we were afraid that she would find her son. She went over to the van, and believe it or not, the German guard had a little bit of human blood in him. He said, "Don't come in. I don't want you to come in." She said, "Please, I want to know. Find out whether my child is there." Finally, the guard told her that the boy was there. She said, "I want to go with my child." The guard tried to explain to her. I don't know how it happened that he had a little bit of human kindness and feeling. He said, "I want you to understand that you will not be with your child anyway." She said, "For as long as I can be with him, I want to go." He gave her permission, and she went with her child to Auschwitz.

Eight of us, friends from Chrzanow, were together in Sosnowiec, and then we were all sent to Ober Altstadt,[28] near Trautenau, Czechoslovakia, in the Sudetenland. We worked in the Kluge factory.[29] It was called *Spinnerei* (spinning mill). We manufactured thread from raw flax. We worked with the raw material.[30] We put raw flax into machines, and this produced much dust.[31] The dust was so heavy that if I was standing about six feet from someone, or even closer, I couldn't recognize the face. This process was called *Carderie* (carding).[32] This process wasn't as dangerous as later work because this was very thick dust that you could spit out. It settled in your throat; it didn't go down into your lungs. After *Carderie* the next step was *Feinsaal*.[33] Here the dust was more fat, heavier.[34] The dust wasn't as thick; it was finer. This dust settled in your lungs. Unfortunately, we had many girls who got tuberculosis because of this work. They were operating the machines that produced finer thread. The first process produced very thick, long strips.[35] The second process[36] produced much thinner thread, and as it came to each machine, it was made finer. The finer the thread became, the finer the dust that was produced, and it entered easily through your nostrils and went down into your lungs.

I was working with the *Schnellaufers* (fast runners). I had to be as fast as the machines. If not, I ran out of material, and it was very hard to connect the threads again. If I had to go to the ladies' room, I had to close down the machine for a few minutes. And I want you to know . . . when we went to the ladies room we had an SS woman accompanying us to watch us, to make sure we came back, and ordering, *"Macht das schnell!"* (Hurry up!)

At the next machine there was a Hungarian girl who arrived from Auschwitz. She had such a rough time. She didn't understand one single word, not Polish, not German, not Yiddish. Only Hungarian. I could help her only by motioning to her, teaching her, or showing her how and what to do only with motions because she didn't understand. She managed. After a little while she started to understand German. I could get along with the German language.

The other seven girls who were my friends were also doing similar work in the factory. We saw each other, standing, operating different machines. But of course, we couldn't talk to each other, we didn't associate, we didn't have anything to do with each other. There wasn't such a thing as lunch hour. Didn't exist. Who says that we have to eat or to rest? We worked shifts from six o'clock in the morning to six in the evening. We were lined up and brought together under the SS women, who walked in front of us and at the end of the column like we were the biggest crooks and murderers.

We worked six days, not on Sunday. On Sundays we washed our things by hand. We cleaned our beds; we took the beds apart to take out the bed bugs. I would like you to know that in comparison with some other concentration camps, ours was luxury because we didn't have the ovens, and we didn't have the terrible conditions that some had.

The Czechoslovakian people were very kind to us. There were Czech civilian workers in this factory who came in in the mornings and went home at night. We saw them as they were passing through. I stood next to the two machines that I was operating. They would pass by and give us a smile. That was everything. Some girls took advantage of them, and the Czechs threw them a piece of bread or some cigarettes. I personally didn't have such experience, and I didn't want to.

There were some nice incidents. One Czech man came to Estia Englander Reichman. He approached her, and he said, "I want to help you, and I want to take you out of here." She said she was afraid (she didn't trust him). "Besides," she said, "I'm not alone. I have seven other friends with me." He said, "I will take you all together." One Czech woman who was working behind me operating a different machine used to bring me a piece of bread, put it into my locker. She didn't say anything; she would just show me with her eyes, motion to me. You understand? They were afraid to speak to us. The Czech people were kind.

There were a thousand women in this place. My room, which was *Stube* 83, had only thirty-six girls. My friends and I slept on four bunk beds, two girls on one straw sack. I slept on an upper bunk with Dora Zeltenreich. Next to us slept Faigusha Gross and Lusia, her cousin, also on an upper. Underneath slept Frieda Elbaum Schein with her friend Estia Englander Reichman. Next to them, below, were Reva Unger Gartner with Aidja Gross. Reva Unger got a big red pot somewhere, and into this pot we took eight portions of soup.[37] We had one spoon, and the soup pot passed from one girl to the next, to all eight girls. In case there was some left over it went around again. As hard and as difficult as our lives were, and as hungry as we were, our behavior and our moral standards were still on a very high level.

We had very narrow closets, lockers. A few girls shared one, not being afraid that one would eat up all the food, which was a question of life and death. We eight shared such a closet, where we kept our belongings that were so precious to us.

Frieda Elbaum was an orphan. She had *yahrzeit* for her mother, and she wanted to light a candle.[38] So I asked one of the Czech women I was working with if she could bring me a candle. She brought a candle, and I went over to the locker to put the candle away. Another woman, a German, a real witch, denounced me to the *Meister*, the supervisor. Luckily, I dug myself out of trouble. I said that I was checking my suitcase, and I saw a candle, and by mistake I put it into my pocket. The candle was disturbing me as I was bending down, so I just wanted to empty my pocket. I went over to take the candle out of my pocket and put it into my locker. How did I get the wisdom to answer this way? This was a *miracle*. Believe me, it was a miracle. It happened that they believed me; otherwise they might have sent me to Auschwitz. They might have cut off my hair to punish me.

Itah was also a *Bais Yakov* friend from Chrzanow. She was a wonderful person; she was in charge of the *Schneiderstube*. She sewed, mended for the girls. They gave us button-down navy blue dresses for work. We didn't have enough underwear; we were imprisoned two years, and we couldn't buy or get new things, so we mended our old ones. Itah was very pious. She remembered the Jewish calendar. I think for one of the years she made some adjustments. I don't remember how, but we knew the Jewish calendar.

Believe it, on *Shabbat* we didn't turn the light on or off.[39] We didn't do anything except go to work. On *Yom Kippur* we fasted, but on *Pesaḥ* we ate *ḥometz* because we couldn't starve eight days and not eat anything.[40] We couldn't get a sufficient amount of potatoes. Otherwise, we wouldn't have eaten *ḥometz*.

We didn't have any prayer books. We could say *Modeh Ani* and *kriyat Sh'ma*.[41] We were brought up like that. There was a lot of bitterness. Each of us was bitter about our fate. But we were used to it, and we used to practice [our religion], some more, some less. It depended on the individual. We didn't check with each other.

One night I went to visit my friend Cesia Zajac,[42] and I slept with her. This was in another part of the same camp, where they were working for a different firm, Ettrich. In the middle of the night, as I was sharing one straw sack with her, she started to cry in a terrible way. That was not like her. [Making gasping, sobbing sounds] Terrible. I didn't know what had happened to her. It was from hunger. One girl happened to have a little bit of sugar. We gave her some on the tip of the teaspoon. She calmed down. That was pure *hunger*. I will never forget it.

I got pneumonia. I was really very sick. They didn't give me any medication. I was moved to the *Krankenzimmer*, a room in the same barrack. In the *Krankenzimmer* Manya took care of me. She was a nurse, a Jewish woman. She was much older than I. If a girl didn't obey her, she cried: "What will I do? They will take you away; they will send you to a worse camp, to Parschnitz."[43] So she cried with tears, begging us not to do this or that and to be careful. She was a *mother*, she was a *mother*. She fought to get more food from the kitchen for the sick girls. She brought me warm tea or something like that. I don't remember exactly. Mostly it was soup. One soup was made from potato peels, and one was cream of farina, very thin, without salt.

The girls used to bring me some food, which I couldn't look at. I couldn't eat. The usual food was bread. We had *Mehl* soup, made from flour and potato peels. When I recovered, I went back to the window where they distributed food. The girls who were working in the kitchen were glad to see me. They gave me a big bowl with noodle soup. They dug the ladle deep into the soup, and they brought up real food, not only the water, with some meat bones. I was so weak I couldn't carry the bowl. Somebody carried it to the table for me. I started to cry, and I ran back to the room. My friends brought this soup into the room, and after this bowl another bowl of soup followed. The girls wanted to rebuild me. As hungry and as weak as I was, I couldn't take their pity; I couldn't take the *rahmones*. I couldn't eat it. I begged my friend, "As long as the soup is warm, you eat this. My throat is closed."

I was lucky that when I was sick my *Lagerführerin*, Irma Hoffman, was at Gross Rosen for training because Ober Altstadt later became a concentration camp.[44] So, I survived. Shortly after this, there was a selection. We didn't know at the time that it was Mengele who did the selection, but I am 100 percent positive that it was Mengele.[45] We were undressed completely nude, and this was in February. We appeared in front of him, and if somebody, God forbid, was a quarter of an inch too close to him, he punched you in the middle of your stomach with his stick: Back! I remember he selected Hessa Ernst from my *Stube* 83 to be sent to Auschwitz. That was when the camp was converted from a labor camp into a concentration camp.[46]

I don't know whether somebody who was not there can understand. The ration of bread we had was very, very little. For the whole week we got a quarter of a small round bread. We kept the bread in our locker. We were not afraid that one would take away from the other one, not even a crumb. Once, my friend Dora Zeltenreich, with whom I was sharing the so-called bed, the straw sack, became sick. She was coughing terribly. As soon as a person started to cough or be sick, they immediately sent you away. We knew that was the end and that was it. We girls were very much afraid; we were very concerned about each other. The girls asked me to go and sleep with somebody else across the room, to share the bunk with another girl who didn't belong to my group so I would not get sick from Dora.

This girl worked in the kitchen. She washed the pots. Because she worked in the kitchen, she was allowed to have some vegetables and potatoes, which was very special. I was lying on my right cheek, turned away from her, and she was sitting on the other side of the bed eating one of the kohlrabies or a raw potato and enjoying herself. I was very proud and still am, and I wouldn't dare ask anybody to give me a crumb. The tears from my left eye were flowing down across my right cheek until I couldn't lie on that side anymore because it was all wet. I had to turn around. If I had asked her, please give me a piece of whatever you are eating, I'm sure she would have given it to me. But I couldn't ask anybody to have pity on me and to give me anything to help me out.

My friends were suffering just like me. Once, for Christmas, the *Lagerführerin* was very "generous." She gave us a tablespoon of jam. You cannot imagine what kind of a feast that was for us. In March, I guess, I became sick, and I was coughing terribly, and some other girls became sick, too: fever and sore throat. They couldn't talk; they needed something to soothe the throat, something sweet. The girls looked around in case maybe somebody had something that would help the sick girls. They came to me. I still had this little bit of jam that they gave me at Christmastime. I kept it in the locker. It was cold there. It didn't dry out; it was wrapped in a piece of cellophane paper. I gave them the jam. All that time I hadn't allowed myself to take a drop. I thought, maybe there would come a worse time when it would be needed.

Together with the letter that my mother sent me in Chrzanow before she was deported, she sent me two wedding rings. One was hers, and one was her sister's. They were four sisters together going to the station to be sent away. I had those two wedding bands with me in Ober Altstadt. I didn't want to touch them. They were very, very precious to me. But the girls started to nag me and to bother me and to beg me. "You don't know what the next hour will bring. We're not going to be alive anyway. You have these rings; exchange them for bread." Finally, I did. I exchanged them, and I got two breads, two round breads.

I gave both rings to a Czech man, Mishka. He was very friendly and a good human being. He worked not far away from me. We couldn't talk to each other, just motion to each other. He brought me two round, black breads. Reva had a huge, loose coat, which she lent me. I hid the breads under the coat and brought them, one at a time, to the barrack. I could have been shot on the spot or sent to Auschwitz. We all shared the bread.

Another time we were starving, and I said to myself, "Whatever will happen, will happen. We cannot go on like this anymore. Our parents are gone. I don't know what we have to return home to . . . " I went to the *Lagerführerin*. Frieda came along. We begged her, "We are hungry. We are very, very hungry. We know that you have some bread in storage. We beg you, before it gets rotten, please have pity. Give us a piece of bread." Irma Hoffman looked at us, and she dismissed us. We went back towards the barrack.

We hadn't reached *Stube* 83 yet, and there was a whistle: *Appell!* We lined up. In front of us was a card table filled with quarters of bread. Everybody lined up, stood in rows, and she chose: you and you and you, and Frieda and I were among them. "Come here." We didn't know what for, to be shot? She gave each of us whom she had chosen a quarter of a loaf of bread, and then she picked up the rest of the bread and threw it into the crowd. And she said, "Kill each other over this. Kill yourselves!" She threw here, and she threw there: "Kill yourselves over the bread!"

We were often depressed. We would lie on our cots up there, crying. We never fought. We never had any disagreements. We never were angry at each other. I cannot understand now how women could live in such harmony in such difficult times because difficult times usually bring anger. The truth was that we did not believe that we would survive the war. We used to say only one thing. If anyone lived through this war, it would be *moshiach tzeiten*.[47] But we won't be here.

We lived with our memories of home. Our real lives were those memories of home. There was one taste of Auschwitz in our camp, a terrible guy, Franz Simolaine, the camp *Kommandant*. His jaw was always working. You could see how it was going back and forth. He had a *Shpitzrute*, a steel whip. He would snap it against his boots. He was huge, and on his face was an expression of an animal, not a person. When he came into the room to check whether we were in bed, we froze. Each and every one of us. We couldn't say a word, but we thought, "He's taking us out. This is the last second of our lives." Franz Simolaine.

But in comparison with some other camps ours was very good . . . They called this *Erholungshause*. A sanatorium, yes, a leisure place as compared to others, especially for women. In 1944 a transport of women from Auschwitz came to us. Suddenly we saw people approaching, lined up. We didn't know if they were men or women, in their striped suits and shaved heads. They were released finally, so we saw they were girls, women. In comparison to their experience, we realized how *good* it was in our camp.

We got liberated last, after the end of the war, which finished on the eighth of May. We got liberated on the ninth. The SS women ran away. The girls caught the *Lagerführerin*, and one woman, Regina Goldberg, who had been slapped by the *Lagerführerin*, hit her. The girls brought the *Lagerführerin* to the camp, and they made her kneel down on her bare knees on the gravel, very sharp pieces . . . They put on her one of the navy blue button-down coat dresses that we wore to the factories. It was two sizes too small. They took pins and pulled the pieces together. They put a scarf on her head, and Regina went over to her and slapped her from one side and from the other side and from one side and from the other side of her face until she was good and red. Then Regina went away, and she let her stay like that. That was the *nekomah*; that was the "revenge" that we could take.

We were told that the Russians were coming. We went to the road to greet them. I cannot describe how happy we were. I don't even know where the girls got flowers and whatever to greet the Russians. We went to the German storage houses where they brought merchandise from all over. We helped ourselves to whatever we needed. We didn't have big aspirations and big desires. What did we take? I got some yarn, and I made a dress. Frieda got some flour from a German woman who was living across the street from the concentration camp, and she baked something to take along on our trip home. We didn't have any bread, so she brought what she baked, and we had something to eat.

We stayed in Ober Altstadt about a week more, and then we just had to run because the Russians were animals. They were wild animals, and we were afraid of them. We put chairs and tables against our doors not to be invaded by them. They invaded the barracks the night before. Thank God they didn't do anything to us . . . We didn't have anywhere to look for rescue, so on *Shabbos* morning we got our belongings, and we went to the railroad station, and the eight of us ran away.[48]

The trip home was also terrible. It was very long. It was crowded. Drunk Russians invaded the train, and Tola Sachs opened a window in the speeding train, and she jumped out and entered another wagon through a window in order to pull the emergency brake and stop the train. It was lucky that she did it. When we came to Katowice, a captain, a high-ranking Russian soldier, came, and he took away the drunk Russians from the laps of the girls. You cannot imagine the scene. This was also something to remember.

We returned to Chrzanow. We all lived together. We slept on the floor because it was a completely empty apartment. We fought with each other, each one getting up earlier to wash the floor so the others wouldn't do it. That was what we fought about.

We went to the Jewish community center, which was reorganized by people who were liberated earlier. Hayyim Henenberg handed over to me a postcard that my brother wrote from Russia and sent to Chrzanow. My brother asked the recipient of the card to put it up on any pole, on an electric pole, telephone pole, to inform his sister of his address so she could get in touch with them. That was how I got back in contact with my brother and with my sister and their family.

Soon after this contact was established Cesia left Chrzanow and moved to Reichenbach with several of her camp sisters. There, Cesia was reunited with the members of her family who survived in Russia. She married her brother-in-law's brother, and the extended family moved to Germany. In Heidenheim, Germany, Cesia's husband was in charge of a Jewish children's home, rescuing Jewish children from convents and Christian institutions where they had been hidden during the war and facilitating their immigration to Palestine.

Although they, too, planned to immigrate to Palestine, Cesia and her husband came to the United States in 1950 with their twenty-month-old son. At first they lived in Omaha, Nebraska, where Mr. Brandstatter worked as a kashrut supervisor and at any other jobs that would support his family. In 1958, with their son and daughter, who was born in Omaha, they left the midwest to live in New York, where they found appropriate Jewish education for their children. In New York, Cesia renewed her close friendship with those of her camp sisters who lived in the area, and they continue to remain in close touch with each other and with those who live in other countries, attending weddings and other happy occasions in each other's families and gathering to offer comfort and sustenance in times of sorrow.

Cesia was widowed in 1986. She is an active volunteer in the cardiology department of her neighborhood hospital.

Being with the other women helped us survive. You have somebody to turn to, to cry on somebody's shoulder, which we did. We helped each other that way. A good word, a ray of hope, something. To be lost and not to trust . . . If you are with strangers, you can't trust. We were very lucky that we were together.

People shouldn't blow unimportant things out of proportion. Life can have much deeper meaning than little things. Remember that we lived in such conditions in such harmony and devotion to each other. We sometimes sit together now and talk about our life in the concentration camp. We cannot understand how we were so devoted to each other in such circumstances. Not one was thinking only for herself and of herself. No, it didn't exist. Whatever we had, we knew we had to share. Estia wouldn't go with that guy who offered to give her freedom without us. She said, "I have friends with me." Each of us was ready to be killed by the Germans, to go to Auschwitz, wherever, but not to leave the other girls. It would have been much better if we hadn't had that experience. We didn't ask for it.

I speak about my experiences gladly because I know that a human being is not forever and that whoever listens to this tape should remember that this happened. This wasn't a *story*; nobody invented this; it is the truth. I had a bitter experience, but mine was not the worst, as I said before. In comparison to some others, it was mild.

When I cannot sleep at night I think about this. Sometimes I want to put myself in the position of my mother and my aunts when they were deported, of my uncles and of my father who went voluntarily. My father knew that my sister and my brother were in Russia, I was in concentration camp, my mother was gone. He was a very bright and aware person, and he didn't fool himself, and he gave himself up. Sometimes I want to feel their feelings, but it's impossible. Sometimes we say, "I understand you, I understand you." Nobody, but nobody, can understand a second person as long as he is not in the same position. As much as you would like to understand, it is impossible. We don't understand *anything* as long we are not in the same position. So whoever is going to listen to this tape, no matter how much you'll cry listening to it because you're hearing me crying now, you will not understand. I just want you to transmit it to your family, to your children, and this should not be forgotten!

—*Interviewed by J. Pery, June 20, 1988, and Bonnie Gurewitsch, October 5, 1994*

Resisters

Resistance during the Holocaust may be defined as any act or course of action taken between 1933 and May 8, 1945, that directly defied Nazi laws, policies, and ideology and that endangered the lives of those who engaged in such actions. Such actions were taken by both Jews and non-Jews, men and women, of all ages. Many paid the ultimate price for their defiance; others survived to tell remarkable stories of heroism, determination, and courage.

Anyone who refused to accept Nazi domination and his or her predetermined fate within Nazi ideology can be considered a resister. It was hardly easier for non-Jews than for Jews. Discovery could mean imprisonment, torture, deportation to a concentration camp, or death, with possible retaliatory action against family and neighbors.

Because of the overwhelming bureaucracy that reached into even the remotest areas of Nazi conquest and controlled so many aspects of daily life, resistance was difficult, if not impossible, to sustain over a period of time. Sometimes a single gesture was all that could be dared. The range of actions that constitute resistance is very broad, encompassing flight, hiding, sheltering those in danger, participating in forbidden activities, maintaining a sense of humanity in a dehumanizing environment, and engaging in military or quasi-military actions that would physically harm the Nazi machine. What characterizes the interviews in this section is the deliberate decision by these women to resist their fates in one way or another and their choice to affiliate with other resisters.

Under Nazi domination, women sometimes benefited from the stereotypes perpetuated by Nazi ideology, which relegated women to the spheres of child raising, the home, and religion (*Kinder, Kuche, und Kirche*). The persistence of the stereotype of the passive, homebound woman dominated by her husband prevented Germans from immediately suspecting women of activities that did not fit this stereotype. Because Jews had, over a period of centuries, developed successful means of accommodation to anti-Semitism and other, more passive forms of resistance to it, Jews were generally viewed by Germans as too stupid and subjugated to resist their brutal occupation.

Jewish men, universally circumcised in a society that did not routinely circumcise male babies, were immediately identifiable. Jewish women, particularly those who had the "Aryan" features of blond hair and blue eyes, were not physically identifiable as Jews. In traditional Jewish families, particularly in rural eastern European communities, Jewish men received little secular education; their language was Yiddish. They often spoke little, if any, of the local language and were therefore handicapped if they tried to "pass" as non-Jews. Religious Jewish men, usually bearded and often wearing distinctive garb, were easily identifiable. Another cultural difficulty involved lack of familiarity by Jews with the pervasive non-Jewish religious customs of the area, not knowing which saints to refer to or when to cross oneself or kneel in church. "Passing" as a non-Jew meant learning a new cultural frame of reference; there was usually no time to do this because the danger was immediate and Jews could not trust anyone to provide this information. Jewish women, who often had more contact with non-Jewish neighbors, would be slightly more familiar with Christian mores, which facilitated their assuming a false identity.

The interviewees in this section are aware of the small advantage that they had as women, and some refer to it explicitly. Yet this was not a crucial factor in their decision to join in resistance activities. They all felt the need to do something, however small and however futile, to resist the Nazi evil. There is a conscious decision to do something right in the face of wrong, to behave consistently with the moral code in which they believed, regardless of personal danger and the threat of death. Some felt that they would die anyway, that their chances of survival were so small that their gesture of resistance simply reinforced their own identities as sentient beings. Others felt that their efforts were intrinsically worthwhile; perhaps they could contribute something that would help defeat the Nazis. *None* feel heroic. None feel that they deserve special credit. They all realize that in the larger pattern of the history of World War II their actions probably had little influence on the course of the war, yet they feel a sense of satisfaction that they took action, that they did what was right, to the extent they could. The women attribute their survival to luck or to God's will, not to any qualitative advantage. All Jewish women, like Jewish men, were earmarked for death; only a fraction survived.

The interviews are arranged, as before, in an order that reflects an ascending degree of danger, from non-Jewish women resisting within a more supportive environment to Jewish women resisting in the Auschwitz death camp.

Took Heroma in the Netherlands and Emilie Schindler in Czechoslovakia both worked together with their husbands. As non-Jews they were free to continue normal civilian activities under Nazi occupation: shopping, doing household chores, moving around the countryside with their own identification documents. Took Heroma and her physician husband did not belong to an organized resistance group, but when mass roundups of Jews began in 1942 in the Netherlands, they and their friends began to shelter Jews in their homes. The Heromas offered more than physical shelter; the Jews they hid became part of their family, eating at their table and sharing household tasks. The Heromas clearly felt a human responsibility for people whose lives were at risk. When Dr. Heroma, whose medical dispensary was used to transmit messages to the underground, was arrested by the Gestapo, Took Heroma was asked if there were other people in her house. Her answer, a partial truth, was disregarded by the Gestapo; they were concentrating on their male prisoner. Took Heroma's involvement in humanitarian activities continued after the Holocaust, with activities on behalf of prisoners, abused women, and others.

Emilie Schindler's husband, the well-known Oskar Schindler, was a flamboyant personality whose public activities were conducted in the full view of Nazi authority and within the Nazi concentration camp system. An adventurer, he delighted in outwitting the system and profited from the expropriation of Jewish property and economic resources. In spite of his philandering, Emilie rescued him from prison several times (even when they were not living together) and finally was an equal partner in setting up the factory in Brünnlitz in which they protected twelve hundred Jews. It was Emilie who made the contacts with the local Czech people, with whom she had grown up, to supply adequate food and medications for the Jews on "Schindler's List." She made the decision to rescue a transport of Jews on a train abandoned on a railroad siding rather than let them die of starvation and exposure. Emilie argued with the SS commander who tortured prisoners in their factory, and she influenced the decision not to burn the corpses of Jews who died but to wait until the ground thawed in the spring so they could be buried with dignity. Emilie Schindler created a haven of humanity within the concentration camp system simply because it was the right thing to do, because to do less would have been a violation of her sense of morality.

For Jews who decided to resist, the stakes were higher and the circumstances infinitely more dangerous. Gertrud (Trude) Groag had been active in community affairs long before World War II. Trained in first aid during World War I and a leader in the Women's Zionist Organization, she, along with others, decided not to let German regulations forbidding health care for Jews adversely affect their community and made the effort to become trained nurses. Even before the period of deportation, ghettoization, and concentration camps, Trude Groag refused to bow to German pol-

icy. Nursing care continued; improvised facilities were also provided, at her initiative, for the welfare of Jewish children in her
town. Working within the system but using it for positive results
also prevailed in Theresienstadt, to which Trude Groag was deported. A Potemkin village set up to mislead Jews and the rest of
the world, Terezin was a cruel hoax. Here, too, Trude Groag refused to allow Nazi intentions to prevail without a fight. With ingenuity and creativity she labored with other Jews in the ghetto administration to improve conditions and raise people's spirits,
creating moments of calm, trust, and reprieve from the devastating
routine in which the Jews of Terezin waited for deportation to
their deaths. Trude Groag literally and figuratively planted seeds of
hope, cultivating seedlings whose leaves improved nutrition, nurturing the sick, and sowing ideas in the hearts and minds of the
children. She worked without illusions, knowing what the fate of
her patients and children would be, knowing the futility of physical resistance in the confined quarters of the Terezin fortress town.
She lived with hope, with belief in the Zionist dream of survival
in a Jewish homeland. She was fortunate to realize that dream.

Zenia Malecki's father and friends were members of the
United Partisan Organization in Vilna. She and her father smuggled food and guns into the ghetto to prepare for possible physical
resistance. She describes clandestine schools, a children's choir,
and other efforts to provide the activities of normal life for children. The *Judenrat*, unable to support resistance activity because
of fears of German reprisals that would seal the fate of the entire
community, demanded that the fighting organization sacrifice
their leader, Yizhak Witenberg. Zenia Malecki followed her conscience rather than the orders of those in command. By assisting
Witenberg with a hiding place and a disguise as a woman, she did
not change his fate, but she delayed it. He died in his jail cell of
cyanide poison. "I was very young then," Zenia Malecki said of

her actions. She was idealistic, acting on her belief in Jewish survival. She was ready to go to the forests with her comrades, but illness prevented her from leaving with them, and she was deported to the Kaiserwald concentration camp in Riga, Latvia, during the liquidation of the ghetto to begin an even more difficult struggle for survival.

Aida Brydbord did leave the ghetto to join partisans in the forest, but her decision was a painful one. Jewish leaders had for centuries survived European anti-Semitism by obeying authority and outlasting difficult rulers. The *Judenrat* in her town of Pruzhany, Poland, objected to partisan activity; only the young believed that resistance was necessary. Until the last minute, family ties determined Aida's actions. At first she could not leave her mother. When it was finally obvious that the community was being liquidated, Aida's father insisted that she escape to the partisans with her boyfriend. One day before the couple left the ghetto, their marriage was registered with the *Judenrat* and consecrated in a religious ceremony. Traditional Jewish values determined their behavior even when the young couple was leaving for a dangerous, unknown future in the forests. Living in the most primitive physical conditions, in danger both from German and Polish pursuers, Jewish partisans were more concerned with physical survival than with military activity. Aida did fulfill the traditional woman's roles, cooking for the fighting groups and nursing the wounded. But she reports that she had a rifle and knew how to use it, and she participated in a raid on a village in order to obtain boots and coats. Aida Brydbord is proud of even the smallest actions of partisan activity because they represent Jews taking control of their own destinies.

Marysia Warman gives us further insight into the varied faces of Jewish resistance. She describes Jews who resisted by simply continuing to live their lives according to human values. Personnel

of the Warsaw Ghetto Children's Hospital, Jewish doctors and
nurses, as well as the *Volksdeutsche Commissar*, continued to treat
hopelessly ill children as if there was a chance for their recovery.
The clandestine medical school provided an intellectual respite
from the devastating chores of daily life in the hospital. It also
gave those who attended a sense of the future and the skills to
deal with the pervasive epidemics in the ghetto. The school gave
purpose to lives that the Nazis deemed worthless. In Warsaw, as in
Vilna and in Pruzhany, Zionist and other youth organizations initiated activities geared to military resistance when they realized that
there were no other viable options to ensure community survival.
When it became clear to them that deportation meant death for
all, they asserted their humanity by choosing to die on their own
terms. Warman tells us of Dr. Adina Blady Szwajger's choice to let
children die in their own beds. She had no illusions about their
chances for survival in Treblinka, as the resistance fighters knew
that they had no chance for military success against the Nazis;
they were going to die as defiant Jews. Marysia Warman's activities
as a courier, carrying money and documents and securing living
quarters for Jewish resisters on the Aryan side of Warsaw, were ultimately insignificant militarily, but that was not their purpose. She
did succeed in raising morale, providing sustenance and information, and hiding Jewish fighters who ultimately survived the Holocaust. Because she looked Polish and was able to evade discovery
as a Jew, she benefited from the stereotyped view that the Nazis
had of women. Because she was young she was able to overcome
her fears and with quick thinking was able to protect herself
against her vulnerability as a woman; she was committed to survival and was ready to risk her life so that others might survive.

In Auschwitz, those who were not gassed on arrival were
stripped of clothing, possessions, name, and even body hair. This
degrading process was the initiation into a system where the indi-

vidual was meaningless, disoriented in time and place, separated from family, and cut off from the familiar details even of ghetto life where lives were threatened but family or friends and Jewish institutions were still present. Anna Heilman and Rose Meth made choices even within this system that did not allow for choices. Anna Heilman had chosen to remain with her family rather than join her resistance group in the Warsaw ghetto uprising. In Auschwitz, bereft of parents, she and her sister chose resistance. Rose Meth had already paid a price for resisting the Nazis, spending time in jail for the "crime" of purchasing shoes for her father. Both women saw the opportunity for resistance in Auschwitz as a chance "not to let ourselves be taken without a struggle." "It gave me a way to fight back." By smuggling gunpowder to the men who planned to use it to blow up the gas chambers, the women were linked to a larger effort, which gave purpose and shape to their lives of drudgery and deprivation. Four other women who participated in the smuggling of gunpowder were hanged in full view of the camp as a deterrent to further resistance activities. Anna Heilman and Rose Meth have told their stories for the purpose of memorializing those who died, those "camp sisters" who were martyred because they resisted. A monument erected at Yad Vashem, Jerusalem, pays tribute to their memories.

Marysia Warman's description of the loneliness of her work may be applied to the experiences of all who faced death every day. The mortal danger that all the resisters confronted isolated each one regardless of the presence of others. Each non-Jew who protected Jews, each partisan, each courier, and each smuggler faced death as an individual. Their loneliness brought them together with other resisters whom they could trust, just as sisters and camp sisters trusted each other and just as trust was intrinsic between mothers and daughters.

The Nazi system was designed to destroy the sense of trust so

essential to humanity. Jews learned that they could trust only themselves; some women, and some who were part of a larger group,
found that they could trust each other. They resisted within a
close circle of trust, with family members, with friends, with other
women. They acted and reacted within the context of Jewish history and culture, resisting with other Jews the Nazi attempt to anni-
hilate them. Some prevailed.

Took Heroma

In 1936 Took Heroma and her husband, a physician, went to live in Dordrecht, a small provincial town fifteen miles south of Rotterdam in the Netherlands. They had no children and very little money. They concentrated on building Dr. Heroma's medical practice.

The very morning that the Germans invaded the Netherlands, they invaded our little town because it was quite near the vital bridges.[1] The parachutists came down, and the fighting started early in the morning. I think it was six o'clock on the tenth of May, 1940.[2] Unlike most other areas of the Netherlands, we were involved in the war from the very first moment. My husband, being a physician, took an ambulance in the afternoon and went around picking up casualties and dead bodies. Holland had an army, and they were fighting, but it was impossible to keep away that big, big, giant German army.[3] The really frightful thing was the bombarding of Rotterdam. Rotterdam was very near to us; you could see the bombarding of the fire. When the heart of the whole city had been blown up, Holland surrendered. Our "Dutch war" lasted five days![4]

First of all the queen went to London.[5] The administration went into exile with the queen. We had no leadership anymore. The Germans controlled the country in collaboration with a lot of the administrators.[6] Some didn't collaborate, and others thought they could influence the Germans. There were fascists, pro-Nazi organizations in Holland also. In Parliament there was a lot of opposition to them. They were a minority. But we had a democracy and those fascist people were selected to Parliament, so it was an accepted situation.

Later, the underground resistance was gradually built up. We were not members of the very active underground groups, but we were, of course, on their side. In 1941 the situation was growing more and more dangerous for the Jews,[7] and when a lot of Jews went into hiding, the question of providing them with ration cards came up. Ration cards had to be distributed and provided for the people who went into hiding, so that's of course what we did.

In my house I had a Jewish friend who came to me the same day the parachutes came down. He had a little cousin, three or four years old. There was shooting going on all the time in the street, so at night we sat in the cellar, the Jewish friend, this little boy, and I. We kept the little boy in the safest place, of course. And then at night, there was a ring of the doorbell. He looked at me, my Jewish friend, and said, a little bit hesitatingly, "Well, I think the best thing is, you go." At that very moment, the first day of my war, I realized, "My God, there we are." Well, it turned out to be nothing dangerous, but I realized at that very moment that the Jewish problem was starting.

At the beginning of 1941 we had a very interesting phenomenon; I don't think there were many countries who had it. We had a big strike in Amsterdam by the people who objected to this action.[8] Amsterdam had a big Jewish population with a big Jewish proletariat. They worked in the diamond business. It was a very poor Jewish proletariat, low salaried, working class. When these Jewish people were chased a general strike sprang up. A lot of people struck, a real big strike. If you ever come to Amsterdam you will see on the place where it happened, a beautiful figure of a man standing upright.[9] It is a beautiful statue, a symbol of that marvelous strike. Every single year we commemorate that strike by the people who said, "We won't accept this persecution." But the Germans killed people, and they picked up a lot of young Jews. This was the first transport of Jewish young people to Mauthausen where they were dead in three months.

In 1942 the *Razzias* started, the chasing and rounding up of Jews.[10] Then the big deportations began. Then it was very important to find hiding places for Jewish people. We had a really good underground group working. They did what they could, but it wasn't really well organized. All the time our friends looked for addresses where Jewish people could go and hide. I have a very good friend who dedicated her whole life to doing that during those four years. Lots of our friends did it. It is impossible to make people who live today understand the difficulty of the whole climate, the whole atmosphere of living under an occupation. For hiding a Jew you would have been treated as a Jew. You would be imprisoned, deported, or shot. One of my neighbors was a brother of the man who headed the fascist Dutch organization. His garden was adjacent to mine. It was dangerous. Many, many people were sent to concentration camps because of hiding Jews.

So, one of my friends, I don't recall anymore who it was, on a certain day came and said, "Could you hide a Jewish woman?" We said, "Yes." We had a small house, but we said, "In the back we have a room, okay." So she came. She was a single woman from Amsterdam, about forty-five years old. We didn't know her. She had a family; they were also in hiding. She stayed with us for two and one-half years. There could be no question of her going out. It was absolutely impossible when you were in hiding. You could only go out during the night when there was no moon to take a little walk. That was the only possibility; even that was dangerous because of neighbors. She became part of our family. She ate at our table.

In the second year, when there was a shortage of fuel, she said, "Perhaps I could buy myself a little more fuel, and then I could sit downstairs without being with you the whole night and the whole evening." You can easily see it was difficult to always have another person around, particularly for my husband. She understood; she felt by herself that we needed privacy. There was a fireplace downstairs too, so that's what we did the second year. She sat downstairs although it was very lonesome, of course. Her laundry she did herself, or we did it together.

One day in 1942, one of my husband's patients said to him: "Oh, my God, doctor, I'm a Jewish girl. I'm a Jewish girl, and I really don't know where to go. I don't know how to escape." So my husband came home and said, "Wasn't your mother saying that she wanted household help? I'll send you a young girl that I met." I can still see her standing at the door. I said, "Well, do come in; let's have a talk." So we talked. She didn't look Jewish. She walked around the whole country, where they didn't know her. I saw she was not suitable for household work for my mother.

Then my husband said, "Well, maybe she can help in the practice a little bit." So she stayed with us. Her father had gone to Westerbork.[11] The mother and two little girls lived quite near to Westerbork. They heard what was going on, and the mother said, "Listen, Carla, here you have five hundred guilders. Go away. See what you can do to save yourself with it." There she was, a girl of seventeen with her five hundred guilders, told to go somewhere. So she came to live with us, and after six weeks she packed her bicycle and went away. I don't know where, but she always came back. She always stayed in that room with that other person, but she went out. She was a rebel. When she came home after she had been away for six weeks, she was so dirty you couldn't touch her. Then she took a bath and cleaned herself up, and she said, "It's good to be home." And after four weeks she went away again. She was that type of a girl.

Now my husband, being a physician, sometimes knew there was a Jewish family hidden in a certain house where he had patients, so he would make a quarantine placard for a contagious disease and put it on the window to keep the Germans away from the house. One day there were three people hiding, a couple and a sister of the woman. On a certain day the house was bombed. The three of them stood in the street, and we had to find a new situation for them. This was an emergency. So the single woman came to stay with us. After the first two and one-half years, the first woman had gone to another address, but we had Carla, and then Elise came. Her husband, a Jew also, was in the military service. People who were in military service were picked up by the Germans as prisoners of war. For him it was particularly risky because at a certain moment the Germans said, "*Juden, austreten.*" The Jews had to step forward, and he ventured not to do it, and he won. It was very dangerous. At first she had letters from him from the prisoner-of-war camp. Later, during the last year of the war, it didn't work anymore. She also had a little girl. Elise longed very much for that little girl. The girl was, I think, two when she left her in Utrecht in a hiding place in a private home. Towards the end of the war, in February or March 1945, she said, "Do you think it's safe? Don't you think the war is over? We could pick her up. We could keep her here." So at a certain moment, someone went with a bicycle and picked up the little girl, but she didn't recognize her mother. They had parted three years before. So you had a difficult situation with Elise and her little daughter. They slept together in one room, and Elise, of course, took care of her. Gradually, a sort of relationship developed, and the little girl also felt something special about "Aunt Elise." Elise didn't say she was the mother. She was afraid to say it because the child wouldn't believe it.

A week before liberation the little girl was standing with her mother in the kitchen, doing some dishwashing together, and I'll never forget it. She was a very little girl, this high, like a little doll with big red cheeks. She came into my living room, with the eyes big like this. She said, "You know what? You know what? I have a mother! I have a mother! I have a mother at hand! All of a sudden I've a mother at hand!" This little girl was dancing like a little doll. The mother had told her. I said, "My God, Elise, what have you done?" She said, "Well, soon it will be over." I said, "Okay, but what if she goes outside? She will tell the boys in the street!" But nothing happened, and the war was over. I will never forget that scene of that little girl dancing with her red cheeks. She had fever afterwards.

And then the war was over. Elise's husband, the prisoner of war, was one of the first to come home, and we saw him, walking with a gun. It was incredible, incredible. There were so many awful things in that time and so many people who didn't come back. You looked around in your little town thinking, who ever will return? We had been supplied with extra food from the underground. They had invaded the bureau where rations were stocked and had stolen most of those rations. Because it was an agrarian area of small farms there were a lot of peasants who had some extra food. But the last winter, I can tell you, my husband and I really suffered because of hunger. That last winter the food was very, very scarce. My husband scarcely had enough medications. All the time you saw all these Germans, ta-dee-dee, singing and marching, all the time. Someone who has never lived through an occupation of this kind doesn't understand the atmosphere of struggle and how it colors everyday life. There was an old lady who died in hiding. Now what could you do? You have to bury her! My husband did it. He buried the corpse in the garden. In '44 the south of Holland had been liberated already. Only the north was occupied, and that was why it was such a horrible winter. My husband's waiting room, where every morning eighty or ninety people were always waiting for the doctor, was a marvelous place for the people from the underground who were spying and bringing messages to the other side of the country. Our door was always standing open; we had people going in and out. So the boys who were working for the underground and spying got their messages there. We knew about it. We consented. My husband wasn't doing any spying himself, but one of those boys wrote down our address in his pocketbook, so on a certain night the Gestapo came and arrested my husband. At that same moment we had three people hiding in the house. And when he was taken away I honestly thought that when they turned around the corner they would shoot him because it had happened to others. Before they went away, at the last moment one of the Gestapo said: "Do you have people here in the house?" I said, "Yes, downstairs there is the assistant to my husband, and there is a nurse." I thought, my God, what are their names? I didn't recall the names at that moment. Those girls were shivering in their beds, but the Gestapo didn't pay any attention to my response.

Then, of course, I had to find out where my man had been taken. So I took my bicycle and went to Rotterdam and from Rotterdam to Utrecht. Finally, I located him in Utrecht in prison with two others. Of course, he said he was not guilty. My husband knew a thing about psychology. When he came in for the investigation he saw one of those boys had been beaten up in a frightful way. My husband said, "Listen, if you beat me like that, I will tell you anything you want me to say; I can't stand it." They said, "No, we've other plans for you." So they talked and talked and talked, and finally . . . My husband was a very strong person. I'm sure there was an influence of his knowledge of psychology. He was a special figure. He influenced others. Well, he came out of the prison in Utrecht.

Going home was another thing, of course. How could you go home? It took me about two or three days on my bicycle. Carla, our dear Carla, was still in the house, and when we came in she said, "Oh, there you are, my God, there you are. I had the Germans here this morning. They wanted to search the house, and I had to show them around, and they'll come back tonight because they thought I was a nice girl." At night, when the Germans came to visit Carla, they saw me of course. I said I was the mother of Carla; it wasn't much fun for them. So I showed them out very quietly. Meanwhile, my husband sat in the hiding place we had in the toilet. For a couple of hours he sat there. Carla became our foster daughter. We were very fond of her. She was eighteen then. She lost both of her parents and her sister; they were deported.

I remember one of those moonless nights with Elise and her sister and brother-in-law. We would sit around the fire and have something to eat. We had a nice evening, and all of a sudden the doorbell rang. It was after curfew time, and there was Carla! "I got a lift on a German soldier's bus. I said I wanted to be home for my father's birthday!" So there we were with the fire, lying on the floor because there were not many beds, the five of us. Carla was telling the story, and we listened to her. Carla always had marvelous stories. She always dramatized things.

In 1971, I was asked to work for a new bill that had passed in Parliament just then for indemnity payments to people who had been in concentration camps and who had been in Japanese camps.[12] The law was giving allowances to people in those circumstances. So I worked in the implementation of this law for eight years, from '72 to '80. I was vice-chairman of that board, and I saw thousands and thousands of files about these cases. You become aware that the important thing is concern for people in the world. In that sense you can say that it has influenced my life. What you see nowadays going on, the cruelty, torture, executing people in so many countries, it makes you hesitate to say that it can't happen again. I wish I could say it will never happen again, but when you see what is happening at the moment, I can't. The only thing you can do is work against it wherever you see the symptoms of what's happening that gives you the feeling that there is the same pattern of cruelty.

We did what we felt was a natural thing to do. Of course, you knew that you took risks, but I think my husband and I had that conviction that when certain things were at stake, you had to take risks because you wouldn't be honest to yourself anymore if you didn't. It was natural. We couldn't do more, but we did something. We lived through the war on the right side.

Please go on with recording. I think it is marvelous that you record for the future, for history. These things have to be done. There have to be convictions and political solutions.

After World War II, Dr. Heroma served for a while as a Red Cross doctor in Indonesia, and Took Heroma became sensitive to the racial problems in a colonial administration. Upon their return to the Netherlands, she became involved in educating women politically and was eventually elected to the Dutch Parliament, where she served for seventeen years. During her service in Parliament Took Heroma also served at the United Nations on UNESCO, the United Nations Economic and Social Commission.

—*Interviewed by Ray Kaner, May 22, 1985*

Emilie Schindler

The character of Oskar Schindler has been immortalized in both the book and the motion picture titled Schindler's List.[1] The story of how he protected the Jewish workers in his factories in Cracow and then in Brünnlitz is one of great daring and compassion. A flamboyant personality, he took great risks to save the lives of "his Jews," who numbered more than twelve hundred. In 1962 Oskar Schindler was cited by Yad Vashem, the Israeli Holocaust Remembrance Authority, as one of the Righteous Among the Nations, an honor given to non-Jews who risked their lives to save Jews during the Holocaust. Less well known, however, is the role played by his wife, Emilie, who was no less devoted to protecting and saving the lives of the Jews who were their responsibility.

In his own memoir, published in Die Unbesungenen Helden (The Unsung Heroes) by Kurt Grossman (Berlin: Arani Publishers), Schindler declared, "My wife Emilia shared my views on the importance of saving Jewish lives, and she often worked a 14 and 16 hour day alongside me, as we faced one crisis after another."[2]

I grew up in my parents' home; I finished public school and agricultural school. We were Catholic, but not very religious. I was nineteen years old when I met and married Oskar Schindler. He worked together with his father running a very successful shop selling agricultural machines.

After the war started, Oskar started working for Abwehr, the secret intelligence service of the Wehrmacht, collecting information. He was dressed as a civilian, not in uniform. First we were in Zwittau[3] and later in Mahrish Ostrau,[4] where I saw a Jewish transport on its way to Auschwitz. Then Oskar went to Cracow and started a small factory called Email in addition to his intelligence work.[5] He was friends with other officers from the Abwehr and with Major Von Korab of the Wehrmacht.

My husband was arrested three times in Cracow[6]; each time I had to struggle for his release from jail. First I went to the German officer who dealt with the Email factory; then I went to the officers dealing with ammunition production. These officers were mainly older officers who were opposed to Hitler's regime.

I came to live in Cracow in 1942. I didn't see much. I knew that the Jews in Cracow were put into a ghetto[7] and then into a *Lager*.[8] I saw some of the Jewish inmates in the Email factory. I never went into the Plaszow concentration camp, but I heard that people were shot there and deported to Auschwitz.[9] The Germans treated the Jews very badly. When my husband had to close the Email factory in 1944,[10] we started the factory camp in Brünnlitz.

Some prisoners who had worked for Mr. Schindler in the Email factory were taken to Plaszow and then sent to Auschwitz.[11] He wanted to take back these prisoners to his factory in Brünnlitz. Mr. Schindler prepared the list of prisoners who had worked for him. He had to give it to the commandant in Plaszow.[12] There were men, women, and families on the list.

Meanwhile, I went to Brünnlitz, which was my birthplace. I knew everyone. Most of the population there were Czechs. They didn't react to our opening a factory there. One day, while my husband was still in Cracow, a German Nazi Party inspector came to inspect and inquire. The factory engineer was really afraid so I myself met this German, called Konig. He was once my swimming teacher. I convinced him to approve the factory. This was the easiest part of what happened in Brünnlitz.

After the machines and the professionals were sent from Cracow, Mr. Schindler was arrested again. He had been going back and forth to Cracow to arrange the moving. In the fall of 1944 the factory was completely installed, but there wasn't much to manufacture. The moment the Jewish inmates were brought into the work camp at Brünnlitz the SS arrived. There was a commandant with them. Mr. Schindler and I lived in a small room. We had to be careful because the SS were around. The SS didn't enter the factory. They only watched outside. Inside the factory were only the *Wehrmacht*. We did not enter the work area either.

The factory functioned twenty-four hours a day in two shifts. I supplied the food; we received more and better rations than those of the civilian population, but this wasn't enough. I had to "organize" food from the black market. I had to seek it out. I went to the mill, which was under German control. The chief miller was a Czech. The owner was Frau Daubek, and the person in charge of the mill was a Czech too. I gave them vodka that we brought from Cracow, and they gave me flour. I also got meat from a veterinarian by giving him coffee and cigarettes, which we also had from Cracow. My husband used to exchange jewelry for bread in a German bakery. I brought some medicine from Cracow and Ostrau.

In the *Krankenstube* there were Jewish doctors.[13] I never entered it because the SS didn't allow me in. I was always quarrelling, and there was always shouting with the SS guards, but I finally always delivered the medications. Food was distributed normally—morning, noon, and evenings. In the factory, the women knitted, and the men worked on the machines.

The German SS guards wanted to show that they were doing their jobs well, so they started searching Mr. Schindler's wagons, accusing him of taking out some goods. Later, they wanted to take away cigarettes from his convoy,[14] so they arrested him for a short time, but they had to release him soon because they knew his arrest would delay the transfer of the factory to Brünnlitz. He succeeded in hiding the cigarettes with the help of one of his Jewish inmates by putting them into ammunition boxes. We needed the cigarettes for getting food and other things.[15]

We tried very hard to get the women on the list back from Auschwitz.[16] There was a lot of going there and back, but nothing really happened. My husband chose one woman, twenty years old, a daughter of a rich factory owner. She was the only girl who was able to get the Jewish women released from Auschwitz. She went herself, as a nice Jewish woman, only for two nights.[17] She knew what to say; she was a character. She brought the Jewish women back to Brünnlitz. You can imagine the excitement. The men were looking forward to their wives' arrival. They thought we would never get their women out of Auschwitz. The men and women were really lucky and happy.

Men and women were separated in Brünnlitz.[18] We had to hide the children, and we made some of the children look older; otherwise, the Germans would send the children to Auschwitz.[19] It was forbidden to keep children. It was a hard life for families.

We didn't deal with false documents for the people. What we did was forge papers to enable us to get additional food to bring into the factory.[20] The SS couldn't enter the work area. There were German women watching over the Jewish women. Inside was under *Wehrmacht* control, but outside it was controlled only by the SS. The *Wehrmacht* always inspected the machinery and the products. The people were inspected by the SS. The SS weren't really seriously interested in production. My husband had to pay a daily tariff for each Jewish worker, similar to the tariff for a German worker. The money was sent to Berlin.

Two railroad wagons that had been traveling for fourteen days arrived in Brünnlitz full of people from *Lager* Golleschau[21] and had probably been destined for some other factory. It was very cold weather. These cattle wagons were left on the railway tracks. The other factory didn't want to take the people because the Russians were approaching already. The Germans watching these wagons came into our factory, telling us, "We are already frozen, and we don't want to deal anymore with these wagons. We are going to shoot the people if you don't take them." We did not know anything about this in advance. My husband was in Cracow at that time, and I had to deal with it myself together with the factory engineer, Schonebrun. We had to prepare space for 100 to 112 people. We used welding apparatus to defrost and move the wagon doors. The SS were watching Polish workers do the job. The people in the wagons were frozen and hungry. I couldn't recognize whether they were men or women. They looked terrible, big eyes, only skin and bones. There were already twelve or twenty dead. We took the poor people. We cleaned them up. We washed them. We gave them some special, better food and gradually put them on their feet, and so they stayed alive — they survived. They got help from the Jewish doctors. This I really saw myself.

The SS did not understand anything about the factory's needs. They knew only to kill, to beat, and to threaten people. Once I saw the SS punishing inmates by forcing them to stand for hours holding a big raw potato in their mouths. I went to the SS commandant and started screaming about it, and so he stopped it. They wouldn't refuse me, knowing that I had control over their food too. They knew that with me it wasn't so easy. My husband dealt with the inspectors. He used to drink with them. They drank very often.

When an older Jew died, my husband dealt with it. First he went to the priest nearby to convince him to bury the Jew in the Christian cemetery. The priest refused. Eventually, there were about twenty dead Jews. They were in a big box. The SS commandant wanted to burn them, but I was against it.[22] I couldn't stand the thought, so the dead people were left in the box over the cold winter. Then my husband dealt with burying them in a kind of special ceremony together with Rabbi Levertov.[23]

At the end of the war, my husband gave the Jews arms to protect themselves.[24] Most of the SS had already run away, more from fear of the Russians than of the inmates who would be liberated. The SS ran two days before the Russians came, May 7, 1945. After liberation, the Jewish committee of our prisoners wrote a letter for Oskar saying that he saved their lives and that he should be treated well.[25] One of the women who went with us hid this letter in the padding of her coat. Later, the lady took out the letter and gave it to my husband.

We left with some Jewish inmates. One of them was a driver [Richard Rechem][26]; also there were Josef Shantz, Enka, Dolek, and Feldstein. There were about ten Jews. We had one truck and a station wagon. We took along some food, cigarettes, and clothing, but when the Russians came they took everything. The Czechs accompanied us to the train that took us to Pilsen in the American zone. We stopped near Pilsen and slept one night in the railroad wagons. Then we marched on foot and passed the American guard. One of our Jews, Feldstein, spoke English to the Americans, and they let us continue. We paid for an ox wagon, and so we moved forward somehow. We were hungry. Then we met an American officer who was a Jew. He was good to us. After the war is a long story. We had a kind of Via Dolorosa [Road of Sorrows].[27] It was cold, and we had no clothing. We had some soup but no meat. We could warm ourselves only by having a warm bath.

In the book about Schindler[28] it says he was a drinker and dealt on the black market. The writer doesn't understand! In order to take care of the Jewish inmates, he *had* to drink with the SS from time to time. He *had* to deal with the black market in order to supply food and other needs. We always lived with one foot in the grave. Our life was no better than the life of a dog. The writer of this book did not understand anything about what was going on there. It really makes me angry. My husband did what he did because he was human; the same with myself. I couldn't stand to see the suffering of innocent, poor people. This I learned from my parents.

"Schindler's Jews" still maintain contact with Emilie Schindler, who lives in Buenos Aires. She was interviewed in New York while visiting some of the Jews she helped save.

—*Interviewed by Bonnie Gurewitsch, with Rose Gurewitsch, May 27, 1983.*
Translated from German by J. Pery.

Gertrud Groag

Trude Groag was born in 1889 to parents who were members of the cultural elite in the small town of Hohenstadt, Austria.[1] Her father was an advocate; her mother was occupied with social welfare and cultural activities and directed a ladies choir up to the time of her expulsion by the Nazis. Their cultural frame of reference was German, and Trude was sent to Dresden at the age of fourteen and one-half to attend high school, where she studied literature, languages, and art history. At sixteen she returned home, worked in a kindergarten, and began to study the profession. In 1911 she developed a model kit of paper and needlework for preschool children[2] and was later certified in Brno by state examination as a kindergarten teacher.

Trude married in 1913. She and her husband lived in Olmuetz,[3] in Moravia. They had three sons within four years. In her leisure time Trude painted, wrote poetry, and did social welfare work. She volunteered for the Red Cross, and in the 1920s she became active in WIZO, the Women's Zionist Organization. Like her parents, her cultural frame of reference was secular and German. She was introduced to the religious aspect of Judaism by Professor Hugo Bergmann,[4] whom she met in 1914, and to Zionism by her youngest son, who became a Zionist when he was asked to leave a swimming club in 1930 because he was not Aryan. As anti-Semitic acts increased and intensified during the 1930s, Trude Groag's Jewish identity deepened, and she "suppressed her feelings of German cultural identity."

Because of the Nuremberg Laws[5] all medical care was withheld from the Jews. I was the leader of *Kasandra Sdenka* [Czech name of the Young WIZO (Women's Zionist Organization)]. I suggested that we take responsibility for helping people who were in need. We made a decision to train and educate ourselves to be competent and qualified nurses. In pairs, we traveled to the Jewish hospital in Ostrau.[6] There we took a four-week basic training course in nursing. The wife of a physician and I were the first two women who graduated as head nurses from this course. Others followed.

Under Nazi rule, it was very difficult to provide social welfare services in the Jewish community. In the so-called Protectorate,[7] Jews could not obtain medical supplies. We nurses immediately started to work. It was necessary to subordinate your private life to your community obligations. The volunteer work that we had done as WIZO women, such as for the Red Cross, now became our professional, but unpaid, employment. The Jews were deprived of all sanitary and medical assistance.[8] The patients of our beautiful old-age home, which the Nazis closed immediately, were taken to an old-age home in Ostrau. Social and hygienic conditions were awful. Although I lived in a suburban village an hour away from Olmuetz, where my husband's factory was located, I was in the regular service of the *Kultusgemeinde*[9] of Olmuetz. When the Jewish community called me to handle a case of sickness, I had to walk for an hour, day or night, to reach the city to do my duty as a nurse. Then I had to walk home again. They would notify me whenever there was a person who needed nursing care, such as a sick or old dying woman who needed a night nurse, a woman who was about to give birth, a baby whose mother could not care for it, or someone who needed nursing care after an operation. We set up competent nursing care in the home.

Jewish children were not permitted to attend public schools[10] or to play in public parks or playgrounds.[11] I arranged to get permission from friends for the Jewish children to use the big garden in Tynecek[12] for relaxation and organized activities. About two hundred children marched there daily to work in the garden. They felt good in pleasant surroundings. Unfortunately, I cannot count on one hand the number of children who survived.

One day we had a visitor in our small home in Tynecek, a well-dressed man. He introduced himself as an "envoy" of our German friends. He said he was on a trip to look at and eventually purchase manufactured goods. He mentioned that he lived in Lodz and had many Jewish friends but that they were not in the city anymore. They were in a camp and could not be visited, and he could not help them. He said he was not sure whether to return to Lodz because he abhorred seeing the suffering, distress, and grief. It was too difficult for him to bear. We were astounded by his report and just did not believe it.

We had German friends who also had a factory in Lodz. They probably wanted us to know what was happening without meeting us in person, so they sent this man. He also told us of a fantastic plan that Hitler had to establish a buffer zone between Germany and Poland where the Jews would be quartered in barracks. They would be expected to serve as an active buffer against the Russian Communists. I had never heard of this plan. It appeared unbelievable to me, just as unreal as the story of the camp. It might be the nature of the Jewish soul, the readiness to bear misfortune, to bear up, to endure, and hope things will turn out well. It must have been that way; otherwise, how is it possible that we walked blindly towards disaster?

Fortunately, we were able to send two of our sons to Palestine in 1939. We also wanted to go to Palestine, but my oldest son, Willi, was still in military service, and we did not want to leave him. When his army service ended we could not get out of the country anymore.[13] I would not have known how to try to leave illegally. My husband was ailing. He had been imprisoned and had severe bleeding in his stomach while in prison. He should have had surgery, but he was in such bad condition that we didn't even consider it. So we were in the same boat together: my mother, my husband, my son Willi, his wife Madla, and I. We stayed together, the five of us; in 1942 we went to Theresienstadt together.

I knew Jakob Edelstein[14] before the war. He was the head of the Palestine office in Prague. He was an eager, enthusiastic worker, who was always overtired from his work for his people. Once he came to Olmuetz. He sat, and people came to see him. He was very fatigued. I said to him, "I could give you good advice, similar to the advice Jethro gave to Moses."[15] "I know," he answered, "create an organization." When he was totally exhausted, ailing with laryngitis, he received permission from the Gestapo to travel from Prague to Ostrau and Tynecek to enter a hospital for a thorough examination. He stayed with us in November 1941, recuperating for eight days, and we became close friends.[16]

I read in a German newspaper that there was a need for trained nurses in Theresienstadt.[17] Furthermore, it said, nurses would enjoy privileges and would also be deferred from transports. This was what gave me the idea to reeducate myself as a nurse. In 1942 I was fifty-three years old.[18]

Everyone became occupied with preparations for transports. We were allowed to take along 50 kilograms [about 110 pounds] of baggage. The Germans issued instructions about what should be brought along: bedcovers, blankets, down comforters, electric heating devices, shaving equipment, and even musical instruments.[19] Before we left I noticed in the city that in one barrack they were opening valises, and the contents were distributed to whomever stood around. It appeared peculiar to me because the valises looked like the valises that I had just bought to bring to the camp. I inquired, but I couldn't get any information. But it seemed to me that Jewish goods were distributed to needy Germans even before the Jews arrived in the camp.

In June people were assembled in a school near Olmuetz.[20] On both sides of the street Gestapo men were cursing and swearing. I worked with the sick, who were lying on the floor of the transport train, which was formerly used to transport horses. A few mattresses were put on the floor for the critically ill. We hoped that illness would exempt people from the transport, but only those with tuberculosis were kept back for fear that they would infect the camp. I also supervised a group of mentally disturbed and deranged people who were brought from an institution. It was a nightmare. Many patients were covered with dirt and terrible rashes. Most of them were not able to control their bodily functions. We nurses still lived with the illusion of keeping the sick clean by observing their needs and bringing them to a toilet. We noticed that not only the deranged patients lost control of bodily functions, but otherwise normal and healthy persons did, too. Our biggest enemy, enteritis, claimed its first victim immediately. On this transport we nurses saw and learned what it meant to nurse people in a concentration camp.

When we arrived in Theresienstadt the sick people were promptly taken over by others. I remained with my deranged people. Jakob Edelstein met us. He offered transportation[21] to me in the midst of the yelling and shouting of the SS, and he personally accompanied us. I asked him, "Do you have institutions for the mentally ill?" He said, "Yes, but they are small. They will all be sent to Poland."[22] "And there?" I asked. He shrugged his shoulders. He noticed my amazement and did not speak.

Jakob Edelstein offered Trude accommodations that he had reserved for her, but she refused to leave her patients. After she saw them transferred to other nurses, Edelstein took her to the administration building, where he offered to assign her to work, but she wanted to join her family, who were in the Schleuse[23] *area where new arrivals were processed. There she registered for work as a nurse and was immediately assigned to work with patients whom she had nursed previously.*

After we arrived in Theresienstadt, we had to pass through the *Schleuse* (control gate), where all our valuables were removed by the Gestapo, including the bedcovers. Before the transport I had been on night duty. When I went on the transport I had no chance to rest, and now I was running from one patient to the next. Dr. Karel Fleischmann,[24] the chief physician (who was also a famous artist) immediately conducted a roll call at the hospital. Every nurse had to appear before him, and he defined our duties. I was so dead tired that I had to hold on to the corner of the table in order not to collapse. In a thunderous voice he shouted at me, "What is the matter with you? Don't you know where you are? Don't you know how a nurse should appear before a superior?" He demoted me from head nurse to nurse. I couldn't believe such awful treatment. I started to cry and returned to my work, heartbroken and shocked.

Everyone had to volunteer to do one hundred hours additional work.[25] I immediately volunteered for a nursing position. We assembled in front of a head nurse, and she organized the work, assigning us to specific hospitals. We were taken in pairs, by a third person, to our destination. You were not allowed to walk alone on the street. On the second night I was delegated to work at the hospital at the *Schleuse*. A constant stream of ailing, unhealthy, and infirm people were routed directly from the transports to this hospital. There they were examined. Depending on their age and condition, they were sent to old-age homes, for surgery, or to other infirmaries.

The *Schleuse* hospital was called *Schleusenspital* L124, after the designation of the street and building number. It was located in a former school building. It had the disadvantages of a makeshift hospital. At first we had no running water at all. There were large classrooms and other tiny rooms. The sick rooms could not be aired. The hospital had about 150 beds, divided into three sections, each on a separate floor with its own doctor and nurse.

The patients were mostly elderly, very sick people. One man with kidney disease was in awful pain, crying and groaning. At 4:00 A.M. I decided to knock on the window of the doctor's room. I opened the door, and saw a young doctor wrapped in *tallit* and *tefillin*, praying. He asked, "What is the problem?" I told him. He answered pleasantly that he would come in a little while, and he did. This made a deep impression on me. In the midst of such a terrible time a young man was saying his morning prayers. I decided then and there to stay and work there so that he would be my boss, and so it was.

We nurses were always dead tired. We slept twenty persons to a room, on trunks. We used our knapsacks for pillows, and we had some kind of cover. In the morning we were crushed and worn, not fit for duty. The head doctor, Dr. Sternbach, had a good idea. In the garden there was a small house with a kitchen and a room. He wanted to set the nurses up in that house. Because

I knew him, I was sent to Edelstein to request this little room, four meters by four meters [approximately thirteen feet by thirteen feet], for three nurses. For us it was a great relief. Linens were available, and we had beds with mattresses that came from transports from Germany. It was a small room, with approximately twenty centimeters [about eight inches] between each bed and a corner to hang up your clothing. My husband made a table for me, which earned him a bread from the head nurse. That's how we lived.

Before we were transported I had put all kinds of seeds into my pockets. When we moved to the house, I and the young doctors dug up the grounds of the school garden, where beautiful trees grew, and we planted the seeds. When the plants grew, people used to pluck their leaves and eat them as a source of vitamins. An apple tree in the garden saved my life. I once suffered terribly from cholera[26] and didn't think I would survive. I was laid up in the little garden house, half unconscious with terrible pain. That was always a sign of the patient's last fight to stay alive, a final signal from the body. Dr. Sternbach came in to see me. To cheer me up he brought me a beautiful apple that he had picked up in the little garden. He probably thought to bring me a last gift of happiness. It was strictly forbidden to pick any fruit. When he left me I used my last energy to bite into the apple, and I ate it, all of it. My body was so depleted that the vitamins in the apple miraculously aided my condition. I fell asleep, and when I woke up I felt much better. An apple!

My work was awfully hard. I had to pump water from the outside and bring it in during the night when it was icy cold. I had to lift patients in and out of bed. About 150 patients died, sometimes three or four a day.[27] When a transport came in, beds had to be added or emptied. Some patients were moved to other infirmaries, and new patients came in from among the new arrivals. The youngest daughter of Theodore Herzl came to our hospital.[28] This poor woman came from a sanatorium for the mentally ill. I could not save her; she was very sick. Like most other people, she died in Theresienstadt of enteritis, an infectious type of diarrhea.[29]

To counter the intentions of the Nazis we had to make a supreme effort, with every ounce of our strength, to save the lives of Hitler's potential victims. I called this action *Mein Kampf,* my own battle. When I was able to nurse a patient back to health I felt satisfaction that I had saved this soul from the Nazis. What normal mind could imagine that sick children would be healed and then sent off to the gas chamber? This was unbelievable! We tried to stay alive, to do our work diligently. In our innocence, we believed that it was a virtue if someone was nursed back to good health and discharged from the hospital.

The Nazis emptied the old-age homes in Cologne and Aachen, and the patients were transported to Theresienstadt. They came to us at the *Schleuse* hospital. They were nursed, but with little success. If anyone fell sick with enteritis, which started as soon as people entered the camp, nothing helped. If there were medications to stop the diarrhea, we did not have them. It was a constant, terrible struggle with death. We were not able to prevent the loss of strength by feeding the patients a decent diet. These people were tormented by this sickness until they wilted away like flowers. Most old people faded away and died in their sleep. In the beginning it was still possible to give the dead a respectable burial. We had enough linens and enough water.[30] I made it my task to wash and wrap the bodies for burial. We also had a Burial Society.[31] They were women from the Rhineland, exceptional personalities, many from the nobility and aristocracy.

I remember an extraordinary, moving scene. A Mrs. Rothschild, afflicted with a heart ailment from before her arrival, loved me very much. She was well aware of her sickness. One afternoon she called me to her bedside and asked me to come very close. "You are now my nearest and dearest," she said. "I want to bless you as a mother blesses her children."[32] She put her hands on my head and recited the ancient blessing.[33] I must say, this blessing was an unforgettable experience for me. I felt myself bound to this Jewish woman who died soon afterward. She left me part of her spirit to take along on my way. I have preserved this blessing in my memory, and it is possible that it somehow helped me to survive.

Jakob Edelstein had already been in Theresienstadt for a year when I arrived there. When I wrote him a note after my arrival he responded in a letter, which I kept, that I should not be presumptuous; he had no time for private audiences. He hardly had time to speak with his wife, let alone with strangers. His secretary, Mrs. Steif, protected him like a broody hen. One terrible morning I tried to see him on a mission for the hospital. I waited without accomplishing my mission. I was told that he was ill. Suddenly his office door opened, and out came a totally absentminded Jakob Edelstein. As soon as he noticed me he asked, "What do you want from me? I am going to say *kaddish*. My mother has died." "When did she die? What happened to her?" I asked him. He said, "Do not ask me. I am going to say *kaddish* now." He did not want to reveal to me that his mother perished in a transport of elderly people that was sent to the east.[34]

Once I said to him, "Why do you not cover your head? You can get sunstroke!" He answered me contemptuously, "I prefer to die of sunstroke rather than doff my hat and make a deep bow to the Nazis. To spare myself the ordeal, I prefer to walk without cap or hat."[35]

Once I approached Jakob Edelstein to ask him to remove a most delightful and charming nurse from a transport. She was from Vienna, an ordinary woman. But she collected Jewish songs, and when she sat at the bedside of a terribly ill patient, she sang delightful, popular Jewish songs. I tried to help this wonderful human being, but I could not move him. He said, "Even you I could not remove from a transport." I felt very sad. Even he suffered the trauma of the transports. He probably knew that even he, the Jewish head of the camp, would also get his turn.

I saw him one more time, when he was already locked up with the rest of the transport.[36] You cannot imagine how numbingly horrible it is not to be able to help someone when you know he has to go. I stood next to a barrier on the main plaza, helpless. He knew everything. He knew the fate of the Jews who went to Poland. Still, he was optimistic that some day we would be rescued and freed. He had a Zionist idealism based on his faith in the rescue of the children and a happy ending.

After working in the hospitals of Theresienstadt for two years, Trude developed thrombophlebitis. The condition endangered her life because there were no medications or proper sanitary conditions to prevent and treat infections. She was forced to choose less physically demanding work and requested a transfer to the youth department in the winter of 1944.

At first I was told that I was too independent and already too old for the Youth Welfare Department.[37] I asked Gonda Redlich,[38] director of Youth Welfare, whom I knew when he was a child, to intercede for me. When my younger son was active in *Maccabi HaTzair* in Bratislava, the young people edited a series of four volumes about Zionist education of youth. I was privileged to write about working with children for this series. My chapters were published. When I applied for the job of handicraft teacher in Theresienstadt the young instructors brought me that book, telling me that this book would teach me how to occupy children with creative work. There were my own charts and suggestions for how to keep children occupied and busy. I told the young leaders that I would study the book well! When Gonda Redlich met me, later on, he said, "Thank God, it turned out better than I thought. I believed I would have to rescue you from the *gendarmes* because you would surely rebel against the system!"

The work was a great comfort to me, and it gave me great satisfaction to work with children again. This was my true profession; I was a licensed nursery and primary school teacher. There was a home for mothers and infant babies where mothers could live in.[39] When the children were grown enough to be transferred without their mothers they were placed in children's homes under the supervision of the Children's Welfare Department. It was important to remove the children from the unhygienic living quarters of the adult population and let them grow up under halfway humane conditions. Considering the circumstances, the homes were very well run. The principal concern was the child, to preserve the lives of Jewish children. Everything was done with this mission: although we live in awful times, our children should have it better.

My first opportunity to work with children in Theresienstadt was in the Kursavy Villa. This building was set up for the Red Cross inspections as a children's sanatorium, where children were brought to convalesce after treatment in the tuberculosis section. The villa was beautifully furnished, with drapes and artistically painted lamp shades. The youngest children were seven or eight years old, but there were girls of fourteen there, too. I paid attention to the order and cleanliness of the bedrooms, checking to make sure that the beds were made neatly, that the rooms were dusted. I prepared the children's portions and ate with the children. The staff watched as the children prepared for bed to be sure they washed themselves. I let the children draw, and I taught them manual skills. I kept them occupied with conceptual teaching (I had no books), teaching the young ones the concepts of round and square, soft and sharp, etc. I did plastic art with the children, small watercolors; the girls painted flowers although there were no flowers in Theresienstadt. I walked with them to the Dresden barracks,[40] where we sometimes saw soccer games. The children did drawings of the soccer games. These activities required daily planning.

When we were preparing for the Red Cross visit I was bringing in a small loom and other things for the children when I encountered a person with a movie camera who was filming what he saw. I was very upset because I was trying to avoid being caught on this "documentary" film.[41]

The former owner of the Kursavy Villa was a Nazi, but a good Nazi, if you can say so. He was the director of agriculture in Theresienstadt. When it was possible, he acted decently to Jews. My daughter-in-law, Madla, was a stunning woman. She was in charge of the cow shed and stable. She kept them immaculately clean. Calves were born there, and she took care of them. In all of Theresienstadt there was not a spot as neat and as spotless as Madla's cow shed. If she noticed a green leaf, she put it in her pocket. In the evening she cooked it in soup for six people. She always shared with those who could not get any vitamins. This energetic, friendly, extraordinary woman became pregnant.[42] I stuffed clothing around her to round her out so she looked fat, not pregnant. Kursavy saved my daughter-in-law from deportation. He declared her to be an irreplaceable worker with the calves in his stable. She was already standing with my son at the transport embarkation point when Kursavy declared, "Groag, irreplaceable!" and so she was saved by him. He acted within certain limits. He did not make big waves, and after the war he was not sentenced as a war criminal.

The Kursavy Villa was set up to keep the children just until they were deported. The children lived there under enormous pressure. There was very strict discipline. One of the children was severely punished because he came out of the toilet with his pants hanging down, buttoned up only on the outside. The doctor in charge disciplined him by ordering him to stay in his bed for three days. Another child, who walked in the garden without permission, was also scolded and ordered to stay in bed. Children recuperating from tuberculosis need a lot of bed rest. It is absurd to make bed rest a punishment. Children were forced to eat when they suffered from throat infections and were unable to swallow. There was a Jewish doctor in charge there, but he was under so much pressure himself that he thought of such peculiar things. He had personality problems and depressions that affected the whole staff. He survived Auschwitz but ended his own life.

This situation depressed me so that I pleaded with Gonda Redlich, the director of Youth Welfare, to relieve me from that position, and I was transferred to a newly setup kindergarten directed by Grete Loewy Sachsl. She was very good at playing and singing with the children, but not as good as I in occupational therapy.

The announcement of an inspection visit by the Red Cross brought a revolution to Theresienstadt.[43] The Nazis wanted the visitors to see the city as a refuge for the elderly. Building facades were freshly painted. Artists painted signs for the street corners, guiding you from the Hohenelbe barracks to the

Hamburger barracks. The distance was actually hardly five minutes away, and everyone knew how to get there.[44] A lot of humbug was displayed to let this asylum appear in a favorable light.

At the time, we had no premonition of what was going on, no inkling that this was a gruesome drama. We were convinced that all the preparations were to impress Bernadotte[45] when he visited and that all the improvements would remain. I was working at Grete Sachsl's kindergarten at the time of the Red Cross visit. It was set up to give the impression of a modern kindergarten. It was situated in a long, narrow ground floor apartment made of wood and sectioned off. In the middle was a shallow, heated pool. Imagine! You could think that the children were able to take a bath in the afternoon. There was a playroom, a dining room with small armchairs, tables and benches. In the first floor rooms, where the beds usually stood very close together, the beds were painted in blue and rose colors for the Danish inmates.[46] The sick were hidden away on an upper floor. The playroom got all new furniture, and new toys were brought in, only for that day. At a large table small chairs were nicely arranged in a square, each in a different color. Facing the garden was a small porch with ten small beds where ten children could rest after a meal.[47] Of course, usually there were so many more children around. All the pictures that we wanted to hang up had to be inspected in a special section in the Magdeburg barracks. Those pictures were stamped, "censored; may be hung." Any pictures that put Theresienstadt in a poor light did not get the stamp.

The whole spectacle was an act. Tragically, after the commission left, all the children were deported. The kindergarten was left vacant. We knew that something was bound to happen; you could feel it.[48]

After the Red Cross visit things changed. The people who came to work last in youth welfare were called in and ordered to work in the war industry plants. Youth welfare became an extra job that we did after our factory work. Sometimes we worked two eight-hour shifts in the factory and four hours with the children, which left us with very little sleep. The "extra" job was many-sided. In Children's Home No. 410,[49] I made drawings with the children, I knitted, I peeled potatoes in the winter. Some of the children probably came to Theresienstadt as infants. They were between four and six years old. They had no impressions of the outside world. They were excited when they saw a cat running across the yard. When we played in the garden, if the children saw a cat they all ran after it, like a herd. They loved to walk to the fortifications,[50] where they were fascinated by the flock of sheep belonging to the Nazis.[51] Another thing they enjoyed was seeing the fire trucks and the fire engine in the firehouse. When I asked the captain to blow the horn, that was their greatest thrill. I taught them a song about firemen. Once, as we were standing near the firehouse, Rahm,[52] riding on his black horse, walked right into my group of children. Only the angels protected them from being trampled to death by the horse.

Children's Home 410 was a home for girls, one of the largest in Theresienstadt. On the ground floor was a small office, a distribution place for bread, and a tailoring shop for the home. There were larger spaces where groups of girls lived. The grown-up girls worked in agriculture. Work in the fresh air was desirable for young people, rather than work in a closed room with a poor supply of oxygen or at forced labor. They left in the morning to work at planting gardens or harvesting fruit and vegetables. They were healthy.

In the basement, below ground, was the schoolroom, a large room with benches for the children. The windows were small airholes at street level. The room was a secret because it was illegal to teach children. We even had a piano in that basement schoolroom. It had no legs; it rested on wooden boxes.[53] The children had piano lessons and practiced on that propped-up grand piano. *Madrikhim* came in to give singing lessons. Next to that room where the children practiced was the music studio of Schaechter, who conducted the Verdi Requiem.[54] All this took place in the basement rooms of Children's Home 410. The director was Mrs. Rosa Englander,[55] and my son, Dr. Willi Groag, was the house trustee. They and the staff made the lives of the children as pleasant as possible.[56]

Friedl Brandeis was a most competent painter and artist.[57] A Bauhaus student, she was the home's soul of artistic accomplishment. She made decorations and sketches for the holidays with the children and devised new embroidery techniques. She celebrated with them and developed close friendships with the young girls. Unfortunately, she was deported with one of the last transports and did not survive.[58]

I did drawings with the children, as well as all sorts of handicrafts. Of course within the limited four hours available to me I could not organize a systematic program, but I did whatever I could each day. One episode haunts me. I was in a room in the hospital with a woman who was a mother. Her little son came to the door, crying bitterly. What happened? He stole a bread from the loaded bread wagon for his mother and was caught, and they took the bread away from him. He said he wanted to give the bread to his mother, and the bad people took it from him. This was a different, primitive morality. Even a six- or seven-year-old understood the misery and wretchedness of his sick mother, plagued with hunger and pain. Why should the child not try to bring his mother a piece of bread?

Today we are blamed for not having done anything, for not resisting. But after nine boys were hanged for smuggling letters out of Theresienstadt,[59] it was obvious that we could all be machine-gunned in a matter of minutes. We saw no solution in physical resistance. The only thing we hoped was to keep the children and ourselves alive as long as possible, until Jakob Edelstein's hope came true: "Drift, you'll yet see *Eretz Yisrael*."

In 1943 a transport of children arrived.[60] They were kept separately. I only knew about them because a doctor who lived in the hospital where I worked asked me to prepare some things for him for an irregular children's center. Another doctor from our hospital was also asked to look after these children. On the day the children were supposed to arrive I met Fredi Hirsch, a *madrikh* who organized sports activities for the children. He told me that it was strictly forbidden to be at the railroad station when the transport arrived. But he believed that nothing would happen to him. He went to the railroad station, and after he saw the children he was arrested and deported. These children had already been in Auschwitz. Their parents had been gassed. After their arrival in Theresienstadt the children were told to take a shower. They cried and wailed bitterly; they feared the shower would be their death. The children were supposed to be sent to Switzerland.[61] Dr. Blumenthal, the pediatrician who was in charge, asked me to pack a suitcase for him; he was to accompany the children to Switzerland. I packed the valise. I saw the train with those laughing and smiling children when they left Theresienstadt. I waved goodbye to Dr. Blumenthal. The train went directly to Auschwitz.

Towards the end the great Dr. Leo Baeck arrived.[62] By then there were fewer young people. I revered and worshipped Dr. Baeck. He was able to harmonize his philosophy of Judaism with his worldly philosophy. He was a marvelous lecturer on Jewish and Christian ideas, giving analytic discourses on both religions. His conclusion was that Judaism was a universal religion, that each Jew should turn to his own religion. Judaism had no dogma, only concepts; it was elastic and therefore all Jewish convictions could flourish within it. He gave many lectures in Theresienstadt, and he wrote a lot. He was blessed with a beautiful voice and a strong hand, like Moses, which he used as an accompaniment to his discourses. He made such a tremendous impression; it is most deplorable that he did not go on *aliyah*.

We owe it to Dr. Leo Baeck that our granddaughter Chava is alive. My son Willi was his assistant. When my daughter-in-law became pregnant, it was forbidden to give birth.[63] The Nazis permitted only ten children to be born in Theresienstadt. This would be the eleventh child. Kursavy saved her from the transport, but when the child was about to be born, Dr. Leo Baeck went to the Gestapo and personally pleaded for the mother and child. He went out of his way because he loved Madla. Dr. Baeck prophesied that the baby would be born on Shabbat and that it would be a son. The child was born a few hours before Shabbat. However, it was a girl. When Willi asked him, "How could you say it would be a boy?" Dr. Baeck answered, "Your wife deceived me." And so we have our Chava, our *ḥayelet*.[64]

In Theresienstadt children were educated without books and without a system. When they were liberated into normal life they were able to make up quickly what they had missed in school. In one year of study two of those girls were able to do their *Matura*, clear evidence that they were prepared for future life. The tragedy is that much of what was done in Theresienstadt was only for paper records. Most people were not allowed to exist.

Everything we did lost its real value. I felt like a marionette that moves, but it is all pretense, all hypocritical. The doctor who tried to promote the patients' well-being did not know whether he would be deported in a few days. When he saved a woman from pneumonia, she was deported two days later. What was the purpose of it all? It was an incomprehensible swindle, a fraud, and we all fell into it.

Trude Groag and her husband returned to Olmuetz after the liberation of Terezin but left Czechoslovakia in 1949 to join their sons in Israel. There, Trude worked for WIZO in one of the temporary tent camps set up to house new immigrants, where she established a sewing workshop for women. She felt fortunate to live in Israel, surrounded by an extended family of sons and daughters-in-law, grandchildren, and great-grandchildren. Gertrud Groag died in 1979.

—Interviewed by Gershon Ben David, September 21, 1965, and October 3, 1965, for the Oral History Division of the Avraham Harman Institute of Contemporary Jewry, Hebrew University of Jerusalem. Translated from German by Alfred Gruenspecht.

Trude Groag wrote poetry throughout her life. The first collection of her poems was "published" in two handwritten copies in Terezin during the first year she was there. These poems, with the addition of others, have been translated into Hebrew and published in Israel. One of her poems appears below.[65] The original German version is reproduced on page 264.

The Sluice

My helpless brother at my side,
Old, sick, a stranger.
I never sought your company,
I never cared for your destiny.
How close I feel to you, my brother,
Helpless as I am myself.

Zenia Malecki

Zenia Malecki was born in Vilna in 1921, the only child of tradi-
tional, middle-class parents. She attended secular Jewish schools and
studied painting at the university. Her artistic talent was useful dur-
ing the Russian occupation, when she was assigned to paint murals
in public buildings. Although there had been refugees from German-
occupied Poland in Vilna since 1939, the Jews of Vilna did not antici-
pate the fury of German occupation. The Germans occupied Vilna
on June 24, 1941, and two ghetto areas were established as of Septem-
ber 6, 1941.[1]

Soon after the Germans came they started to catch men in the street.
People would go to business and not come back. The Lithuanians cooperated, collaborating with the Germans. One day in autumn 1941,
the Germans came into our house and said, "Take what you can," and we
were sent to the ghetto. We had a good friend, a very handsome young Pole,
who had come to my parents before that and said that there would be a
ghetto. He wanted to make some papers for me as a Karaite.[2] But I said,
whatever will happen to my parents will happen to me. My parents also hesi-
tated. Somehow they didn't trust him. But later, when we were in the ghetto,
he waited at the entrance, and when we went to work, he brought bread. He
risked his life and hid, and he waited for me and my father. He probably
wanted to prove he was a good human being.

The Germans didn't *ask* anything. They *ordered*. There was no conversation. Sometimes I see in the movies that Jews talked to Germans. It didn't
exist. There was an order, and you were afraid, and you did what they said.

There were two ghettos. Ghetto 2 was closer to our house, so they took
us there. It was the old Jewish area. It had very narrow streets. People were
already living there, and other people came as well, so we didn't have anywhere to live. My mother, my father, and I lay on the floor in a corner of a
room. We didn't go out to work yet because we had the feeling that this was

only temporary. It couldn't continue like that. We weren't at all organized. We were there three weeks or so.

Then came the liquidation of the second ghetto. They took people to Ponar[3] and killed them. There were constant *Aktions*. They used to come in and take whomever they wanted, old people, young people. Germans came with Lithuanians. They just accumulated a group of people and took them away and that was that. We knew that Ponar was a place where they killed them. One girl escaped from Ponar, and her mother was still in the second ghetto. She told about it. We believed anything. Anything. We understood that this was it. We go to death.

When the second ghetto was liquidated we went to the first ghetto.[4] With our bundles in our hands we looked for some spot, some corner. We went to the apartment of the parents of some people who were in the same business as my father. Again, we slept on the floor because it was impossible to get a regular room.

From there, my father[5] organized a bakery called The Public Bakery, *Die Gesellschaftliche Bekerei*, located at Oszmiana 8. The idea was that everybody who belonged to the FPO, the *Fareynitke Partizaner Organizatsye* (United Partisan Organization) could get bread.

At the same time, the FPO was organized in the first ghetto, intending to prepare the youth and whoever wanted to belong to resist.[6] That was the resistance. The partisan staff had a command post at Oszmiana 8. That was the place where we could hide rifles and whatever we could "organize." When we came to the first ghetto everything was already organized. My friend Sonia Madeysker was one of the leaders in the partisans. She was a very, very important member of the FPO. She perished, unfortunately. At that time she was very active, and that was actually how I got into the underground.

The resistance consisted of people from all shades of political inclinations: Zionists, Revisionists, Betar, HaShomer HaTzair, Communists, Bundists; everybody was in FPO. That was why it was called the United Partisan Organization. We knew we would have to do *something*. We couldn't be passive anymore. Our leader was Witenberg, Yizhak Witenberg. There were also Jewish police in the ghetto. Thanks to an uncle of my friend, Hershke Gordon, who was in the *Judenrat*, I got a kitchen in one apartment. They took out the stove and everything, and that was a room that was used for an emergency. I lived there with my mother. My father lived nearby at Oszmiana 8.

There were times I worked with my father besides being in the bakery.

My father used to go out of the ghetto on purpose to bring in whatever he could. Everyone who had a yellow *Schein* could work. Otherwise, you were really condemned to death. So whoever could, got a yellow *Schein* from the *Judenrat*. My father got one in order to be able to go out to get ammunition for the rifles or other parts for the FPO. He smuggled things in. I also smuggled them in. You couldn't carry a whole gun; you had to smuggle it in parts. It was a holy task. We *had* to do it. It was our goal. We didn't have anything, just survival.

Whenever there was some order from the Germans, they transmitted it to us, and we had to carry it out. There might be an order that on a certain day they would want a number of people. Gens[7] and Dessler,[8] our *Judenrat* leaders, had to provide the people. After every *Aktion* they let us rest for a couple of days, and then again and again they demanded people. It is difficult to admit, but when our own people got the order they had to take the people. The Jewish police would come and take the old people first.

There was great hunger. We had rations, but because we were involved in the bakery we had a little bit more bread. Some people used to smuggle food into the ghetto when they went to work. I had long narrow pockets sewn into my clothes so I could smuggle in flour or peas. One time I was caught, and, oh my God, I was beaten. When we walked back into the ghetto with the SS someone walking with another group, or even someone from the Jewish police, would walk towards our group, just saying, "Kittel[9] is at the entrance." Kittel was a murderer. He threw me in the corner, and I was beaten—oh God!—because he found some peas.

We had schools for the children in the ghetto. We had a choir. We had theater. We had discussions. It's just unbelievable. Can you imagine? We wrote poems and songs. We did whatever we could. The mothers were called to special discussions. I'll never forget what they said: "Now we are in a cage, but we have to do everything, everything possible that when the children come out of the cage, they will be able to fly." They did everything they could to create a normal atmosphere. A leader from Warsaw, Jozef Muszkat,[10] really taught the women to do everything for the children so that they wouldn't feel that they were in a cage.

The resistance had a lot of trouble with the *Judenrat*. As a matter of fact, when the Gestapo demanded that the *Judenrat* give up Witenberg,[11] the FPO leaders tried to convince the *Judenrat* that liquidation would come anyway, so why should we give away our leader?

Abba Kovner's mother lived at the same address as our bakery. She wore long, old-fashioned skirts. I got a skirt from her, and I dressed Yizhak Witenberg as a woman and took him to my room, which we used in emergencies. Witenberg was hidden in my room, and I was the contact between him and the staff. I had the key to the room, and we communicated like in a prison. Three short taps and one long; that was our signal. Then I got the order that the FPO staff decided to give him up because they said if Witenberg was not given up to the Gestapo the liquidation of the entire ghetto would come. If he was delivered to the Gestapo, there would be no liquidation. When I got this order, I just couldn't bring myself to do it. I just couldn't.

I went up to my room, to Yizhak Witenberg, and I said, "Yizhak, the staff decided to give you up." I said, "Look, we will go up to the attic." The criminal police were downstairs; it was a bright, sunny day. He dressed himself again, with a scarf; I will never forget his face. I took him up to the attic even though the criminal police ordered all the attics to be closed. You hanged the laundry in the attics, which were connected from one building to another, but the connecting doors were locked. I went up to Mrs. Davidowich, and I said: "I don't have my key for my attic; give me your key." She said, "Oh no, I'm not going to give it to you." I said, "Please," but she didn't give it to me. I searched until I found one hole that he could squeeze through because he was very skinny. I left him up there. When somebody came and asked, "Where is Yizhak?" I said, "I don't know." I just couldn't tell them, and I couldn't give him up. I couldn't, no.

By doing this I worked against the staff of the FPO, and I want you to know that we were very much like soldiers. We had discipline. We had to obey orders. Witenberg tried to run from one attic to another, and the criminal police found him anyway. It took a whole day. Then I felt guilty that I didn't follow orders, so I wrote a letter to the staff in which I said, "I committed a crime," so to speak. I didn't follow orders. I had a small trial, but they understood and didn't punish me. The leaders of the FPO at that time who were making the decision to give up Witenberg were Abba Kovner, Abraham Chwojnik, Sonia Madeysker, and Nissan Reznik and the *Judenrat*. This was the Witenberg chapter in my life that I think created my character. I was very young then.

Meanwhile, Witenberg's wife, Etel, and younger son were hiding because she didn't have a yellow *Schein*.[12] Since I was the connection between Witenberg and the staff, he asked me to go to his wife and tell her that he was all right. I went in there, and she said: "Zenia, I can't take it anymore. All the women are saying, "Nu, nu, did they catch him already? Did they catch him? . . . " She was sitting there with the child.[13] She was a little woman, slim. She said: "I probably will have a heart attack here." But she didn't.

After Witenberg was taken away,[14] Abba Kovner took command.[15] We had our meetings. We had also connections with the Polish partisans. Sonia Madeysker[16] looked like a Christian girl, and she was very important. She organized everything. We were trained to work with rifles, and we also filled up bulbs with acid. In case we would have to resist, we planned to throw the bulbs because we didn't have enough armament. We did everything ourselves. There were some people who had some military experience with the Polish army; they knew how to train us. We had our meetings, and we were indoctrinated. We knew what we had to do. We had our plan in case it would come to resistance. Everyone had a position. My position was next to the library.

Once, at Straszuna 12 there was an incident. Two Germans were killed. A Jewish girl shot even though she didn't receive the order to shoot, so the gun was taken away from her. After that, as a result we had an *Aktion*.[17] I was standing there; I'll never forget it. It was about three o'clock in the morning. It was my shift. I saw cars with German military insignia; the SS came. We gave the signal, and soon everybody knew what was going on. It didn't take long; you could hear crying and screaming, and you could see groups of people being gathered together, and you knew those people were going to die. That's all. Some Jews were against the resistance, and some joined. It was hard to make decisions. You only knew that today you were here and that tomorrow you didn't know where you'd be. You really couldn't think clearly.

The policy of the Jewish commandant Gens was to save any number he could. When he had to deliver to the Germans a certain number of people, he took the old people first. I am sure that his state of mind was terrible, but he felt this was the right thing to do. Did he have a choice? The partisans said, "No, whoever has to go will go. The selection shouldn't come from the *Judenrat*." That was our position. The *Judenrat* shouldn't decide who had to die first, the old people or the sick people from the hospital. Who was I to say that a sick person in the hospital had to die first? That was our misunderstanding with the *Judenrat*. This was something I will never forget.

I was also prepared to go to the forest. I was ready and had prepared whatever I had to take along with me, but I developed the flu. I had a 104-degree temperature, and I couldn't make it. I couldn't make it. We were organized in groups of five, called *finiftlekh*. Boyfriends and girlfriends were not allowed to be in the same *finift'l* because if they got caught they might be more concerned for each other. We were planning to escape through the sewer. We also planned future actions, like sabotage or putting bombs under trains. We had some very brave people, and many perished.

We had emissaries from Bialystok, and from Vilna we sent emissaries to Bialystok and to Grodno and to Warsaw. We were constantly in contact. We had a choice: either we would resist, put up resistance in the ghetto, or we would try to go with as many as possible to the forest. In the beginning, we preferred resistance, of course. But then we realized that it was very difficult because the people in the ghetto weren't on our side. It was then, I remember, that we decided that as many as possible should go to the forest. At least we would be "safe" there, if possible, and work in the forest.

After my group left for the forest, when I was sick with the flu and couldn't go with them, the liquidation of the ghetto started. I was hidden with my parents. We were sitting there, and we heard the steps, the German steps. When we were caught the men were sent to Estonia, and I was sent with my mother to Riga.

In Kaiserwald concentration camp in Riga, Latvia, Zenia and her mother were "processed": hair shaved, personal belongings taken away, and striped dresses given to wear. From there they were sent to Dunawerke, where they dredged canals. Zenia's mother became too sick to work and was sent back to Kaiserwald, where she perished. Her father was sent to Klooga concentration camp in Estonia and from there to Freiburg in Breisgau, Germany, where he perished with one thousand men who were burned to death. Zenia's group was sent to Ghetto Shavli (Siauliai), Lithuania, and then to Freudendorf concentration camp near Danzig, where she worked at hard manual labor. She describes beatings and primitive means of trying to cope with illness and injury. By the time she was liberated by the Russians, she was unconscious with typhus. After a series of encounters and coincidences, Zenia was reunited with an uncle in Bolivia, South America. She married and came to the United States in 1953.

—Interviewed by Aviva Segall, March 14, 1986

Emilie Schindler in the home of "Schindler Jews," Plainview,
New York, 1983. *(Emilie Schindler File, Yaffa Eliach Collection,
donated by the Center for Holocaust Studies, Museum of Jewish
Heritage, New York)*

Gertrud Groag and her sons, Olomuec, Czechoslovakia, 1936. *Left to right:*
Jan, Lev, Gertrud, and Willi. *(Courtesy Dr. Willi Groag)*

Gertrud Groag, Jerusalem, Israel, 1965. *(Frenze Gruber, courtesy Dr. Willi Groag)*

Schleusse*

Hilfloser Bruder neben mir,
Alt, krank und fremd,
Nie hat mein Herz nach Deiner Näh' verlangt,
Nie hab ich mich gesorgt, nach Dir gebangt.
Wie nahe bin ich Dir,
Hilfloser Bruder, hilflos wie ich selbst. –

* Kontroll-und Durchschlagsplatz für Neuankömmlinge

Poem by Gertrud Groag as it appears in the book of her poetry; calligraphy by Dr. Willi Groag. *(Courtesy Dr. Willi Groag)*

Zenia Berkon Malecki, Vilna, Poland, 1933. *(Courtesy Zenia Malecki)*

Zenia Malecki, New York City, 1986. *(Courtesy Zenia Malecki)*

Rose Grünapfel Meth, Frankfurt, Germany, 1946. *(Courtesy Rose Meth)*

Rose Meth, Brooklyn, New York, 1986. *(Courtesy Rose Meth)*

Aida Brydbord

When World War II began, the Soviet Union occupied the town of Pruzhany, Poland, where Aida Brydbord (Chaja Czerczewska) was born and raised. The Russians confiscated her father's small grocery store, and the family subsisted on their savings and on the proceeds of clandestine sales. Aida was the youngest, the only one of six children still living at home in this religious family. With the German occupation, the Czerczewska family was living in Linovo, a small town near Pruzhany. Two sisters were living in Palestine, and two were in the United States; another, Esther, was married and living with the family in Linovo.

Aida became a teacher of Russian in a village school near Pruzhany. The Jews in Pruzhany were fairly isolated from the growing cataclysm engulfing European Jewry. Radios were scarce, newspapers reflected the political agenda of the occupying power, and although Jewish refugees who passed through the town told frightening stories of their experiences with Nazism, they did not influence the opinions of Pruzhany's traditional Jews. Aida remembers her father describing his impression of the Germans as "the same Germans (as in) the First World War."

During the first few days they didn't mistreat us too badly.[1] They called us to the marketplace, and they announced that the Jews were the biggest enemies of the people and that the Gentile people should have nothing to do with us. Within a week or two they said that all the Jews were supposed to wear round yellow circles on the front left side and on the back of their clothes.

One day they called my father in. My father was a very educated man. They asked him to be the head of the *Judenrat* in Linovo.[2] He didn't want to. He said that he was too old and that he wouldn't be able to send another Jew to do whatever they would demand of him. After that, my parents decided to move to Pruzhany and lived in the ghetto there. In Pruzhany, Mr. Janowicz,[3] who knew German very well, was chosen to be president of the *Judenrat*. He was a Zionist and a wealthy man. Another man, Siegel,[4] had lived in Danzig. He came to visit his parents in Pruzhany and was stranded there when the war broke out. He was the spokesman to the Germans because he knew German very well. Rabbi Mandelbaum was not an official member of the *Judenrat*. He was very smart, very intelligent. His word was taken into consideration when any decisions had to be made. Dr. Goldfein, a woman doctor,[5] was also on the *Judenrat*. She was responsible for medical services. Her husband was also a member of the *Judenrat*.

The ghetto was formed three or four weeks later.[6] The *Judenrat* had to carry out German orders: to see that people went to work when they were called, to dig ditches, to go to a farm to dig potatoes, to clean the streets. There was barbed wire all around the ghetto, with a gate. We could go in or out only when a policeman was standing there checking us. We were counted when we walked in or out. When we walked in we were searched. There were two Jewish and one German policemen or a Polish policeman appointed by the Germans. I did all kinds of work: cleaning toilets, washing floors, cooking for the Germans, milking cows, chopping wood, going to a farmer to dig potatoes, and working in a hospital. People my age tried to work outside the ghetto because the farmer sometimes let you have something. We tried to sneak in a potato or maybe a handful of greens or a little bit of butter. We didn't get paid by the *Judenrat* because the *Judenrat* didn't get paid by the Germans. The food in the ghetto was very poor quality. There was a lot of sickness. Tuberculosis was a constant killer.

I remember working in the hospital in the ghetto.[7] It was originally a Polish *Gymnasium*. The doctor in charge was Dr. Goldfein. The head of the laboratory was Dr. Avram Treger. He taught me how to use the microscope and to detect tuberculosis and other diseases. A lot of people died of tuberculosis because conditions were very poor. You have to understand that in one small room seven or eight people lived. There weren't enough beds. Bathrooms were outside. Sanitary conditions were absolutely terrible.[8]

I had a niece. She was five or six years old. Do you know what children played in that environment? They played "Germans": *Farbalten zach* (hidden thing) hiding from the Germans. The Germans are coming. Where shall we hide? Where shall we run away? That's what children played.

The *shul* also moved into the ghetto. Rabbi Mandelbaum was the head of the *shul*. People went to *daven*. The religious Jews went every morning and every evening. Everybody tried to observe Jewish holidays any way they could.

The Germans gave us some food. You had to stand in line to have your little bit of milk, some flour, and whatever you could try to get. We exchanged things with the natives through the wires as long as the Germans weren't watching us. You gave them a blouse, or you gave them a dress, and they gave you some butter or a chicken. There was a *shoḥet* in the ghetto, so you could kill a chicken and have some meat. As a matter of fact, once, in the middle of the night, they smuggled a cow into the ghetto. My house was on the edge of the ghetto near the wire. They put regular shoes on the cow to disguise its footprints. The *shoḥet* slaughtered the cow in the middle of the night. We already had customers, and everybody was begging for a little bit of meat. By the next morning there was no sign that the cow had been in the ghetto.

In the ghetto the situation changed slowly. People were brought to Pruzhany from all the small villages and even from bigger towns.[9] More and more they asked the *Judenrat* to send people to outside work, to *Arbeitslagers*, from which they didn't return. Sometimes people volunteered for the *Arbeitslager* because conditions in the ghetto were so bad. They didn't have a place to sleep. They had to sleep on the floor. I was living with my parents and my aunt and my uncle, five in a tiny little room. We had two beds and a sofa and a little stove. This room was our bedroom, our bathroom, our toilet, our eating room, everything.

We heard that ghettos were being liquidated. In the summer of '42 a group of people from Ghetto Pruzhany went out to work at Linovo twelve kilometers away. They told us that the Jews of Linovo were taken and killed.[10] Among them were my sister Esther and her family. The Germans pretended that they were taking everybody to work, but they took them to a special place and they killed them. The Germans promised Mr. Siegel of our *Judenrat* that our ghetto was very valuable to them because Pruzhany was on a strategic line between Warsaw, Baranovichi, and Moscow. But it looked like our safety wouldn't last too long.

In 1942, two partisans came into the ghetto. One was a Jew, Josef Friedman; one was a Christian. Josef Friedman was originally from Bereza Kartuska. They came to talk to a group of young people in our ghetto who had already tried to organize a group. We didn't know about the partisans, but there were people who were willing to escape the ghetto.[11] They tried to bring in pieces of rifles, pieces of shells, bits of ammunition, and slowly assemble them for a future date to escape from the ghetto. News traveled very quickly that the Germans would finally liquidate the ghetto and kill us. Those people came to talk to the group, and they gave us advice, and they told us where to go in case we wanted to escape.[12] I heard about this from my boyfriend. He told me: "Two partisans came, and I want to go away. My younger brother is also going." My mother cried so much about our leaving that I felt I had to stay. The reaction of the *Judenrat* was terrible. They said, "You will ruin us! The minute the Germans know that a group of people went to the partisans, there will be absolute disaster!"[13] My boyfriend's brother, Tuvia, was fifteen years old. He went with the first seven boys to the partisans. They took ammunition and food, and they left.

My boyfriend, Paul, came to visit me, and he talked to me. You know how young people are, always secretive. No one else knew anything about what was going on. We whispered because everybody lived in one room. Paul's friend asked me one night, "Why do you let Paul get mixed up with all those people? Why are you in it? See to it that he withdraws from the group and does not have anything to do with them." There was a second group that formed to run away from the ghetto. It was boys and a very few girls. Mostly young people. But in this particular group there were a few elderly men. We took them because they knew the surrounding area. We didn't have any leader. Every night Paul assembled ammunition in the cellar; because he and others smuggled it in, he was a valuable part of the group. He told them, "I want my girlfriend to come with me."

We got married on our last day in the ghetto, January 27, 1943. We had to register with the *Judenrat* so they would know that we were a couple. We got a piece of paper. There was a rabbi from a *shteibel* for *ḥuppah-kiddushin*. There was no meal, no wine, nothing, just to *shtell the ḥuppah* (set up the marriage canopy) and *mazel tov*, and that was all. I had a small ring. We didn't have any gold rings anymore because in the ghetto the Germans took every piece of gold away from us. Everybody had to give their gold away.[14] How did you make sure that people were being honest and bringing *all* their gold? You made a room dark. You put out a *sefer Torah* and lit two candles. The head of each family had to go into this room and swear that he or she had given away everything that they had. Some religious men were there to see to it. I think my father was even there. The head of the family, the father or the mother, said, "*Dos vos ikh hob und dos gib ikh eikh aveck*" (This is what I have, and this is what I give you). Everything was done spontaneously, without any reason or rationalization if it was wrong or right. Things were done on impulse.

Within a week, we had to run away. It was the last days of January 1943.[15] The Germans surrounded the ghetto, and they said tomorrow everybody had to be ready with a little package. We were going to the railroad station twelve kilometers away. They said they would take us on sleds and bring us to the railroad station.[16] That's when our group decided to escape. I went to the house where I lived with my parents. I told my parents I didn't want to leave them because I was the young one and I could supply them with food and everything. "I don't want to leave you!" My father said to me: "You are running away. You are *not* coming with us on the sleds. You will be the one who will survive and tell your sisters in the United States how we suffered." I said, "But I want to go with you." "No," he said, "you are not coming." Those were his last words to me.

I ran away from the house, and I saw the Germans at the beginning of the street coming to the house to pick them up. I ran away to another street. Meanwhile, Paul sent out a man to look for me. He took me to the hiding place where there was a bunker. We hid in this bunker for the day. At night we went out; the streets were empty. My parents went on the transport, and they were taken to Auschwitz. They perished like everybody else.

My husband, Paul, and I and the group of twelve people ran to the forest. At first we didn't make contact with anybody.[17] The first group that left was supposed to be in touch with us. If they heard that something happened in the ghetto, they were supposed to be on the road to meet us. A day went by, and nobody met us. We didn't know what to do. We sat under the trees, and we asked ourselves, "What shall we do? Which way should we turn? We don't know where to go." Then, most of the group left us. Paul and I remained, and another girl and boy remained. The girl from the other couple said to me: "I had a maid. She worked in our house a long time. I know where she lives. I'll go there." But she never reached that place because the Germans caught her. The rest of the group came back at night, and they said, "Oh, we didn't leave you. We just went to look for a place where we can settle." They were jealous that we were couples. The next day we met more people from the ghetto, and the next night more people came, and we were around sixty or seventy people. We decided to divide ourselves into smaller groups but not to separate too far from each other.

We lived like that for a few days, but we were hungry. We had nothing to eat. We didn't take any utensils with us. We found a little container in the woods for warming up a little bit of snow to get water. The older people knew the surrounding areas. They said, "We will go out to the village, and we'll bring some food." Six or seven men took the four or five rifles, and they went to the village. Morning came, and they returned with a couple of sleds of food. We were very happy. The people who went to bring the food went to rest, and the people who stayed behind started to unload the food. But the people in the villages got mad at us for grabbing all the food. They immediately went to the Germans and squealed on us, and right away the Germans were on our tracks. They brought the Germans straight to our camp. There we were, unloading the food, and we heard shooting from all over. Like animals we started to run, not knowing what happened but knowing that we were in danger. I was running; I didn't know where Paul was, he didn't know where I was. As I was running, I met him. As we ran we grabbed some bread. I said, "If I have to die, let me not be hungry because my stomach is so empty." We ran all day long. The Germans were after us, shooting constantly. By night, everything quieted down, and like animals we started to crawl out of the hiding places wherever we were. We lost twelve people, including my husband's older brother, Avrum. He was then twenty-one.

We still didn't meet any partisans. The partisans didn't know anything about us. We were afraid the Germans would return the next day. Now we divided up into small groups, and each went in a different direction. We took what food we had because we knew that we could not depend on anybody. We were afraid to show our faces in any village. We walked all night, and we came to a place that was just swamps and woods and settled down there for the night. In the morning, we saw that we were not near any villages, so we decided to stay there. We started to dig holes to live in. You dug a hole, and you cut tree branches, and you camouflaged the hole with leaves.[18] It was winter, it was February, and I didn't have any shoes. I wrapped my feet with *shmattes*. Whatever food we had with us we ate, but after a couple of days we were hungry. I don't have to tell you what the sanitary conditions were. We were full of lice. They were eating us alive. Our bodies were bloody from our scratching.

One day we saw, from afar, something like a mountain. That was the way the peasants protected their food for the winter. They didn't have any cellars, no refrigeration. The climate is cold, so they piled up potatoes and carrots and beets and covered them with straw and with dirt and used the food as they needed it. At night we went over there, dug up the potatoes, covered it up again, and went back to our little *ziemlanka*. We found a pail, and we cooked the potatoes. We had no salt; we just washed one off a little bit in the snow, and we cooked it. One potato was shared by the whole group, two women and ten men. The peels were eaten, everything. Nothing was thrown away. Everything was full of sand. You just ate the potatoes without salt, bread, nothing with it. Everybody had heartburn constantly.

We lived like this for a couple of weeks, always cold and hungry. We saw light from afar, but we were afraid to go closer. One day one of our fellows looked around the surrounding area, came back, and said: "There is only one house in the vicinity. Maybe we should take a chance and go in and talk to them. First of all we want some kind of news of what's going on in the world. Also, we can get something to eat." That was what happened. Two of our fellows went out. They made up a story that they got lost, but the woman said to them, "We know who you are. You are not lost. We know that a group from the Pruzhany ghetto ran away and that they are hiding some place near here. I don't care. What do you want?" They told her that they were hungry. The man told them, "I'll give you something to eat, but you have to be very careful. I cannot show you the way out of here because the Germans come here constantly."

From that day on, that Russian peasant was our contact. To us he was a lifesaver. He provided food for us. He gave us all the news. He didn't take any money from us; we didn't have any. I remember I gave him my coat. It was a maroon coat with a black collar. I paid him for the bread with it. Whatever article of value somebody had they gave to him for bread. We lived like that all winter. Spring started to come. The sun was out. A partisan never takes off all his clothes, only one piece at a time, which you smoke out over the fire till all those insects are dead, and then you put it back on. You couldn't dig a hole by the water and wash yourself. We smelled terribly. At night we never all slept at once. Two or three people were always on watch to know and see what was going on. One night the watchman alarmed everybody. What was it? Partisans, the real partisans![19] Russians, organized partisans, were walking in our direction. It was a group of about four or five people. One of them was Paul's younger brother, Tuvia. They got news that a group of people ran away from the Pruzhany ghetto and was hiding. Tuvia made sure that his group would go through the woods looking for us. He didn't know exactly who it would be, but he knew that a group of Pruzhaner Jews were in the woods. Tuvia's name was now Anatole, a Russian name. He wore a uniform, and with a machine gun he was going on a mission. He said he'd be back this way. That was how it happened. On their way back, they took us to the partisan *otrad*.

It was the Kirowsky *otrad*. Our commandeer was Juzef Samulik. The group was composed of about five hundred people: non-Jews, Jews, runaways from the army, officers and soldiers, Russian soldiers. They were mostly men, but there were some women too. All the "houses" were *ziemlankas* underground. As long as it was quiet, the Germans didn't attack us; we lived like this in a little "town." We went to villages and took food. If they betrayed us, the next day the whole village was on fire. In this particular *otrad* there were thirty Jews. We were treated nicely but with sarcasm: "A Jew is not a fighter." The Russians called us *"Abrashas."* "Abrasha" means a Jew, from the name Abraham. But the truth was that the Jews were very loyal and brave fighters in the partisans.[20]

I had a gun, and I had a rifle. I knew how to take them apart and put them together. I cooked for the group that went out on military missions. Another group went out to bring food. Another group sewed and repaired the uniforms. If we stayed long enough in one place, we gathered stones and built a little house with an oven, heated up the stones, and threw water on them, like a *shvitz* bath.[21] We wore pants and boots. Boots were the most important. You got your boots where you got your food, in the villages. We went for what we called a *"bombioshka."* You "bummed" whatever you could. One night I went out with a group of other partisans. I climbed up to an attic of a house probably owned by a rich man. I threw down boots and overcoats and fur coats from the attic for the other people to take. That was when everybody got dressed so nicely in boots and coats.

We had a radio for transmitting, and we had a printing press on which we printed news flashes. We had a Jewish doctor, Dr. Smolinsky, who also ran away from the ghetto. One day a group of five men and I went to dynamite a bridge. As soon as we started out the Germans began to shoot at us. We hid in the woods, but the mission wasn't a loss. The bridge was destroyed, and they couldn't find us even though the dogs were after us because once you come to water they lose your track.

After this incident Dr. Smolinsky said to me: "I need a nurse to help me. You will be my assistant instead of going on this kind of mission." After that I worked in the dispensary. I rode a horse to check if the dispensary was in a secure hiding place.[22] This dispensary was for the very badly wounded. Nobody in the partisans was sick with ordinary illness. The doctor amputated legs and arms with an ordinary saw. In the middle of the night, I would go there to look at how they were, to cook something for them, change their dressings, make them comfortable. Then I would come back to the camp and talk over the problems with the doctor. He would give me the medications that we got through our connections with Moscow. The Communists trusted the Jewish partisans. When airplanes flew in from Moscow with parachute drops of medication or very important news, Jewish partisans went to pick them up.

There was an epidemic of typhus once in the partisan camp, and as soon as I got everybody well, I got sick. But nobody died of illness in spite of the conditions. A few wounded died. We had a cemetery. We had even a clubhouse. After the missions were done, we went to the clubhouse; we read, the Russian *garmushka* was played. We danced.

We Jews knew when the Jewish holidays were, but we didn't have any means of observing them. We knew when *Pesah* was. Nobody ate bread on *Pesah*. We knew that we had to be very careful with the Russians. There were partisans who were killed because they were accused of being spies. It was very cruel; they were shot. In our group, every Jewish partisan was well treated and respected because we never said "no" to a mission no matter how big, how small, how dangerous. We were always saved for the most dangerous missions. For sleeping on the guard post, the punishment was death. That was the law of the camp. Because you were asleep, the whole camp could be killed. One day a young Jewish boy either fell asleep or they told him that he was asleep. We started to beg them, "So few of us are alive. He's just a young boy. Nothing happened to the *otrad*. Please let him live!" And they did.

Once my husband was sent out on a big mission. In the back of someone's mind was the hope that he wouldn't return. One of the officers made a pass at me. A guy with whom I was working came to me and said, "Tonight, don't sleep in your regular place. Go to where all the girls are sleeping." I didn't, so he got mad at me, and he sent me to the Kirowsky family *otrad*, where they had a special place for families with children. I worked there as a nurse with the doctor's permission. There were sick children, sick people. The Russians were afraid to harm me because I had a husband and because my brother-in-law, Tuvia, was a very influential person in the *otrad*. He got a lot of medals. The Germans offered a big reward for him, dead or alive. They knew who he was because he came in the middle of the day and shot at them in public places, like at the airport, where Germans sat at their posts. He killed them without any warning.

We lived like this till the end of the summer 1944. The day when we were liberated there was a very big fight. I was alone with our part of the *otrad* without my husband or brother-in-law. A lot of boys went out on a mission, and they didn't return. News came to me that Paul was killed. His brother came back from a mission. Immediately, he asked me, "Where is Feivel (Paul)?" I said, "Paul is not here. They told us that he probably got killed." But soon he returned with the group. After the liberation our child was born, 1945, in Pruzhany. Then things got very hot for us. My brother-in-law Tuvia got arrested by the Russians and was sentenced to death. He was accused of being a spy, even though he was so highly decorated.[23] His parents were rich; this was "evidence." They found a Polish book in his possession. This was "evidence." It was enough to arrest him, and he got a death sentence. By the time we found out about him his sentence was changed to a life term in Siberia. When he walked out of the courthouse, an officer was sitting at the desk and asked him, "What is your last wish?" Tuvia said, "I don't really have any last wishes, but one thing I would like. I have very valuable medals: Stalin's medal and the Red Cross medal. I would like them sent to my hometown." The officer said: "I don't see that you are such a spy, such an enemy of our country. Sign this paper." Instead of death, he sent him to Siberia. When we heard about it, we started to search for him. We hired a lawyer from Moscow, and he said to us: "Are you crazy? Your brother was sentenced for spying; he is in Siberia. Your sister from the United States sent you papers to come to the United States. With this combination of events, you'll be on the list for Siberia too." Then he told us that we had better do something for ourselves. We forged documents, and a friend of ours gave us his truck to take us to the railroad station to get out of Russia.

The Brydbord family reached Lodz, Poland, and then were smuggled across the border to Berlin. After a series of mishaps, including the arrest of their baby daughter, they finally reached the American zone of occupation, where they had to go through two more marriage ceremonies in order to obtain the proper documents for immigration to the United States. Paul's brother was eventually liberated from Siberia and immigrated to Israel.

—Interviewed by Collette Krause, February 28, 1986, and Rachel Licht,
October 9, 1986

Marysia Warman

Bronislawa Feinmesser was born in 1919 in Warsaw, the third and youngest child in an assimilated family.[1] She remembers little of her father, who traveled a lot on business and died when she was seven years old. The family lived in a non-Jewish neighborhood; Polish, not Yiddish, was spoken in their home, and she attended a Polish primary school. Bronka chose to attend a Jewish Gymnasium because of its academic excellence. She did not continue her studies beyond Gymnasium level but took over the management of her grandfather's store in order to assist her mother to provide for her family.

Bronka describes a climate of growing anti-Semitism in the 1930s, with epithets and stones hurled through the windows of the family stores. When Warsaw was occupied by the Germans, Bronka and her mother transferred ownership of the stores to Poles whom they knew, thereby hoping to retain their source of livelihood, but the Poles never provided any of the promised income.

When the ghetto was established, Dr. Braude-Hellerowa, director of the Berson and Bauman children's hospital,[2] whom I knew very well, hired me as a telephonist.[3] I lived in the hospital. I slept in the operating room on the operating table. I became very, very friendly with almost all the personnel. In the evening, after my work in the office, I stayed in the hospital, and I worked as a nurse, although I was not qualified or registered, but I worked with the children, giving them food, changing their hospital clothes, even giving injections, massages, various things. Whatever was needed. As an employee of the hospital I was immunized against typhus, but I caught it. I was moved to the adult hospital, and thanks to the injection, my friend and I were the only ones among forty typhus patients to recover.

As the Germans reduced the area of the ghetto the hospital had to move several times. Finally it moved to the *Umschlagplatz*, where all the Jewish people went to the trains, and all the children were taken to the camp, to Treblinka. It didn't look like a hospital; it was in a school building; conditions were terrible.

At the beginning, in '41 and part of '42, there was a nursing school and medical school in the ghetto.[4] I attended this medical school for two years. The head of this medical school was Dr. Professor Hirszfeld.[5] I studied medicine, anatomy, different subjects. We had books, lectures. The lectures were given in private apartments; it was informal. There was no laboratory, only lectures. I went because I was interested. I was *very* interested. Of course this was a medical school without any rights, you know, it was underground.

I wasn't in touch with many people. I was busy working all day long. My mother and my sister lived far away from the hospital in the ghetto. Once or twice a week I went to see my mother and sister. On the way, through the ghetto streets, I saw plenty of people, mostly children, lying in the street, swollen with hunger, begging for food, or dead, covered with newspaper. There were some stores; I bought food with my salary from the hospital and brought some to my mother and sister.

The director of this children's hospital, Dr. Anna Braude-Hellerowa, was absolutely committed to helping the children of the ghetto swollen from hunger, dying on the street, transported at the last moment to the hospital. Some of them recovered; most of them died in the hospital.[6] The children, especially from Orthodox families, hardly spoke Polish, and communication with such sick children was very, very difficult. Besides typhus, the majority of the children were dying of hunger.[7] It was terrible.

Dr. Braude-Hellerowa established this hospital many years before the war. She was widowed long before the war, and I can compare her devotion to this hospital and to these children with the devotion of Janusz Korczak[8] to his children, even though they fought a little bit, Korczak and Braude-Hellerowa, about the food, about the children, about admission to the hospital from the Korczak orphanage. But Dr. Braude-Hellerowa was an absolutely fantastic person. She was completely devoted to the children, even the children who were too sick without any hope of recovery. The children were the most important thing for her. She didn't leave them until the end.[9] A hiding place was prepared for her by friends on the Aryan side, but she refused. About her death there are different stories. As far as I recall, she went together with the children from the hospital to the trains on the *Umschlagplatz*. But her nephew told me that she was found in the cellar and that she was shot in this cellar.[10] The basic truth is that to the last moment she remained in the hospital. She was an absolutely unusual person.

Marek Edelman was working as a courier for the hospital.[11] He was in touch with different Jewish organizations in the ghetto. He took messages or correspondence from the hospital, whatever was needed. At that time he wasn't a doctor. He studied after the war in Lodz.[12]

We had a commissar of the hospital, Dr. Waclaw Skonieczny, who was appointed by the Germans.[13] He was a very nice, very honest man. He was probably a *Volksdeutscher*. Thanks to his help with medicine for the hospital, with food, with different things, the hospital could exist.[14] My friend, the head nurse, Debora Keilson, was very close to him. I got a pass from him to leave the ghetto to go to the Aryan side. I don't remember whose idea it was. Maybe I spoke to him; maybe the head nurse spoke to him. With that pass I went from the ghetto to the Aryan side and back. The pass allowed me to do things for the hospital on the Aryan side. When I left the ghetto, I was very elegantly dressed; I had a winter coat with fur cuffs. On the Aryan side I pulled down my arm band so it was inside the cuff, and nobody noticed it.[15]

On the Aryan side I organized and looked for apartments and shelters for our people on the Aryan side,[16] bringing Aryan papers back to the ghetto, transferring documents and different things. When I came back to the ghetto I brought some food, arms only once or twice, because I was searched by the Germans or the Jewish police to see what I was bringing.

I put things in different places, in my pockets. I put some bread on top of the bag that I carried. My document, issued by the German authorities, allowed me to leave the ghetto, so although I was searched, they were not very thorough, and I didn't usually smuggle weapons. Today I would be very scared. At that time when I was twenty something; I wasn't scared. I wanted to do it. I wanted to be active, to help people, and I had my group that needed me to do this.

On July 22, 1942, they gathered the population of the Warsaw ghetto in the front of the *Judenrat*.[17] Dr. Braude-Hellerowa got a few "life passes" for all the employees of the hospital, which meant that they wouldn't be sent to the *Umschlagplatz* and that they had a right to live in the ghetto.[18] It is very difficult to say exactly, but for approximately two hundred employees of the hospital, doctors, nurses, supporting personnel, and so on, she got around twenty-five to thirty of these passes. How can one person decide who has a right to live and who will die?[19] It was an enormously difficult decision, but she had to distribute those tickets of life.[20] The *Umschlagplatz*, where all the ghetto people were gathered, had an entrance with guards, and only the people with those passes had the right to go outside this place. All other people were taken to the trains. Dr. Braude-Hellerowa didn't give those life passes to her closest colleagues, to her friends, to the doctors, to many people who used to work for the hospital. Her decision, which was very characteristic of her, was to give those passes to the youngest ones.[21] Among others, I got this pass, although I didn't have an important position in this hospital. Marek Edelman also got this pass. In my opinion, this was a heroic decision. Very heroic. She didn't even give her family members any passes! Her nephew recalled that at this time, he was on the *Umschlagplatz* with his parents, and suddenly somebody held his hand and forcibly took him to a cellar somewhere. It was Marek, Marek Edelman, who knew him. No one in Dr. Braude-Hellerowa's family got the ticket, no. She didn't keep one for herself either.

As a young hospital employee, I got the ticket, the life ticket. My mother and my sister were taken to the *Umschlagplatz* with the others. I believed that if I would take two white hospital gowns, I would be able to rescue my mother and my sister by claiming that they were patients in the hospital. I went to the *Umschlagplatz*, and while looking for my sister and my mother, I met my cousin with her son. They knelt and held my skirt, didn't want me to go further, asking for rescue, asking me to remove them from the *Umschlagplatz*. I couldn't take more people, only two, and I was concentrating so on rescuing my mother and my sister that somehow I went further. I never found my mother, but I found my sister. My sister had a boyfriend who was a Jewish policeman, and he protected her, but he couldn't get her outside the *Umschlagplatz*. When I found her I gave her this white gown, and then I started to look around for my cousin, but I couldn't find her. She was probably taken right away to the train. This ends the story of my immediate family.

After the *Akcja* of the twenty-second of July I didn't have any more work to do in the hospital. Most of the personnel went to the *Umschlagplatz* and got killed. We knew what was going on; there was no work for me. For doctors, for Dr. Szwajger, there was a little bit, but for me, nothing. At that point I still had my pass to go outside the ghetto. Although I still had things to do in the ghetto, we realized that our work was not finished, that I would be more helpful on the Aryan side than in the ghetto. Then the Germans recalled all the passes, and Dr. Skonieczny asked me to return my pass to him. That was when I decided to leave the ghetto. I told him that I would give the pass back to him on the Aryan side. I met him on a street corner on the Aryan side. I didn't have any hiding place prepared, and I wondered where to go.

Dr. Skonieczny lived outside the ghetto with his wife and two children. He couldn't offer me a place in his own apartment, but suddenly he remembered that he had the key to an office where I could spend a night or two. I had to promise to leave the office very early in the morning before the personnel came to work. I didn't find a place to stay immediately, and I spent a second night in this German office. Then I started to work as a typist in an office on the Aryan side. I rented a small room, and I established contact with Antek Zuckerman[22] and later with Marek, after the ghetto uprising. After a few weeks I had to quit my office work because so many people escaped from the ghetto and I had to place them on the Aryan side.

The Polish underground provided Bronka with the name of a deceased woman and the address of the parish where she was baptized. With the documents she obtained from the parish priest she was able to obtain genuine identity documents from the German authorities. She assumed the name Maria Radlow, which became her underground pseudonym: Marysia with the blue eyes.[23]

My friend, Dr. Adina Blady Szwajger (Inka), who wrote very detailed accounts of the children in the children's hospital and her experiences as a doctor, left the ghetto a few months later than I did. In this last hospital on the *Umschlagplatz*, she knew that all the children would be sent to the death train, to Treblinka. She somehow got access to morphine, yes, and because she had promised the children that nothing would happen to them, she gave them injections to put them to sleep in their beds, to die, instead of sending them to the death camps.[24]

How did this come about? One of our nurses from the Jewish adults' hospital on Czyste Street had a mother who was a patient in the hospital on the *Umschlagplatz*. The mother was very sick and couldn't walk, and it was very difficult for the daughter to give a morphine injection to her own mother. The daughter came to Dr. Szwajger and asked her to give her mother an injection to put her to sleep, and after consideration, Dr. Szwajger did it.[25] Later on came the idea that she could do the same for the children instead of sending them to their deaths.[26]

Somebody who was there[27] brought the news about Treblinka and the gassing, that all the people were dying. I don't remember when I first heard about it, but it was very, very early. I was already going back and forth to the Aryan side. I believed it because one man somehow managed to get out and brought the news that all the people were gassed. He saw it.

I was not aware of preparations for an uprising. It was a surprise for me. I knew that arms, revolvers, were being smuggled into the ghetto. But that was really secret. Nobody knew about that except the people who took part in organizing and preparing for the ghetto uprising.

Somehow I managed to get my sister out of the ghetto. She had light hair, a straight nose; she looked more Aryan than I. She didn't look at all Jewish. I got her a false document, and I rented her a room in Zoliborz on the Aryan side. She was very scared of everything, and that was the *worst* thing for survival because the look in your eyes, if you were scared, betrayed everything. But I told her that with her looks, she could really walk through the streets and nobody would bother her, and she could live in this room, not even hiding, going outside; she could survive.

I started to work for the Bund organization.[28] My duties were: finding hiding places, organizing false documents, distributing money, paying rent to the landlords; these were my main tasks. After a few months, Dr. Szwajger also left the ghetto,[29] and she was also involved with the Bund organization. The two of us lived officially in one very small room, with a gas burner for cooking, at Miodowa Street 24, with an outside lavatory, not a bathroom but a public lavatory in the corridor. Before the war the building was some kind of higher court.[30] There were corridors and plenty of rooms on each corridor, which were rented. Our room was the location for the Bund organization gatherings.[31] When these gatherings took place we girls (Inka and I) didn't take part; we left the apartment. They told us when we should come back. The meetings were secret. In this room we stored files, documents, underground literature, and plenty of money that we distributed.[32] It was decided that in this room we would not hide people. We would follow all the conspiracy rules.[33] But it wasn't always possible because sometimes if someone was without a roof for the night we couldn't send them out on the street after curfew; we had to hide them. We tried not to, but if it was absolutely necessary, we had to.[34]

We were out in the city from very early morning until the curfew.[35] We were always exhausted, completely, because every day we were in danger of being recognized. Remember that I was born in Warsaw, and I used to live in the center of the city, and plenty of people knew me. This was not a question of Jewish looks or language. Thanks to my language and looks, I could pass easily; until I met somebody who could denounce me, I could walk around freely.

Many times our friends from the Jewish Fighting Organization came after curfew to discuss many things, to help, to plan for the next day or days.[36] We had to sit quietly and talk in this apartment. Then they stayed for the night. It was necessary because they couldn't go outside in the street. We used to drink plenty of vodka, plenty, but we never were drunk.[37] It was necessary in order to continue our work. I cooked in this apartment, fed them [laughing]. We had in this room a record player, and all evening while we were talking the record player would play on and on and on so that nobody would hear what we were talking about, what we were doing; nobody would know that others were in the room. The worst thing for our guests was going to the bathroom. They had to look in the corridor to see if somebody was in there or in the corridor; then they slept in there. Fortunately, it was directly across from our door. We were considered by our neighbors to be "light girls," you know, who were meeting many men.[38] Maybe they suspected that we were prostitutes; I don't know what they thought, but that was how it looked. To create a cover for our activities, my future husband, who left the ghetto in January 1943 and had a false identity, came quite often to our room when we were not home and put flowers outside our door.

I have to tell you about the people who were helping us. There were many, many different kinds of people. There were Christian people who were very religious, and they thought that they were doing what God told them to do. There were people who wanted money because they didn't have any source of income to live on except their apartment. For example, women whose husbands were in Germany in the prisoner-of-war camps didn't have anything to eat. The superintendent of the building was a drinker, always drunk, always drunk. But he was working for the *Armia Krajowa*,[39] and when we were in urgent need to hide someone for one or two nights, he always took them and hid them under the staircase. The hiding place was very small and very dirty, but he never refused. He considered that that was his duty, to save the people. We were afraid because he was drunk that he might slip some words about our people, but it never happened, never happened. He suspected that I was Jewish, yes. I didn't openly tell him, but he knew that I was working for a Jewish organization. It wasn't said openly, but it was not necessary because he surely recognized that people whom I located there were Jewish. He was shot in a German raid on his building because of his activities for the *AK*, not because of Jews because at that time nobody was there, and they had an eye on him about his underground activities for the Polish organization.

One woman, the wife of a Polish officer who was in a camp in Germany, took a lot of money from us for each person. She fed them, she hid them. She fed them very poorly, but somehow she was reliable. She also told us that in the ruins there were two Jewish boys, hiding and hungry. She spotted them in the neighborhood and gave us the tip that somebody had to take care of them. We had an agreement with her. There were many people already in her apartment. For each person we paid a lot of money. The Jewish Fighting Organization agreed to pay for these two boys, and the next day they were taken to her apartment, and she took care of them. She didn't tip us off because she wanted to hide them, no, no. It was simply her human feeling that they were in very much danger. When she realized that somebody knew that she was hiding Jews, she relocated all the people hiding in her apartment in different places, with her friends for a few days. For those few days she invited plenty of people to spread the news that she was living alone. After a few days she took the Jews back. I had very mixed feelings about her. After the war she came to me, and she asked me for certification that she rescued Jews. That was true, but the other part was that she took a lot of money. I didn't know what to do. I didn't want to have this on my conscience because I realized that somehow she did this for money. I spoke to some people who were working in the Jewish committee in Warsaw after the war, and I told them. "You decide, I can't." They gave her the certification.

We needed a lot of apartments to hide people who were escaping from the ghetto. I had to rent an apartment for the organization headquarters, so I pretended that I was getting married. For this apartment I needed a second identity and a second set of documents. I went to rent the second apartment together with my friend, Marysia Sawicka, a Polish Socialist woman who rescued many Jews, many children.[40] We pretended to be sisters. The apartment was at 18 Leszno Street.

During the time that the ghetto was burning, my sister knew that I was going to get another document in another name. I wasn't afraid to go to the official authority to get this document because it was enough to have a birth certificate of a dead person, which was easy to get from the church. With that you had to go to the German authority to get the *Kennkarte*. When she learned that I needed the second set of documents in another name for this new apartment, she insisted that she also wanted a second set, or she would not survive. But she didn't have the courage to go to the German authority to receive a new document. Together with her was Dr. Keilson from the children's hospital, who also was afraid to go officially to get the papers. We were in contact with a man from the Polish underground organization who was making the false documents. We all met in the cafe of Dr. Keilson's friend: I was there with Dr. Szwajger and my sister and Dr. Keilson. We were supposed to meet the man who had promised to bring the documents for my sister and Dr. Keilson.

We had an address of an apartment not far away from this cafe, and because this man was not on time, Dr. Szwajger and I decided that meanwhile we would go and look at this apartment. We told the remaining people that we would come back in a half hour. We took the tram, saw the apartment, and immediately tried to go back to the cafe. As we came by tram to the corner of the street we saw that the street was completely closed. We saw a big German car in front of the cafe, and they were taking people into the car. Later on we learned that they took everybody from this cafe to Pawiak; that was the prison during the war for Jewish people. This is the worst part. That man who was supposed to prepare the false document, as I mentioned, was in the underground organization, and he was carrying a gun. The Germans knew whom to approach; they killed him right away in the cafe, and the remaining people they took to the Pawiak prison. Later on I tried to find some sign of life of my sister, but without success. Dr. Keilson survived. Many years later she told me that my sister was called for interrogation. I can only suspect that she was very scared and weak and that she simply admitted that she was Jewish. Dr. Keilson was never called for interrogation. I tried to contact some people who took money to get information. They took money, but I got no information. Dr. Szwajger and I were lucky that we left the cafe for a short time because if we had been there we would also be dead.[41]

Sometimes I had trouble because I grew up in a Polish neighborhood. Plenty of people knew me from childhood or from when I helped my mother in the store. They were the most dangerous because they could recognize me.[42] Among other people whom I was taking care of were a very old couple, parents of Hela and Debora Keilson, who was the head nurse in our ghetto hospital. I rented an apartment for them in Swider, outside Warsaw, where they survived the war.

I had to take the train to go there to visit them. It was in the evening before the curfew, and when I got out of the train, I noticed a man who knew me from childhood. He came over to me, and he said, "We are going to the Gestapo." I asked him, "Why?" "Because you are Jewish." "No, you made a mistake. I don't know you, and I won't go with you." "So, let's not go to the Gestapo; we'll go to the hotel. We'll spend the night together." Near the station there was an open candy store. I went into the store, and the man followed me. There were two men inside, and I told them, "Listen, this man is accusing me of being Jewish, and he proposed to me to go either to the Gestapo or to the hotel. Please tell him to go away!" The man got a little scared, and he went out of the store. I waited there for a while, maybe half an hour, maybe an hour, and I asked them, "I'm afraid of this man. It is dark, it is curfew. . . . Can I ask you to go with me?" And one of the men went with me. Of course I didn't go to the place where those old people were living, but I told him, "OK, I live here. Thank you very much." I hid in the woods for some time, and then I went to them. I'm giving you only some examples because I have many such stories.

One day we were on the bus, and we were in a hurry because an operation was scheduled for Kazik Ratheiser[43] to remove his circumcision. It was going to be in the doctor's office, and we had to assist the doctor, and so we didn't notice who else was on the bus. Someone who knew Inka must have recognized her. When we left the house where the operation took place, there was a policeman. "What happened?" we asked. "Oh, somebody told me that you were Jewish." He took us to the entrance of a building. He took our documents; he asked hundreds of questions, where we lived and so on. He put our documents in his pockets, and he said, "OK, we are going to the Gestapo." It just happened that I was wearing new shoes, very uncomfortable. He was walking with us, and at one point I told him, "Listen, I am not going further because my foot hurts me very, very much. I can't walk. Take a taxi or something else, and then we will go." At that moment he looked at me and at Inka and saluted us and told us, "I'm sorry, this is a real mistake," and he returned the documents to us. As he went off we asked him, "What happened that you . . . " "Oh, somebody told me that you were Jewish." Today I am completely different, but at that time I had *hutzpah*.

Inka and I didn't hide; we lived officially in our apartment. But we hid documents and money in different places in the room, in the table, under the mattress. Different places. I had a very unpleasant experience in that period of time with some of the people I took care of. Many people were escaping the ghetto and didn't have anywhere to go, like my friend who was a nurse in the hospital. First, when I had the pass, I rented a room in an apartment for her, and then I transferred her possessions. I bought food for her, and she had everything she needed, but she was very scared. Then one day a friend of hers exited the ghetto, and I didn't have anywhere to place her. I went to the first woman, and I told her, "Listen, I have to bring Zosia here. I don't have any other place. I can't take her to our place because you know that we are not supposed to hide anybody in our apartment." They knew each other very well. And she told me, "Over my dead body." Then I told her, although it was very hard, "If you refuse, if you feel that you won't be safe, I can't do anything. But I promise you that I won't come to you any-more. You'll have to manage by yourself," and then I left, and I didn't go to that apartment anymore. I placed Zosia as a servant in the house owned by the wife of a Polish officer who was a prisoner of war in Germany. Both women survived, but that was very, very difficult.

I had different places to hide people. Private places, like a bunker that I organized in a very small wooden house on Rakowiecka Street. The owner of this house was the dispatcher of the trams. He worked at the last stop of the tram in an almost deserted, empty area. I contacted him and discussed preparing a hiding place under his house for six people. Of course he took money for this. He dug out a large space under the house. On two walls he built six plank beds, three on each wall. The entrance to the hiding place was through the metal plate at the foot of the tiled heating stove on the ground floor of his house. The landlady prepared meals for the six people who were hiding. Tuvia (Tadek) Borzykowski[44] and Stefan Grayek were in this group of six people who had escaped the ghetto to the forests and needed to find a safe refuge.

During the ghetto uprising I was already on the Aryan side. The only thing I could do was take care of the people who escaped from the ghetto, to find some place to hide them, to make documents for them, and to give them money. I was told about them by Antek, by Marek. Until they crossed the border of the ghetto nobody knew they were coming. Somehow, they were in touch with the people from the underground. Information about avail-able rooms would reach me through different people. I always had open ears for any possibility to rent a room that could serve as a hiding place. Dr. Szwa-jger and I were still living together, but we each had our separate assign-ments to take care of a number of people. I did have enough food. I was getting some money from the organization for our expenses. For example, we couldn't meet with the people anywhere in the city and walk openly through the street. So maybe ten times a day we were in various cafes as meeting places. We needed money for this.[45]

Almost at the end, before the Warsaw uprising, the apartment of the heads of the organization, Antek Zuckerman, Marek Edelman, and several other people, was in danger. I was in touch with them. They asked me to transfer them. It was not simple. It was very hard to organize something, to transfer them from the previous apartment. We decided that I would make all the arrangements. I used the excuse that I was going to be married, and together with my "sister," Marysia Sawicka, we rented an apartment at 18 Leszno Street.[46] This apartment hid eight people, mostly from the command of the ZOB: Marek, Antek, Zivia, Rivka Steiner, and Bernard Goldstein, who was very active in the Bund organization.[47] Who else? My future husband played a role as my fiancé, and he came every day to me, to this apartment. Sometimes he also stayed there for the night, and it was relatively safe.

When the Polish uprising broke out,[48] Antek and Marek went to the higher officers in the Polish army[49] and asked them to take us as a group, as the Jewish Fighting Organization.[50] They refused.[51] "Individually, please come, but not as a group; we won't give you any commander." So they went to the *Armia Ludowa*,[52] and they took us as a group. They gave us a commanding officer. First we fought in the Old Town, hiding at night in the cellar together. There was very heavy fighting. We had ammunition, guns. I didn't fight; the men fought. The women didn't fight. There were maybe six or eight women. There was heavy, heavy bombarding, and the old city was leveled to the ground.[53]

Then we decided that there was no sense in remaining there, and somehow they found a guide to lead us to the Zoliborz quarter of Warsaw through the sewers.[54] The water was going with such speed and rising higher and higher.[55] It was very difficult even for a strong person to stand or walk. I had a bundle with my personal things, some photographs, some documents, and one moment I fell under the water; I was drowning. My husband, who was very, very tall, held my arm and he pulled . . . He pulled me up, and I dropped my bundle and lost all my documents and photographs, and by then the whole group was far away. We didn't know where we were, where the exit was, but somehow we found it. When we came to Zoliborz, it was so beautiful and peaceful. We thought the quiet would last forever.

At the beginning, we were located in some houses. The men took part in the fighting; the women did not. They tended to some wounded people. My husband was hit.[56] He was wounded, and it was very difficult. Terrible. We were there almost a month, and at the beginning of October we learned that the uprising was finished.[57] The *Armia Krajowa* surrendered, and its troops were treated as prisoners of war. We didn't know what to do. As members of *Armia Ludowa*, and as Jews, we were not covered by the terms of surrender. We tried to go to the other bank of the Vistula where the Russian army was already. We were gathered on the shore of the Vistula, waiting for a boat or some help to cross, but there wasn't any. We had to make a decision.

With our Jewish faces, we needed a hiding place. In that quarter of Warsaw, I had a friend, a Jewish doctor, an older woman, whom I located in a small house.[58] She was living there with her friends, and I visited, taking care of them. This doctor was very afraid. We went to the house where the doctor was hiding, which was familiar to me. The owner of the house was away; only the grandmother of the owner was there with Dr. Tosia Goliborska and her friend Sabina. There were fifteen of us, including our Polish AL commander. We decided as a group, with the agreement of Dr. Goliborska, that we would hide in the cellar. This cellar had a wooden shelf with glass jars on it behind which there was a space where we could sit. There were Marek, Antek, Zivia, my husband, Tuvia Borzykowski, Leah Silverstein, Zosia (Regina Frydman), Yulek Fiszgrund, Tosia Goliborska, and I, and there was also an older Jewish woman, Stefa, who was working in the hospital. We decided that we would sit in the back and that the four old women would be in front, as an excuse for sounds in the cellar. They also lived in the cellar, but they used the beds openly. We were behind the wooden shelf; it was impossible for us to stretch our legs or to lie down on the floor to sleep.[59]

Then there was no more water for so many people.[60] After five days Antek and Marek suggested that five people, including the Polish commander,[61] leave the bunker during the night with their revolvers and look for another place. Then five people together with this officer went somewhere else, to another cellar. They all survived.[62] Ten people remained in our cellar.

After a few days, the German army took a position on the Vistula in front of the window of the house where we were hiding. We heard their conversation, and for people who understood Yiddish it was not difficult to understand what they were talking about. Then we got actual news from their conversation.

It is very difficult to describe the whole six weeks in there.[63] There was a kitchen in the next cellar, and during the night we would cook food scavenged from other houses, and of course the Germans smelled the food. Several times the Germans came down to the cellar to look. Fortunately, the kitchen was next door, and the Germans did not see how much food was being prepared. Between all those private houses, because of the war, there were trenches that we used as passages to several houses. The houses were all empty because the whole population of Warsaw was evacuated by order of the Germans. Warsaw was a ghost town. Nothing.

About the water . . . I went with my friend through the cellars of those houses collecting water. I took a container with me. Sometimes the water was very dirty. At night we went out to the garden to take care of our natural needs. . . . Later on we couldn't go outside to the garden, and the only place we could do it was far away from us, but it was smelly. We had to kill the dog there because he was barking.[64] The doctor who was hiding with us tried to commit suicide with some cyanide tablets. How angry I was at her! How could she do something like that, knowing that we all were in danger? What were we supposed to do with her body? But we gave her an injection, and somehow she survived.

My husband was wounded. He was in the cellar with us, and he would cough and make noise, and we had to put the pillow over his mouth so that nobody would hear. It was very difficult to take care of him. We were not clean. His wounds got infected; he was feverish, very sick.

One day it was the turn of Lodzia (Leah Silverstein) to look for water. On the way she met German officers, and they asked her, "What are you doing here?" "I am taking care of four older women who are very sick and couldn't leave this place." The Germans went to the place where the four women were lying down, and they decided to come back with a horse and wagon, and after a few hours they took the four "Polish" women, together with Lodzia, from our group, and they were transferred to Pruszkow, the camp outside Warsaw, but they released them.[65] But Lodzia alerted the people in Pruszkow who were in charge of our situation.[66] Dr. Anna Margolis (Marek Edelman's mother-in-law) was working in this camp. When she was transferred another woman doctor came in her place. As she was leaving, she told this doctor, "Listen, if somebody from Zoliborz, from Promyka Street, appears here, please do everything, whatever is possible, to release them from the camp and give my address. Because of lack of food, because of terrible illness, they are in a terrible state; they can't survive any longer."

One evening Antek and Marek, as our commanders, decided that we couldn't stay any longer in our dangerous position because the old women were no longer there.[67] Antek and Marek said they would go during the night to the inhabited places where the people from Warsaw were evacuated. But I knew that would be suicidal. I told them, "Listen, we know that around the house, and around the German positions in the front lines, there are several hiding places, tunnels and barbed wires. You can't go because you don't know where they are. It is dangerous because at night you won't see anything; you don't know where the inhabited places are, and you will get caught." We made a deal that I would go with Zosia,[68] pretending to be civilians returning to the city to get their personal possessions.

We left on Sunday, six o'clock in the morning, with the promise that when we encountered inhabited places, we would come back and take them. We agreed with the remaining people, with Antek and Marek, that if we didn't come back by Wednesday noon, then they would follow the previous plan, but with the promise that they would take my husband with them. He was very sick, but they promised to take him. If not, I said, I would not go; I would stay with him and with this doctor who wanted to commit suicide, whom they didn't care about, and they could do what they wanted. They promised, and we left.

Zosia also had very good looks. We were so hungry. We hardly had strength, certainly not for carrying possessions, but we had to have some excuse for being in that area. We didn't know the terrain. We saw the Polish cemetery, Powazki, which is adjacent to the Jewish cemetery. We went there and walked through this cemetery, and then we heard Germans driving on the street nearby, and we knew that this was German territory. But where was the exit from the cemetery? Finally we found the exit. We went to the main street outside the cemetery, and we saw plenty of cars with Germans driving, and they were afraid of fleeing people, and they passed us by, no reaction to us. They were scared. From the distance we saw the exit from Warsaw with the German guards, and we went straight to them. I didn't have any documents because I lost them in the sewer, but Zosia had some documents. She knew Yiddish, so she could communicate in German.

There were two *gendarmes* at the end of the main street. We went straight to them and told them the story that we had come back to Warsaw to take our things because we didn't have any clothing, anything, and now we wanted to go back to where we were living. They bought this story, and they gave us directions how to reach the inhabited areas. We went as they told us, and suddenly, on the right-hand side, we saw some people near a building, and we thought that we were already in an inhabited area. We went there, and there were plenty of Germans and horses with wagons, and they ordered us to go to the second or third floor to carry down the belongings of an old couple who were being evacuated. We were absolutely exhausted. . . . We couldn't tell them that we didn't have strength. Then we went, and we barely managed to load those belongings on the wagon.

The Germans told us, "Come sit on the wagon." We didn't want to sit down because we thought there was still some possibility that we could escape, but it was impossible. They didn't let us, and then the whole caravan, we, the Germans, and this old couple, went to the Pruszkow camp. This was the transfer camp for Poles who were being sent to Germany for forced labor. We had some money with us, and we tried to bribe some Ukrainian soldiers to let us go. They took the money, but they didn't do anything. We hid one night in a train station, and we were very worried because we only had until Wednesday. We had to get out! We spent the night on the train platform hiding behind a large wooden bin.

The next day was Monday. We saw a very nice-looking doctor; we didn't know if she was Polish or German, but we didn't have anything to lose. We went to her, and we told her, "Listen, doctor. . . . We have to leave the camp." She was Polish; she understood. She told us, "Girls, you will come to my office in the evening." OK. We hid because there was a transport. Then we came back to her office, and she asked us, "You came from Warsaw?" "Yes." "From Zoliborz?" "Yes," "From Promyka Street?" "Yes," I told her, and I was shaking. "What about the others?" she asked us. She had been told by Dr. Anna Margolis, "If somebody from Warsaw comes here to the camp, do everything, whatever possible, to let them leave the camp." She gave us passes to leave the camp. It was already evening, curfew, and she told us, "Listen, you have to hurry"; people couldn't be outside. She gave us the address of Dr. Margolis, and we left the camp.

We were completely exhausted, you understand, and it was a long, long way. We rushed. We rushed about two or three miles, and we got there after the curfew. Several people were living together with Dr. Margolis. They looked at us as if we were ghosts. They boiled water and filled up the *bania*, and they told us, "Take off everything." There was plenty of water, and it was hot, and it was, ah, what a pleasure it was! They burned all our clothes, and they gave us clean clothes. They fed us, and Dr. Margolis took care not only of us but of the plan for how to rescue the others. It was already Monday evening.

Because I didn't have any documents and this was the time when Germans took people from the street to send to Germany to forced labor, they didn't let me out. Absolutely not. Dr. Margolis took action. She went to Dr. Stanislaw Swital, the director of the Red Cross hospital nearby. She told him that she knew that some Polish fighters were in Warsaw, in very big danger, and she asked him to send people with stretchers to go there and rescue them. She did not mention that we were Jewish. The whole action was scheduled for Wednesday morning.[69]

The only person who knew the place where Antek and Marek and my husband and the others were hiding was Ala Edelman, the daughter of Dr. Margolis, because she used to visit Dr. Goliborska.[70] She guided a group consisting of Dr. Zylkiewicz, his wife, Maria, and Janusz Oscka. Warsaw was empty; there was no one to ask.[71] This was a miracle, what happened. They left very early in the morning on Wednesday, and they came to the place, to that house near the Vistula five minutes after twelve. This was very important because the Germans were having lunch, and they left their position at twelve o'clock. If the whole action had been five or ten minutes earlier, everybody would have been killed.

I wasn't there; they did not let me out of the camp because I had no papers. What I am telling you is beyond human imagination. They had two stretchers with them. They put Marek on one stretcher because he looked very Semitic, dark, and my husband on the second stretcher.[72] He was very sick. My husband wore German boots, and he was very tall. The rest of the people were carrying their belongings and also on foot. They went to the German checkpoint carrying Marek first, and the guard shouted, "He's a Jew," and Maria Zylkiewicz, who knew German very well, shouted, "No, this is not a Jew. He has typhus." The Germans were very afraid of catching typhus, and they didn't wait for the answer. Our people went through with Marek, and the second was my husband, who didn't look Jewish, but he was very tall, and he wore German boots. Again, "Oh, this is a bandit." And our people said that he also had typhus. The Germans were scared, and they didn't wait for the answer, and our people brought them to the Red Cross hospital.[73]

Dr. Margolis and Ala had arranged everything. The whole group spent one night in the hospital, and the next day they left the hospital, and a place where they could hide was already organized. The only person who stayed in the hospital, who was really very, very sick, was my husband. He stayed in this hospital ten days or so.

My friends didn't let me go out. I couldn't visit him in the hospital. Dr. Margolis had a place in a village, and when he was ready to leave the hospital she offered my husband and me a place to hide until liberation, January 17, 1945.

After liberation Marysia and her husband retrieved Mr. Warman's daughter Anya from the convent where she had been hidden and went to Lodz,

where they lived with Dr. Margolis in the apartment she had vacated
when the Germans occupied the city. In 1947 their son, Jerzy, was born,
and then they returned to Warsaw. Marysia worked first for a newspaper
and then for a scientific publisher. Her husband worked as an attorney
and then became a justice of the supreme court of Poland. He died in
1965. In 1968 all the Jewish employees of Marysia's firm were dismissed
during a government-sanctioned anti-Semitic purge, and in 1970
Marysia came to the United States with her son. She worked as a parale-
gal until her retirement.

My father died when I was seven years old. I was the youngest one of
three children, and I felt that I had to help my mother. So before the war,
I was working, helping my mother, going to school, studying, but I didn't
finish studying. In the ghetto there was the medical school organized by Dr.
Hirszfeld. Right after the war, I worked, and when I came to Lodz, I started
to work, and my husband didn't have work for two months. My family life
was not easy. So, I am used to working from my very early years. But now I
am an old woman, and all my energy is up here [points to her head]. I used
to be very energetic.

I was not involved with the Jewish heritage. But Jerzy, when we came
here, he was involved with the Second Generation,[74] and I talked to young
people; he forced me to make a speech. What did I tell them? Not as pre-
cisely as I am telling you now. No, generalities. But it's important for young
people to know about the Holocaust because we survivors are disappearing
from this world. I had plenty of friends here. When we came here in 1970,
fifty people gathered to greet us. Now, it is a very, very small group, very small
group.

What I told you is not precise; it is not everything, no, but my memory is
very weak now. What I remember are very, very important moments in my
life.

—*Interviewed by Rachel Kalifowicz Waletsky, March 8, 1992, and Bonnie*
Gurewitsch, October 9, 1996, for the Museum of Jewish Heritage, New York

Anna Heilman

*Anna Heilman was born in 1928 in Warsaw. During the Warsaw
ghetto uprising she was living with her parents on the Aryan
side, going back and forth from the ghetto as a courier for
HaShomer HaTzair, the Socialist Zionist organization active in
resistance to the Nazis. Eventually, she was forced to choose between remaining permanently in the ghetto and participating in
the uprising or remaining with her family on the Aryan side. She
opted to remain with her family. In May 1943 she was arrested
with her family and taken to Majdanek. From there, she was
transferred to Auschwitz.*

We were first in *Lager* A,[1] which was called the quarantine camp.[2]
There were all kinds of rumors flying; we heard it was good to say
that you were a metallurgist, so we did. We were transferred to
Lager B,[3] and from *Lager* B we were assigned to the Union Werke, a German
munitions factory.[4]

At that time we did not know exactly what the factory produced. We
knew that this was an ammunition factory. Now we know that V2 missiles
were made there. Two shifts worked in the factory, one night shift and one
day shift. The day shift worked from very early in the morning till five, and
the night shift worked immediately after. My sister and I worked the day shift.

Alma was our *Kapo*.[5] She was German, non-Jewish. There were German
SS women who were *Aufseherin,* and there were also four Jewish *Arbeiterin*
who were responsible for the Jewish girls. This was the hierarchy.

My job was to inspect some of the manufactured pieces on the production line. They were round Bakelite pieces very much in the shape and size
of a checker. Each piece had a little indentation. My job was to check those
indentations and move the pieces on to the second person on the line. My
sister[6] also worked in the Union factory, but she worked in the *Pulverraum*

together with Ruzia Meth.[7] The *Pulverraum* was the *only* place in the factory where they handled gunpowder. Nine girls were involved in this small department.

We smuggled the gunpowder from the factory into the camp. It was smuggled in tiny little pieces of cloth tied up with a string.[8] Inside our dresses we had what we called a little *boit'l*, a pocket, and the *boit'l* was where everybody hid their little treasures wrapped in pieces of cloth. Often there were searches. When they conducted searches we used to untie the string and spill the gunpowder behind us on the ground so it wouldn't be found.

My sister brought the gunpowder out. She gave it to me and to other girls, whose names I don't remember.[9] I gave it to another girl in the camp,[10] and this girl gave it to another girl who was running between Auschwitz and Birkenau. The fourth girl,[11] who was executed, was the one who used to give it directly to the man who worked in the crematorium. I think we were involved in it for about eight months.

Very little contact was permitted between men and women, but we managed somehow. None of the people in charge had any idea that gunpowder was being smuggled out. There was one man I knew, a Belgian Jew whose name I don't remember, who was participating in the resistance in the men's *Lager*. He was my link with the men. He was blond and slight and had green eyes. He was about thirty or thirty-five years old. I had contact with him. When my sister was taken to the bunker,[12] which was a prison in the men's *Lager*, I approached him to ask for information. I needed to know what others were saying so that my explanation would coincide with theirs. But he pushed me away saying, "Don't ever come near me. I don't want anybody to see you with me." That was the end of my contact with him.

I'm not sure how many people were involved because there was such great secrecy. I only knew about myself, about Ruzia,[13] about Estusia,[14] and I think Alla.[15] I cannot remember anybody else. We only knew each other, and we were very, very careful.

It began this way. A small group of girls would get together after work in Auschwitz, dreaming of Israel, singing Hebrew songs, and talking about life outside or in the future if we survived. I remembered my agonizing decision in Warsaw, whether to go with *HaShomer HaTzair* into the ghetto or to stay with my parents. It left me terribly guilty. The last order of the day in *HaShomer HaTzair* was that we were not going to let ourselves be taken alive.[16] We were all going to die, but we were not giving our lives for nothing. I survived the Warsaw ghetto, and I felt guilty. Nobody in Auschwitz, unless they came from the Warsaw ghetto, knew about what happened there. We, too, decided that we were not going to let ourselves be taken without a struggle. We came from different countries, from different walks of life, from different organizations, and some were not affiliated with any organizations. We were about seven or eight girls, no more.

Out of this friendship evolved the idea of resistance. I can't tell you who initiated it . . . The idea was, what could we do, each one of us, to resist? I thought, "You are working in the *Pulverraum*. How about taking gunpowder?" We started to talk about the idea. The gunpowder was within our reach. We thought, we can use it! Somebody in the group knew that the *Sonderkommando* was preparing resistance. We said, "Let us give the gunpowder to them!" We gave it through Marta[17] to Anitchka, who was working in Birkenau. She ran between Auschwitz and Birkenau and gave it to Roza Robota. Roza Robota gave it to the men in the *Sonderkommando*. This was how it went.

Among a very select few there was talk about a plan for mass escape, but we didn't know who or when or where. We only knew that they would use the gunpowder for blowing up the crematorium. We knew that the *Sonderkommando* had decided to burn the crematorium because they knew that every *Sonderkommando* was going to be executed.[18] There was contact between the resistance in the camp and the PPR,[19] the resistance outside of camp. In our group there was a girl who had direct contact with PPR. We waited for word from the PPR to tell us when they would start from the outside.[20] We would then start to rebel from the inside, to break the camp down because the Russians were coming. But somebody from the *Sonderkommando* snitched on them, and they were attacked by the Germans before they had a chance to carry out their planned revolt. A crematorium was blown up.[21] And then the time to die approached.

We went on the famous death march in January.[22] We walked on foot in snow piled so deep we felt we were walking on our knees. We didn't see our legs anymore. Marta took me bodily. She had to force me to come; I wanted to stay in Auschwitz. It was worse than a nightmare. We stayed in Ravensbruck[23] just a few days. Then we were transferred to Neustadt Glewe[24] by train in cattle cars.

After liberation I was in a hospital. I was operated on several times for gangrene, and then I refused to be operated on again. Finally we were repatriated, but I decided that I didn't have anything to go back to Poland for. I convinced my camp sister, Marta, to come with me to Belgium because one of the nurses told us that the best ice cream in the world was in Belgium. I said, "We are going to Belgium." We were flown there by the Red Cross plane, and I stayed in Belgium for a year before I went with Youth Aliyah to Israel. I married in Israel in 1950. We came to the United States in 1958, and after two years we went to Canada.

I find it very difficult to speak about it; I find it very difficult to remember, but I understand that this is my responsibility, and I want to bring about the commemoration of the four girls who were executed in Auschwitz. This is what I wanted to do; this is the essence of my talk.[25]

My Auschwitz number was forty-eight, one hundred and fifty (48150). The numbers add up to *ḥai*.[26] The girl who tattooed my numbers told me: "You are going to come out alive because your number is *ḥai*."

— *Interviewed by Bonnie Gurewitsch, October 14, 1985*

Rose Meth

Rose Meth was born in 1925 into a prominent Hasidic family in Zator, Poland, a small town between Oswiecim and Cracow. She was the fourth of six children. In prewar years, Rose's father, as representative of the Jewish community, welcomed the president of Poland on a state visit to Zator. When the Nazis occupied Poland in September 1939, the family tried to escape eastward, but the effort was futile. Rose and her sisters were taken to clean German army lodgings; her father was forced to scrub the German carriages. As a result of this his shoes were ruined. The purchase of a new pair of shoes for her father was a "crime" for which Rose was imprisoned for six months.

From the Zator ghetto, where she lived after serving her sentence, Rose and other young people were sent to the Wadowice[1] ghetto to sew uniforms for the Wehrmacht. They were hoping that their labor would protect their families in Zator when they learned of the liquidation of the Zator ghetto and the deportation of the Jews to their deaths in Belzec,[2] July 1942. In August 1943 the Wadowice ghetto was liquidated. Rose and her three sisters were deported with the Wadowice Jews to Auschwitz.

We arrived in Auschwitz late in the afternoon of August 10, 1943. It was *Tisha B'Av.* My sisters and I were fasting. There was a selection on the platform by SS man Tauber.[3] He was in charge next to Mengele.[4] We dressed up my little sisters to make them look older, and we all passed the selection. Then we were brought to Birkenau. I can't begin to describe the shock and the humiliation. We were sheltered children. They made us undress completely naked in front of the Nazi soldiers. We wanted to die. They shaved our heads. They shaved all our hair, everywhere. We were given numbers. Mine was *Vier und funfzig, drei sieben achtzig* (54387). I'm alive because of confusion with those numbers, 54387. [The numbers]

3,8,7 add up to 18. You know what that is in *gimatria?*[5] There was a selection in October 1943. My number was taken down. As you read the number in Polish it's 54387. In German, the seven is read before the eight. We had to dictate our numbers to the *Kapo*, and I translated from the Polish: 54387, but in German the *Kapo* wrote down the seven before the eight. When they were calling the numbers, I knew my number was written down, and I wanted to step forward, but my friend Estusia[6] grabbed me by my arm and said, "That's not your number." I asked, "What if somebody else goes?" She said, "You'll have time to go then." The correct number never came up.

First we carried rocks from one place to another and back. Just cruel, busy work. Nothing constructive was being done with the rocks. I was in a state of shock because my sisters were taken away. I had typhus. I swelled up with what we called the "elephant sickness," and I also developed some sort of joint ailment, but I continued going to work. Finally, I was taken on a litter to the *revier*. I was so very sick that I couldn't walk.

In the *revier* there was a lady, Mrs. Oleander, from Cracow. She said to me, "Quickly, get off that bed and go back where you came from." I cried. I said, "I can't walk." She said, "I don't care what you say. You'd better go." She chased me out of the *revier*, and I came back to the camp. The entire *revier* was sent to the gas chamber. I don't know why she did it. I don't know why she picked me.

In the late fall of 1943, just before Hanukkah, I was taken to work in the Union factory,[7] and in the fall of 1944 I was transferred from Birkenau to [a new block in] Auschwitz [I]. In the Union factory I was working in the *Pulverraum*.[8] It was an enclosed room about ten feet by six or seven [feet]. On one side were tables with six or seven press machines.[9] We made the part called a *Verzögerung* that ignited a bomb. The *Verzögerung* itself was a little smaller than a checker, and there was a hole in it, one-eighth inch in diameter. This hole had to be filled with gunpowder. We used a certain measure, a tiny spoon, to pour the gunpowder into that hole and then press it down in the machine. That was our job. The *Meister*, Von Ende,[10] brought us allotments of powder. Each girl got a certain allotment, and she had to produce I don't remember how many hundreds of *Verzögerungs* with her allotment. After we finished our allotment, it was put on a tray the size of a cookie sheet, and it was tested to see whether the caps exploded. *Meister* Von Ende pulled out a few at random. We were not punished if there were five or ten that did not pass the test, but if there were more, then we had to do it all over, or we had our rations taken away. Most of the time we were careful not to be caught with poor work. We were extremely careful. Regina Saperstein[11] had to stand next to *Meister* Von Ende and watch when he pulled caps out of the tray at random for testing. He had a habit of doing it in a certain pattern. Since we were allowed some defective pieces, Regina tried to put them on the tray in such a pattern that she more or less felt sure the defective caps would not be pulled out. When we pressed down the handle on the machine, some of the powder had to overflow because we had to put enough in the hole to pack it down. The overflow was a little mangled. It was not powerful enough. It was called *Abfall*. We saved this *Abfall*, and sometimes we mixed it with the good powder even though we were supposed to discard it. Von Ende collected the *Abfall*, but we made sure that there was always enough so that they couldn't catch on that we were stealing some of it.

No one was permitted to come in, only *der Meister* who collected the finished product and one more person; I don't remember who that was. We didn't know where the part we made belonged or how they assembled it. In the part of the Union factory that I saw, they were producing all sorts of pieces of metal and tubes. We were so isolated that I don't know what they were. We found out from people who worked in the plant that V2 rockets were made there.

We started working at daybreak. Sometimes it was dark. There was a *Zahlappell* at daybreak. We got our tea or coffee and a slice of bread, and we marched to work in formation. We continued working till noon, when they blew a siren. We went into formation again, and they dished out our bowl of soup and then we continued working until five o'clock or later. I think only one shift worked in the *Pulverraum* because I don't remember ever seeing any other. The other parts of the factory had two shifts, day and night. In the *Pulverraum* were eight or nine girls. There was Estusia from Warsaw, and there were Inge Franke[12] and Ilse Michel[13] from Germany, Genia Fischer,[14] whom I approached to work with us, another girl, and myself. Regina Saperstein was a *Vorarbeiterin*. We were all more or less the same age. Not all of those girls were working in the underground. Regina Saperstein was a lovely person, quiet and very nice. She was a Jewish girl, one of us. She helped us with the powder.

In March 1944 Estusia approached me. She told me that resistance was being organized and that we were in a position to help because we were the only ones who had access to powder. Would I be willing to risk the danger of being caught? Of course I agreed right away because it gave me a way to fight back. I felt very good about it, and I didn't care about the danger. None of us did. She taught me how to collect and save powder. She told me to try and mix the *Abfall* with the good powder and fill several of the *Verzögerungs* with the bad powder in order to accumulate good powder. The good powder we put in little pieces of cloth. We tied them up, and we put them either in our bosom or into a pocket, if we had one. We tore off a piece of a shirt, or you gave away a piece of bread for a kerchief, and you cut it up. You could do many things when you forced yourself to do them. We kept the powder on our bodies or in our pockets.

Very often before we entered the camp, they stopped and searched us. When we saw from afar that there was going to be a search, we sprinkled the powder on the ground and stepped on it, ground it into the ground so there was no way of catching us. The powder was charcoal gray. Very dark. Almost black. It wasn't powderlike, it was more like tiny grains. It couldn't get under the nails. In a day three of us could collect about two teaspoons full.

We observed the other girls. We talked to them. We asked them: "What would you do if you had a chance to do something?" It was done very subtly. One friend whom I approached refused. She didn't give me a reason. After the war, we met, and she said her conscience bothered her. She had to get it off her chest; she said, "I was afraid that I would not be strong enough under duress, if they would catch me, whether I could withstand pain." I gave her credit for being honest. She's a very good friend, and I never held it against her, even though I didn't know the reason at the time.

When I accumulated this gunpowder, Estusia took it from me, and she gave it to someone. We did not know many names for safety reasons, so I really don't know exactly, but I know that there was a girl who was a runner, and she delivered the powder to other people who had connections with men, and the men used it.[15] I knew that we were going to try a mass escape. The men would go first and maybe the women later. Whether anyone would survive was doubtful, but at least we would try. That was our main goal.

Only later on I learned the names of two of the girls, Roza Robota[16] and Alla Gaertner.[17] They did not work in the *Pulverraum*. I started the stealing sometime in March of '44 and continued until the crematorium was blown up, October 7, 1944. Regina Saperstein, Estusia, Genia Fischer, and I participated. Three others did not.

The *Sonderkommando* was changed every few weeks.[18] They didn't want the same people. These three hundred men knew that they were going to be gassed,[19] so they blew up the crematorium and tried to escape, but they were caught.[20] From what I heard it was a gruesome story. They were caught and shot. Then they made a *Zahlappell* of shot bodies to make sure that no one escaped.[21] That's what I heard. I didn't see it, but it was immediately repeated to us. It was the general talk in the *Pulverraum*, where we were immediately isolated. An SS woman was assigned especially to us.[22] We called her "the frog"; she was the ugliest thing in the world. She was a huge woman, and she watched us. She listened to whatever we were talking about, and whenever we went out, she searched us. It was bad before, but it was miserable after the crematorium was blown up. They knew there was no other way of getting gunpowder but from this *Pulverraum*.

With Estusia, there was a tragedy. One day she had sick leave. There was a Russian girl, Klara, and she saw Estusia on the *Block* talking to a man and denounced her. I heard that right after the explosion they caught this Klara with something that she was not supposed to have, and she made a deal with them that if they went easy on her, she'd tell about Estusia's connection with the men.[23] About two weeks afterwards they took Estusia and Regina to Block 11[24] into a bunker. Regina was taken because she was responsible for the room.[25] They were beaten up beyond description. Their bodies looked like pieces of raw liver.

Since I always worked next to Estusia, they took me, too, for interrogation.[26] Well, the beating that I got was not as severe as theirs. They showed me a drawing of a man and asked me whether I ever saw this man.[27] They told me right away: "This is Estusia's friend. Did you see him often?" They started interrogating me. Of course I denied I had ever seen the man or been in contact with him, which was true. They threatened me with shooting and all sorts of things, but they couldn't get anything out of me, so they sent me back. From their questioning, I thought that they suspected the whole world. All the Jews were their enemies. They couldn't even suspect Regina or Estusia of anything specific because they didn't have anything on them, except that Regina was responsible for the *Pulverraum*, and the *Pulverraum* was the only source of gunpowder. That much they could suspect, but they couldn't know who gave it.[28]

Two weeks later, Estusia and Regina were released. The SS didn't have any tangible evidence that they could tie to them. So Estusia and Regina were released and were sent back to work. They were in such agony after their beating. They were with us for a very short while. Before Christmas the Gestapo took them back to Block 11, and of course January 6 was the hanging, the execution of the four girls.[29] All the women of the camp were outside, and they called the *Pulverraum* to the front, right next to the gallows where the chairs were. This I remember. I marked it down in my notes. Hoessler,[30] the camp *Führer*, called, "*Pulverraum nach vorne*," which means "*Pulverraum* to the front," and he read the verdict: "In the name of the German law, you are sentenced to death."[31] What a paradox that was: "in the name of law." In Auschwitz, to read a verdict in the name of law! I passed out. I hardly remember anything afterwards. Complete numbness set in for me. I didn't care about anything. Nothing mattered to me. We were all silent. We couldn't talk for quite a while. Thirteen days later we were evacuated from Auschwitz.

I wrote down some notes in Auschwitz, but when we were evacuated, I threw them away. I tore them up because I thought perhaps I'd be searched and there might be incriminating information in the notes. I traded bread for paper, or I sewed little aprons for the *Blockalteste*. She gave me the needle and thread, and for the apron she gave me an extra piece of bread. My father always wanted us to remember what was happening, to be able to tell the world, so the world would know of the heinous crimes the Germans committed. He always said, "Remember what is happening." It was my father's strong message to survive and tell the world.

Estusia and I were like sisters. People never knew that we were not really sisters. As soon as all my sisters were taken away from me and Estusia saw my condition, she helped me a lot morally. She told me I must be strong and survive. I had told her things that my father said. He prepared us for the hardship. He was a very unusual, very unique person. Through *meshalim* he gave us courage and taught us how to live in spite of difficulties.

Just before we were separated, before we went to Wadowice, my father took us four girls aside. He told us a parable of two men. They were tired of life. They had difficulties and problems. They went to a river, stood on the bridge, and contemplated suicide. One of the men courageously jumped into the water and was gone. The other one shivered and went away. Which was the coward and which was the brave man? Of course, as children, we said it was the one who had the courage to jump into the river. My father said, "No, you're wrong. The one who took up the fight and continued to live and fight for what he wanted, this one was the brave man." I had told this to Estusia before, and she kept on repeating it to me. Other things that he told us made us have faith, to believe that some good would come of it. I feel that it was my father's blessing that helped me survive.

Rose Meth was evacuated from Auschwitz on January 19, 1945, on a death march to Wroclaw on the Polish-German border. From there they were transported to Ravensbruck and then to Neustadt-Glewe, where they were liberated by the American army on May 3, 1945. In Neustadt-Glewe Mrs. Meth again wrote an account of her experiences in Auschwitz. Those original pages are in the archives at Yad Vashem. She arrived in the United States in May 1946.

Rose Meth, Anna Heilman, and other women survivors of Auschwitz were instrumental in the erection of a monument to the four women who were hanged for smuggling gunpowder to the men at Auschwitz. The monument now stands on the grounds of Yad Vashem in Jerusalem. A memorial plaque to the four Jewish women was unveiled at the Auschwitz concentration camp site on October 7, 1994.

—Interviewed by Bonnie Gurewitsch, October 28, 1985

❧ Afterword

Jewish Women and Jewish Responses during the Holocaust

This book is neither comprehensive nor a scientific survey of Jewish women's Holocaust experiences. Nevertheless, common responses can be identified among the twenty-five women in this book and may serve as criteria for such a study in the future. The Jewish women whose interviews are included in this volume had a distinct sense of themselves as Jews that accompanied them during the Holocaust. Even young children knew that Jews have certain behavior patterns, values, and beliefs and risked their welfare or even their lives in asserting their Jewish identity during the Holocaust.

One of the distinguishing religious observances of Jews is their adherence to the dietary laws known as *kashrut*. Five-year-old Eva Schonbrun knew that Jews do not eat ham. Eating the ham given to her by the *Blockalteste* was justified because the starvation rations were a threat to life, but she remembers it as forbidden food. Estelle Alter rejected pork in the Belgian convent even though food was scarce. She doesn't even remember how, at five years old, she knew it was forbidden to Jews; her action was instinctive. Edith Wachsman describes how even her two-and-one-half-year-old brother refused to eat nonkosher meat when it was given as charity to their family by their non-Jewish neighbors who pitied them. Hannah Bannett said she was a vegetarian, providing a rationale for her avoidance of meat in the home of the German for whom she worked as a housekeeper. Smuggling a cow into the Pruzhany ghetto in order to allow it to be slaughtered according to the rules of *kashrut* endangered the entire community, but the benefits of adding even a small bit of protein to their subsistence diet made the risks worthwhile. Concentration camp prisoners were so desperately hungry that they risked their lives to scavenge and steal anything remotely edible. Yet some Jews in concentration camps refused to eat food that was clearly not kosher.

Rita Grunbaum remembers a North African Jew named Labi, marvelling at his self-discipline because he did not eat the soup that contained horse meat in Bergen Belsen. Rozalia Berke's camp sister Dorka risked her life in Stutthof when she approached the barbed wires separating the men's and women's camps. If the men threw a potato or a carrot over to her, she shared the bounty with her camp sisters. When a piece of bacon was thrown over the wire Rozalia refused at first to eat it; Dorka insisted. Another important *kashrut* issue was eating bread on Passover, normally forbidden. Edith Horowitz reports that the women in Zillertal ate only potatoes on Passover, not bread. Tilly Stimler was offered a piece of bread on Passover by a woman who was not going to eat it; Tilly was reluctant to take it, but the woman insisted, arguing that she did not think she would survive and that Tilly, as a youngster, had an obligation to try to survive. This argument is in keeping with Jewish tradition, which permits the eating of normally forbidden foods when life is at stake. Rita Grunbaum recalls that in Bergen Belsen in 1944 the rabbis permitted the eating of bread but that few Jews did. The following year, when conditions had deteriorated, there was no bread. Ironically, the flour and water that were available were used by the prisoners to bake *matzah*, the biblical bread of affliction. "We were slaves now, and God would save us from our enemies. History had become reality." Rita Grunbaum, not religious herself, nevertheless interpreted what had happened to the Jews in the context of Jewish history and derived a measure of hope from that history.

Jewish education was a primary Jewish value. Edith Wachsman describes in detail her efforts to continue her education in spite of persecution and discrimination in Czechoslovakia. When Jewish children were dismissed from local schools, Jewish communities opened special schools for their children, or families hired tutors to continue educating their children. In the Warsaw ghetto, Vladka Meed's mother gave part of her tiny bread ration to the tutor who was preparing her twelve-year-old son for his bar mitzvah.[1] Zenia Malecki describes clandestine Jewish schools in the Vilna ghetto; Adele Bay transcribed music from a score retrieved secretly from an abandoned Jewish apartment in Vilna, arranging the music for a children's orchestra in the ghetto.[2] Rachel Garfunkel's first act of resistance was the rescue of Jewish books from the Nazi fire when she was eight years old. Later, in the home of her protector, she read the leather-bound books looted by her illiterate Polish protectors from a Jewish home, reassuring herself that although she was scrubbing their floors she was not their inferior.[3] A sense of Jewish history and culture informed the daily lives of Jewish women in concentration camps and reinforced their sense of worth even when the external world was despising them. Rachel Silberman's mother and other "older" women kept up the spirits of the younger women by reminding them of miracles that had happened in the Jewish past. Edith Horowitz tells of the education she got in the Zillertal forced labor camp by listening to the stories told by a woman who was a teacher. Edith describes this education as *Torah be'al peh,* oral tradition, the same idiom used to describe the Talmud and commentaries on the Bible. From this teacher the young girls learned geography and history; some wrote poetry. In the ghetto/camp of Terezin, where Jews were held until they were transported to their deaths in Auschwitz, Trude Groag taught young children manual skills and basic conceptual skills: round and square, soft and sharp, as well as basic hygiene and other life skills. After the young children were deported she worked with older girls, who studied in an underground classroom. Groag also mentions Dr. Leo Baeck, the renowned and beloved rabbi from Berlin, whose lectures in Terezin taught Jewish history and philosophy and provided spiritual sustenance for the adults. For Trude Groag, as for other Jewish educators during the Holocaust, education was a value in itself even if it would have no practical application.

As soon as they were able, many women resumed their interrupted educations after the Holocaust. Edith Wachsman finished high school in the United States but is particularly proud of the advanced level of Jewish education that her children achieved. Rozalia Berke formalized her wartime nursing experience with advanced professional training in nursing and midwifery and pursued a successful career in the United States. Hannah Rigler, who is so proud of her mother's university degree, also resumed her education and pursued careers in nursing and in feeding the homeless. Tilly Stimler, Marysia Warman, and Rywka Diament, whose own educations were stymied, take pride in the educational achievements of their children and grandchildren.

Jewish prayers are both individual and communal. Jews can speak to God directly, expressing their needs and emotions without an intermediary. Some prayers are part of the rituals learned at home in the earliest years of a child's life. Margie Nitzan remembers learning the *Sh'ma,* the basic affirmation of monotheistic Judaism, and specific blessings that are said upon eating certain foods. Edith Wachsman began to pray every day, not just on the Sabbath, at the age of ten or eleven because of her need for spiritual expression and comfort at a time of increasing persecution of Jews. Rachel Garfunkel and Edith Wachsman repeated the words of the *Sh'ma* in moments of stress, when they felt imminent danger. Cesia Brandstatter and her seven camp sisters also said the *Sh'ma* and *Modeh Ani*, prayers that they learned as very young children at home. In times of stress and danger Jews often read the Psalms, which express dependence on God and affirm one's personal faith. Tilly Stimler remembers that while the girls were being tattooed in Auschwitz, some were saying aloud parts of Psalms that they remembered, and others were repeating them over and over. She attributes the fact that she never received a tattoo to this affirmation of her faith in God.

A particularly important women's religious observance is immersion in the ritual bath, or *mikvah*, at prescribed times. Observance of this commandment enables marital relations to resume at prescribed intervals after childbirth and menstruation. During the Holocaust Jews went to great lengths to facilitate the observance of this ritual by traveling to the closest *mikvah* even when travel was forbidden to Jews and then maintaining *mikvaot* even when they were ordered shut by German authorities.[4] Observant women in ghettos, hiding, or transit camps who were still living with their husbands made special efforts to observe this important commandment. When the Jewish community of Czechoslovakia was decimated by the first wave of deportations in 1942, one family that remained continued to maintain and use the *mikvah* in their town.[5] Nina Matathias describes the measures she took that substituted for the *mikvah* ritual when water was a scarce commodity in the little Greek village where she and her husband were hiding. In Italy, Sara Rothstein, her husband, and two children and another married couple were hiding in a village in the mountains. Mrs. Rothstein and the other Jewish woman immersed themselves in a stream in the absence of a real ritual bath.[6] In the Westerbork transit camp in the Netherlands, Pepi van Ryk and other observant women received permission from the commandant to leave the camp, under guard, in order to use the closest *mikvah*.[7] Because of the issues of discretion and privacy that are part of the *mikvah* ritual, it is remarkable that women went to such lengths, endangering themselves, to observe this women's ritual.

Another, better-known Jewish woman's observance is the kindling of Sabbath and holiday candles. Traditionally, women have added their own personal prayers to the usual ritual. When she lit the candles for *Yom Kippur* just before the Diament family escaped from France, Rywka Diament prayed for their safe arrival in Switzerland. In ghettos, where Jewish community life still existed, many women were still able to light Sabbath and holiday candles. In hiding, observing this ritual posed the danger of discovery. Edith

Wachsman's mother said the blessing on the electric lights so as not to draw attention to a Jewish family in a hostile environment. Nina Matathias had no Sabbath candles in the remote Greek village where she was hiding. She simply rested on the Sabbath, observing it in mind and spirit. In concentration camps there was no question of lighting Sabbath candles, but some marked the Sabbath in their own way. The eight camp sisters from Chrzanow did not turn the lights on or off, observing the commandment against lighting or extinguishing a flame. At first, in Zillertal, Edith Horowitz's mother made wicks from threads stolen from the cloth the Jewish women spun in the factory. She lit those wicks as Sabbath candles. Then a Christian woman who worked in the factory but lived in the town brought her a candle from a Christmas tree. This candle was lit and extinguished each week to welcome the Jewish Sabbath for the Jewish slave laborers in Zillertal. "Everyone was waiting, watching her, so she did it," regardless of the risks.

How did Jewish women in concentration camps know when to observe Jewish holidays? Their belongings were confiscated on arrival; calendars and prayer books were almost unknown. Nevertheless, there was a need to know this information, and Jews in the camps went to great lengths to calculate the Jewish calendar and to disseminate the information about when a Jewish holiday should be observed. The Jewish calendar is lunar, determined by the waxing and waning of the moon, which was visible even in the dark skies of the concentration camps. Knowledgeable Jews, men and women, were able to calculate the progression of Jewish months and determine the dates of Jewish holidays. Sometimes a Jewish calendar was smuggled into the camp, perhaps from among the confiscated belongings that were sorted by prisoners in the warehouses. Edith Horowitz reports that in Zillertal someone had an old calendar, and the Jewish women always knew when the holidays occurred. In addition to lighting "candles" for the Sabbath, Edith's mother lit lengths of yarn to celebrate Hanukkah, the festival of freedom. We have already listed several instances of Passover observance, and Miriam Rosenthal reports that as she labored to deliver her son in Kaufering, the doctor who assisted her informed her that the men in the nearby hut were saying Psalms for her safe delivery and added that it was Purim day, the holiday of Jewish deliverance from a genocidal threat in ancient Persia. Golda Finkler wrote down the calendar that she calculated in one of the HASAG forced labor camps in Leipzig, Germany, on the backs of unused production cards. She also transcribed the daily morning prayers for herself on the pages of a discarded German memo book.[8] Dina Kraus Ehrenreich wrote a substantial part of the Passover *Haggadah* from memory in the Unterluss labor camp in Germany and used this to conduct a clandestine *seder* for the women in her barrack.[9] It should be noted that stealing the paper used to write the calendar or prayer books was considered sabotage by the Nazis, punishable by death.

Yom Kippur, the Day of Atonement, is the most solemn of Jewish holidays. A day of soul searching, Jews fast for twenty-five hours, removing themselves from worldly concerns and concentrating their thoughts and intentions on prayer and repentance. Edith Horowitz reports that the women knew which day to fast, as did the eight camp sisters in Ober Altstadt. Rachel Silberman and her mother, doing agricultural work in Germany, were isolated on a farm. Her mother was calculating the calendar in order to fast on *Yom Kippur.* When she made contact with another Jewish woman in an adjacent field whose calculations differed from hers, she realized that she was mistaken, that she and her daughters would have eaten on the holy fast day. This invalidated what for her was an act of spiritual resistance. She became bitter, wounded, and although she did say a prayer with her daughters, she never regained her sense of competency and control.

Viktor Frankl describes how keeping track of family events, such as his wife's birthday, sustained him in the concentration camp. For another prisoner the hope of seeing his beloved child sustained him.[10] Thus, family time was a point of reference for some prisoners and a beacon of hope for them. Similarly, Jewish time was a point of reference for Jews in concentration camps, giving Jewish prisoners a measure of control over time in a universe that allowed them no control over their physical environment. By calculating the Jewish calendar and marking the Sabbath and Jewish holidays, even if just in their minds, Jewish prisoners retained a sense of their Jewish identities. Keeping track of the Jewish calendar allowed Jews to retain the Jewish sense of the consecration of time, a basic concept in Judaism. This phenomenon was common to Jewish men and women. It served communal needs by uniting Jewish prisoners in hope and comfort and sustained individuals by giving them a sense of identity and autonomy.

Faith in a Jewish future, inspired by prayers that express the hope for a return to Zion, was also a factor that contributed to maintaining Jewish identity. Eva Schonbrun remembers the girl who was not afraid to sing Zionist songs at night in the Bergen Belsen barracks. Estelle Alter may have sung the same songs in the Belgian orphanage. Anna Heilman also sang Zionist songs at night in the dark Auschwitz barrack. Out of this grew her involvement in resistance activities. Margie Nitzan's childhood memories of learning

Hebrew and imitating Zionist agriculture are some of her few positive memories. Marrying an Israeli helped to ground her in reality, but only temporarily. Rachel Silberman's mother sang Sabbath hymns in her barracks in Stutthof; Trude Groag and Zenia Malecki taught Jewish children so they would be prepared for life in the future, even though they knew most would not survive. Hannah Bannett saw God's hand in her survival, and Cesia Brandstatter saw her ordeal as part of the Messianic era, portending a better future.

Zionists looked forward to living in a Jewish state in which Jews would determine their own futures. For religious Jews, return to *Eretz Yisrael*, the Land of Israel, was part of their Messianic dream, which they hoped would be realized at the end of the cataclysmic disaster of the Holocaust. Some were preparing the way for immigration to Palestine even before World War II. Hannah Rigler's parents owned an apartment in Haifa, as did Hannah Bannett and her husband. Helen Foxman recalls that she and her husband had the opportunity to immigrate to Palestine before the outbreak of World War II, but her husband deferred to her very strong family loyalties, and they did not take advantage of the immigration certificate that was offered to her husband. Edith Horowitz and Trude Groag immigrated to Palestine after the Holocaust. Edith Horowitz participated in the Zionist struggle for self-determination. Trude Groag, who came to believe in Zionism out of the depths of Jewish powerlessness in the Holocaust, settled in Israel and was proud of her soldier granddaughter and the accomplishments of the State of Israel. Edith Wachsman remembers her father encouraging his family by telling them about the Land of Israel when they were in hiding. She assumed that after the miraculous survival of her family, they would immigrate to Israel and was bitterly disappointed that her parents chose to go to the United States. Helen Foxman articulates the choices faced by families in the postwar period. Because the British severely limited Jewish immigration to Palestine, many Jews joined the "illegal" immigration movement, which involved physical hardship and risk. Parents of young children were reluctant to subject them to those risks. Hannah Bannett waited in Europe until legal immigration certificates were available for herself and her children and made a new life for herself in Israel.

Many of these women saw God responding to their prayers and personally protecting them, sometimes through the intermediary of their parents. Rywka Diament followed the instructions given to her husband by his father in his dream, which brought their family to a safe haven. Hannah Rigler believes it was her father who carried her, ran with her, and protected her when she escaped from the death march because her feet were frozen in her clogs. Miriam Rosenthal felt her parents "looking down" on her, watching over her and protecting her. She felt she was in God's hands. Hannah Bannett prayed frequently in times of distress and believes that God protected her and her children, perhaps because of their complete trust in God, perhaps just so she could tell her story. Rose Meth drew courage from the support of Estusia, her camp sister, who encouraged her to live and resist by repeating her own father's words to her. Rose considered them her father's blessing. Tilly Stimler also regards her survival as a gift from God, whose protection she felt in Auschwitz and in the Hundsfeldt labor camp. Edith Wachsman feels that she and her family were personally redeemed by the hand of God; the experience of the Nazis skipping over their door is parallel, for her, to the redemption of the Children of Israel at Passover from slavery in Egypt. Other women, such as Edith Horowitz and Rachel Silberman, attribute their survival to luck or good fortune. Estelle Alter and her sister, Regina, clearly depended on each other and gave each other vital moral support. Cesia Brandstatter says she survived because of her camp sisters, who supported each other physically and morally. Anna Heilman saw an omen for her survival in the number eighteen, meaning "life," which was the sum of the numbers on her arm. While these women may feel particularly blessed in their survival, some also have feelings of guilt. None suggests that those who perished were unworthy.

Whatever their rationale for survival, the women in this book have retained their identities as Jews. Religious observance is, for many, the way in which they express their Jewish identity. For many it is Jewish continuity that they see in their children and grandchildren. For others, such as Marysia Warman, being Jewish is simply who they are. Some, such as Rywka Diament and Edith Horowitz, have increased the degree of their religious observance. Brandla Small says that God has been good to her since the Holocaust, but nothing compensates for her losses; she "will never be happy." Others have not changed their lifestyles, but none have denied their Jewishness. The event that broke Margie Nitzan's hold on reality was her baptism; it destroyed her sense of who she was. Tragically, she is quite aware that she has never fully regained her hold on her identity.

There are no "happy endings" to these testimonies; in most cases the story has not ended. The interviewees still live in their experiences; their memories are part of their post-Holocaust identities, informing their lives on a day-to-day basis. Some survivors have come to terms with part of their experiences, articulating "lessons" that they have learned or wish to teach future generations. Most are ambivalent, reflecting contradictions within the experience and in their adjustments to post-Holocaust life. The reader should beware of attributing meaning and interpretation either to the Holocaust experience or to the survivors' perceptions of it. The experience remains with them always, defying meaning. The reader is challenged, both by the survivors and by the experience, simply to know, to transmit to future generations.

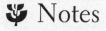 Notes

Preface

1. See Joseph Friedlander, ed., *Pinkas Pruz'any* (Tel Aviv: United Pruziner and Vicinity Relief Committee/Pruz'ana Landshaft Association, 1983), 59–62. Referred to hereafter as *Pinkas Pruz'any*.

2. See Joan Ringelheim, "Women and the Holocaust, A Reconsideration of Research," in *Different Voices: Women and the Holocaust*, ed. Carol Rittner and John Roth (New York: Paragon, 1993), 376.

3. See interview with Sara Silber. Sara Silber's interview and other oral history interviews that are not included in this book are listed in the bibliography.

4. See Sybil Milton, "Women and the Holocaust: The Case of German and German-Jewish Women," in Rittner and Roth, 229–30, for a discussion of this phenomenon.

5. Milton, 229.

6. See oral history of Miriam Rosenthal in Camp Sisters section.

Mothers

1. The British government policy on Jewish immigration to Palestine, as stated in the White Paper of May 17, 1939, limited Jewish immigration to fifteen thousand a year for five years, with subsequent Jewish immigration subject to Arab approval. See Israel Gutman, ed., *Encyclopedia of the Holocaust* (New York: Macmillan, 1990), 1649 (referred to hereafter as *EH*).

2. The original certificates are in the Rita Grunbaum file.

3. Ringelheim, 378–79.

4. Y. Arad, Y. Gutman, and A. Margaliot, eds., *Documents on the Holocaust: Selected Sources on the Destruction of the Jews of Germany and Austria, Poland and the Soviet Union* (Jerusalem: Yad Vashem, 1981), 450.

5. Milton, 227–28.

6. See Edith Horowitz interview.

Rywka Diament

1. Born in 1858, Tsvi Hersh Szmerlowski served in the Russian army. The medals he earned saved his life during the early, violent days of World War I when a cossack demanded his money or his life. The sight of the medals awarded by Tsar Alexander III cooled the cossack's fury. See Theo Richmond, *Konin: A Quest* (New York: Pantheon, 1995), 42–43.

2. In addition to the religious library at the house of study, Konin's 2,902 Jewish residents supported a large, well-patronized lending library. The library had a total of 5,225 books in Yiddish, Hebrew, Polish, Russian, and other languages. It had more Polish books than any other lending library in Poland. See Richmond, 298–99.

3. In return for an alliance with Germany, on June 24, 1940, Italy occupied a small bit of French territory on the Mediterranean coast. See William Shirer, *The Rise and Fall of the Third Reich: A History of Nazi Germany* (New York: Simon and Schuster, 1960), 746. In this occupied

zone Italians prevented the arrest and deportation of Jews. See Leni Yahil, *The Holocaust: The Fate of European Jewry* (New York: Oxford University Press, 1990), 433.

4. The Jewish Boy Scouts, *Eclaireurs Israelites de France*, were a recognized youth organization in Vichy France. These scouts, who worked with French resistance groups, assisted refugees in crossing to the Italian occupation zone in southern France. They also provided false documents to Jews who needed them. See oral history of Harry Evan, *Newsletter* (New York: Center for Holocaust Studies, 1991), 36.

5. Henri Diament explains in his interview: "The local [train from Antibes] gets into Nice station on a separate track, and the people who get off this local train are not checked." Henri says they arrived in Nice in mid-1941. See "Oral History of Henri Diament."

6. "Soon a number of philanthropically minded Jews organized a local 'Joint' in Nice, which functioned illegally." This committee provided asylum and sufficient funds so the refugees could demonstrate financial independence to the police. See Zajwel Diament, "Jewish Refugees on the French Riviera," *YIVO Annual* (1953): 265.

7. Nice and other resort towns on the French Riviera were empty of tourists, with many vacant villas and apartments. If a refugee could pay rent the police left him alone.

8. On September 9, 1943, the Germans entered Nice, and the Italians retreated to Italy.

9. "Some were in favor of evacuation [to Italy] without organization; others felt that without Allied permission to move to North Africa, flight to Italy entailed more dangers than staying on the spot." Z. Diament, "Jewish Refugees," 278.

10. See "Oral History of Harry Evan" for details of how the French Jewish Scouts provided false identities for Jewish refugees.

11. Henri says he was told that his name would be Blanc and thinks he probably kept his own first name, but he was not told that they were going to Switzerland. See oral history of Henri Diament.

12. The date of Yom Kippur was October 8, 1943.

13. Henri describes the train similarly: "During the war, on trains at night, all lights were out. It was dark." See oral history of Henri Diament.

14. Annemasse, a small town on the Swiss border opposite Geneva, was known to Jews as a good spot to cross the border. See "Oral History of Sascha Stein." On a current road map, roads numbered 40 and 41 lead to Annemasse; number 40 crosses the border into Switzerland.

15. Zanvel Diament wrote in his memoir, "The townspeople had drawn a map for us. We believe we are on the right road." Zanvel Diament, memoir, 1943; Yiddish manuscript in Rywka Diament file.

16. "We go forward through forest, stones, water." They had to cross a stream and walk up a steep hill. Z. Diament, memoir. Maps of the area show several streams, tributaries of the Rhone and Arve rivers, at Annemasse.

17. "Jews who come with their families which include old people over 70 and children under the age of 6 are accepted." Z. Diament, memoir. Swiss immigration policy was restrictive and changed frequently. The Diament family benefited from Paul's young age.

18. "We surrender our false papers . . . which enabled us to go through the German control in Annemasse." Z. Diament, memoir.

19. Zanvel Diament says they were taken by car to a refugee camp named Cropettes, near Geneva.

20. Zanvel Diament describes several days of thorough interrogation and reports how other Jewish refugee families were sent back to France as a result of investigation. One man could not prove that the children who were with him were his own.

21. Zanvel Diament mentions refugee camps named Charmille and Champel.

22. Henri describes the wife of the professor as an anti-Semite, cold and uncaring toward him.

23. The American Joint Distribution Committee, called the "Joint," provided relief funds for refugees, wherever permitted, before, during, and after World War II.

Rita Grunbaum

1. This was the final major roundup of Dutch Jews; "the total liquidation of Dutch Jewry was about to be consummated." See Jacob Presser, *Ashes in the Wind: The Destruction of Dutch Jewry* (Detroit: Wayne State University Press, 1988), 213.

2. Members of the Dutch Nazi Party (NSB) participated in this final roundup of Dutch Jews; they collected and held the keys to homes abandoned by the Jews who were deported. Presser, 212.

3. Westerbork, in northeastern Netherlands, was established by the Dutch government in October 1939 to house Jewish refugees who had entered the Netherlands illegally. In late 1941 the Germans decided to use Westerbork as a transit camp for Jews who were awaiting deportation to Poland. The camp was expanded, and SS were sent in to reinforce the Dutch police who were originally in charge. The internal camp administration remained in the hands of the German Jewish refugees who were its original inhabitants, even after the Dutch became the majority of the prisoners as a result of the systematic rounding up of Dutch Jews in 1942. The camp housed a large, well-equipped hospital. In addition, entertainment activities were encouraged, and food supplies were adequate. The weekly transports from Westerbork, which took Jews to the Polish death camps, were a great source of tension. *EH*, 1645–48.

4. Most women worked at peeling potatoes and similar chores. Some women worked as domestics, cleaning the homes of the SS or the German Jewish doctors. Presser, 445.

5. Philip Mechanicus, a Dutch Jewish journalist who kept a diary in Westerbork, reports that on February 8, 1944, those deported from Westerbork whose transport was destined for Auschwitz were greatly "disappointed," knowing that Auschwitz was a less desirable destination than Bergen Belsen, where prisoners with special papers were sent for possible exchange. Nowhere, however, does Mechanicus indicate that the nature of Auschwitz as a death camp was known in Westerbork. See Philip Mechanicus, *Year of Fear: A Jewish Prisoner Waits for Auschwitz* (New York: Hawthorne Books, 1968), 247–48.

6. Rita Grunbaum kept a diary in Westerbork and Bergen Belsen. The paragraphs in brackets are excerpted from this diary, which Rita Grunbaum translated. A copy of the translation is in her file.

7. There was excellent medical attention at Westerbork, with a well-equipped hospital, outpatient clinics, and pediatricians. Prisoners of Westerbork could receive immunizations and x-rays, their medical records were kept up to date, and the medical staff would hold weekly consultations at "the highest scientific and clinical level" (Presser, 424–25). Mechanicus reports that Dutch Jewish doctors were in charge of the hospital huts, and Jews were employed as nurses (31).

8. Mechanicus refers to the incidence of infantile paralysis several times in his diary, beginning with September 23, 1943, prior to the arrival of the Grunbaum family. Other cases are reported on October 12, November 1, and November 4 (nineteen cases). Dr. Spanier, head of the hospital, instituted quarantine measures and ordered prisoners to follow specific rules of hygiene, but in view of overcrowding in the camp these measures were unrealistic (164, 174, 182–83).

9. Mechanicus reports on a "small child with inflammation of the inner ear" who was taken to the Academic Hospital in Gronningen in an open bus, unaccompanied by a parent. "The ear was lanced and the child was put on the bus for Westerbork straight after the operation and the father took charge of it again at the camp entrance. . . . Inflammation of the middle ear [and other upper respiratory illnesses] . . . occur frequently" (50–51).

10. Some privileged prisoners had private accommodations in the camp in a number of small huts that were allotted to prisoners who worked in the camp administration, mostly run by German Jews who came to Westerbork in the early days of its existence.

11. A painting of Doctor Samuel di Lion Benavante, 1643–1722, is reproduced in the Dutch *Memorboek,* dedicated to Dutch Jewish history. This doctor seems to have been a prominent member of the community; perhaps the Dr. Benavante in Westerbork was his descendant. See Mozes Heiman Gans, *Memorboek: Platenatlas van het leven der joden in Nederland van de middeleeuwen tot 1940* (Netherlands: Baarn, Bosch and Koening, 1971), 51.

12. February 14, 1944, was a Monday. Presser lists a transport of 935 people who left Westerbork for Bergen Belsen on Tuesday, February 15, 1944. At that time, Belsen was listed as a "residential camp" by the Germans, reserved for specific groups of Jews who might possibly be exchanged for German prisoners of war (Presser, 513–14). One such group were holders of Palestine certificates, like those that had been obtained for the Grunbaums by their relatives in Mexico. According to Mechanicus, this deportation train was composed of passenger cars, not cattle cars, and the transport included all holders of Palestine certificates who had not yet been deported (Mechanicus, 249, 255). Because these prisoners might be used for exchange, the German administration sought to keep them alive. Living conditions were slightly more humane, the rations were better, and not all of the prisoners were assigned to the harshest labor. This situation changed, beginning in March 1944, as the camp gradually became a regular concentration camp and began to absorb large transports of prisoners from other camps. The Grunbaums, imprisoned in the "Star Camp" with other prisoners designated for exchange, experienced the transition from relatively privileged conditions to the chaotic, death-factory conditions of the end of the war, when tens of thousands of prisoners were dumped at Bergen Belsen from other camps. By then, mass deaths from starvation and typhus were common.

13. Celle, in the province of Hanover, Germany, was the town closest to the Bergen Belsen camp.

14. Although Bergen Belsen in February 1944 was still not classified as a concentration camp, the SS were as brutal and the regime as harsh as some others with that classification. "The work commandos were set to the hardest of labour, sometimes for nineteen hours at a stretch, guarded by merciless SS men, who set their dogs on them, and followed this up with blows" (Presser, 515–16).

15. In the "Star Camp" *(Sternenlager),* where the Dutch Jews were taken, men and women lived in different barracks, but members of the same family were allowed to meet. They wore their own clothes but had to wear the yellow star. On July 31, 1944, the Star Camp held forty-one hundred Jewish prisoners designated as exchange prisoners (*EH,* 187).

16. There were many unaccompanied children (see interview with Eva Schonbrun). Presser quotes several eyewitness accounts that describe the children as wild, "neglected waifs and strays" (521).

17. "More than one report speaks of the murderous roll-calls, which even the oldest camp inmates had to attend—people had to stand from 6 am in the morning, poorly clad, in streaming rain, in snow, in mud, sometimes for eight, nine or even twelve hours at a stretch—dreading all the time that they were about to be picked for an extermination camp" (Presser, 516).

18. Mrs. Grunbaum brought a small enamel potty among the belongings that she took with

her from Rotterdam. This potty was donated to the Museum of Jewish Heritage, New York. Eva Schonbrun and her sister Theresa were allowed to take a potty for their baby brother when they were deported from Czechoslovakia in 1944.

19. The Hungarians were the 1,684 Jews of the Kasztner transports brought to Bergen Belsen in July 1944 in an exchange deal negotiated by Reszo Kasztner. Many of the Jews on these transports were Orthodox; some were prominent rabbis. Three hundred and eighteen of these Jews were released in Switzerland in August 1944, and the others were released in December 1944 (*EH*, 187). Rita Grunbaum's testimony about religious observance relates to the presence of these Orthodox Jews from Hungary.

20. "Everyone stole, not only those from the poorer classes but leading businessmen as well. The deputy manager of one of the biggest Dutch banks was once caught cutting slices from a fellow-prisoner's loaf of bread" (Presser, 518).

21. Presser describes intellectual debates held while the men were working, including introductory lectures on sociology and debates on justice, religion, and history. Children would be taught history, biology, and even beginning Latin, clandestinely (519).

22. In the late fall of 1944 Allied governments and Jewish leaders were pressing the International Red Cross to send inspectors to exercise control in the concentration camps until the Allies liberated them. By then, Heinrich Himmler was receptive to making a deal with the Red Cross that would be to his advantage in the postwar reckoning. While negotiations were taking place the Red Cross actually visited some camps and distributed packages. Edith Horowitz and her mother received a package in Gunskirchen, a subcamp of Mauthausen, but Andrew Burian's package was confiscated by the SS moments after he received it (see interview with Andrew Burian). The shipping labels of Rita Grunbaum's packages are in her file.

23. The Star Camp held two hundred Jews from Tunisia, Tripoli, and Benghazi, North Africa, who had been in the Fossoli di Carpi camp in Italy (*EH*, 187).

24. Presser quotes a description of a Passover *seder* held in the children's barrack in the spring of 1945. "At the nadir of their suffering . . . the Jewish spirit touched its zenith with this celebration, this time-honoured observance, this feast of freedom, this token of inviolable faith" (521).

25. In the spring of 1945 tens of thousands of Jewish concentration camp prisoners were marched on foot westward from camps in the east to evade the Allied liberators. Twenty thousand women, including Anne Frank, arrived in Bergen Belsen on death marches from Auschwitz and the satellite camps of Buchenwald, and thousands of men came from Sachsenhausen and Buchenwald. "The camp administration did not lift a finger to house the prisoners who were streaming in. There was now total chaos in the camps, and a [spotted] typhus epidemic was at its height" (*EH*, 189).

26. Presser reports that two trains left Bergen Belsen for Theresienstadt in early April on orders from Berlin. One left either April 6 or 8; this train was liberated in Magdeburg. The second train, with the Grunbaums aboard, left Belsen at midnight, April 10, 1945. It had just carried a load of people with typhus and had been neither cleaned nor disinfected. During its thirteen-day journey the train made occasional stops, when those who could still stand could beg for food and drink in villages or isolated farms. Many of the prisoners on this transport died (522–23).

Nina Matathias

1. The Fascist anti-Jewish movement, the EEE (Greek National Union), perpetrated attacks on Jews between 1931 and 1934. In 1936 Jewish participation in the Greek army officer corps was forbidden, although Greek Jews were serving in the Greek army (*EH*, 1325).

2. Germany occupied Salonika on April 9, 1941, and immediately began the systematic persecution of its Jews. On July 11, 1942, Jewish men were ordered to assemble in Liberty Square and forced to do calisthenics in the blazing sun (*EH*, 1325).

3. Two thousand Jewish men were sent to forced labor. By October 1942, 250 had died (*EH*, 1326). Because systematic German persecution of the Jews in Salonika did not begin immediately, an illusion of safety was created that did not encourage Jewish emigration from Salonika. The Salonika Jews suffered great hardship during the winter of 1941–1942, and Red Cross and Jewish community relief efforts tried to supply food, shelter, and medical care. This "stable" situation was rudely shattered in July 1942 when Jewish men were sent to forced labor. See Michael Molho and Joseph Nehama, *The Destruction of Greek Jewry, 1941–1944* (Jerusalem: Yad Vashem, 1965), 46–47.

4. Volos had a prewar Jewish population of 882 (Molho and Nehama, 224).

5. When Germany conquered Greece in the spring of 1941 the country was divided into Italian and German occupation zones. Salonika, with the largest Jewish population of fifty-six thousand, was under German rule from the start. Volos, in the center of the country, was occupied by the Italians (Yahil, 408–9).

6. In December 1942 a *Judenrat* was established in Salonika, and in February 1943, with Eichmann's arrival, the Nuremberg Laws were implemented, isolating Salonika's Jews (*EH*, 1326).

7. On February 25, 1943, Jews in Salonika were concentrated in the Baron de Hirsch quarter, near the railroad station. From there, transports left for Auschwitz, where most Jews were gassed on arrival (*EH*, 1326).

8. Deportations to Auschwitz began in mid-March of 1943. The first transport arrived in Auschwitz on March 20, 1943 (*EH*, 1326).

9. On September 30, 1943, the first day of Rosh Hashanah, the mayor of Volos informed the rabbi, Moshe Pessah, that he was ordered to appear at the German commandant's office immediately. When the rabbi explained that because it was a holy day he would not report until the following day, he was threatened with arrest. The rabbi was told by the mayor that the city's census office was ordered to prepare a list of all its Jewish inhabitants and their addresses. The mayor gave orders to delay the preparation of this list in order to give the Jews time to escape. Rabbi Pessah appeared at the German commandant's office that afternoon, where he was berated for not appearing immediately, and was ordered to appear again the following day. Rabbi Pessah immediately went to see Metropolitan Joachim, head of the Greek Orthodox church in the area, and asked him to recommend to the Greeks who lived in the nearby villages to assist Jews to hide and escape. The rabbi was spirited away that evening from his home by two resistance fighters and taken to a village in an area not under German occupation. The rabbi's escape served as a signal to the Jewish community to seek hiding places, which was done by most of the Jews of Volos. Only about 130 of Volos's 882 Jews were caught by the Germans (Molho and Nehama, 157–58).

10. After the September 8, 1943, capitulation of the Italians, Germany moved into areas previously occupied by the Italians.

11. Jewish boys are normally circumcised on the eighth day. Not being able to observe this cardinal tenet of Jewish life was very distressing to the Matathiases.

12. Sweets, often including nuts, are an important ingredient in the Sephardic holiday cuisine.

13. Sephardic Jewish women, even those who do not observe other rituals meticulously, are often strict in their attendance at the ritual bath, the *mikvah*. This ritual facilitates the resumption of marital relations after childbirth or menstruation.

14. In the *mikvah*, women immerse themselves in the ritual bath after having bathed.

15. Of close to eighty thousand Greek Jews, about ten thousand survived the Holocaust. In Volos, where most of its 882 Jews hid, 760 survived. A ruling of November 21, 1944, by the Greek Ministry of Religion restored official status to Greek Jewish communities that had more than twenty surviving Jewish families (Molho and Nehama, 218, 224).

Helen Foxman

1. An abortion.

2. May 1, 1940.

3. A kerosene stove with one burner.

4. The Red Army entered Vilna on September 9, 1939, but handed the city over to the Lithuanians a few weeks later. In July 1940 Lithuania, including Vilna, became a Soviet republic (*EH*, 1571).

5. On June 24, 1941, two days after invading the Soviet Union, the Germans occupied Vilna (*EH*, 1572).

6. In late June 1941, a series of anti-Jewish decrees were established, including the order to wear the yellow star, a curfew, and putting certain streets out of bounds to Jews. After *Aktions* in July, August, and the beginning of September, in which several thousand Jews were murdered in the nearby forest of Ponar, two ghettos were established in the area from which the Jews had been cleared for the September 3 *Aktion* (*EH*, 1572–73).

7. The ghettoization *Aktion* took place on the Sabbath, September 6, 1941, and through the ensuing night. See Yitzhak Arad, *Ghetto in Flames: The Struggle and Destruction of the Jews in Vilna in the Holocaust* (Jerusalem: Yad Vashem, 1980), 112.

8. This prohibition was among the first anti-Jewish decrees issued on German occupation of Vilna (*EH*, 1572).

9. Thirty thousand Jews moved into ghetto number 1 and nine thousand to ghetto number 2. Jews with work permits (*Scheinen*) were in ghetto number 1; others were transferred to ghetto number 2. This ghetto was soon liquidated, its inhabitants massacred at Ponar (*EH*, 1573).

10. There was no authority within the ghetto to allocate housing. "Within a few hours all the vacant apartments were occupied," and latecomers crowded into already occupied rooms, basements, hallways, or even open yards (Arad, 120–21).

11. Jewish workers were not paid. Their non-Jewish employers were paid, and the Jews received ration cards that entitled them to very small rations of a few commodities, which were distributed in the ghetto.

12. A Jewish police force was created by order of the Germans soon after the ghetto was established. They were responsible for law and order in the ghetto and also manned the ghetto gates (Arad, 126).

13. *Aktions* took place on Yom Kippur, October 1, 1941, and on October 3–4, 15–16, and 21, in which ghetto number 2 was liquidated and its inhabitants taken to Ponar and shot. In additional *Aktions* on October 24, November 4–5, and several in December, the population of the ghetto was reduced to approximately twenty thousand Jews, from the fifty-seven thousand in Vilna at the beginning of the German occupation (*EH*, 1573).

14. The first protective documents were yellow work passes (*Scheinen*), which protected the bearers and their families from the *Aktions* on October 24 and November 4–5, 1941. They were permitted to remain in the ghetto after those mass roundups and murders. Early in December, pink passes were issued to relatives of those holding yellow passes and to others who were living in the ghetto illegally and did not hold any pass. On December 20–22, in the "Pink

Pass *Aktion*, Jews without passes were rounded up and taken to Ponar. This was the last in the series of mass exterminations of Vilna Jewry" (Arad, 149–63).

15. The Revisionist Zionist group was active in Jewish defense efforts. Joseph Glazman, a leader of the Revisionist-sponsored Betar youth group, took over the leadership of the Revisionists in the Vilna ghetto. On January 21, 1942, a meeting took place in his home at which the United Partisan Organization (FPO) was formed, a coalition of Zionist youth movements and Communist party groups. Glazman became part of the FPO staff command (Arad, 189, 236).

16. The resistance groups in the Vilna ghetto did not have the support of the majority of the population and never mounted a full-scale uprising against the Nazis. Before the final liquidation of the ghetto some escaped to the forests and joined partisan groups that fought independently or under Russian command.

17. Glazman left the Vilna ghetto in July 1943 and formed a Jewish partisan group in the Naroch Forest. They fought first under Russian command and then under the Lithuanian partisans. Glazman was killed fighting the Germans on October 7, 1943 (*EH*, 587–88).

18. Vilna, Bialystok, and Warsaw were in three separate zones of German administration. Travel between them was forbidden to Jews in part to prevent the spread of information from one zone to another. Jewish couriers, often women, for whom disguise as non-Jews was easier, risked their lives to travel, bringing news and messages from one ghetto to another. (See interview with Marysia Warman.) Henryk Grabowski brought the first news of the Vilna massacres to Warsaw in September 1941. The manifesto written by Abba Kovner in Vilna on January 1, 1942, and distributed to other ghettos by these couriers, called for armed resistance: "Let us not be led as sheep to the slaughter! . . . The only answer to the murderer is: To rise up with arms!" (Arad, 221, 230–32).

19. The Warsaw ghetto uprising took place between April 19 and May 16, 1943. It was the first urban uprising in Nazi-occupied Europe and lasted longest of the Jewish uprisings (*EH*, 1625).

20. Ponar (Paneriai), in a forest ten kilometers from Vilna, was used as a mass extermination site. The Soviets had excavated huge pits that they planned to use for fuel storage, but they left the area before the storage tanks were installed. The Nazis massacred tens of thousands of Jews and Soviet prisoners of war at Ponar. In September 1943 they used slave labor to open up the pits and exhume the bodies, which were burned in order to destroy the evidence of mass murder (*EH*, 1180).

21. Arad says that about seventy of these prisoners were Jews, caught after the liquidation of the Vilna ghetto, and ten were Soviet prisoners of war suspected of being Jewish. They were housed in an underground bunker surrounded by barbed wire. A ladder was the only access to the bunker; it was hauled up at night to prevent escapes. The prisoners were chained at the ankles, which allowed them to walk but not run (444–45).

22. They dug for three months, using their hands and spoons, and escaped from the tunnel on April 15, 1944. They sawed off their chains using a file they had found. About forty prisoners got out of the tunnel before the escape was discovered. Twenty-five were caught or killed, and about fifteen eluded capture. Eleven reached the Rudnicki forests and joined the partisans (Arad, 445).

23. "On April 20, 1944, 70 people were taken from the Kailis camp to continue cremating the corpses. They were murdered before the Germans retreated from Vilna" (Arad, 445).

24. In *Aktions* on August 4 and 24 and September 1 and 4, 1943, more than seven thousand men and women were deported from Vilna to concentration camps in Estonia. September 4 was a Saturday (*EH*, 1574). (Also see interview with Zenia Malecki.)

25. Klooga was a subcamp of the Vaivara camp in northern Estonia, near Tallinn. It was opened in the summer of 1943 and held about two thousand to three thousand Jewish men and women prisoners, most of whom arrived in August and September 1943 from the Vilna ghetto (*EH,* 806).

26. Helen Foxman explained that there were Jewish policemen in charge of the gate. Many knew her.

27. Beards were usually worn by observant Jewish men and would identify her husband immediately as a Jew.

28. Without makeup or a fashionable hairdo she looked like a peasant woman rather than a city person and was thus less likely to attract attention in a rural setting.

29. The official rations in the ghetto were totally inadequate to sustain life. A flourishing black market existed, based on smuggled goods and commodities, which supplemented the official rations.

30. She probably means fastidious.

31. Abe Foxman remembers that the first time he was taken to the synagogue was at the end of *Sukkot,* on *Simhat Torah,* a festive holiday that celebrates the finishing and beginning of the annual cycle of weekly Torah reading in the synagogue. On this day there is dancing and singing, and children are given candy and participate in the festivities (interview with Abraham Foxman).

32. Polish citizens in the Russian zone of occupation were given the option of returning to Poland after the war.

33. At the end of the war there was a large movement of Jewish refugees toward port cities from which they could embark for Palestine. Zionist organizations were involved in facilitating the crossing of borders, usually illegally, from country to country or from one occupation zone to another.

34. Because of the severely limited Jewish immigration quota imposed by the British, most Jews who wanted to go to Palestine had to do so illegally. Boats that took these refugees to Palestine picked them up on the Italian coast of the Mediterranean. To get to Italy, groups of refugees, assisted by Palestinian representatives of the *Haganah,* had to make a hazardous and difficult journey over the Alps. This was even more difficult for families with young children.

35. In the fall of 1945, in response to the intractable problem of tens of thousands of Jewish displaced persons in camps in Europe, the Anglo-American Committee of Inquiry conducted a plebiscite in the displaced persons camps to determine where the Jewish refugees wanted to go. In response to their expressed desire to go to Palestine, the committee report recommended in April 1946 that 100,000 Jews be allowed to immigrate to Palestine, that the British Mandate in Palestine be ended, and that a binational state be established in Palestine. See Yehuda Bauer, *A History of the Holocaust* (New York: Franklin Watts, 1982), 342–43.

36. YIVO is the Yiddish acronym for the Institute for Jewish Research, founded in Berlin in 1925, with its main center in prewar Vilna. "With particular emphasis on Yiddish speaking Jewry, YIVO sought, from its inception, to collect and preserve material mirroring Jewish life, to rescue Jewish folklore from oblivion, and to study various Jewish problems scientifically." The central directorate of YIVO shifted to the New York branch when Vilna was occupied by the Nazis. See Cecil Roth, ed., *Encyclopedia Judaica* (Jerusalem: Keter Publishing, 1972), 837–38 (hereafter referred to as *EJ*).

37. The Barton's candy company, established by the Klein family, Jewish refugees from Vienna who reached New York in the late 1930s, had stores all over the New York metropolitan

area. This company was particularly sympathetic to the needs of Holocaust survivors and hired many in the postwar years.

38. While the Barton stores were owned by the Klein family all their stores were closed on the Sabbath and Jewish holidays.

Hannah Bannett

1. "Aaron Marcus (1843–1916) . . . was one of the few Orthodox Jews in Germany who totally adopted Hasidism in theory and in practice" (*EJ*, 944).

2. Between 1862 and 1866 he made several long visits to the Hasidic rabbi of Radomsk, Solomon Rabinowicz (*EJ*, 949).

3. The Germans occupied Brzezany on July 7, 1941 (*EH*, 184).

4. On September 30, 1941, the eve of the Day of Atonement, "all male Jews aged 18 to 65 were ordered to assemble the following day in the central town square." Seven hundred Jews were taken to a nearby forest and murdered (*EH*, 185).

5. The *Judenrat* had to collect and hand over the valuables to the Germans (*EH*, 185).

6. On December 18, 1941, twelve hundred Jews were moved out of the city on the pretext that they were being transferred to a nearby town. They were machine gunned by Germans and Ukrainians (*EH*, 185).

7. Other *Aktions* took place at the end of 1941 and throughout 1942.

8. By March 1941, forty thousand Jews had been expelled from Cracow. The Cracow ghetto was established in the Podgorze section for the remaining eleven thousand Cracow Jews and Jews from neighboring towns. Jews were no longer permitted to live in Cracow at all (*EH*, 830–31).

9. Hans Frank (1900–1946) became governor general of Poland in October 1939. He was tried with the major Nazi war criminals at Nuremberg and was hanged (*EH*, 524–26).

10. On October 10, 1942, the remaining Jews of Brzezany were confined to a ghetto. In an *Aktion* on December 4 and 5, 1942, several hundred Jews were sent to the Belzec extermination camp. Many Jews attempted to go into hiding or sought refuge in the forests. In the spring of 1943 there were additional murders, with the final liquidation on June 12, 1943 (*EH*, 185).

11. This notorious prison was used by the Gestapo from the end of September 1939 to January 1945. It housed political prisoners, convicted SD and SS men, Soviet and British parachutists and spies, and common criminals. Jewish prisoners suffered brutal tortures and the worst conditions of incarceration (*EH*, 988).

12. The Joint Distribution Committee, an American Jewish international relief organization that entered the Allied occupied zones soon after their liberation to assist the survivors.

13. *Aliyah Bet*, the "illegal" immigration to Palestine during the period of the British Mandate, when legal Jewish immigration was severely restricted.

14. Legal immigration certificates were issued to fifteen thousand immigrants a year, usually to those with prior ties to the Zionist movement.

15. United Nations Relief and Refugee Agency, established after World War II to care for refugees and displaced persons.

Edith Horowitz

1. As one of the first steps in making Germany *Judenrein*, Germany began to expel Jews in 1938, beginning with Jews of foreign birth. In the Zbaszyn affair in late October 1938, thousands of Jews of Polish origin were rounded up in Germany and deported to the area of no-man's land outside Zbaszyn, Poland. The Polish government denied entry to holders of Polish passports after October 19 unless their passports were stamped by an examiner. In retaliation,

they also prepared to deport Jews of German origin to Germany. A stalemate, in which thousands of Jews were stranded in no-man's land, was finally broken by a compromise in which Poland admitted about seven thousand Jews, the Germans admitted some, and others returned to their homes. See Raul Hilberg, *The Destruction of European Jews* (Chicago: Quadrangle Books, 1961), 258.

2. Transports of children, called *Kindertransports*, were sent to England and Palestine in an effort to rescue German and Austrian Jewish children from the Nazi regime. Those children survived the Holocaust.

3. See interview with Cesia Brandstatter for background on the *Bais Yakov* schools.

4. Rosh Hashanah, the Jewish new year, occurred on September 25 and 26, 1939.

5. In the early days of German occupation, the German policy in areas annexed by Germany was to expel the Jews. Ghettoization followed later.

6. Moshe Merin was first the chairman of the Jewish Council *(Judenrat)* of Sosnowiec, with the title of *Judenalteste*, then chief of the *Zentrale*, the central office of the Jewish Councils of Elders in eastern Upper Silesia. The Jewish councils were the administrative bodies that implemented German orders. See Isaiah Trunk, *Judenrat: The Jewish Councils in Eastern Europe under Nazi Occupation* (New York: Macmillan, 1972), 26.

7. The first series of "resettlements" in eastern Upper Silesia took place from May to August, 1942 (Trunk, 422). The *Judenrate* were forced to make all the preliminary preparations, including making lists of Jews for deportation. Some chairmen refused to cooperate with German orders, which often led either to their immediate death or to their being among the first to be deported. Moshe Merin considered labor a means of rescuing young people from a worse fate. He urged them to report voluntarily to the German labor office for work in camps. He failed to achieve voluntary compliance, however, and young people were sent to camp against their wills (Trunk, 403–4). In May 1942 Merin "took an active part in setting up . . . [a] transport of about 1200 people to Auschwitz" (Trunk, 428).

8. Merin justified his participation in this kind of action: "I state that I have saved . . . people from resettlement" by selecting some so that others remained (quoted in Trunk, 422).

9. Zillertal was a subcamp of Gross Rosen. Women worked at the manufacture of thread and cloth. See *Vorlaufiges Verzeichnis der Konzentrations Lager un Deren Aussenkommandos, 1933–1945* (Arolsen: Comite International de la Croix-Rouge, Service International de Recherches, 1969), 129 (hereafter referred to as Arolsen).

10. An area of mountain ranges in the Sudetenland between Germany and Czechoslovakia.

11. For additional information about the process of making cloth from flax, see interview with Cesia Brandstatter.

12. There were French and Russian prisoners of war, German criminal prisoners, and Ukrainian workers in the factory. Only the Jews and the German criminals were incarcerated in the camp; the other workers left the factory after work.

13. According to camp lore, bromine was put in the coffee to prevent menstruation. Edith mentions that her mother never drank the coffee because she wanted to get her period. Nonetheless, malnutrition will cause cessation of menses, which usually resume when the body recovers and a normal proportion of body fat is attained. Also see interview with Miriam Rosenthal, note 10.

14. The prisoner groups who worked in the gas chambers were called the *Sonderkommando*. When the Hungarian Jews arrived in Auschwitz in the spring of 1944, Polish Jews may have formed the majority of this commando. The *Sonderkommando* itself was periodically killed, however, to prevent information about the gas chambers from circulating. See interviews

with Rose Meth and Anna Heilman for information about the revolt of the *Sonderkommando* in the fall of 1944.

15. Maramures (Maramaross-Sighet, Rumania) in the Carpathians was given to Hungary in 1939. It had a large, traditional Jewish population before World War II and was a center of Jewish religious life. The Carpathian Jews were generally religious, many following Hasidic rabbis. There were, of course, religious Jews among the Budapest Jews as well, but urban Jews were apt to be more cosmopolitan.

16. Candles are lit on the festival of Hanukkah every night for eight nights, beginning with one candle and ending with eight, in celebration of the Maccabean victory over the Assyrians and the rededication of the Holy Temple in Jerusalem, ca. 586 C.E.

17. Literally, oral tradition, or education transmitted orally without the benefit of books or a formal classroom.

18. Lot, Abraham's nephew, who was saved from the destruction of Sodom and Gomorrah, thought that he and his family were the last human beings on earth.

19. Miriam Rosenthal, who was also pregnant, tells of receiving extra food from the women she worked with, who were eager to protect her and her unborn child. She gave birth in Kaufering; she and the baby survived. See interview with Miriam Rosenthal.

20. An administrative subcamp of Buchenwald, Nordhausen was in the Hartz mountains of Germany. Secret weapons, including V1 and V2 rockets, were manufactured there in underground installations, some of which were subcamps of Nordhausen. It was liberated by the Americans on April 11, 1945.

21. Traditional standards of modesty followed by religious Jews assure that daughters do not see their mothers without clothing.

22. Germans convicted of certain criminal offenses were sent to concentration camps. They were often chosen to be *Kapos*, in charge of other prisoners.

23. Mauthausen is near Linz, Austria. It was a major camp, whose main feature was a stone quarry that served as the site of brutal forced labor. Prisoners hewed out a flight of 186 steps, carrying the stones by hand. Work in the quarry was notorious for its senseless cruelty and high death toll. It was liberated by the Americans on May 5, 1945.

24. Prisoners were sometimes pushed off the top of the steps to their deaths at the bottom of the quarry. It was called "Parachutists Leap."

25. Located in a forest near Lambach, Austria, Gunskirchen was an administrative subcamp of Mauthausen. It was liberated by the Seventy-first Infantry Division of the United States Army on May 5, 1945.

26. Andrew Burian also describes a visit of the Swiss Red Cross shortly before Gunskirchen was liberated. His package was confiscated by the Germans as soon as he received it. See interview with Andrew Burian.

27. The Jewish Brigade Group was a unit of Jewish soldiers from Palestine who volunteered to fight with the British army. At the end of World War II soldiers from this unit sought out Jewish Holocaust survivors and facilitated their immigration to Palestine. Also see interview with Estelle Alter.

28. Units of the Polish army, organized in exile, waited in England for the invasion of Europe and then fought with the Allies to liberate eastern Europe.

29. Dr. Horst Schumann, who began his Nazi pseudo-scientific experiments in the euthanasia program as director of the killing center at Grafeneck, and Dr. Wladislaw Dering, a Polish prisoner doctor, sterilized and castrated prisoners in Auschwitz. See Robert Jay Lifton, *The Nazi Doctors: Medical Killing and the Psychology of Genocide* (New York: Basic Books, 1986), 246, 278.

Rachel Silberman

1. ORT are the initials of a worldwide network of Jewish vocational schools. Originating in Russia in 1880, the organization established schools on every continent and is now a major provider of vocational skills to Jewish communities. Its schools are also sources of technological innovation (*EJ* 12: 1481–85). The network in English is called the Organization for Rehabilitation and Training.

2. The Russians occupied Siauliai from June 15, 1940, until June 26, 1941.

3. One thousand Jews were murdered in Siauliai by Germans and Lithuanians in the first two weeks of German occupation (*EH*, 1239).

4. Two areas of the city were designated as ghettos, Kaukazas and Trakai. Kaukazas, located near the Jewish cemetery, included about five streets and had previously housed four hundred poor people. About twenty-eight hundred Jews crowded in there. See Eliezer Yerushalmi, *Pinkas Shavli: A Diary from a Lithuanian Ghetto, 1941–1944* (in Hebrew) (Jerusalem: Yad Vashem, 1958), 18.

5. The second ghetto, Trakai, was more isolated, surrounded by factories, including the Frankel leather factory, the Bata shoe factory, and a large lake (Yerushalmi, 18).

6. This refers to the children's *Aktion* of November 5, 1943, which was a traumatic experience in the ghetto. Hannah Sara Rigler also remembers it and describes it as she saw it. Adults had to go to work, leaving their children behind. *Hauptsturmführer* Forster, the security police, and other Nazis who came from Kaunas for the occasion supervised the *Aktion*, in which the Jewish police were forced to assist the Ukrainian collaborators. The *Aktion* lasted from 7:00 A.M. until 4:00 P.M. The adults watched from the square or from the factories where they worked. Seventeen children and eight elderly Jews were killed; a total of 796 children under the age of thirteen and elderly and ill Jews were taken away in the *Aktion*. Yerushalmi reports that the adults were shot at the German border and that the children were gassed on arrival at Auschwitz (Yerushalmi, 302–9).

7. In July 1944 Siauliai was one of the last ghettos to be liquidated. About two thousand Siauliai Jews remained, along with two thousand Jews from other places who were working in the factories in and around Siauliai. Transports left Siauliai on July 15 and 17. The transport that was supposed to leave on July 19 could not travel because of damage to the rail lines. The transport of July 17 went to Kaunas and then to Stutthof (Yerushalmi, 379–92).

8. See interviews with Hannah Rigler and Rozalia Berke for other experiences in Stutthof. Stutthof was located thirty-four kilometers northeast of Danzig. It was opened in September 1939 and remained in operation until World War II ended in May 1945. It had several dozen administrative subcamps and was located near the Baltic Sea. Its prisoners suffered from extremes of hot and cold weather, harsh labor, and little food. Most died of the severe conditions. In 1944 large numbers of Jewish women were brought there from the Baltic countries and Auschwitz. See Konnilyn Feig, *Hitler's Death Camps: The Sanity of Madness* (New York: Holmes and Meier, 1981), 191–203.

9. Feig points out that the coast of the Baltic Sea was a major resort area of eastern Europe. SS personnel who worked in Stutthof could lie on the beach after a hard day's work. There was an unusual fountain in front of the camp headquarters building (Feig, 191–92).

10. Although Stutthof was not officially classified as an extermination camp, most of the fifty thousand prisoners who were brought there died. There was no systematic killing, but the harsh conditions and brutality of the guards took a huge toll.

11. There was a small gas chamber in a far corner of the camp. Many prisoners did not know of its existence. See *Obozy Hitlerowski na Ziemiach Polskich, 1939–1945* (Warsaw: Panstwowe Wydawnichtwo Naukowe, 1979), 496 (map). Invalids were gassed at Stutthof.

The camp commandant was ordered to kill "all the Jews who were old, sick or unable to work. . . . The great majority of them were women." See Eugen Kogon, et al., *Nazi Mass Murder: A Documentary History of the Use of Poison Gas* (New Haven: Yale University Press, 1994), 191–92.

12. Keeping track of the Jewish calendar was an important act of spiritual resistance for Rachel's mother. When she realized that her calculations might be inaccurate, her sense of control and competence was destroyed.

13. Elbing was a subcamp of Stutthof. Rachel says they worked at dredging. According to *Obozy*, prisoners dug canals (503). Arolsen lists the *Todt* organization as the labor contractor at Elbing.

14. Northwest of Gdansk (*Obozy*, 503 [map]).

Brandla Small

1. On September 4, 1942, Chaim Rumkowski, chairman of the Lodz ghetto *Judenrat*, announced the imminent resettlement of twenty-five thousand Jews (those under the age of ten or over sixty-five). A curfew was imposed, and Jewish policemen, accompanied by Gestapo, systematically assembled residents of each ghetto block and selected those who were to be deported. See Lucjan Dobroszycki, ed., *The Chronicle of the Lodz Ghetto, 1941–1944* (New Haven: Yale University Press, 1984), 248–55. This *Aktion*, called the *Szpera* by the Jews of Lodz, was a traumatic one for the community and is described frequently by survivors.

2. People selected for deportation were loaded onto wagons or five-ton trucks with high plank siding (*Chronicle*, 252).

3. As a center of garment manufacturing before World War II, the Lodz clothing factories were impressed into forced labor for the German war effort, producing uniforms, insignia, and other garments for Germany.

4. People seized for deportation while waiting in lines to receive food may have carried their family's ration cards with them. Such seizures were random and unpredictable, and remaining family members sometimes starved to death before they could arrange for new ration cards (*Chronicle*, 254).

5. All ghetto residents had to demonstrate *produktsye* (productivity) in order to receive food rations (*Chronicle*, 433).

6. After the September 1942 *Aktion*, two thousand children were accounted for in the ghetto. On February 23, 1944, however, the *Chronicle* reports five thousand unemployed persons, most of whom are presumed by the writers of the *Chronicle* to be children. Natural population growth would not explain three thousand children (459). Obviously, many children eluded the September 1942 *Aktion*. Presumably, some of the five thousand unemployed were also elderly or sick.

7. The last *Daily Chronicle Bulletin* in Lodz was issued on July 30, 1944. It listed 68,561 inhabitants. All but fourteen hundred people were deported to Auschwitz-Birkenau in August 1944.

8. As of July 2, 1944, the *Chronicle* reports that "the ghetto still has no idea where the transports are headed" (519).

9. A caustic solution was poured on areas that were shaved of body hair during the disinfection process at Auschwitz.

10. Christianstadt was a subcamp of Gross Rosen. Prisoners worked in and around a munitions factory (Arolsen, 111).

11. At Parschnitz there were several forced labor camps, subcamps of Gross Rosen, at several factories, including Kluge (Arolsen, 122).

12. The Polish *Armja Krajowa* (Home Army) was known as *A-Kovtses*, from the initials AK. They were antagonistic to Jews and often attacked Jewish partisan groups or informed on them to the Nazis.

13. This interview was recorded at a gathering of Lodz Holocaust survivors at the Concord Hotel in the Catskill mountains of New York State. Mrs. Small's daughter accompanied her to the gathering.

Sisters and Camp Sisters

1. Ringelheim, 382.
2. Ringelheim, 384.

Estelle Alter

1. The Germans occupied Belgium in May 1940.

2. On March 3, 1942, a general labor draft was issued in Belgium, and on March 11 special forced labor was imposed on the Jews (*EH*, 162). "Thousands of men between the ages of 16 and 60, as well as women from 16 to 40 were rounded up for forced labor in projects of the *Organisation Todt* at Audinghem and other areas" (Hilberg, 387).

3. "As of December 31, 1941, Jewish children were excluded from the public schools." See Lucy S. Dawidowicz, *The War against the Jews, 1933–1945* (New York: Holt, Rinehart and Winston, 1975), 364.

4. Deportation of Jews from Belgium began in the summer of 1942. A transit camp at Malines served as the collection point for deportees. Foreign Jews were deported first, but by September 1943 Jews of Belgian nationality were deported as well. Most perished in Auschwitz (Hilberg, 387, and *EH*, 162). The name of Estelle's father, Abraham Feld, appears on the list of Belgian convoy number 17, which arrived in Auschwitz on November 3, 1942. See Serge Klarsfeld and Maxime Steinberg, *Memorial de la Deportation des Juifs de Belgique* (Paris: Beate Klarsfeld Foundation, 1982). Research at Yad Vashem by a member of Estelle's family yielded the information that her father died in Auschwitz on December 6, 1944 (conversation with Estelle, July 20, 1992).

5. In Belgium, Jews had to wear the Star of David as of June 3, 1942 (*EH*, 162).

6. As of August 29, 1941, Jews in Belgium were subject to nightly curfew from 8:00 P.M. to 7:00 A.M. (*EH*, 162).

7. A Jewish underground organization, Comite de Defense des Juifs, affiliated with the Belgian resistance movement, was instrumental in assisting some twenty-five thousand Jews to hide from the Germans. Many Belgians participated in this effort, including church institutions (Dawidowicz, 365, and *EH*, 165).

8. Estelle's mother's name appears as Leni Schwimmer-ova, her maiden name, on Belgian convoy number 18, which arrived in Auschwitz on January 15, 1943 (Klarsfeld and Steinberg).

9. Wezembeek-Oppem is a suburb east of Brussels, Belgium.

10. The Jewish Brigade Group was a fighting unit of the British army and was composed of volunteers from the Jewish community in Palestine. It was formed in September 1944 and fought in Italy from March to May 1945. After the end of the war men from the Jewish Brigade traveled throughout Europe seeking survivors of the Holocaust and facilitating their immigration to Palestine through the "illegal" *Briha* [escape] network (*EH*, 746–47).

11. A working-class neighborhood at the seashore in Brooklyn, New York.

12. A busy commercial street with apartments above the stores. The subway train runs on an elevated track past the windows of the apartments.

Margie Nitzan

1. Work permits were not granted to refugees in Switzerland because their status was supposed to be temporary.

2. Although anti-Jewish prejudice was part of Italian Fascist ideology from its beginnings, Italy was not perceived as being anti-Semitic in the 1930s. See Meir Michaelis, *Mussolini and the Jews: German-Italian Relations and the Jewish Question in Italy, 1922–1945* (Oxford: Clarendon Press, 1978), 8.

3. The prayer "Hear, Oh Israel, the Lord our God, the Lord is One" is the ultimate declaration of monotheistic belief. Devout Jews cover their eyes when they say it to eliminate any distraction from the seriousness of this prayer. It is one of the first prayers taught to young children.

4. Observant Jews say a different blessing before eating different varieties of food and say grace after meals.

5. Until 1938 the civil and religious rights of Jews in Italy were respected (*EH*, 722).

6. "By 1938 over 10,000 Jewish refugees were in Italy" (Dawidowicz, 340).

7. The first anti-Jewish laws were enacted in 1938, as Italy's ties with Nazi Germany strengthened. In September 1938 Jewish refugees and all Italian Jews who became citizens after January 1, 1919, were ordered to leave the country within six months. Jewish civil and economic rights were taken away (Yahil, 422).

8. Before Italy entered the war there were mass arrests on June 10, 1940, of Jews who had not left the country when ordered to do so earlier (*EH*, 726).

9. Dawidowicz describes the San Vittorio prison in Milan as "notorious . . . where torture and murder were common" (340).

10. Ferramonti was the largest of the forty-three Italian detention camps in which foreign nationals were interned (Michaelis, 292).

11. Jewish children were banned from public schools in Italy by the racial laws of 1938 (Yahil, 422).

12. The Union of Communities established schools and social service institutions, such as soup kitchens, to assist children and the poor (Yahil, 423).

13. After the fall of the Fascist regime on July 25, 1943, most of the Jews of Italy were caught between the German occupation, with its relentless search for and deportation of Jews, and the push of the American forces from the south (*EH*, 726–27).

14. Margie is petite, about five feet tall, and is very slight.

15. Possibly the Comitato di Assistenza agli Ebrei profughi dalla Germania, a Jewish community organization that assisted German Jewish refugees. See Klaus Voigt, "Jewish Refugees and Immigrants," in *The Italian Refuge: Rescue of Jews during the Holocaust*, ed. Ivo Herzer (Washington, D.C.: Catholic University Press, 1989), 154.

16. "German raiding parties had lists of the names and addresses of the Jews and were assisted . . . by the Italian Fascist armed forces." The large *Razzia* (roundup) in Milan took place on November 8, 1943. Arrested Jews were first held in local jails, then in nearby concentration camps, and then deported to Auschwitz or other extermination camps (*EH*, 727).

17. The Vatican newspaper. The Vatican expressed opposition to the implementation of Nazi racial ideology in its own newspaper, which was constantly under the threat of being banned. By 1943 the newspaper confined itself to printing the vague and ineffectual expressions of Pope Pius XII's messages about human rights abuses (Michaelis, 254, 288, 371).

18. The chief rabbi of Rome, Rabbi Israel Zolli, was born in Brody, Poland, in 1881, and "had personal memories of anti-Semitism. As a rabbi in Trieste for nearly thirty years before coming to Rome in 1940, he had talked with hundreds of Jewish refugees from northern

Europe during the 1930's. He was much more wary of the Nazis than most of his Italian colleagues." He vainly argued in favor of closing the synagogue and warning the Roman Jews to go into hiding, but the Jewish lay leadership ignored his warnings. Zolli's absence from the synagogue on Rosh Hashanah 1943 was attributed to illness, thus not allowing his actions to constitute a warning to others. Zolli and his family survived the war in hiding ("according to some, in the Vatican"). After Rome's liberation he was relieved of his duties by the Jewish community leadership. In February 1945 Zolli converted to Catholicism, in a shocking resolution of his differences with his community. The issue is still a controversial one. See Susan Zuccotti, *The Italians and the Holocaust: Persecution, Rescue, Survival* (New York: Basic Books, 1987), 114, 300 n. 18, 301 n. 34; and Yahil, 426–27.

19. Her father had recognizably "Jewish" features, and her mother wore a wig, traditionally worn by very Orthodox Jewish women who cover their hair for reasons of modesty.

20. Margie calls her la Georgetta, la Milanola, la Francesca, la Principessa.

21. Lago Orta, in northern Italy near Lake Como.

22. A group of approximately one thousand refugees, mostly Jews, who were liberated by American troops in the southern part of Italy were allowed to enter the United States in 1944 temporarily and were interned in the Fort Ontario army camp in Oswego, New York, with the understanding that they would leave the United States after the war. With no place to go, however, after the war they were allowed to reenter the United States from Canada as immigrants.

23. In European synagogues women usually sit in a balcony where they look down at the proceedings.

24. ORT: see interview with Rachel Silberman, note 1.

25. Pioneer Women is a women's Zionist organization affiliated with the Israeli Labor Party. The women raise funds to support social service projects in Israel. Margie is a member.

26. A Jew who rejects a conversion to another religion may return to Judaism without any ceremony.

27. A German-language newspaper published in New York City that caters to the German-Jewish refugee community.

Edith Wachsman

1. Rabbi Moses Sofer, known as the Ḥatam Sofer (1762–1839), was a renowned *halakhic* authority and leader of Orthodox Jewry. His sons and disciples were active in promoting the growth of Jewish settlement in Palestine in the nineteenth century (*EJ* 15: 77–79).

2. Rabbi Glasner served as rabbi in Klausenberg (Cluj), 1878–1922. He participated in the first Mizrachi [Religious Zionist] world conference in Pressburg in 1904 and was a delegate to the Twelfth Zionist World Congress in Carlsbad in 1921. See Herman Dicker, *Piety and Perseverance: Jews from the Carpathian Mountains* (New York: Sepher-Hermon Press, 1981), 65.

3. Jelsava, Czechoslovakia, twelve kilometers south of Revuca, fifty miles west of Kosice.

4. The Jewish Code, based on the Nuremberg Laws, was passed on September 9, 1941, depriving Jews of their civil and legal rights (Dawidowicz, 378).

5. Orthodox Jews do not write or carry things outside their homes on the Sabbath.

6. The first Jewish badge was a yellow arm band with a Star of David. Jewish apartments also had to be identified with a star. See Avigdor Dagan, ed., *Jews of Czechoslovakia: Historical Studies and Surveys* (Philadelphia: Jewish Publication Society, 1984), 3: 184.

7. Variants of these regulations were locally promulgated and enforced. On September 22, 1941, all Jews over the age of six had to wear the yellow star (Dagan, 3: 184).

8. Orthodox men, with beards and earlocks, were particularly vulnerable to attack in which their beards and earlocks would be cut or torn out.

9. The deportations began in March 1942.

10. *Ovinu Malkeinu*, a supplicatory prayer usually said on fast days.

11. Very pious Jews would fast on Mondays and Thursdays, the days when the Torah is read in the synagogue. In times of grave danger this practice would be instituted for all adults.

12. Deportation of families from Revuca occurred in June 1942 (comment by Edith Wachsman, July 14, 1994).

13. Ritual slaughter is normally prohibited on the Sabbath. Because lives were in danger, however, the rabbi slaughtered chickens on the Sabbath.

14. Normally the soaking and salting would take an hour and a half. This prescribed time was shortened because lives were in danger.

15. The usual mode of transportation was in cattle cars.

16. Before Zyklon B was used in large, stationary gas chambers, truck motors were used to generate carbon monoxide that would kill the victims, who were either in sealed vans or in sealed chambers that were connected to the engines. This method was used at Majdanek, near Lublin, in 1942.

17. Rabbi Klein had a travel permit, issued August 27, 1942, that permitted him to travel to specific Czech towns. A copy of this document is in Edith Wachsman's file.

18. The Kleins were Slovak citizens, but they, like the other Jews, lost their citizenship when the Nuremberg Laws were instituted in Slovakia. Mrs. Klein's mother, Rebbetzin Mindel Lichtenstein, who lived in Hungary, bribed and cajoled the Hungarian authorities to obtain a Hungarian passport for the Kleins in late 1942 or early 1943. This document enabled Mrs. Klein to travel back and forth to Hungary and smuggle Slovakian Jewish children across with her, including her own child Yehudah, who eventually perished in Auschwitz (comment by Edith Wachsman, July 14, 1994).

19. March 19, 1944.

20. Yehudah was sent to relatives in Balkany, Hungary, to get a "proper Jewish education." See *Z'chor Y'mot Olam*, memoir of Rabbi Abraham Klein, Edith Wachsman file, 5.

21. One of the earliest calls for resistance to the Nazis came from the left-wing Zionist Socialist group, *HaShomer HaTzair*, in August 1940. The general Slovak uprising began on August 29, 1944, and included several Jewish units (Dagan, 3: 224–33).

22. Copies of Rabbi Klein's false documents are in Edith Wachsman's file.

23. Murany is nine kilometers northwest of Revuca.

24. Riecka, Czechoslovakia, 48.46N, 19.05E (Klein memoir, 9).

25. This is consistent with Orthodox Jewish practice in which married women cover their hair for reasons of modesty. It was also common practice among European peasant women to wear kerchiefs over their hair, however.

26. She could not use one of her own pots because the meat was not kosher.

27. Podlavice, Czechoslovakia, sixty-two kilometers east of Czestochowa.

28. German soldiers often came to the village to search for partisans or arms. The first time they came all the Klein children hid under the beds, hoping they would not be found. Edith remembers it was on the Sabbath; the Germans did not search their apartment (conversation with Edith Wachsman, July 18, 1994).

29. An egg is one of the symbolic foods eaten at the Passover *seder*, as is a fresh vegetable. The egg is a reminder of the daily sacrifice in the Holy Temple in Jerusalem, and the fresh vegetable a symbol of spring and the renewal of nature.

30. Thursday, March 29, 1945.

31. Bread is normally forbidden on Passover.

32. The second day of Passover, Friday, March 30, 1945.

33. The slaughtering knife was hidden with Rabbi Klein's *tallit* and *tefillin* in the woodshed. These ritual objects were kept near the family throughout their experiences.

34. Tornalja, Czechoslovakia, seventy-five kilometers southwest of Kosice. It is called Safarikovo today in Slovakia.

Eva Schonbrun

1. Theresa's story is based on her oral history. See oral history of Theresa Beilush.

2. The first deportations from Slovakia began in March 1942 and continued through October 1942. At that time, transports were concentrated in five concentration camps, including Novacky. During the period of no deportations from Slovakia, the camps served as labor camps. When deportations resumed in the fall of 1944, Novacky and the other four camps were again used as concentration and staging points for transports to the Polish death camps.

3. For two weeks Theresa continued her vigilant attention to her remaining brothers and sisters, until she was denounced as a Jew and arrested. Her adamant denials of Jewish identity, in spite of interrogation and severe beatings by the Gestapo, kept her with the non-Jewish prisoners for two days. On the third day, the Czech woman who was hiding her sister Eva, and the superintendent of her parents' apartment building, confronted her with their accusations and identified her as Jewish. When they brought in five-year-old Eva and their nine-month-old baby brother, who had been denounced and brought to the Gestapo by their Czech protectors, Theresa could not deny her relationship to them. They were reunited as Jewish prisoners.

4. Sered, one of the original five Czech camps, was the second largest concentration camp in Czechoslovakia. As of July 1, 1943, it had 1,095 inmates. The camp was noted for its carpentry shop, whose production was of very high quality. Commandant of the camp was Alois Brunner (Dagan, 3: 214–15, 234).

5. Bergen Belsen was near Celle, Germany. Established in 1941 as a camp for Russian prisoners of war, it was designated in 1943 as a preferential camp for Jews holding documents or passports from enemy countries who would be used for prisoner exchange. There were five subcamps, among them several that housed families and children. The children are described in *Inside Belsen* (Sussex, U.K.: Harvester Press, 1982) by Hanna Levy-Haas, who arrived in Belsen in August 1944. Czech nationals in Belsen are described in United Nations War Crimes Commission, *The Belsen Trial* (New York: Howard Fertig, 1983), 74. Theresa estimates their arrival in Belsen at the end of October or the beginning of November 1944. Eva says she was in Belsen nine months, which would put her arrival there sometime in September 1944. Theresa explains that their transport left Sered and traveled toward Poland. At the Polish border it was stopped for two days and then rerouted to Oranienburg like other transports from Sered. Strangely, however, their transport left Oranienburg after only one night and brought them to Bergen Belsen, where they were put with the Hungarian Jews of the Kasztner transport. Also see interview with Rita Grunbaum, note 19, regarding the Kasztner transport.

6. A similar experience is described by Jona Oberski in *Childhood* (New York: New American Library, 1978).

7. Theresa tells of tearing her slip into four pieces, which she used as diapers. Every night she washed the "diapers" and dried them on her body for use the following day.

8. She was a Polish prisoner in charge of her barrack; her name was Luba. In her interview, Theresa describes Eva as a "charming child."

9. Coming from a strictly Orthodox home, Eva knew, even at the age of five, that ham

was not kosher and was therefore forbidden. She probably did not know that when a person's life is in danger, the rules of *kashrut* may be abrogated.

10. In her interview, Theresa called herself "the only unwed mother . . . like the miracle of the Block." There was a daily ration of about eight ounces of milk for each child under the age of two. Theresa and Eva's brother was the youngest child in their barrack, but Theresa would often share this ration with mothers of children over two, who received no milk at all. Theresa also "mothered" many of the motherless children in their barrack, talking to them, consoling and caressing them.

11. In *Childhood*, Jona Oberski describes the same structure.

12. The British entered Bergen Belsen on April 15, 1945.

13. A children's home for one hundred child survivors of Bergen Belsen was established in the Warburg family home at Blankenesee, Germany, near Hamburg. See interviews with Michael Gelber and George Schwab and untitled, confidential JDC Report number 341, June 28, 1946; subject: report on Bergen Belsen by Shlome Michael Gelber, director, JDC Activities in Paris.

14. At the time of liberation, Theresa was ill with typhus in the camp hospital. After ten days she located her sick brother and sister in the *revier*, the barrack designated for sick people, where they were being cared for by the British. Theresa threw what she called a "hysterical fit" until she was allowed to be reunited with them and was moved with them to the sanatorium.

15. According to Theresa, this English doctor took the baby to a tent he set up on the highest spot in the area so the baby's lungs would benefit from cleaner air and nursed him until he was healthy enough to move.

16. Theresa tells that when her parents were arrested in Bratislava after Yom Kippur in 1944, they were taken to the camp at Novacky. In a series of daring escapes, they eluded deportation and finally survived the war in Budapest, Hungary. All the children who remained in hiding in Czechoslovakia also survived. Only the oldest daughter was deported and perished with her two children in Auschwitz.

17. Theresa said the transport was supposed to go to Sweden, where many of the sickest survivors of Bergen Belsen were taken for medical treatment and rehabilitation.

18. Theresa made a list of all the children she had contact with in Bergen Belsen. When she returned to Prague she was bombarded with questions from mothers seeking their lost children. Because of her list, Theresa was able to furnish pertinent information to a few mothers about their children. Most of the children Theresa knew in Bergen Belsen were Dutch, however.

19. According to Theresa, Eva and her baby brother were cared for in the Masaryk Sanatorium in Prague.

Hannah Sara Rigler

1. A photo on page 1439 of the *Encyclopedia of the Holocaust* shows a group of men, including the prominent rabbis Nochomovsky and Baksht, in front of the "White Prison" in Siauliai before they were taken to the nearby forest to be shot. See interview with Rachel Silberman for additional historical background of the German occupation of Siauliai.

2. Two areas of the city were designated as ghettos, Kaukazas and Trakai. Kaukazas, located near the Jewish cemetery, included about five streets and had previously housed four hundred poor people. About twenty-eight hundred Jews crowded in there. Trakai was more isolated, surrounded by factories, including the Frankel leather factory, the Bata shoe factory, and a large lake (Yerushalmi, 18).

3. Mendel Lejbowich was the head of the *Judenrat* in the Kaukazas ghetto. A prominent citizen of Siauliai, he was a well-to-do merchant before the war who had many contacts among the non-Jewish population (Yerushalmi, 18).

4. Diary entries for May 1942 by Yerushalmi describe conditions at forced labor camps in three neighboring towns, where groups of several hundred Jews from Siauliai were sent to mine peat. The camps were surrounded by barbed wire, minimal food rations were distributed, and the regime was harsh. The camps were supervised by Lithuanian collaborators (Yerushalmi, 79–83). Also see interview with Rachel Silberman.

5. Yerushalmi reports in his diary entry of November 4, 1943, that the ghetto of Kaukazas has been liquidated (301).

6. Georg Pariser and Mendel Lejbowich were appointed leaders of the ghetto/concentration camp that was established in Trakai after the November 5, 1943, children's *Aktion*. Pariser was appointed head of the Labor Office (*Arbeitseinsatz*). A German Jew, he was married to a German woman who followed him willingly into the ghetto with their two children. Because of his German origins and wife, Jews in the ghetto suspected him of ulterior motives, but Yerushalmi insists that Pariser did not attain special privileges, was jailed for a while and suffered hunger like the others, and assisted the weak and helpless in the ghetto (Yerushalmi, 318).

7. Under the concentration camp administration, everyone had to work. Most people worked in one of the local factories.

8. Also see interview with Rachel Silberman.

9. See Rachel Silberman interview, note 6.

10. See Rachel Silberman interview, note 7.

11. The gas chamber in Stutthof was originally built for delousing clothing. The first gassing of people at Stutthof took place on June 22, 1944, and subsequent gassings occurred until November 1944. The camp commandant received orders to kill "all the Jews who were old, sick or unable to work." Most of these victims were women, selected to die on the basis of superficial appearance or the inability to do certain physical exercises (Kogon, 193).

12. The original wooden crematorium in Stutthof burned down and was replaced with a larger brick structure. It is located at the far end of the camp, near the gas chamber. Today the crematorium building serves as a museum with eight exhibition halls. The ovens are still there (Feig, 193–94, 200).

13. Arolsen lists Stutthof as *KL Hauptlager*, a main concentration camp with administrative subsidiary camps (Arolsen, 221).

14. The German euphemism for this action, in which thousands of prisoners were marched on foot deeper into Germany to evade the approaching Allied armies, was "evacuation." In actuality it was a death march, as the prisoners themselves called it.

15. In the Danzig corridor. This part of Hannah's story is corroborated by the diary of William Fisher, a British prisoner of war who was held with nine other British soldiers in Stalag 20B in Gross Golemkau. He had been a prisoner for about five years when he began a diary on scraps of paper in January 1945. The diary is in the collection of the Museum of Jewish Heritage, New York, and William Fisher's letters to Hannah Rigler, written years later, are in the Hannah Sara Rigler file.

16. William Fisher describes the column of women on Hannah's death march in his diary entry for January 25, 1945: "I have seen today the filthiest, foulest and most cruel sight of my life. God damn Germany with an everlasting punishment. At 9 am this morning a column straggled down the road towards Danzig—a column far beyond the words of which I am able

to describe. I was struck dumb with a miserable rage a blind coldness which nearly resulted in my being shot. . . . They came straggling through the bitter cold, about 300 of them, limping, dragging footsteps, slipping and falling, to rise and stagger under the blows of the guards and SS swine. Crying loudly for bread, screaming for food 300 matted haired, filthy objects that had been—Jewesses!"

17. Her father, Mr. Zilberstein, was the assistant principal of the Gymnasia Ivrit Bialik, which Hannah and her sister attended in Siauliai (conversation with Hannah Rigler, September 1, 1994).

18. The man was Stan Wells, a prisoner of war like William Fisher. From Fisher's diary entry for January 26, 1945: "Stan comes to me after dinner and tells me a Jewess has got away and has her hiding in cows crib. I suggest moving her to loft over camp. Plenty straw and the chimney from our fire will keep her warm."

19. The British prisoners of war lived in a room above a barn. William Fisher's diary entry for January 26 says that he crossed the road with Hannah under the pretext of going to repair a wireless radio at the farm across the road. He explained to the guards that Hannah was a Russian girl. At the barn another prisoner of war "had a good fire going all day and the brick chimney is hot. Hot water[,] soap[,] towel—old clothes, slacks[,] food rushed up to her. One of the lads stays with horses (there are nine in the barn) and watches for crovies. Take all clothing off kid, give her paraffin for lice in her hair and bid her goodbye. She grabs my hand and kisses it—and tries to thank me, calls me *Herr*—I say roughly, we are all comrades, only doing what we can."

20. William Fisher's diary entry for January 27: "Everyone brings in food for our escapee! Hundred weight peas—ducks, hens, best part of a pig, bread by loaves—and believe me she's ate 3 loaves today and 5 bowls of soup—somewhat around 22 lb. of food. She's ill now—sick diarrhea. Suggest only milk for a few days."

21. William Fisher's diary entry for January 26: "We had a good look at her. Her eyes are large as is usual with starvation, sunken cheeks, no breasts. Hair has not been cut, body badly marked with sores caused by scratching lice bites. Head still a bit matted and lice still obviously in. I got my forefinger and thumb easily around the upper part of her arm. About 5′7″ in height. Sonia is her name. Feet blue and raw with frostbite. The right heel is eaten away by frost and constant rubbing of badly fitting clog. We have stolen clothing and a pair of shoes off the refugee wagons to replace hers which is marked with the Jew star in red dye. She sat till twelve making a new hat from material and sewing and talking. She will keep harping on her mother and sister and the concentration camp, but we forbid her to mention them. She says it is very lonely and the time passes so slowly in the daytime. We arrange for fellows to pop in and out during the day."

22. William Fisher's diary entry for February 9: "2 PM. Suddenly ordered to move off in two hours. Stan escapes. I determined to escape but not here. Ask Jewess to follow us tonight and go through Russian lines, but she is too afraid. Leave her enough food for three weeks. Push off 8:30."

23. Everyone had to have identification papers. As a concentration camp prisoner, Hannah had no papers.

24. A direct route from the Danzig area to Bialystok, Poland, is approximately 225 miles.

25. The Rescue Committee of United States Orthodox Rabbis was established in November 1939 by the Union of Orthodox Rabbis of the United States and Canada for the purpose of rescuing rabbis and rabbinical students from occupied Europe. After World War II the committee was involved in relief and rehabilitation work in the displaced persons camps and also facilitated the immigration to the United States of Holocaust survivors (*EH*, 1557–58).

26. Decommissioned U.S. Navy ships were used to transport large numbers of immigrants after World War II.

27. New York State has uniform examinations in academic subjects that are administered by the regents of the state Education Department. High school students must pass a required number of regents' examinations to qualify for an academic diploma.

28. Hannah married William Rigler, now a judge on the Supreme Court, State of New York.

Rozalia Berke

1. The Germans marched into Lodz on September 8, 1939 (*Chronicle*, xxii).

2. The Germans followed a policy of Germanizing Lodz. After they occupied the city they annexed it to the Reich as part of the Warthegau region. Renaming the city Litzmannstadt in honor of the German general Karl Litzmann, who had conquered it in World War I, the Nazis resettled in Lodz Germans from the Old Reich and ethnic Germans from other areas of German occupation. There was also an effort to identify ethnic Germans among the local population, and they were accorded special privileges (*Chronicle*, xxiv).

3. "In the first few weeks [of occupation], hundreds of Jewish apartments were confiscated and their tenants deported, without prior notice" (*EH*, 902).

4. Drewnowska Street was at the southwestern perimeter of the ghetto (*Chronicle*, street map of the ghetto of Lodz).

5. The public announcement of the formation of the ghetto was made on February 8, 1940. The ghetto was designated in the Baluty area, a poor, rundown neighborhood of mostly wooden houses with no running water or sewers. The ghetto was sealed on April 30, 1940 (*EH*, 902).

6. Two wooden bridges were built over Zgierska Street, and one was built over Limanowski Street. These major thoroughfares, which were fenced off from the ghetto, passed through the ghetto and served as links to the city. Residents crossed the bridges to go from one part of the ghetto to another (*Chronicle*, street map of the ghetto of Lodz).

7. Food could no longer be obtained from outside the ghetto. Supplies in the ghetto were severely rationed.

8. On November 4, 1940, Jews were instructed to wear a yellow arm band. On November 17, 1940, this order was amended, and Jews now had to wear yellow Stars of David on the right front and back of their outer clothing (*EH*, 902).

9. On May 25, 1940, the ghetto administration ordered factories to be set up that would provide cheaply manufactured goods for the Nazis. Jews worked in return for meager rations (*EH*, 903). Rozalia Berke describes the daily ration as a portion of "soup and a slice of bread per person for working people. Wives of secret police and Rumkowski's advisors had food in abundance" (written comment, September 25, 1994). Dobroszycki describes the ghetto hierarchy, with heads of workshops and departments receiving better food and the majority of the working people living at subsistence level or below. "Undoubtedly, an equitable distribution of food would have contributed greatly to improving the ghetto's mood and morale but only to a negligible, even microscopic degree could it have altered the general situation of hunger" (*Chronicle*, xlviii).

10. Henryk Neftalin, a young legal apprentice before the war, organized many of the ghetto's administrative branches and was a confidant of M. C. Rumkowski, Jewish head of the ghetto administration. "An honest man without pretension, he was concerned with the good of the ghetto and its people" (*Chronicle*, x).

11. Initially there were five hospitals in the ghetto with a total of 1,225 beds (Dobroszycki, 4–5).

Hospital No. 1, for internal diseases, also housed an outpatient clinic and was located at 34/36 Lagiewnicka Street. Other hospitals were a mental hospital on Wesola Street (Hospital No. 3); the contagious diseases hospital on Drewnowska Street; and two clinics, one at 17 Zgierska Street and one at 40 Brezezinska Street. In July 1942 the ghetto had a total of 1,550 hospital beds (*Chronicle*, 225). Hospital patients were deported in September 1942. One wing was left open until 1944 for privileged residents of the ghetto (Rumkowski's confidants), as was the outpatient department headed by Dr. Ser (Rozalia Berke written comment, September 25, 1994).

12. With the permission of the Germans, the ghetto Education Department reopened forty-five schools at the end of October 1939. This educational network existed for about two years. Rumkowski opened a number of orphanages within the ghetto in the agricultural suburb of Marysin, and schools were also established there (Yahil, 212–13). One of those schools was the Eldest of the Jews' Lyceum, which held a graduation ceremony in January 1942, conferring diplomas on eighty-five graduates. The *Chronicle* describes Rumkowski's affection and concern for children: "Everyone in the ghetto knows that children and young people are the apple of Chairman Rumkowski's eye. . . . He has established and maintained . . . a school system that will stand out like golden threads in the history of the ghetto" (122).

13. The *Chronicle* describes frequent inspections of ghetto hospitals by German medical commissions.

14. At the beginning of September 1942 all the ghetto hospitals were emptied of their patients in a series of brutal roundups. This *Aktion* was followed by a *Gehsperre* (Yiddish/Polish: *szpera*), a curfew, from September 5 through September 12, in which escapees from the hospitals, old people, and all children under the age of ten were rounded up and deported to Chelmno. This was a terrible trauma for the entire ghetto population (*Chronicle*, 248–55). Also see interview with Brandla Small.

15. In the spring of 1944 more and more Jews were drafted for forced labor outside the ghetto. Rations for these workers were even less than for those in the ghetto. Others were sent out of the ghetto for "resettlement." Some of these transports did, indeed, go to labor/ concentration camps. Others went to death camps.

16. "Sunday, June 25, 1944: Everyone knows that the situation is serious, that the existence of the ghetto is in jeopardy. . . . And yet—Jewish faith in a justice that will ultimately triumph does not permit extreme pessimism. . . . God only knows who will be better off: the person who stays here or the person who leaves!" (*Chronicle*, 515).

17. Touching the electrified barbed wire fence was a form of suicide.

18. See interview with Rachel Silberman, note 10.

19. It was not unusual for prisoner-trusties, who often were not Jewish, to have a Nazi who protected them in return for sexual favors. Sexual relations between Germans and Jews were forbidden under the Nazi racial laws.

20. V2 rockets, which made a distinctive sound.

21. Rabbi Solomon Schonfeld (1912–1982) was an English rabbi, educator, and rescue activist. He created the Chief Rabbi's Emergency Council in London as a vehicle for his work in which more than 3,700 Jews were brought to England before and immediately after World War II. After the war he brought several transports of children, mostly war orphans from Poland and Czechoslovakia, to England (*EH*, 334).

Tilly Stimler

1. Ruscova, Rumania, also known as Visooroszi in Hungarian, was a small town (population 1,034) in the Carpathian Ukraine, Maramaros County. The area was seized by Hungary in

1939, then occupied by Germany on March 19, 1944. See Randolph L. Braham, *The Politics of Genocide: The Holocaust in Hungary* (New York: Columbia University Press, 1981), 168.

2. A neighboring town (conversation with Tilly Stimler, October 20, 1994).

3. This sister was twenty-four years old in 1944 (conversation with Tilly Stimler, October 20, 1994).

4. Tilly's brother was twenty years old in 1944.

5. This sister was three years older than Tilly (conversation with Tilly Stimler, October 20, 1994).

6. Arriving prisoners had to line up in rows of five to pass a selection by an SS officer.

7. Irma Grese, an attractive blonde SS woman, was trained for her job at Ravensbruck, the women's concentration camp, in 1942. She was transferred to Auschwitz, where she rose in the ranks because she was good at her job. Women survivors at Grese's trial after liberation testified to her cruelty, which earned her the name "Bitch of Belsen," where she worked at the end of the war. She was one of three SS women hanged for their war crimes in December 1945. She was twenty-two years old (Feig, 137, 188, 381–82).

8. Dr. Josef Mengele, the notorious SS doctor in charge at Auschwitz. He selected inmates for death and for pseudo-scientific experiments that he conducted in the camp.

9. Auschwitz was a large complex of thirty-nine camps, covering fifty kilometers. It was divided administratively into three main groups: Auschwitz I, Auschwitz II (known as Birkenau), and Auschwitz III, which included the Buna synthetic rubber plant and the petrol works at Monowitz (Feig, 340).

10. The Hundsfeld women's concentration camp was located in Breslau. An administrative subcamp of Gross Rosen, it was opened in July 1944. The women worked in the Rheinmetall ammunition factory. The camp was "evacuated" to Gross Rosen on January 25, 1945 (Arolsen, 110).

11. Gross Rosen was a major concentration camp. Located in Lower Silesia, it was established in August 1940. It was the site of a large-scale euthanasia program in which 100,000 people were killed between 1939 and 1941. Prisoners who were being transferred from one camp to another within the Gross Rosen administrative unit were sometimes brought to Gross Rosen for a few days (Feig, 204–8).

12. Mauthausen, located near Linz, Austria, was also a major concentration camp with administrative subcamps of its own. In addition to death by gassing, prisoners also died of starvation and overwork, particularly in the infamous granite quarries (Feig, 116–17).

13. Bergen Belsen, located near Celle in northern Germany, was the destination of thousands of Jewish concentration camp prisoners who were brought there as the Germans retreated from the advancing Allied armies in the winter of 1945. Originally established as a prisoner-of-war camp, then used to house civilian prisoners who were to be used for exchange, by 1945 it was horribly overcrowded, and the administration of the camp had deteriorated into chaos. (Also see interview with Rita Grunbaum.) When the British liberated Belsen on April 15, 1945, there were 10,000 corpses that had to be buried in mass graves, and an additional "28,000 typhus-ridden and starved human beings died after liberation" (Feig, 271). (Also see interview with Eva Schonbrun.)

14. "Learning" refers to the study of the Talmud, Bible, and other holy Jewish texts. Setting aside time for daily or frequent study is an important part of traditional Jewish life not only for youngsters in school but also for adults.

15. *Ḥesed,* or acts of kindness, refers to participation in charitable activities, helping the less fortunate either privately or within an organized framework.

Miriam Rosenthal

1. In 1941 a system of conscription to the Hungarian army's labor service, called *Munkaszolgalat*, was instituted in Hungary and its annexed territories. Jewish men of military service age were drafted to labor battalions and worked on war-related projects by building roads, clearing forests, and digging ditches, often on the front lines under enemy fire. Some battalions worked in Hungary. Others worked in the Ukraine, Serbia, and eastern Galicia, and some were sent to Germany. Unarmed, poorly equipped, and living under appalling conditions, tens of thousands of the Jews in these battalions perished (*EH*, 1007–9).

2. Letter from Miriam Rosenthal, October 28, 1997.

3. His name was Szendrei; he worked for Bela's father. Miriam and her family consider him a Righteous Gentile because he saved her life. Their efforts in recent years to ascertain whether he was still alive were unsuccessful (letter, October 28, 1997).

4. At Orthodox weddings it is customary for the bride to circle the groom several times at the beginning of the ceremony. Miriam's wedding took place on April 5, 1944.

5. Jews in Hungary had to wear the yellow star as of March 29, 1944.

6. The women's camp was located in Birkenau (Auschwitz II), first in sector BIa (mid-August 1942). In July 1943 BIb was added to the women's camp. Jewish women arriving from Hungary in the spring of 1944 were held in BIIc. See Israel Gutman and Michael Berenbaum, et al., *Anatomy of the Auschwitz Death Camp* (Bloomington: Indiana University Press, 1994), 394–95, and *EH*, 110.

7. Polish Jews first arrived in Auschwitz in 1941, Slovakian Jews in 1942. By the time the transports arrived from Hungary and its annexed territories in 1944, those prisoners who were still alive were hardened to the Auschwitz routine and mentality and had little sympathy for the shock experienced by those who had been comparatively sheltered from Nazi brutality until their arrival at Auschwitz.

8. Ernushka's family was among the escapees from Vienna who stayed on the Schwarcz family farm. Her mother died in Komarno, and Ernushka was informally adopted by the Schwarcz family and lived with them. Her father survived in hiding in Budapest, and her brothers eventually reached Palestine illegally (conversation with Miriam Rosenthal, October 21, 1997).

9. Plaszow, in the city of Cracow, Poland, was established in 1942 on the site of two Jewish cemeteries. It was first a forced labor camp and became a concentration camp in 1944. By May and June 1944 it held twenty-two thousand to twenty-four thousand prisoners, including six thousand to eight thousand Hungarian Jews. Plaszow was known for the brutality of its regime. It was the scene of massacres of Jews (*EH*, 1139–41).

10. Part of camp lore was that a substance, variously described as bromine or bromide, was put into the food to prevent menstruation. Livia E. Bitton Jackson, in her memoir, *Elli: Coming of Age in the Holocaust* (New York: Quadrangle, 1980), mentions bromide. Dr. Gisella Perl, a Jewish gynecologist who worked as a doctor in Auschwitz, attributes the cessation of menstruation to the "psychic trauma caused by the circumstances we lived in" rather than to any chemical added to the food. See Gisella Perl, *I Was a Doctor in Auschwitz* (Salem, N.H.: Ayer Co., 1984). Also see interview with Edith Horowitz, note 13.

11. Dr. Josef Mengele, called the "Angel of Death" by Jewish prisoners because he decided prisoners' fates with a flick of his finger at the infamous selections. He also conducted medical "experiments" on the prisoners.

12. The concentration camps at Augsburg, Germany, were administrative subcamps of Dachau. The men's camp was opened on April 14, 1942, and the women's camp was opened

on September 7, 1944. The Messerschmidt factory is listed as a men's camp in the Arolsen catalog of concentration camps (57).

13. In the fall of 1997 Miriam's niece met a woman at a wedding and in conversation with her mentioned that her mother's aunt brought home a baby from a concentration camp. "Is her name Miriam?" asked the woman. She, too, had worked in the Messerschmidt factory in Augsburg, side by side with Miriam. She did not know that Miriam was pregnant and asked her why she was always begging for food from her and the other girls. Only when the two SS men took her away did she realize that Miriam was pregnant. For fifty years she felt guilty that she did not give Miriam some of her food, for she too was hungry. Miriam is now in touch with this woman (letter from Miriam Rosenthal, October 28, 1997).

14. Women were sometimes punished for sexual offenses by having their hair shaved off. After the war this was done to women who were accused of collaboration or consorting with the enemy.

15. She was in Kaufering I. There were fifteen camps around the village of Kaufering, four miles north of Landsberg, Germany. The camps were administrative subcamps of Dachau. The prisoners worked at slave labor in underground aircraft factories.

16. Of the fifteen Kaufering camps, four were for women, and eleven were for men. This group of women was kept in one of the men's camps.

17. *Tehillim*, Psalms, are recited when a person's life is in danger, as in case of illness or childbirth.

18. February 27, 1945. Purim is the holiday on which Jews remember their deliverance from the evil edict of Haman, a viceroy of Persia, who wished to kill them because they refused to bow down to him. It is a day of feasting and rejoicing. The biblical book of Esther tells the story.

19. For other descriptions of death marches, see interviews with Edith Horowitz, Rachel Silberman, Hannah Sara Rigler, and Rozalia Berke.

20. The railroad tracks in the town of Dachau are in the middle of the town; houses are across the street from the tracks, which run right outside the gate of Dachau concentration camp.

21. Dachau was liberated on April 29, 1945.

22. One Jewish soldier, First Lieutenant Ben Rosenthal, in charge of a platoon of twenty-two black soldiers from the 567th Medical Ambulance Company, reported in the *Jewish Monthly* that he entered Dachau [on April 30, 1945] the day after it was liberated. He saw twenty women and seven babies in the camp. See *Jewish Monthly*, December 1991, 43. The newspaper clipping is in Miriam Rosenthal's file.

23. The United States Army set up field hospitals to care for the sick and malnourished survivors. American nurse Charlotte Chaney, of the 127th Evacuation Hospital, wrote home on May 8, 1945: "I and three other nurses were on duty from 9 till 4:30, delousing over eighty women and seven babies, what were prisoners here and are now in our hospital. . . . Many of the girls were Hungarians, Polish and Jewish." See Yaffa Eliach and Brana Gurewitsch, eds., *The Liberators: Eyewitness Accounts of the Liberation of Concentration Camps* (New York: Center for Holocaust Studies, 1981), 46.

24. The six other women went to the American army hospital. A United States Army Signal Corps photographer shot a picture of them there with their babies some time later (copy of photograph in Miriam Rosenthal's file). Miriam preferred to return to Komarno as soon as possible.

25. Canned, condensed milk used for babies' formula.

26. Jewish baby boys are normally circumcised on the eighth day after birth. Also see interview with Nina Matathias.

Cesia Brandstatter

1. *Bais Yakov* (Beth Jacob), a network of religious schools for Jewish girls. Founded in Cracow in 1917 by Sara Schnirer, some, like the school in Chrzanow, were supplementary schools that the girls attended after their classes in public schools. Others were day schools or teachers' seminaries. The network of schools was under the auspices of the Orthodox Agudat Israel movement. In 1938 there were 230 Beth Jacob schools in Poland, with about twenty-seven thousand pupils (*EJ* 6: 426–28; 16: 1260). The *Bais Yakov* school in Chrzanow was established after World War I, the first institution founded in Chrzanow for the religious education of Jewish girls. See Solomon Gross, ed., *Sefer Chrzanow: The Life and Destruction of a Jewish Shtetl*, trans. Jonathan Boyarin (Roslyn Harbor, N.Y.: Chrzanower Young Men's Association, 1989), 46 (hereafter referred to as *Sefer Chrzanow*).

2. Bnos Agudat Israel was the youth movement for girls sponsored by the Orthodox Agudat Israel movement.

3. She describes a fairly advanced curriculum that covers much of biblical literature, including the Five Books of Moses, Prophets, and Later Writings (wisdom literature).

4. Samson (ben) Raphael Hirsch (1808–1888) was an Orthodox rabbi and writer, the leader and foremost exponent of modern Orthodoxy in Germany. His ideal was the *Jisroelmensch*, an enlightened Jew who observed the precepts of Jewish law. His philosophy of enlightened Orthodoxy is embodied in one of his most significant works, *Neunzehn Briefe uber Judentum* (Nineteen Letters on Judaism), which Cesia Brandstatter reports that she read in her Beth Jacob school (*EJ* 8: 508–9).

5. Except for the Mizrachi Zionist movement, which sponsored its own network of schools, Zionist movements in the prewar period were secular. Some were explicitly atheist or antireligious. Hebrew, as the language of political Zionism, was not used as a living, spoken language by the *Agudat Israel* movement in the prewar period.

6. *Sefer Chrzanow* describes a variety of active, well-organized Jewish philanthropic organizations that provided for the needs of the Jewish sick, elderly, and poor. These organizations were run by volunteers from the Jewish community (47–50).

7. In October 1938 the German government deported thousands of Polish-born Jews to the no-man's land between Poland and Germany at Zbaszyn, Poland. About seven thousand of these Jews were eventually admitted to Poland; Germany accepted some of her own citizens, and the rest of the deportees eventually returned home (Hilberg, 258). Also see interview with Edith Horowitz.

8. Helen Sendyk reports that her family provided refuge for relatives who had been deported in the Zbaszyn *Aktion*. The presence of the refugees, and their reports of persecution and terror at the hands of the Nazis, worried Polish Jews, who wondered what their fate would be in case of German attack. See Helen Sendyk, *The End of Days: A Memoir of the Holocaust* (New York: St. Martin's Press, 1992), 47.

9. "The proximity of the German border and the concentration of Polish military personnel in Upper Silesia inspired the [Jewish] population to do some hard thinking." From August 23, 1939, when the German-Soviet pact was signed, Chrzanow, on the main highway between Katowice and Cracow, witnessed evacuation of civilians living near the German border and disruption of economic life, which created a "sense of panic" (*Sefer Chrzanow*, 82).

10. Chrzanow was occupied by the Germans on September 4, 1939 (*EJ*, 5: 534, and *Sefer Chrzanow*, 83).

11. About three hundred Chrzanow Jews succeeded in reaching Soviet-held territory (*EJ*, 5: 534).

12. Helen Sendyk reports that before March 1940 Jews in Chrzanow had to put on a white arm band with a blue Jewish star on it (73). *Sefer Chrzanow* concurs, stating that the decree was issued at the beginning of 1940 (92). Photographs in the book show Chrzanow Jews wearing white arm bands with Jewish stars (163, 164, 166).

13. The *Judenrat* was the "self-government" council that was set up by German decree in occupied eastern European towns. In some regions, a regional council was appointed. The *Judenrate* were, in effect, puppet governments that had to carry out German orders. *Judenrat* officials who were not cooperative were often shot or sent to their deaths in concentration camps. They were then replaced by more compliant people.

14. Betsalel Cuker and Kalmen Teichler were members of the second *Judenrat*, reorganized in March 1940 by Moshe Merin. (See interview with Edith Horowitz.) Cuker was chairman; Teichler was second vice-chairman and director of social assistance (*Sefer Chrzanow*, 114).

15. The Chrzanow *Judenrat* was under the jurisdiction of the Sosnowiec regional council, of which Moshe Merin was chairman. In March 1940 the regional council reorganized the Chrzanow *Judenrat* and changed its composition. "Later on, however, the chairman and two members of the reorganized Council were arrested, and Merin sent his own man over to serve as chairman." The first chairman of the Chrzanow *Judenrat*, Betsalel Cuker, was sent to Auschwitz "for dealing with the Gestapo with self respect and for resisting Merin's servility toward the Germans" (Trunk, 37, 331). *Sefer Chrzanow* reports that Cuker, Teichler, and Mendel Nussbaum were sent to Auschwitz in January 1942. "Several days later telegrams were sent by the Auschwitz camp administration to their families, announcing the deaths of their husbands and fathers, even listing a 'disease' from which they had died" (105).

16. Helen Sendyk describes how she and her brother "scavenged the city for food every day. . . . One had to stand on line for hours to obtain a quarter loaf of bread" (74).

17. One of the largest labor enterprises in the area was a "plant for sewing uniforms run by a German named Rosner. From a workshop employing a few dozen people, it grew into a factory with three thousand workers." Rosner apparently treated his employees with respect and even warned them when an *Aktion* was about to take place (Yahil, 208). Helen Sendyk also worked there at the age of thirteen, sewing buttons on uniforms on the night shift (Sendyk, 97).

18. Sendyk, too, reports that several times her family had to leave their apartment suddenly, on German orders, and find other living quarters. "The invading German army, police and civilian staff forcefully seized the better living places in the city. . . . In the fall of 1941, the ghetto became much more crowded and shrunken. . . . The Jews were left with only the small, narrow streets around the marketplace" (*Sefer Chrzanow*, 94, 101).

19. Sendyk describes a similar *Aktion* that occurred in the summer. *EJ* says that in June 1942 the Germans rounded up four thousand Jews for deportation to Auschwitz. In 1942 the holiday of *Shavuot* occurred on May 22 and 23.

20. Sendyk and her parents were taken to the Jewish old-age home. She managed to escape; her older sister bribed the Germans with some valuables, and her parents were released (Sendyk, 127).

21. Edith Horowitz tells of Moshe Merin making the selection during an *Aktion* in Jaworzno, near Chrzanow, in the summer of 1942. *Sefer Chrzanow* reports that Merin made the selection during an *Aktion* on May 30, 1942, in Chrzanow (107).

22. Shmuel Yosef Weiss, member of the *Judenrat*, was the director of its charity bureau, and carried out its work with "tact and deep understanding" (*Sefer Chrzanow*, 94–95).

23. Sendyk also describes various colored stamps, at times green, blue, or red, that were put into Jewish identification papers. Not having the stamp deprived one of rations and was also a pretext for deportation. Having a stamp might also mean deportation (Sendyk, 129).

24. Sendyk describes this hanging. "Israel Gerstner and his two sons were arrested when a Pole informed on them for allegedly baking bread illegally . . . a lie. Shaye Malach was caught with illegal onions in his possession. Seven such criminals were . . . put . . . to death in a big spectacle attended by the whole town" (87). *Sefer Chrzanow* dates this hanging in mid-May of 1942 and lists the names of six of the victims. A statement by the surviving son of Israel Gerstner, written in 1988, asserts that his father, a baker, had German permission to use the oven in the *matzah* bakery for reheating food for the Sabbath. A Polish neighbor informed the German police of smoke from the bakery oven. About nine hundred people were forced to witness the hanging of the seven Jews, including their families. A photograph of the monument erected on the spot, listing names of six Chrzanow Jews and an unknown Jew from Olkusz, appears on page 165 of *Sefer Chrzanow*.

25. The German police confiscated the identity cards of the Jews who were ordered to witness the execution. "To reclaim them they were compelled to be present" (*Sefer Chrzanow*, 107). "Everyone's document would be stamped at this time; anyone later found with an un-stamped document would be punished by death" (Sendyk, 87).

26. *Sefer Chrzanow, EJ*, and Sendyk all date the liquidation of the Chrzanow Jewish community on this date. This time the Germans did the selection (*Sefer Chrzanow*, 112).

27. Orthodox Jews wash their hands and recite a blessing upon arising in the morning, before eating, and upon retiring at night.

28. In Arolsen, Ober Altstadt is listed as a women's forced labor camp until March 1944, when it became a concentration camp. According to the catalog the women were given numbers when the camp's status changed (121). Cesia Brandstatter, however, says that she had a number from the beginning, number 21263, which she sewed onto her blanket.

29. J. A. Kluge is listed as one of three firms that contracted to use slave labor at Ober Altstadt. The Kluge enterprise is described in Arolsen as *Flachsspinnerei* (flax spinning). The other firms were Ettrich, which also had a spinning factory, and Siemens, which had a munitions plant where the workers built fortifications (Arolsen, 121).

30. Cesia Brandstatter describes the material she worked with as long, bent, ribbonlike strips about six inches wide, which were placed in cans (conversation, November 10, 1994). These strips were processed to produce fibers of increasingly thinner width, which were used to manufacture fine types of linen fabric. See Dorothy S. Lyle, *Modern Textiles*, 2d ed. (New York: Macmillan, 1982), 90.

31. "It is interesting to note that dust is an expensive problem in spinning flax fiber. More money is spent for machinery for the treatment of air and dust extraction than for production machinery" (Lyle, 91–95). This comment reflects a concern with environmental hazards (in 1982) that were not considered in 1943. The comfort or health of Jewish slave laborers was certainly not a concern of the German firms that contracted to employ these workers.

32. The part of the process called carding involves cleaning and straightening the fibers by the use of combs. The fibers are cleaned, drawn out, and doubled into strong yarn for warps and filling. *Encyclopedia of Textiles*, 3d ed. (Englewood Cliffs, N.J.: Prentice-Hall, 1980), 140–46.

33. She is probably referring to the area where finer thread was drawn from the thicker lengths obtained in earlier processes. *Fein* = fine; *Saal* = room.

34. "In its raw state [flax] contains over 70% cellulose with water, fat, wax, ash and inter-cellular matter making up the remainder" (*Encyclopedia of Textiles,* 140).

35. "Hanks of combed flax pass through a drawing machine where they emerge in a con-tinuous wide, ribbon called a 'sliver' " (Lyle, 91).

36. "Repetition [of the combing process] draws the flax thinner until all small fibers lie parallel ready for spinning" (Lyle, 92).

37. When they worked a day shift the girls ate in the dining room. When they worked a night shift they had to bring their food to the barrack.

38. On the anniversary of a parent's death, it is customary to light a candle that will burn for twenty-four hours.

39. Orthodox Jews do not turn lights on or off on the Sabbath, nor do they engage in any of several categories of activities defined as "work" on the Sabbath or holidays.

40. Orthodox Jews are usually strict about not eating foods on Passover that have yeast or other leavening agents. These laws could not be observed in camps, where the diet was so limited and permitted foods not available. It is permitted, according to even the strictest inter-pretations, to eat any food on Passover when observing the prohibitions would endanger life.

41. These prayers are taught to young children in the home by their parents. They are brief and easy to memorize. *Sh'ma*, the affirmation of monotheistic belief, is said on retiring at night and is repeated twice more during the day in morning and afternoon prayers. *Modeh Ani* is said on arising in the morning. It thanks God for restoring sentience to the person who awakens.

42. Cesia Zajac's parents are described in *Sefer Chrzanow*. Her father, Reb Yehiel Zajac, was a respected merchant, the son of a rabbi. He was a learned man who made Jewish educa-tion his personal mission. Children and adults were influenced by his kindly manner and char-ismatic personality. He was a talented preacher and drew large audiences to his lectures on Jewish morality and the weekly Torah portion. Mrs. Miza Zajac, described as "Ḥasidic, . . . highly intelligent and refined," was active in the WIZO women's organization, which brought together the "best and most refined women of Chrzanow" who worked to improve the lot of needy Jewish women and children (*Sefer Chrzanow*, 35, 49).

43. In nearby Parschnitz (also a subcamp of Gross Rosen) there was a *revier*, an infirmary for sick prisoners. However, the women mistrusted unfamiliar arrangements. They could not be sure that sick prisoners were not sent to Auschwitz for gassing from the *revier* in Parschnitz (conversation with Cesia Brandstatter, November 10, 1994).

44. This happened in March 1944 (Arolsen, 121).

45. The other women with whom Cesia Brandstatter is still in touch told her that they were told by the *Judenalteste* that the German officer who did the selection was the infamous Dr. Mengele from Auschwitz (conversation, November 21, 1994). This cannot be verified from pub-lished sources about Dr. Mengele.

46. Workers who were judged unfit, from both Ettrich and Kluge, were sent to Auschwitz, presumably to be gassed. At that point the remaining workers were consolidated in the Kluge factory (conversation with Cesia Brandstatter, November 10, 1994).

47. *Moshiah tzeiten*, the Messianic era. The Jewish Messianic belief is that the time of the Messiah will be preceded by a war between the forces of good and evil, a major cataclysm. The events that the women experienced seemed to them to presage the coming of the Messiah. They thought that if any Jews survived the war they would witness the Messianic era, but they did not expect that they would survive. The title of Helen Sendyk's book, *The End of Days*, reflects the same belief.

48. Orthodox girls would not normally travel on the Sabbath, but the threat of rape by the

Russian soldiers was so great that they felt their lives were in danger, which would permit travel on the Sabbath.

Took Heroma

1. "The key to the German plan was the seizure by airborne troops of the bridges just south of Rotterdam over the Nieuwe Maas and those further southeast over the two estuaries of the Maas (Meuse) at Dordrecht and Moerdijk. . . . In no other way could this entrenched place, lying behind formidable water barriers . . . be taken easily and quickly" (Shirer, 721).

2. Just after dawn on the morning of May 10, 1940, the minister of the Netherlands in Berlin was informed by Ribbentrop that German troops were entering his country "to safeguard their neutrality against an imminent attack by the Anglo-French armies" (Shirer, 713).

3. By the evening of May 10, 1940, Dutch infantry, supported by artillery, were able to drive the Germans from three airfields surrounding the Hague, momentarily saving the capital and the government. Dutch forces were also able to hold off German tank forces at Rotterdam until the massive German bombing of May 14, perpetrated while surrender negotiations were under way, led to the surrender of Rotterdam and the rest of the Dutch forces (Shirer, 721–23).

4. The official surrender documents were signed at 11 A.M. on May 15, 1940 (Shirer, 723).

5. Queen Wilhelmina and the Dutch government arrived in England on May 13, 1940 (Presser, 4).

6. Although the prewar Dutch civil service continued to operate, increasing responsibility was given to Dutch National Socialists (Presser, 4).

7. Anti-Jewish decrees were introduced gradually, beginning with the proclamation on August 31, 1940, that abolished Jewish ritual slaughter. Other decrees followed along the German pattern, which defined the Jews in racial terms, required Jews to register with the census office, and registered Jewish businesses in the beginning of an Aryanization process. On February 12, 1941, a Jewish Council (*Joodsche Raad*) was formed, which was charged with carrying out Nazi orders and maintaining order in the face of Jewish resistance to Nazi attacks (Dawidowicz, 367).

8. In mid-February of 1941, Jewish resistance to Nazi attacks led to a reprisal in which 389 young Jews between the ages of twenty-five and thirty-five were seized and deported to Buchenwald and then to Mauthausen. The arrests and deportations outraged the Dutch population, which reacted on February 25 with a wave of strikes that paralyzed public transportation and industry in Amsterdam and northern Holland. The strike was suppressed after three days; martial law was established, and the death penalty was threatened for infractions. Huge fines that penalized the Dutch population were imposed on Amsterdam, Hilversum, and Zaandam (Presser, 50–57; Dawidowicz, 368; Hilberg, 372–73).

9. Presser points out that the strike was particularly significant for its message of solidarity between the Dutch and their Jewish compatriots. The statue of the dockworker stands near the Portuguese synagogue on the broad avenue named Mr. Visserplein in Amsterdam.

10. During the spring of 1941 various decrees were issued that abolished Jewish civil rights and expropriated Jewish property. The Central Office for Jewish Emigration was charged with rounding up Jews and deporting them. Forced labor camps for Jews were established in January 1942, and Jews were concentrated in a ghetto in Amsterdam. Deportations began in July 1942 (Dawidowicz, 368).

11. See interview with Rita Grunbaum, note 3.

12. On March 7, 1942, the Netherlands Indies (Indonesia), a Dutch colony, fell to Japan, an ally of Germany. Dutch nationals were interned in Japanese camps there until the Japanese surrender in 1945.

Emilie Schindler

1. See Thomas Keneally, *Schindler's List* (New York: Simon and Schuster, 1982) and the Steven Spielberg film with the same title, released by Universal Studios, December 1993.

2. Quoted in "Saving Jewish Lives Was a Moral Obligation," by Ernie Mayer, *Jerusalem Post Weekly*, November 5, 1974.

3. Oskar Schindler was born in Zwittau (Czech name, Svitavy, population, 8,983, in western Moravia), the Sudetenland, in 1908 (*EH*, 1331).

4. Moravska Ostrava, Czechoslovakia. The first wave of deportations from Slovakia began in March 1942 and continued through October 1942. Those transports went to Auschwitz.

5. As a *Volksdeutscher*, Oskar Schindler was able to take over two Jewish firms. He operated one as *Truehander* (trustee). Both factories produced and distributed enamel kitchenware. Schindler also established his own enamelware factory in Zablocie, outside Cracow, in which he employed mostly Jewish workers (*EH*, 1331). David Werdiger described Oskar Schindler, the "Nazi *balabus*" (owner) of the Email factory, as "one of the good people. . . . Schindler gave his word to our people that he's not going to let nobody kill in our place, promised that . . . whatever will happen, he will not let kill nobody there." See interview with David Werdiger.

6. He was arrested for black market dealings (Keneally).

7. The Cracow ghetto was established in the southern suburb of Podgorze on March 3, 1941. The Schindlers lived on an elegant street in central Cracow in an apartment formerly owned by Jews.

8. After a series of *Aktions* and deportations, which took place from May through October 1942, the population of the Cracow ghetto was drastically reduced, and after the liquidation of the ghetto in March 1943, the remaining eight thousand Jews were put into the Plaszow camp in Cracow. In 1944 Plaszow became a concentration camp, and SS Death's Head units took over its command. Also see interview with Miriam Rosenthal, note 9.

9. Even before its designation as a concentration camp, Plaszow was known for the brutality of its regime and for massacres of prisoners. Miriam Rosenthal witnessed a massacre of prisoners in Plaszow in the fall of 1944.

10. As the Russians approached Cracow in October 1944, Schindler received permission to reestablish his factory as an armaments production company in Brnenec, in the Sudetenland. The German name of the town was Brünnlitz. The factory was designated as a concentration camp, an administrative subcamp of Gross Rosen. Arolsen lists the arrival of the men as October 21, 1944, and the arrival of the women as November 1944. Firma Schindler is listed as the labor contractor.

11. During the liquidation of the Cracow ghetto in 1943, some of Schindler's workers were sent to Plaszow. Schindler's connections with high-ranking German officials helped him obtain their release. When some of his workers were later sent to Auschwitz, he used bribery and political connections to effect their transfer to his factory in Brünnlitz (Keneally; conversations with Emilie Schindler, May 27, 1983).

12. Amon Goeth, well-known for his brutality and irrational behavior. Schindler cultivated a friendship with him, which Schindler then used to his advantage.

13. Victor Lewis confirms this in his interview. The doctors' names were Duberstein and Helfstein. See interview with Victor Lewis.

14. Schindler sent "convoys" of vehicles from Cracow to Brünnlitz with supplies for his factory.

15. Cigarettes were used as currency on the black market and in the barter economy among civilians.

16. Several hundred of the women who worked in the Email factory were deported to

Auschwitz before the move to Brünnlitz. Schindler went to extraordinary lengths to retrieve them.

17. She was sent in a car stuffed full of bribes for German officials: cigarettes, liquor, jewelry, and other valuable commodities. When asked what this woman was instructed to say or do in the effort to free the Jewish women, Mrs. Schindler moved her shoulders suggestively and replied, "She did what she had to do." The woman who was sent was not Jewish.

18. This was the usual arrangement in all labor camps.

19. The Nazis defined children as those under the age of fourteen. In the ghettos, they were not issued ration cards, nor were they supposed to work, which meant that they starved or that families had to stretch their less-than-subsistence rations even further. Some *Aktions* were directed specifically against children, such as those described by Rachel Silberman and Hannah Sara Rigler in Siauliai and the Lodz children's *Aktion* described by Brandla Small. Like Brandla Small's little girl, children were usually condemned to immediate death in the initial selection on arrival in Auschwitz. When the SS discovered five-year-old Ryszard Horowitz at Brünnlitz, Ryszard and his father were sent to Auschwitz, where they remained until liberation. See Ryszard Horowitz interview.

20. Normally, only starvation rations were provided for concentration camp prisoners. "The average diet in Auschwitz permitted a prisoner to remain alive no more than three months, after which time symptoms of emaciation and 'hunger disease' set in" (Lifton, 187). Some other work camps were marginally better, but prisoners often died of malnutrition. Mrs. Schindler's efforts to provide better food were crucial in saving the lives of the Schindler Jews.

21. A concentration camp located in Goleszow, Poland, an administrative subcamp of Auschwitz. Arolsen lists "evacuations" on three dates in January 1945, including one to the Brünnlitz camp. In Golleschau, the prisoners worked in a Portland cement factory and in a quarry.

22. Corpses were usually burned on pyres in concentration camps. Only the larger camps had crematory ovens.

23. Rabbi Menashe Jacob Levertov, one of the prisoners, originally from Cracow. Rachel Levertov, the rabbi's widow, reports in her interview that her husband told her that he conducted a Jewish burial ceremony for the Jews who died in Brünnlitz.

24. Victor Lewis describes contacts between the Jews in Brünnlitz and the Czech partisan underground. Lewis was involved in the smuggling of guns into the camp, which was facilitated by the camp blacksmith, Joe Jonas. When Lewis asked Schindler after liberation whether he was aware of underground activities in the camp, Schindler responded evasively. See Victor Lewis interview.

25. Expecting to be liberated by the Russians, the Schindlers, as ethnic Germans (*Volksdeutsche*), were vulnerable to charges of collaboration with the German enemy. This letter was designed to protect them from reprisal and prosecution by the Russians.

26. Victor Lewis supplied the name of the driver (conversation, March 26, 1998).

27. They had a difficult odyssey, moving from place to place, penniless for several years. Oskar was unable to earn a living. They eventually settled in Argentina, where Oskar was unsuccessful at operating a farm. The "Schindler Jews" provided financial support for Oskar Schindler for several years during the 1960s until his death in the late 1960s. On February 10, 1998, the *New York Times* reported that the president of Argentina, Carlos Menem, approved a $1,000 a month pension for Emilie Schindler. Conversation with Victor Lewis, March 26, 1998, and *New York Times*, February 10, 1998, p. A6.

28. *Schindler's List*, the novel by Thomas Keneally.

Gertrud Groag

1. Hohenstadt is the German name for Zabreh, twenty-six miles from Olmuetz, in north-west Moravia. In 1889 it was part of the Austro-Hungarian empire.

2. The kit is now on exhibit at the Oranim Teachers Seminary, Kiryat Tivon, Israel (letter, Dr. Willi Groag, December 26, 1996).

3. Olmuetz, in north-central Moravia. Its Czech name is Olomouc.

4. Professor Hugo Bergmann (1883–1975), philosopher and classmate of Franz Kafka, espoused a philosophy of cultural Zionism that was blended with an appreciation of traditional Jewish prayer and a personal relationship with God. See Hillel J. Kieval, *The Making of Czech Jewry: National Conflict and Jewish Society in Bohemia, 1870–1918* (New York: Oxford University Press, 1988), 99–115.

5. The German Nuremberg Laws, which defined and discriminated against Jews, were applied as of March 15, 1939, in Bohemia and Moravia (Dagan, 3: 76).

6. Mahrish Ostrau (Moravska Ostrava), the provincial capital of northeast Moravia.

7. After the occupation of Bohemia and Moravia by the *Wehrmacht* on March 15, 1939, Hitler proclaimed a German "Protectorate" in those territories, thus incorporating the heart of Czechoslovakia into the Reich (*EH*, 227).

8. In an order dated February 20, 1940, "hospitals, homes for the aged and similar institutions were ordered to segregate Jewish patients from non-Jewish patients and see to it that Jews and non-Jews should not use their facilities at the same time." By 1942 treatment of Jews by non-Jewish physicians and admission of Jews to hospitals was limited to emergencies (Dagan, 3: 78–79).

9. *Judisches Kultusgemeinde*, the Jewish Culture Administration, was in charge of all Jewish community affairs.

10. Between July 1939 and July 1942 orders were issued that at first restricted the education of Jewish students and finally prohibited it entirely (Dagan, 3: 86–87).

11. Jews were restricted from wooded areas as well as from parks and certain public thoroughfares in decrees of 1940–1942.

12. A village five miles north of Olmuetz.

13. By June 1941, emigration from the Protectorate became almost impossible (Dagan, 3: 89).

14. Jakob Edelstein was the director of the Palestine office in Prague. "The leading personality in [Czech] Zionist leadership," he was in charge of Jewish immigration to Palestine and served as official Jewish representative to the Germans. A religious Zionist, he traveled to other communities to share information and warn of new developments. In spite of several opportunities to escape, he always returned to Prague. He was deported to Terezin on December 4, 1941, and was the first chairman of its *Altestenrat* (*EH*, 415–16).

15. The biblical Jethro, father-in-law of Moses, recommended that Moses appoint judges to help him administer God's law to the tribes of Israel during their wanderings in the desert (Exodus, chapter 18).

16. Ruth Bondy confirms Edelstein's visit with the Groags, who "promised not to reveal his presence to the Jews of Olmuetz and its vicinity, so that he could finally have a few days of uninterrupted rest." See *Elder of the Jews: Jakob Edelstein of Theresienstadt* (New York: Grove Press, 1981), 191.

17. Deportations from the Protectorate to Theresienstadt, the former Czech garrison town of Terezin forty miles north of Prague, began on November 24, 1941, and continued until March 16, 1945 (*EH*, 230).

18. In Terezin, young people assumed leadership positions. Edelstein was thirty-six when he became *Judenalteste*. Gonda Redlich was twenty-five when he took over responsibility for thousands of children as head of Youth Welfare. Whoever was over age fifty was old. See Vojtech Blodig and Miroslav Karny, *Theresienstadt in der "Endlosung der Judenfrage"* (Prague: Terezinska iniciativa, Panorama, 1992), 84.

19. Jews were forbidden to use these valuable items. They were confiscated on arrival in Theresienstadt (letter, Dr. Willi Groag, December 26, 1996, 2).

20. Three transports left Olmuetz for Terezin: transport number 43, AAf, on June 26, 1942; transport number 44, AAg, on June 30, 1942; and transport number 47, AAm, on July 4, 1942. The three transports totaled twenty-seven hundred people. Another transport, number 126, AE7, left on March 7, 1945, with fifty-five people (Dagan, 3: 56–58). The Groags were on transport AAm, which left on July 4, 1942 (letter, Dr. Willi Groag, February 4, 1997).

21. A tractor that towed a platform, driven by a very young SS man, used to await incoming transports (letter, Dr. Willi Groag, December 26, 1996, 3).

22. Ehrmann reports that there were about 240 mentally ill patients who were kept isolated at Terezin until they were sent away on transports. See Frantisek Ehrmann, *Terezin, 1941–1945* (Prague: Council of Jews in the Czech Lands, 1965), 120.

23. *Schleuse*, literally, sluice. This was where newcomers to Theresienstadt were checked and their belongings confiscated.

24. Dr. Karel Fleischmann, a dermatologist, was deported to Terezin in April 1942. There he worked as a doctor and also did paintings, woodcuts, lithographs, and drawings and wrote poetry. He and his wife were transported to Auschwitz in October 1944, where they were gassed. Many of his artworks and poetry were preserved (Ehrmann, 318).

25. All able-bodied inmates between the ages of fourteen and sixty-five were assigned to work by the Labor Department. The official work week was fifty-two hours for manual labor and fifty-seven for office workers, but "in fact the average working week was much longer" (Dagan, 3: 116).

26. Trude Groag refers to it as *"cholera nostra."*

27. Between August 1942 and the end of March 1943 there were 20,582 deaths, averaging more than 85 a day (Ehrmann, 119).

28. Herzl's daughter Margarethe, known as Trude (1893–1943), was previously hospitalized many times. She was sent to Terezin in 1943, where she died (*EJ*, 8: 421).

29. Bondy reports that Trude Herzl appealed to the ghetto leadership for special privileges because of her lineage, and "the nurses tried to satisfy her wishes to the best of their ability." Trude Groag paid special attention to the mentally ill woman, and the nurse who was present at Herzl's death on March 17, 1943, gave Trude Groag as a memento the scraps of paper on which Herzl recorded her diary (Bondy, 300–302). Trude Groag gave half of these diary scraps to Jakob Edelstein for preservation; these are probably lost. The other fragments she placed in the Zionist archives in Jerusalem shortly after her arrival in Israel (letter, Dr. Willi Groag, February 4, 1997).

30. "By order of the German command it was forbidden to place any textiles in the coffins but we had paper shrouds to clothe the dead" before burial. Up to August 1942 every corpse was buried separately. Afterward, mass graves were dug, and from October, 1942 bodies were cremated and ashes stored in paper boxes (Ehrmann, 54).

31. The Burial Society, or *Hevra Kaddisha*, is an important part of Jewish community life. Its members wash and prepare the dead for burial according to Jewish law.

32. It is customary for Jewish parents to bless their children when the Sabbath or holidays begin.

33. The text is the words of Jacob, who blessed his grandchildren on his deathbed (Genesis, chapter 48).

34. On December 28, 1941, Mattel Edelstein, Jakob's mother, was killed at Horodenka, Poland, together with her husband, Mottel Meir, daughter Dora, and half the Jewish population of Horodenka. Edelstein learned of this in the spring of 1942, probably through Franta Friedman, head of the Jewish community of Prague (Bondy, 319).

35. This conversation is reported in Bondy (257).

36. On December 18, 1943, Jakob Edelstein and his family were transported to Auschwitz, where they were shot on June 20, 1944 (*EH*, 416).

37. The Youth Welfare Department saw to the separate housing and schooling of children and teenagers (Dagan, 3: 116).

38. Mentioned in note 18.

39. "There was an infant home, where mothers, mostly employed in the home, lived with their babies" (Ehrmann, 91).

40. Block V. The Dresden barracks housed women and children. Football (soccer) was permitted in the barracks yard. See Vojtech Blodig and Ludmila Chladkova, *Ghetto Museum Terezin* (Terezin: Memorial Terezin, 1993).

41. The SS-produced film, *The Führer Presents the Jews with a City*, was made for propaganda purposes to show that Jews were enjoying a pleasant life in Terezin while German cities were being bombed by the Allies. Many Terezin inmates were ordered to join the cast of the production (Dagan, 3: 137–38). The filming ended in September 1944 when transports began going eastward again. Most Terezin inmates "carried out passive resistance" and tried to avoid being filmed (Ehrmann, 183).

42. Pregnancy meant immediate deportation (letter, Dr. Willi Groag, December 26, 1996).

43. Preparations began as early as December 1943 (Dagan, 3: 135).

44. Until the arrival of the Red Cross, streets in Terezin had no names, only numbers (Ehrmann, 91).

45. Count Folke Bernadotte, a Swedish diplomat who represented the Swedish Red Cross. In March and April 1945 he successfully negotiated with Himmler for the release of Scandinavians from Nazi concentration camps, including more than four hundred Danish Jews from Terezin (*EH*, 206).

46. In October 1943 the first of three transports of Danish Jews arrived in Terezin. As a result of persistent Danish government requests to allow representatives of the Danish and Swedish Red Cross to visit the Danish inmates, the status of these prisoners was better than that of others.

47. This description closely matches the excerpts from the diary of Helga Weissova-Heskova (Ehrmann, 8).

48. Dr. Paul Eppstein, who replaced Jakob Edelstein as chairman of the *Altestenrat*, told some close friends after the Red Cross left that "he did not believe that the committee had been duped—they had seen through the cosmetic job. The children enjoyed their new home for exactly twenty-four hours" (Bondy, 441).

49. L410, on Hauptstrasse, is described in Blodig and Chladkova as a children's home for girls between the ages of eight and sixteen.

50. Behind the Magdeburg barracks were part of the fortifications that were dug around Terezin. Between two ramparts were moats. It was a grassy area (Ehrmann, 305).

51. A photograph of "the sheep from Lidice" appears on page 296 of Ehrmann.

52. SS *Obersturmbannführer* Karl Rahm was in charge of the beautification process prior to the Red Cross visit (Dagan, 3: 136). He was the camp commander from February 8, 1944, to

May 5, 1945. After the war he was found guilty of crimes against humanity and responsible for the deportation of prisoners. He was condemned to death by a Special People's Court in Litomerce (Blodig and Chladkova, *Ghetto Museum Terezin*).

53. Rafael Schaechter, pianist and founder of the Chamber Music Opera in Prague, practiced on a "half demolished piano without feet, in a little cellar room . . . where it was often so cold that . . . the singers froze" (Ehrmann, 231).

54. Rafael Schaechter was deported to Terezin on November 27, 1942. He formed a mixed choir and worked with an orchestra and soloists. He directed performances of opera and major choral works as well as a children's opera in Terezin (Ehrmann, 323-24). *Terezin Requiem*, by Josef Bor, a former inmate of Terezin, is a memoir describing the rehearsals and performance of the Verdi Requiem in Terezin for an audience of Jews and Nazis.

55. Drawings of Raja Englanderova are reproduced in the *Ghetto Museum Terezin*. She lived in L410 and was a daughter of Rosa Englander.

56. In his article "Jewish Youth in Resistance," Hanus Schimmerling analyzes the efforts of Dr. Willi Groag and others of the young leadership of the *maavar* Zionist group. They tried to create a new, ideal social structure in the children's homes in Terezin that would empower Jewish youth and imbue them with Zionist ideals (Blodig and Karny, 184).

57. The painter Freidl Dicker Brandejsova was a graduate of the Bauhaus. She studied with Klee, Kandinsky, and Walter Gropius (Dagan, 2: 489).

58. A photograph of her appears in *Ghetto Museum Terezin*. The caption says that she was deported to Auschwitz in October 1944, where she perished.

59. On January 10, 1942, nine inmates were hanged for engaging in "prohibited" activities (Dagan, 3: xxxiv). According to paragraphs 8 and 10 of the Common Order of the Jewish Self Government, "The smuggling of letters is punishable by death. Any attempt is judged as the completed act itself" (Ehrmann, 75).

60. This children's transport arrived in late August 1943 from Bialystok, Poland. The twelve-year-old spokesman told one of the medical orderlies that their parents had been shot or gassed. Early in October the children were placed in strict isolation, and the nurses who cared for them were sworn to secrecy (Dagan, 3: 134).

61. The children were supposed to be sent to Britain via Switzerland, but the offer was sabotaged by Adolf Eichmann's office (Dagan, 3: 150 ff.).

62. Dr. Leo Baeck (1873-1956) was the president of the Reich's Representation of German Jews, acting as the accredited Jewish representative to the Nazis. He refused to avail himself of opportunities to leave Germany and was deported to Terezin at the beginning of 1943. He became a member of the *Altestenrat*. His sermons and speeches had a great effect on morale (*EH*, 144-45).

63. "There were only a very few infants in the ghetto and an extremely small number of births. . . . In a few isolated cases it was possible to get permission from the camp head to carry the child to the end" (Ehrmann, 121). Women who came to Terezin already pregnant had to have an abortion, which was performed by Jewish doctors (Ehrmann, 92).

64. The Groags settled in Palestine after liberation, where Willi and Madla's daughter served in the Israeli army.

65. Trude Groag, *Lieder Einer Krankenschwester, im Schleusenkrankenhaus L-124 im Ghetto Theresienstadt*, handwritten and illustrated by Willi Groag (Israel: Beit Theresienstadt, 1989). This poem was translated from Hebrew and German by Brana Gurewitsch. In an essay about Trude Groag as poet, "Die Dichterin Gertrud Groag (1889-1979)" (*Judaica Bohemica* 25 [1989]: 1), Ludvik E. Vaclavek tells the history of the Terezin poems and provides literary analysis.

Zenia Malecki

1. The ghetto *Aktion* began at 6 A.M. on September 6, 1941. See Arad, 110.

2. The Karaite sect of Jews, which developed in the eighth century, rejected the Talmudic-rabbinical tradition. In the twentieth century, after World War I, the largest group of Karaites, estimated at ten thousand in 1932, lived in Russia. Vilna also became a Karaite center, and the Polish Ministry of Culture and Education gave the sect official recognition. "On January 9, 1939 the German Ministry of the Interior expressly stipulated that the Karaites did not belong to the Jewish religious community; their 'racial psychology' was considered non-Jewish." As a result of this policy the Karaites were ordered to be spared from the massacres of Jews by the *Einsatzgruppen* [mobile killing squads under SS command] in eastern Europe. When queried by the Germans, Jewish rabbinical authorities gave the opinion that the Karaites were not of Jewish origin in order to protect them (*EJ*, 10: 776).

3. Ponar (Paneriai) was a wooded area located eight miles south of Vilna and formerly used for recreational activities. The Soviets had dug deep pits for fuel tank storage, surrounded by embankments created from the excavated earth. Lithuanian collaborators first used Ponar as a killing site for small groups of Jews, and *Einsatzkommando* number 9 subsequently massacred tens of thousands of Vilna Jews and other prisoners in these pits (Arad, 75).

4. At first, people were assigned to the ghetto closest to their former residence. By mid-September 1941 holders of work permits, craftsmen, and artisans were moved to ghetto number 1, and those without permits, the sick, orphans, and the elderly, were moved to ghetto number 2. Eventually, the Jews in ghetto number 2 were taken to Ponar to their deaths (Arad, 133–35, 139).

5. Zenia's father was Abram Berkon. Procurement of food was a major preoccupation in the ghetto. The subject of food appears on the agenda of every meeting of the *Judenrat* of ghetto number 2 (Arad, 130). In addition to Mr. Berkon's supplies and the meager rations allowed to the *Judenrat*, flour was also smuggled into the ghetto. See Zenia Berkon, "Zichroinos fun Genia Berkon," *YIVO Bletter* 30 (winter 1947): 206.

6. By December 1941 the Zionist organizations in Vilna were considering options for resistance. Reports of the massacres at Ponar and of the fates of Jewish communities elsewhere in Lithuania and in Poland were brought to Vilna by reliable eyewitnesses. The questions of collective responsibility, armed resistance, and escape were hotly debated. On January 1, 1942, a manifesto composed by Abba Kovner, "Let us not be led like sheep to the slaughter," was read aloud for the first time to members of several Zionist Youth movements. It proclaimed: "Brethren! Better fall as free fighters than to live at the mercy of murders. Rise up! Rise up until your last breath!" On January 21, 1942, the FPO was formally established (Arad, 229–32).

7. Jacob Gens, a Jew and former captain in the Lithuanian army, was appointed by the *Judenrat* as commander of the Vilna Ghetto Jewish Police Force in September 1941. On July 12, 1942, the Germans dissolved the *Judenrat* and appointed Gens "Ghetto Representative," responsible for law and order in the ghetto (Arad, 328).

8. Salk Dessler was Gens's chief deputy in the Vilna Ghetto Jewish Police Force.

9. Bruno Kittel, born in Austria, was a member of the security police. He was called the "Liquidator of the Vilna Ghetto" (Arad, 368).

10. Josef Muszkat was the second in command of the Jewish Police and was a Zionist-Revisionist. He was trained as a lawyer and arrived in Vilna in 1939 as a refugee from Warsaw. In May 1942 he organized the many orphans in the ghetto into the Transport Brigade, which took charge of transporting food from *Judenrat* stores to distribution centers. Muszkat also put them in charge of hygiene and cleanliness in homes and courtyards. The youngsters reported breaches of rules to the ghetto police (Arad, 26, 319–20). Trunk credits the "high standard" of

the Vilna *Judenrat*'s "professional expertise [that] protected the ghetto inmates from the outbreak of severe epidemics, which decimated such ghettos as Warsaw and Lodz (165).

11. Yizhak Witenberg, a former member of the Communist Party, was appointed chief commander of the FPO at its general meeting on January 21, 1942. He, Abba Kovner, and Joseph Glazman comprised the resistance group's staff command. "Witenberg's personality, aptitudes and experience in the Communist underground in Poland . . . served to recommend him to command the organization" (Arad, 236-37). In the course of interrogating a prisoner about activities of the Communist Party, the German security police discovered the party's contacts with Witenberg and demanded that Witenberg be surrendered. Witenberg went into hiding but attended a meeting at the home of Jacob Gens, not suspecting that the meeting was a ruse to lure him into the hands of the Germans. As Witenberg was arrested by Dessler and led toward the ghetto gate, FPO fighters attacked, wrenched him away, and escaped to their own quarters. Gens threatened to begin the liquidation of the entire ghetto if Witenberg was not turned over to the security police (Arad, 387-95).

12. Yellow work passes *(Scheinen)* were issued in October 1941 and were valid until March 31, 1942. Three thousand such passes were issued by the German *Arbeitsamt* (employment office), of which four hundred were given to the *Judenrat* for distribution in the ghetto. The *Schein* was a passport to life because it (temporarily) protected the bearer against deportation (Arad, 145).

13. Yizhak Witenberg had two sons. The younger son was with his mother. The older son, Hirsh, age sixteen, was caught with Abraham Chwojnick and Jacob Kaplan of the FPO staff command by a German patrol as they attempted to leave the Vilna ghetto for the forests on September 23, 1943. They fired on the German patrol and killed one of the policemen. The four Jews were hanged by Bruno Kittel in Rossa Square as other Jews watched (Arad, 434).

14. Witenberg was taken to the security police headquarters on July 16, 1943. The next morning he was found in his cell, dead of cyanide poisoning. From other interviews with survivors, Arad concludes that it was Gens who gave the poison to Witenberg (Arad, 393).

15. Before Witenberg parted from his FPO comrades, he named Abba Kovner his successor as FPO commander (Arad, 392).

16. Sonia Madeysker, also a member of the Communist Party, was part of the nucleus of Jewish activists in the ghetto. In September or October 1942 she and another woman left the ghetto in a risky attempt to make contact with Soviet authorities in the hope that assistance and rescue would result. Unfortunately, their heroic actions were fruitless. Sonia Madeysker participated in other activities that necessitated her leaving and re-entering the ghetto. When the FPO leadership decided to leave the ghetto, she was one of three women who met them at the exit from the sewer tunnels to lead them to the forest. She remained active in the leadership of the Communist Party in Vilna almost until liberation, when she was caught by German security police. She attempted suicide and died of her injuries in a hospital (Arad, 253, 260, 456).

17. Arad describes the *Aktion* of September 1-4, 1943, as a clash between the FPO and German and Estonian police forces (410-13).

Aida Brydbord

1. Pruzhany was occupied by the Germans on June 23, 1941 *(EH,* 1200).

2. A *Judenrat* was formed in Pruzhany in mid-July of 1941, consisting eventually of twenty-four members *(Pinkas Pruz'any,* 92). *EH* dates the formation of the *Judenrat* in Pruzhany as July 20, 1941.

3. Yitzhak Janowicz was head of the Pruzhany *Judenrat* *(Pinkas Pruz'any,* 339).

4. Zavel Siegel is mentioned in *Pinkas Pruz'any* as a spokesman (378).

5. Dr. Olia (Olga) Goldfein, born in Pruzhany in 1889, received her medical training in Geneva in 1913 after being excluded from Russian medical schools by the *numerus clausus* (Jewish quota). She served in a Moscow hospital during World War I and then returned to Pruzhany, where she established a flourishing medical practice among Jews and Christians. During Russian occupation in World War II she was appointed director of the city hospital. She and her husband were on the first transport to Auschwitz from Pruzhany. She escaped from the train at nearby Linovo and made her way back to Pruzhany in spite of a head wound caused by a German rifle butt. Dr. Goldfein sought refuge in the convent at Pruzhany and was warmly received by Sister Dolorosa, whom she had once cured of a serious illness. The mother superior, however, ordered her to leave the convent. Dressed as a nun, accompanied by Sister Dolorosa, Dr. Goldfein reached Sister Dolorosa's home in a faraway village, where she worked as a nurse for the duration of the war. After liberation by the Red Army the women returned to Pruzhany, where Sister Dolorosa was expelled from the convent. They then went to Lodz, where Sister Dolorosa settled. Dr. Goldfein became a medical officer in Marshal Zhukhov's army. After the war she was reunited with her daughter in France and eventually settled in Israel, where she worked as a doctor for *Kupat Holim*. She died in 1964. Sister Dolorosa was honored by Yad Vashem as a Righteous Gentile (*Pinkas Pruz'any*, 59–62). Also see Ilya Ehrenburg and Vasily Grossman, *The Black Book* (New York: Holocaust Library, 1981), 206–12.

6. The Pruzhany ghetto was formed in early September 1941, and on September 18 thousands of Jews from Bialystok and neighboring towns were brought to the Pruzhany ghetto (*EH*, 1200).

7. See Trunk for a description of this hospital: "A group of dedicated doctors and nurses worked miracles" (170).

8. In the Pruzhany ghetto the population density reached unusual proportions, with two square meters per person, after forty-five hundred Jews from Bialystok were forced to move in (Trunk, 126).

9. *EH* lists the towns of Ivanovichi and Stolbsty as locations whose Jews were brought to Pruzhany in March 1942.

10. This massacre is described in *Pinkas Pruz'any* (151–53). It took place at the end of July 1942.

11. *EH* describes two underground groups operating in the ghetto. The Antifascist Organization established contact with a Belorussian underground group. Twelve members of the Jewish group left the ghetto for the forest in January 1943. A group of eighteen armed fighters from another underground group left the ghetto in December 1942 and joined the Russian partisans. They maintained contact with the ghetto and helped other Jews leave.

12. Trunk, 465–66.

13. Trunk, 462.

14. The first order given to the *Judenrat* in Pruzhany, as soon as it was formed, was to collect a huge ransom of gold, silver, and cash from the town's Jews. *EH* estimates the value of this ransom at $95,000 in terms of the 1940 value of the ruble.

15. The Pruzhany ghetto was liquidated on January 28, 1943 (*EH*, 1201).

16. *Pinkas Pruz'any*, 380. They were going to the railroad station at Linovo.

17. Because of increased German activity in the area connected with the liquidation of Pruzhany, it would have been particularly dangerous for Jews already living in the forest to make contact with newly escaped Jews who were hiding close to Pruzhany. It took the Germans three days to place almost ten thousand Jews of Pruzhany on three transports that deported them to Auschwitz from the railroad station at Linovo (*EH*, 1201).

18. This structure, called a *ziemlanka*, was a camouflaged underground dugout that sheltered partisans in the forests. It was designed to blend in with the trees and the foliage.

19. Aida Brydbord stresses the improvised nature of their existence. As urban Jews, they were totally unprepared for living in the forest and had no fighting experience at all. Tuvia Bielsky, commander of the largest Jewish partisan group in Europe, stressed this in his interview, calling the members of his group "big fighters, my partisans. . . . I didn't have five such people." See Yaffa Eliach and Brana Gurewitsch, eds., "Oral History of Tuvia Bielsky," in *Oral History Manual* (New York: Center for Holocaust Studies, 1991), 52. For Bielsky, the main purpose of his group was to save Jewish lives. Survival was the primary goal of all Jewish partisans. Rarely did military considerations override this goal.

20. Bielsky, too, had to prove to the Russians that his Jewish partisan group was an asset to the Russian military effort. He did this by having his family camp provide support services to the small nucleus of fighters. He reports that Russian partisan commanders would usually refuse to take Jews into their units, particularly if the men were with wives or children, and would send the Jews to "Bielsky in Jerusalem," as his unit was derogatorily described.

21. The Bielsky group also built a bathhouse, which was essential for maintaining minimal personal hygiene. Bielsky reports that after his people started using the bathhouse there was no more typhus among them.

22. Like in the Bielsky group, the larger group of partisans was divided into several smaller groups who lived near each other in the forest. Sick people were isolated to minimize the spread of infection. Little medicine, if any, was available to supplement bed rest in the partisan "hospital."

23. Tuvia Bielsky, too, became a "wanted" man after the liberation and had to flee Poland to escape arrest by the Russians, who were determined to eradicate all leadership or political movements not controlled directly by the Communist Party. The usual tactic was to accuse Jews who had survived the Holocaust of collaboration with the Nazis. The punishment was either execution or exile into the gulag.

Marysia Warman

1. Her colleague in the resistance, Kazik Ratheiser, describes her background: "Marysia was from an assimilated family, wasn't a Zionist, and didn't know a thing about Judaism." See Simha (Kazik) Rotem, *Memoirs of a Ghetto Fighter: The Past within Me* (New Haven: Yale University Press, 1994), 110.

2. Charles G. Roland's book, *Courage under Siege: Starvation, Disease, and Death in the Warsaw Ghetto* (New York: Oxford University Press, 1992), is a comprehensive study of the health care system in the Warsaw ghetto, which sought, against terrible odds, to preserve life under deadly conditions. He devotes a section to the Berson and Bauman children's hospital (94–97).

3. Bronka's job as telephone operator is mentioned by Vladka Meed, *On Both Sides of the Wall: Memoirs from the Warsaw Ghetto* (Israel: Ghetto Fighters House, 1973), 140, as well as by Rotem, 109.

4. Roland devotes a chapter to this medical school. Established with German permission as a vocational course for combating typhus, the school conducted clandestine university-level courses in the ghetto. While communication was still possible with Warsaw University, student records were secretly transferred there to enable students to receive university credit for work completed. Roland also mentions clandestine courses in dentistry, chemistry, and pharmacy (187–98).

5. Ludwik Hirszfeld (1884–1954) "was by far the most scientifically prominent member of

the faculty." His research on blood groups and their inheritance was in a field bastardized by the Nazis for their theories of racial purity, and during his military service in World War I he worked to control epidemics of typhus and bacillary dysentery. His baptism as a Catholic did not protect him from Nazi racial laws. He escaped the ghetto in 1943 and survived the war (Roland, 194).

6. "Children died in the hospital at a staggering rate. . . . During the last quarter of 1941, 24% of the 724 children confined to the hospital died there" (Roland, 96).

7. A scientific study of the effects of starvation was conducted by physicians in the Warsaw ghetto. Dr. Braude-Hellerowa and other staff members at the children's hospital participated in this research. See Myron Winick, ed., *Hunger Disease: Studies by the Jewish Physicians in the Warsaw Ghetto*, trans. Martha Osnos (New York: John Wiley and Sons, 1979), and Roland, 96.

8. Henryk Goldszmit (1878 or 1879–1942) was a prominent Polish Jewish pediatrician, educator, and writer. Janusz Korczak was his pen name. He became a legendary figure because of his extraordinary devotion and loyalty to the children in his charge at the Krochmalna Street orphanage. Although he had opportunities to save himself by accepting the protection of Aryan friends, he chose to accompany his children to Treblinka, where they perished together.

9. "As long as there are Jews in the ghetto I am needed here, and here I will stay" (quoted in Roland, 92).

10. Roland cites a similar report that Braude-Hellerowa's body was found in the courtyard of the hospital (92). Dr. Adina Blady Szwajger, a pediatrician in the children's hospital who left the ghetto in January 1943 before its liquidation, reports that she and Bronka wrote to Braude-Hellerowa from the Aryan side "begging her to leave because we had everything ready for her. We got the reply, 'Don't worry about me. I've got my own plans.' And we really don't know how she died. Whether in the flames of the burning hospital or in the cellar. Or maybe she was amongst those who were taken away. We don't know." See Adina Blady Szwajger, *I Remember Nothing More: The Warsaw Children's Hospital and the Jewish Resistance* (New York: Pantheon Books, 1990), 65.

11. Edelman (b. 1921) represented the Bund on the coordinating committee that later became the Jewish Fighting Organization (ZOB) and was a commander of the Warsaw ghetto uprising. See Yitzchak Zuckerman, *A Surplus of Memory* (Berkeley and Los Angeles: University of California Press, 1993). "The children's hospital was a terminus in operations by the Polish underground in cooperation with the ZZW, the Jewish Military Organization. . . . They were deeply committed to smuggling medical supplies, flour, rice, and other foods to Berson and Bauman hospital" (Roland, 96–97).

12. He became a cardiologist after World War II.

13. Szwajger reports that Dr. Waclaw Skonieczny, the trustee administrator appointed by the Germans, "did all he could to help." Szwajger also assumes that he was a *Volksdeutscher* (20).

14. Roland reports that Skonieczny headed a delegation that tried but failed to persuade the Nazis to increase food allotments to the ghetto hospitals (95).

15. Jews in Warsaw were forced to wear a white arm band with a blue Jewish star, which identified them as Jews.

16. Vladka Meed mentions several apartments and hiding places located by Marysia for members of the Jewish underground (Meed, 201, 235).

17. "Early on the morning of Wednesday, July 22 [1942] the walls and gates of the ghetto were placed under the guard of special forces." The *Judenrat* was ordered to provide six thousand people for the deportation transport of that day, and the plan was to deport all Jews in the ghetto with only a few exceptions. See Israel Gutman, *The Jews of Warsaw, 1939–1943: Ghetto, Underground, Revolt* (Bloomington: Indiana University Press, 1982), 203–4.

18. Gutman says that staffs of Jewish hospitals were exempted from the deportation orders. Szwajger and Roland explain that only a limited number of exemptions, called "life passes" or "life tickets," were issued (Szwajger, 55; Roland, 91).

19. "German inventive cruelty put Jews in the awful position of having to choose among their own people" (Roland, 91).

20. Szwajger reports of Dr. Braude-Hellerowa: "I remember her saying that she didn't want to distribute the 'life tickets.' I remember telling her: 'If you don't, Doctor, then none of us is going to survive because the director of the adults hospital is going to do it instead' " (Szwajger, 55).

21. Szwajger reports that after the war she asked Dr. Braude-Hellerowa's son Arik "if he knew why it was us who got 'tickets'; that is, people like myself and not the older ones who were a thousand times more valuable. He told me then that his mother had staked her bets on youth, that we might live through it all and still do something with our lives" (55).

22. Itzhak (Antek) Zuckerman was active in the Dror Zionist organization. He was not in the ghetto during the uprising but was organizing the rescue of the Jewish fighters at the end of the uprising.

23. Vladka Meed and Simha Rotem both corroborate Bronka's use of the name Marysia in her Aryan identity (Meed, 201; Rotem, 109). Rotem describes Marysia as looking "like a typical Pole, spoke perfect Polish, and had big, somewhat sad blue eyes. She was always calm and didn't get excited, something we all needed in those days" (110).

24. Dr. Szwajger describes giving the older children morphine to drink and pouring morphine into the mouths of the little ones from a spoon (57).

25. Szwajger, 56. It was Sister Mira who asked Dr. Szwajger to give her mother a morphine injection.

26. "Yet sometimes, even now, when I can't sleep, I wonder whether any of them woke up. But it's better not to think about it" (Szwajger, 54).

27. Marysia explained that the Jewish underground organization sent someone on a transport to Treblinka to report on the fate of Jews deported there. This was probably Zalman Friedrych, who was sent by the Bund to bring back information about Treblinka. On his way, in Sokolow, he encountered Azriel Wallach, an eyewitness who had escaped from Treblinka. The Bund organization immediately published Wallach's report in a special edition of their newspaper, *Storm*. See Bernard Goldstein, *The Stars Bear Witness* (New York: Viking Press, 1949), 118. Jacob Podos, who was not involved politically, reports that he found out about gassing in Treblinka at the end of 1942 from a friend, Yitzhak Unterbuch, who hid among bundles of clothes in the deportation train and jumped off as the train returned to Warsaw from Treblinka. "In 1943 we knew, already, what they [were] doing to people. We had the whole picture" (see interview with Jacob Podos).

28. Salo Fiszgrund, a leader of the Bund organization, was her contact.

29. Dr. Szwajger left the ghetto on January 25, 1943. She reports that she was given papers for a false identity (79–80). Dr. Szwajger became known as Irena Meremińska, or Inka to her comrades. She became Marysia's partner in resistance work, and for a while she also lived with her. Copies of Dr. Szwajger's false documents are reprinted in her book after page 74.

30. Szwajger describes this room as being in the building at 24 Miodowa Street, formerly the Supreme Administrative Court. The two women lived there, using their false Aryan documents, from the spring of 1943 through the first half of 1944 (Szwajger, 102–3). Szwajger's description of the room as both a meeting place and a refuge for those who needed to hide is consistent with Marysia's.

31. Vladka Meed describes several such "clandestine lodgings," which served as Bund

headquarters on the Aryan side. "The house at Miodowa 24 was of special importance to our work, especially during the early meetings of our couriers. Following the ghetto uprising, Inka Schweiger and Bronka Feinmesser (Marysia) had rented this one room dwelling with money supplied by the Coordinating Committee. This was the rendezvous of all our co-workers" (234–36). Simha Rotem calls the room "A Warm Corner at Miodowa Street 24. . . . It was good to come there, like an oasis in the desert, where you could relax a bit. Marysia, who was optimistic and quiet by nature, created a pleasant atmosphere" (110).

32. Rotem explains that the "money to support the Jews in hiding came from the Jewish Agency, the Joint and special Bundist sources" and was transmitted to the Jewish resistance members through the Polish government-in-exile in London (98).

33. Rotem corroborates this policy. He tried to avoid staying there overnight because of fears that if they were discovered as Jews, the safety of the entire group would be jeopardized (110).

34. Rotem reports that on the few nights when he had to stay with Marysia and Inka, he slept at the foot of the bed that the two women shared (110).

35. Szwajger writes: "Usually I went everywhere with Marysia because it was safer. We used to walk together smiling and chatting like two young girls—just like all the other girls who filled the streets of Warsaw. But if one of us went out alone, she might forget herself, and have 'sad eyes,' eyes that betrayed the past within" (83).

36. Vladka Meed, who was also part of the leadership of the Bund, describes the dangers of using one meeting place for a long time. The "hideout was also visited by Bund couriers to pick up money, doctored documents and illegal literature obtained from the Polish underground for distribution among disguised and hidden Jews" (234).

37. Szwajger describes one incident shortly before the ghetto uprising when she was stopped by a patrol and ordered to open her bag in which ammunition was hidden under some potatoes. Having just drunk some vodka for "Dutch courage," she smiled "broadly and opened the bag wide." The German gendarme, disarmed by her manner, told her to move on (82). Rotem tells that a glass of vodka was their "only luxury on the menu—and we insisted firmly on that" (99).

38. Rotem comments: "Naturally, young men came calling on two Polish girls" (110).

39. The Polish Home Army, an underground military organization.

40. Vladka Meed calls Marysia Sawicka a "devoted collaborator" (275). Szwajger says of her: "No amount of love and respect would ever be enough to repay Marysia Sawicka" (163). A photo of her and her sister, Anna Wonchalska, who played the part of Meed's "mother," appears before page 273 in Meed's book. Simha Rotem also mentions both women (21). Both Polish women were designated as Righteous Among the Nations by Yad Vashem, Israel's Holocaust Remembrance Authority.

41. Szwajger describes this incident on pages 21–22 and 88–90. She dates the episode as April 23, 1943, during the ghetto uprising and confirms that "Marysia and I were left out in the street with no documents, money or anything else . . . while Hela [Keilson] and Marysia's sister, Halina, were taken to the Pawiak prison." Halina was shot when she admitted to being Jewish (21–22).

42. Szwajger concurs: "Every familiar face was hostile" (111).

43. Simha Rotem (Kazik Ratheiser), a commander of the Jewish Fighting Organization in the ghetto, set off an explosion on the second day of the ghetto uprising, which killed and injured scores of Germans. He and Antek Zuckerman escaped from the burning ghetto on the eleventh day of the uprising through a tunnel dug by the Revisionist fighters. They found shelter with their colleagues on the Aryan side (Rotem, 43–45). They tried to join the Polish parti-

sans in the forest but were met with so much hostility that they were forced to return to Warsaw (Meed, 203). In Warsaw, Kazik continued the struggle against the Germans as a courier for the Jewish underground (Meed, 310).

44. Borzykowski confirms that it was Marysia who found him and Stefan Grayek a hiding place at 10 Rakowiecka Street, in "a small house surrounded by fields." Access to the hiding place was through a "trapdoor in the floor" that led to a basement, where other members of the Bund organization were already hidden. See Tuvia Borzykowski, *Between Tumbling Walls* (Israel: Ghetto Fighters' House, 1976), 143.

45. Rotem says that the Jewish resistance members had "a monthly budget, which was spent on the most necessary items" such as cigarettes, trips, warm winter clothing, and one meal a day (99).

46. Szwajger mentions that "near the end . . . Marysia moved to Leszno Street" (111). Meed mentions a house at Leszno 18 "which had been purchased through Marysia, . . . converted into a hideout for Zivia Lubetkin, Antek [Zuckerman] and Marek Edelman," and served as a coordinating center for the surviving ghetto fighters, the Jewish partisan groups and the fighting organizations in various concentration camps throughout Poland (235–36).

47. Meed adds to her description of this house that Bernard Goldstein and Rivka Rosenstein also used it, as did various couriers (236).

48. The Warsaw Polish uprising began on August 1, 1944, and lasted until October 2, 1944. The insurgents did not succeed in holding the city until the arrival of the Soviet army (*EH*, 1632).

49. They first approached the *Armia Krajowa* (AK), the Polish Home Army. Rotem says that their contacts with the AK in early 1944 did not inspire confidence. The AK did not tell the Jewish resisters of their plans for an uprising (Rotem, 120). Also see Zuckerman, 534.

50. Borzykowski reports that "the group staying at 18 Leszno Street resolved to remain a unit, never to part no matter what the circumstances" (169). He mentions the names of twelve people in this group and adds that there were a few others.

51. "Everyone in Warsaw threw himself completely into the fight against the hated occupiers. . . . The surviving officers of the Jewish Fighting Organization . . . urged all their fellow Jews by radio to participate in the struggle against the Germans" (Meed, 322–23). Szwajger found work in a Polish hospital, and she reports of her colleagues in the Jewish underground: "Our men reported to the commander of a unit which was stationed on the same yard. They were not accepted. There was no need for a unit of Jewish fighters. So they went to the AL [*Armia Ludowa*], where they were accepted" (168).

52. The Communist-supported People's Army was more likely to accept Jewish groups into its ranks. Borzykowski reports that the group of Jewish fighters that joined the *Armia Ludowa* was the only one that "fought officially as a Jewish group" (169). The *Armia Ludowa* provided material support for the Bielsky Partisan Brigade as well as for other Jewish partisan groups in various locations in Poland (see interviews with Tuvia Bielsky and Samuel Gruber). Rotem reports that the AL "accepted the fighting group of the ZOB into their service on the spot" (121).

53. The Germans began systematically to level the center of the city with their superior firepower. Buildings in which Jewish fighters were hiding in bunkers were demolished by bombardment; the Jews had to find other hiding places. In spite of their participation in the Polish uprising, Jewish fighters were still in danger of being identified by the Poles to the Germans as Jews. Small groups of Jewish fighters escaped from the Old Town to the Warsaw suburb of Zoliborz, which soon capitulated to the Germans.

54. Szwajger, who was separated from Marysia at this point, also left the Old Town through

the sewers, in an ordeal similar to Marysia's (Szwajger, 170–71). The Jewish fighters went through the sewers in early September 1944 (Zuckerman, 541–43).

55. Borzykowski describes whirlpool currents in the sewers, waterfalls created at the confluence of several sewer branches at different levels, walking through the stinking waters in total darkness, and explosions of German grenades lobbed into the sewers. Nevertheless, all the Jewish fighters survived the ordeal in the sewers and emerged safely in the Zoliborz quarter on August 28, 1944 (178–83).

56. Borzykowski notes that "Zygmunt Warman came back—wounded." Antek Zuckerman's hearing was impaired as a result of proximity to explosions (191).

57. *EH* dates the surrender as October 2, 1944 (1780).

58. Szwajger says that [Dr.] Tosia Goliborska lived in a house on Promyka Street near the Vistula from before the Polish uprising and that Szwajger's friends found shelter in the cellar of that house (174). Borzykowski says that the house was inhabited by several Jewish women who had been hiding there throughout the war: an eighty-year-old paralyzed woman and two other elderly Jewish women who had not been evacuated in the general evacuation of civilians from the Zoliborz area (195).

59. "There were fifteen of us, in a space which could hold only six lying side by side. . . . When one wanted to turn over, all the others had to sit up. . . . We kept quiet—stifling coughs, speaking in low whispers" (Borzykowski, 100–102).

60. "What caused us the worst suffering in the hideout on Promyka Street was the lack of drinking water" (Borzykowski, 203).

61. Borzykowski says this was "Lieut. Witek, our closest friend" (195).

62. Borzykowski lists their names and confirms that they survived (208).

63. Borzykowski describes more details of their daily routine, which, in addition to the constant search for food and water, also included keeping track of the calendar and having lectures by various members of the group with expertise in different academic disciplines, followed by discussions, and an entertainment hour, where they would share jokes, riddles, and puzzles (208–9).

64. The Polish owners of the house had left behind a cat and a dog, which kept begging to be allowed into the cellar. Their noises created a serious danger to those who were hiding. The cat had to be strangled, and the dog was buried alive in the garden (Borzykowski, 206).

65. Pruszkow is described by Simha Rotem as a transit camp "populated by several thousand Warsaw residents, who had been taken out of their homes and sent there at the height of the [Polish] uprising. . . . Young people were sent to forced labor in Germany; old people, women and children were released" (135). Borzykowski describes this incident on pages 212–15.

66. Szwajger says that people from the Coordinating Committee of Jewish Organizations were hiding in Pruszkow and other suburbs on the outskirts of Warsaw (175).

67. Another problem was their lack of water and the constant proximity of the German soldiers, who were likely to discover them (Borzykowski, 218).

68. "Marysia and Zosia were assigned to the task." Borzykowski says the two girls left at dawn, before the arrival of the German soldiers. "It was arranged that we should wait for them until the next evening; this would give them two full days and one night to carry out their mission" (219).

69. The rescue is described in Borzykowski, pages 220–22.

70. Szwajger says that "the director of the hospital in Jelonki sent out a sanitary patrol. One of our girls went with them" (174).

71. Szwajger was not with them, but she knew that "while walking across the mine field"

the girl who went with the rescuers "took her shoes off, because it seemed to her that it would be safer in bare feet" (174).

72. Szwajger's and Borzykowski's accounts of the typhus ruse are similar to Marysia's (Szwajger, 174; Borzykowski, 221).

73. Marysia learned the story of the rescue mission from the memoirs of Dr. Zylkiewicz, who worked in the Red Cross hospital, and from others who wrote their memoirs of this mission. Borzykowski dates the rescue as November 15, 1944 (222).

74. Jerzy Warman was among the founding members of the International Network of Children of Jewish Holocaust Survivors and served as its second president.

Anna Heilman

1. *Lager* A in the main camp, Auschwitz I.

2. Prisoners stayed in the quarantine camp for a few weeks, where they were physically and psychologically "broken in" to the inhuman routine and torture of the camp. See Kazimierz Smolen, *Auschwitz, 1940–1945: Guidebook through the Museum*, 6th ed. (Oswiecim: State Museum at Auschwitz, 1976), 45–46.

3. *Lager* B, also in Auschwitz I.

4. The Union Werke munitions factory was located near the base camp. See Jadwiga Bezwinska, ed., *Amidst a Nightmare of Crime: Manuscripts of Members of the Sonderkommando* (Oswiecim: State Museum at Auschwitz, 1973), 155. Its full name was Weichsall-Metall Union Werke. Anna Heilman's presence as a worker in the Union Werke factory is confirmed by several testimonies in Lore Shelley, ed., *The Union Kommando in Auschwitz: The Auschwitz Munitions Factory through the Eyes of Its Former Slave Laborers*, Studies in the Shoah, vol. 13 (Lanham, Md.: University Press of America, 1996).

5. Salomea Baum remembers the *Kapo* "Alma with the drunken voice," a German woman (Shelley, 15). Ada Halperin also remembers a peasant German *Kapo* named Alma who supervised the women checking the quality of manufactured pieces (Shelley, 78).

6. Esther Wajcblum, born in 1924. Ilse Michel remembers her as "a beautiful, vivacious girl, who cared deeply for her younger sister, Hanka." This description is echoed by other women who knew the two Wajcblum sisters (Shelley, 136). Esther, also known as Estusia, was eventually executed for her part in smuggling gunpowder to the men of the resistance.

7. This is confirmed by several eyewitnesses in Shelley.

8. Eugenie Langer says they "placed a tiny quantity of powder into a paper and put it in our pockets." If they were warned of a search they "just took the powder out of [their] pockets and threw it away" (Shelley, 130).

9. Explosives were brought from the Union factory by several women, including Esther Wajcblum, Alla Gaertner, and Regina Saperstein, and given to Roza Robota, who worked sorting clothing and luggage in Birkenau BIIg, adjacent to crematorium IV.

10. Anna Heilman's role in transferring the gunpowder is confirmed by Mala Weinstein (Shelley, 141).

11. Roza Robota. According to Israel Gutman, a woman named Hadassah transferred the explosives to him or to a fellow prisoner in the *Sonderkommando*. See Israel Gutman, *Men and Ashes: The Story of Auschwitz-Birkenau* (Merhavia, Israel: Sifriyat Poalim, 1957). A footnote to the diary of Salmen Lewental says that it was Roza Robota who transferred the gunpowder to a Jewish prisoner named Wrobel (Bezwinska, *Amidst a Nightmare of Crime*, 155).

12. Her sister, Esther Wajcblum, was interrogated in Block 11, the punishment barrack of the men's camp, as were other girls from the Union factory. "The upper windows were sealed off and the basement windows barred." Most survivors of interrogation in Block 11 were shot at

the "Black Wall" (Feig, 347). Obviously, the Germans decided to make a public spectacle of the hanging of the four women.

13. Rose Grunapfel Meth.

14. Her sister, Esther Wajcblum.

15. Alla Gaertner.

16. Clara Heyman says that Anna and her sister, who slept just below her in the Union Werke block, "had already fought in the Warsaw ghetto uprising" (Shelley, 245).

17. Marta Cige tells of a small parcel that was given to her by Esther Wajcblum to hold until Roza Robota picked it up. This happened several times. Marta Cige also smuggled Esther's last note to Anna, written before Esther was executed (Shelley, 301–2, 395).

18. Salmen Lewental, a worker in the *Sonderkommando*, wrote in his diary, which was hidden in Auschwitz and unearthed after the war: "We believed that the Germans would want at all costs to obliterate all traces of their crimes . . . by killing our entire *Kommando*" (Bezwinska, *Amidst a Nightmare of Crime*, 154–55).

19. Polska Partja Robotnicza, a resistance group formed by Polish communists who escaped and returned from territory initially held by Russia, together with the remnants of the Polish Communist Party. See Stefan Korbonski, *The Polish Underground State* (New York: Columbia University Press, 1978), 110.

20. Additional assistance came from Soviet prisoners of war who were brought to Auschwitz from Majdanek and assigned to the *Sonderkommando* on April 16, 1944. They helped organize plans for a mutiny and escape. It became clear, however, that assistance from outside the camp would not be forthcoming. When two hundred men of the *Sonderkommando* were taken and killed, it became obvious that "the date of the final liquidation was approaching." The *Sonderkommando* decided "to act, to act, over" (Bezwinska, *Amidst a Nightmare of Crime*, 157–63).

21. One crematorium was blown up on October 7, 1944. See Rose Meth's interview, notes 19 and 20.

22. "Evacuation" of KL Auschwitz started on January 18, 1945. Columns of prisoners on foot left in groups of five hundred all day and night and were marched west for days. Those who could not keep up died where they fell or were shot. See *From the History of KL Auschwitz*, vol. 1 (Oswiecim: State Museum at Auschwitz, 1967), 215.

23. Ravensbruck concentration camp, near Furstenberg, Germany. They must have walked more than 150 miles.

24. Neustadt Glewe, Germany, near Ludwigslust.

25. Anna Heilman was active in the effort to erect a monument to the four girls who were hanged in Auschwitz for smuggling gunpowder to the men.

26. Hebrew letters have numerical equivalents. The sum of the numbers on her arm is eighteen, which is the same as the sum of the letters of the Hebrew word *ḥai*, meaning "life."

Rose Meth

1. Wadowice, Poland, twenty-three miles west-southwest of Cracow. Pope John Paul II was born there, as Karol Wojtyla, on May 18, 1920.

2. Belzec extermination camp, located 120 kilometers southwest of Warsaw, was built for the exclusive purpose of murdering the Jews of southeastern Poland. It was in operation between March 17, 1942, and June 1943 and claimed an estimated 600,000 Jewish lives in its six carbon monoxide chambers (Feig, 276–77).

3. SS *Rapportführer* Tauber is mentioned by Sara Nomberg-Przytyk in her memoir, *Auschwitz: True Tales from a Grotesque Land* (Chapel Hill: University of North Carolina Press,

1985), 53. He "was famous in Auschwitz for his ability to kill a person in two motions," knocking the prisoner unconscious with a blow to the head, then strangling the prisoner with pressure of his foot on the prisoner's throat.

4. Dr. Josef Mengele, highest ranking doctor of Auschwitz.

5. *Gimatria* is Hebrew numerology. The total value of her numbers added up to eighteen, which in letters is *ḥai*, meaning "life." Also see interview with Anna Heilman, note 26.

6. Estusia was Esther Wajcblum, referred to in other sources as Toszka, sister of Anna Heilman. See testimony of Marta C., "New Testimonies: Women's Resistance in Auschwitz," *The Voice of Auschwitz Survivors in Israel*, no. 34 (April 1986): 11. Also see interview with Anna Heilman.

7. Weichsel Union Werke Factory in Auschwitz I produced rockets and munitions, among which were shell fuses. See Jadwiga Bezwinska and Danuta Czech, eds., *KL Auschwitz As Seen by the SS: Hoss, Broad, Kramer* (Oswiecim: State Museum at Auschwitz, 1972), 185.

8. Rose's presence in the *Pulverraum* of the Union factory is confirmed in the testimonies of Eugenie Langer and Ilse Michel (Shelley 129, 136).

9. Rose's description of the work is corroborated by the testimonies of Eugenie Langer and Ilse Michel, who also worked in the gunpowder room (Shelley, 129, 136–37).

10. Shelley says that Paul Von Ende, foreman of the gunpowder room, was a German civilian employee of the Union firm (127). Eugenie Langer says he was a decent person who left extra food for the girls every day; Ilse Michel says he was a "man of few words and he treated us fairly" (129, 136).

11. Regina is mentioned in Bezwinska, *Amidst a Nightmare of Crime* (155), in Marta C.'s testimony, and in several of the testimonies in Shelley. Eugenie Langer describes her as a young married woman, the forewoman of the group (129).

12. Paula Stern says that Inge Franke came to Auschwitz in a transport from Neuendorf, Germany. Lore Shelley says that Franke worked in the gunpowder room (Shelley, 367).

13. Her testimony is published in Shelley, 133–39.

14. Ilse Michel mentions Genia Fischer (Shelley, 136).

15. This was probably Roza Robota, who worked sorting clothing in the *Effectenlager* at Birkenau (BIIg), which adjoined the area of crematorium IV. She transferred the gunpowder to the male prisoner Wrobel, a member of the resistance movement who worked in the *Sonderkommando* (Bezwinska, *Amidst a Nightmare of Crime*, diary of Salmen Lewenthal, 155). Israel Gutman describes another girl, Hadassah, whom he says was the courier who would bring the gunpowder to him or to a prisoner named Yehuda. See Gutman, *Men and Ashes*, 151. "A Russian technician named Borodin fashioned a kind of hand grenade." Another prisoner, Porebski, an electrician, acted as liaison between resistance groups in the camp (Gutman and Berenbaum, 500).

16. Roza Robota was twenty-three years old, from Ciechanow, Poland, an active member of the Zionist organization *HaShomer HaTzair*. She was an early active recruit to the resistance organization in Auschwitz (Gutman, *Men and Ashes*, 155).

17. According to the testimony of Marta C. (12), Alla Gaertner was deported to Auschwitz from Sosnowiec, Poland, and was a work foreman in Auschwitz (conversation with Rose Meth, May 15, 1990). In Shelley, Marta Cige says that she came from Belgium (302).

18. "All our *Kommando* had always been of the opinion that we were in a much greater danger than all the other prisoners in the camp, much more even than the Jews in the camp. We believed that the Germans would want at all costs to obliterate all traces of their crimes committed till now. They would not be able to do this otherwise than by killing our entire

Kommando, leaving not a single one alive" (diary of Salmen Lewental in Bezwinska, *Amidst a Nightmare of Crime*, 154–55).

19. On Saturday, October 7, 1944, resistance members in the *Sonderkommando* were informed that the camp commandant planned to reduce the size of the *Sonderkommando* from 663 to 300 men. Specific prisoners were named, and they decided to resist. A German prisoner who threatened to inform on the conspirators to the SS was killed by them, and they then attacked the SS guard unit with hammers, axes, and stones. "They set Crematorium IV on fire and [threw] several self-made grenades." See Danuta Czech, *Auschwitz Chronicle, 1939–1945* (New York: Henry Holt, 1990), 725.

20. In the revolt of the *Sonderkommando* on October 7, 1944, crematorium II was exploded (Gutman, *Men and Ashes*, 153–54, and conversation with Tsippi Tichauer, May 16, 1990). Crematorium III was burned (oral history of Henry Fuchs and copy of original notes of Rose Meth). Professor Erwin Tichauer reports that a fire damaged the ceiling and roof of crematorium IV (conversation, May 16, 1990). Damage in crematoriums II and IV is confirmed by the report of Henryk Tauber: "The revolt . . . also spread to Krematorium II. . . . Before fleeing, we set Krematorium IV on fire." See Jean Claude Pressac, *Auschwitz: Technique and Operation of the Gas Chambers* (New York: Beate Klarsfeld Foundation, 1989), 498.

Gutman reports in *Men and Ashes* that the revolt of the *Sonderkommando* involved about six hundred men, that one of the cruelest *Kapos* was thrown alive into the flames, that four SS men were killed in hand-to-hand combat, and others were wounded. In the chaos, some prisoners broke down the fence and tried to escape, but most were killed by a force of two thousand Nazi guards who were alerted.

Professor Tichauer stressed the lack of coordination and cooperation among the several resistance groups. He explained that the explosives experts worked at crematorium II. When the noise of the explosion in crematorium II was heard by the others, the fires were started in crematoriums III and IV.

21. They counted all the dead bodies. This is confirmed by Gutman (*Men and Ashes*, 153). Danuta Czech sees the actions at crematorium IV as precipitating the revolt. Her chronicle reports that the bodies of all the prisoners who were killed in the revolt were brought to the grounds of crematorium IV. Prisoner firefighters who were brought there to put out the fire in crematorium IV witnessed the SS shooting the survivors of the *Sonderkommando* who had worked there (726). Her account adds up to 451 prisoners killed by the SS. Gutman and Berenbaum agree with this tally (501).

22. Erich Kulka reports that after Esther Wajcblum and Regina Saperstein were released, SS women were assigned to supervise the work in the *Pulverraum*, which was a new policy (Shelley, 304).

23. Mala Weinstein says that Alla transferred gunpowder to Roza Robota (Shelley, 141). She points out that Klara, a night-shift supervisor at the Union factory, informed the Germans that Alla was involved with stealing the gunpowder (Shelley, 368). Erich Kulka links Klara's denunciation to the arrest of Esther Wajcblum (Shelley, 304). Several testimonies in Shelley claim that Alla Gaertner could not withstand Nazi torture and confessed to smuggling the gunpowder (Shelley, 368–69).

24. Block 11 was the punishment block in Auschwitz I, where interrogations and torture took place. It was known for the harshness of the interrogations. Gutman confirms the account of the interrogations of the girls (*Men and Ashes*, 154–57).

25. Czech's *Chronicle* dates Regina's arrest, together with that of Alla Gaertner and Estusia Wajcblum, as October 10. She says they were arrested in the women's camp of Auschwitz I and

"charged with stealing explosives . . . and giving them to the prisoners of the Special Squad [*Sonderkommando*]" (728). Czech says that on October 11 "two female prisoners were taken from the women's camp in Auschwitz I to the Political Department for an interrogation" and adds that "the interrogation is probably related to the investigations into the uprising of the Special Squad" (729). Their names are misspelled in her account.

26. Eugenie Langer says: "To this day I do not know why Esther was taken and not Rose or myself" (Shelley, 130). There is no corroboration in the testimonies in Shelley's book of Rose's interrogation. Rose distinguishes between interrogation and arrest and does not claim to have been arrested (letter of Rose Meth to Erich Kulka, June 10, 1986, quoted in Shelley, 396). Danuta Czech, in her diary entry for October 16, lists additional women who were interrogated: "Another female prisoner is locked in the bunker of Block 11 and yet another is brought from the women's camp in Auschwitz I to an interrogation" (732). Later in that same entry: "Three female prisoners remain under camp arrest, i.e., in the bunkers of Block 11, and . . . 77 female prisoners have been taken to the Political Department to be interrogated." The names of the prisoners are not specified.

27. In her letter to Erich Kulka, June 10, 1986, Rose Meth said that during a search of Esther's cot on the block, a drawing of her boyfriend was found (Shelley, 304, 408).

28. Gutman points out that initially, the possibility that Jewish women could be involved in transferring explosives was inconceivable to the Gestapo, and after the initial investigation they tried other avenues of inquiry. According to Gutman, the *Kapo* Eugene Koch, who had befriended Alla Gaertner, informed to the Gestapo and told them what he knew of the resistance and the role of the women. After Koch's testimony the Jewish women were arrested again and interrogated further. In spite of severe torture, Gutman says that the women did not reveal any information (Gutman, *Men and Ashes*, 155).

29. Roza Robota, Regina Saperstein, Alla Gaertner, and Esther Wajcblum were hanged. Roza Robota's last word prior to her execution was: "*Nekamah!*" (Revenge!) (Gutman, *Men and Ashes*, 157). Shelley says that the consensus of survivor testimony is that Regina Saperstein and Alla Gaertner were hanged first, in the presence of the night shift, and that Roza Robota and Esther Wajcblum were hanged later, in the presence of the day shift (367).

30. SS *Hauptsturmführer* Franz Hoessler, appointed in June 1944 *Lagerführer* of the men's camp at Auschwitz. He was executed as a war criminal on December 13, 1945 (Bezwinska, *Amidst a Nightmare of Crime*, 50).

31. Czech reports that Hoessler screamed, "All traitors will be destroyed in this manner" (775). Kulka points out that "there is no proof that the Gestapo found gunpowder at the crematorium" that was exploded. Surviving members of the *Sonderkommando* have said that they threw the gunpowder and handmade grenades into the latrine during the revolt. Kulka therefore concludes that the four Jewish women were the scapegoats for the sabotage that the men of the Auschwitz resistance had been practicing on a much larger scale (Shelley, 304-5).

Afterword

1. See interview with Vladka Meed, United State Holocaust Memorial Museum, Research Institute, Record Group 50, Oral History, USHMM Collection, call number RG-50.030*0153.

2. See interview with Adele Bay.

3. See interview with Rachel Garfunkel.

4. See Shimon Huberband, *Kiddush Hashem: Jewish Religious and Cultural Life in Poland during the Holocaust*, ed. Jeffrey S. Gurock and Robert S. Hirt, trans. David E. Fishman (Hoboken, N.J.: Ktav, 1987), 193-99.

5. See interview RG1606 (name withheld by request of interviewee), oral history file, Yaffa Eliach Collection.

6. See interview with Sara Rothstein.

7. See interview with Pepi van Ryk.

8. This artifact is on loan to the Museum of Jewish Heritage, New York.

9. The *Haggadah* is in the collection of the Museum of Jewish Heritage, New York.

10. See Viktor Frankl, *Man's Search for Meaning: An Introduction to Logotherapy* (New York: Pocket Books, 1963), 60–67, 126.

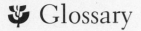
Glossary

Abfall (German) Waste, shavings.

Abwehr (German) German intelligence service, the Foreign Bureau/Defense of
the Armed Forces High Command.

Achtung! (German) Attention!

afikoman (Greek) The last piece of *matzah* eaten at the Passover *seder*.

Agudah, Agudat Israel (Hebrew) Union, Association of Israel; an Orthodox Jewish
political group formed in 1912 representing German, Hungarian, and Polish Orthodoxy. It sponsored cultural activities, youth groups, and educational institutions (*EJ* 2: 421–26).

aḥdus (Hebrew) Unity.

akcja (Polish) Roundup.

Aktion (German) Roundup.

aliyah (Hebrew) Ascent. Refers to being called up in synagogue to the reading of
the *Torah* or to immigration to Israel.

Altestenrat (German) Jewish leadership in Terezin, similar to *Judenrat*.

Appell (German) Roll call in concentration camp.

Appellplatz (German) Open area in concentration camp where roll calls took
place.

Arbeiterin (German) Female workers.

Arbeitslager (German) Forced labor camp.

Artz (German) Doctor.

Aufseher(in) (German) Overseer of work in concentration camp.

austreten (German) Step forward.

Ave Maria (Italian) Hail Mary.

Bais Yakov (Yiddish, Hebrew) Beth Jacob school system for Orthodox girls.

bania (Polish, Russian) Bath.

bar (bat) mitzvah (Hebrew) The assumption of adult religious obligations by a
Jewish boy at the age of thirteen and by a girl at the age of twelve, usually marked by a family celebration.

Batei Midrash, Beit Midrash (Hebrew, pl., sing.) Houses of study.

bekher (Yiddish) Wine goblet used for *kiddush* on Sabbath and holidays.

bentch (Yiddish) To say a blessing.

Block (German) Barrack.

Blockalteste (German) Prisoner in charge of a barrack in concentration camp.

blockhova (Polish) Prisoner in charge of a barrack in concentration camp.

boḥur (Hebrew, Yiddish) Young man.

boit'l (Yiddish) Little pocket.

bombioshka (Russian) Raid carried out by partisans.

borukh HaShem (Hebrew) Thank God; lit. blessed is the name [of God].

brakha, brakhot, brokhos (Hebrew, Yiddish) Blessing(s); there is a blessing for each food and many daily actions.

Briḥa (Hebrew) Escape. Refers to the illegal immigration to Palestine organized by Jewish Palestinian volunteers.

bris (Hebrew, Yiddish) Circumcision ceremony for a Jewish male child, usually held on the eighth day of his life.

Burgermeister (German) Mayor.

daven (Yiddish) To pray.

devushka (Russian) Darling, term of endearment for a female.

Dror (Hebrew) Freedom, a Zionist youth group.

Effektenlager (German) Lit. "personal belongings camp"; the area called "Canada" by the prisoners in Auschwitz because of the abundance of goods and commodities, where confiscated belongings of deportees were sorted and bundled for use by the *Reich*.

emunah (Hebrew) Faith.

Entlousung (German) Delousing.

Eretz Yisrael (Hebrew) The Land of Israel, biblical name.

erev (Hebrew) The evening before, usually before the Sabbath or a holiday.

Erholungshause (German) Sanatorium.

farfluchter (German) Damned (obscenity).

fiacre (French) Small hackney coach.

finift(lekh) (Yiddish) Group(s) of five people.

frum (Yiddish) Religiously observant.

Führer (German) Leader.

garmushka (Russian) Accordion.

Gehsperre Aktion (German) Curfew roundup, referring to a specific roundup that occurred in the Lodz ghetto in September 1942 that targeted children and the elderly.

gemara (Aramaic) The Talmud.

gendarme (French) Policeman.

Gestapo (German) Acronym of *Geheim Staatspolizei,* secret state police in the Third Reich.

gimatria (Hebrew) Hebrew numerology. Each Hebrew letter has a numerical value.

goy(im)(a) (Hebrew) Non-Jews, lit. "nations"; *goya* is feminine form; *goyish* is the adjective.

Gymnasium (German) European academic secondary school.

Häftling. (German) Prisoner.

Haganah (Hebrew) Jewish defense forces of the Palestinian community prior to Israeli statehood, lit. "defense."

Haggadah (Hebrew) The book of prayers and history that is chanted at the Passover *seder,* lit. "telling."

hai (Hebrew) Life. In Hebrew numerology the number eighteen is the same as the word for life.

HaKadosh Barukh Hu (Hebrew) The Holy One, Blessed be He, a name for God.

hakhsharah (Hebrew) Agricultural training camp run by a Zionist youth organization that prepared youth for immigration to Palestine.

halakhah, halakhic (Hebrew) The body of Jewish law.

halef (Yiddish) Knife used for kosher slaughtering.

hallah (Hebrew) The special, often braided, bread eaten on the Sabbath and holidays.

Halt! (German) Halt!

Hanukkah (Hebrew) Feast of Lights, celebrating the victory of the Maccabees, 168 B.C.E. The eight-day holiday usually occurs in December.

HaShem (Hebrew) The Name; a reference to God's name.

HaShomer HaTzair (Hebrew) Young Guardians, a Socialist Zionist youth organization whose members established many of the early *kibbutzim* in Palestine.

Hatikvah (Hebrew) The Hope, a poem that became the Jewish national anthem.

Hauptsturmführer (German) SS rank, equivalent of captain.

hayelet (Hebrew) A woman soldier.

heder (Hebrew, Yiddish) Jewish primary school, lit. "room."

Herr (German) Mister.

hesed (Hebrew) Loving-kindness.

hometz (Hebrew) Food containing leavening, forbidden on Passover.

humash (Hebrew) The Five biblical Books of Moses.

huppah-kiddushin (Yiddish, Hebrew) The wedding canopy and the wedding ceremony that consecrates a Jewish marriage.

hutzpah (Hebrew, Yiddish) Nerve, arrogance.

ivrit (Hebrew) Hebrew language.

Jude, Juden (German) Jew, Jews.

Judenalteste (German) Head of the Jewish community, usually appointed by the Germans.

Judenfrei (German) Free of Jews, declared after Jews were expelled from a locale.

Judenrat (German) Jewish Council, formed by German command, which was forced to carry out German orders and administer the affairs of the Jewish community.

Judenrein (German) Cleansed of Jews, declared after Jews were expelled from a locale.

Jud Süss (German) Title of a German anti-Semitic propaganda film, September 1940, depicting the rootlessness of the Jews and their alleged criminality.

kaddish (Hebrew) A prayer said by mourners that reaffirms faith in God.

Kapo (German) Prisoner-trusty in charge of other prisoners in a concentration camp.

karpas (Hebrew) A vegetable, eaten during the Passover *seder*.

kashrut (Hebrew) The Jewish dietary laws. To *kasher* is to make something conform to the dietary laws.

Kehillah (Hebrew) The organized Jewish community, its representative body.

kein ayin harah (Hebrew, Yiddish) An expression inserted into a description, which minimizes the importance or beauty of what is described, in order to deflect the attention of the "evil eye," lit. "without the evil eye."

Kennkarte (German) Personal identification card.

Kesuvim (Hebrew) The biblical books of the Hagigographa.

kibbutz (Hebrew) Commune or collective settlement.

kiddush (Hebrew) The blessing on wine said at the beginning of Sabbath and holiday meals.

kind(er) (Yiddish) Child(ren).

klei kodesh (Hebrew) Ritual objects, lit. "holy vessels."

klop(ping) (Yiddish) Bang(ing).

Kohelet (Hebrew) The biblical book of Ecclesiastes.

Kol Nidrei (Hebrew) "All my vows," the prayer with which the *Yom Kippur* service begins.

Kolonne (German) Column, refers to a work detail.

Kommandatur, Kommandant, Kommando (Polish, German) Police station, commander, commando/work group.

kosher (Hebrew) Proper, referring to foods permitted by the dietary laws.

Krakenzimmer (German) Sickroom, infirmary.

Krankenstube (German) Infirmary.

Kristallnacht (German) Night of Broken Glass, November 9 and 10, 1938, when organized mobs of Nazis attacked and destroyed synagogues and Jewish homes and businesses in Germany and Austria, a crucial turning point in Holocaust history.

kriyat Sh'ma (Hebrew) "Hear Oh Israel," said upon retiring for the night, one of the first prayers taught to children. See also *Sh'ma Yisrael*.

Kupat Holim (Hebrew) Sick Fund, a major health maintenance organization in Israel.

KZ (German) Abbreviation of *Konzentrationslager*. The letters are pronounced "*Ka-Tzet*"; prisoners sometimes called each other *Ka-tzetniks*.

Lager (German) Camp; a generic term for concentration camps.

Lageralteste(r) (German) Head of a concentration camp section.

Lagerführer(in) (German) Head of a concentration camp section.

Lampe (German) Lantern.

landsman (Yiddish) Person from the same town.

lekovod (Hebrew, Yiddish) In honor of.

links (German) To the left.

Litvak (Yiddish) A Lithuanian.

lomer gayen (Yiddish) Let's go.

maavar (Hebrew) Transfer, transition.

Maccabi, Maccabi HaTzair (Hebrew) Maccabees, Young Maccabees. A network of Jewish sports organizations in prewar Europe.

madrikh(im) (Hebrew) Youth leader(s), counselor(s).

magasin (French) Warehouse.

magen David, mogen Dovid (Hebrew) Six-pointed star of David.

mahzor (Hebrew) Holiday prayer book.

malekh (Hebrew, Yiddish) Angel.

matonos l'evyonim (Hebrew) Gifts for the poor, charity, given on the Purim holiday.

Matura (German) Final examinations prior to finishing secondary school; a certificate is given to the successful student.

matzah, matzot, matzos (Hebrew) Unleavened bread eaten for eight days during the holiday of Passover.

mazel tov (Hebrew, Yiddish) Congratulations; lit. good luck.

mehallel Shabbos (Hebrew) To violate the Sabbath laws.

Mehl (German, Yiddish) Flour.

Meister (German) Master, work foreman.

melamed (Hebrew, Yiddish) Teacher of young children.

mensch, menschen (Yiddish) Respectable man, people.

meshalim (mashal) (Hebrew) Parables (parable).

mikvah, mikveh (Hebrew, Yiddish) Ritual bath.

minyan (Hebrew, Yiddish) A group of ten Jewish men over the age of thirteen, who constitute a quorum for communal prayer.

Modeh Ani (Hebrew) "I Praise Thee," the first prayer said upon awakening in the morning, one of the first prayers taught to children.

mohel (Hebrew) One who does ritual circumcisions.

moshiaḥ (Hebrew) The messiah.

Musselman(ner) (German) Lit. "Moslem." Concentration camp terminology for prisoner(s) who had become totally emaciated and had lost the will to live.

natchalnik (Russian) Comrade.

Navi (Hebrew) The books of the Prophets in the Bible.

nebekh (Yiddish) Unfortunate.

nekamah, nekomah (Hebrew, Yiddish) Revenge.

Oberscharführer (German) Noncommissioned SS officer.

otrad (Russian) Partisan unit.

Ovinu Malkeinu (Hebrew) Our Father, Our King. A prayer of repentance, said on fast days.

oy vey! (Yiddish) Woe is me!

parsha (Hebrew) Portion, sometimes paragraph, of the Bible read weekly in the synagogue.

partigiani (Italian) Partisans.

payes (Yiddish) Earlocks.

pension (French) Small hotel or boarding house.

pepita (Czech) A wool skirt in a checked pattern.

Pesaḥ (Hebrew) Passover, the seven-day holiday commemorating the biblical exodus from Egypt, when Jews refrain from eating bread and unleavened foods.

pinteleh yid (Yiddish) The essence of one's Jewishness, lit. the "point" of Jewish identity.

Poilishe hit (Yiddish) Polish hats.

pritch (Yiddish) Wooden shelf on which prisoners slept in concentration camps.

Pulverraum (German) Gunpowder room.

raḥmones (Yiddish, Hebrew) Pity, compassion.

Raus (German) Out!

Rav (Hebrew) Rabbi.

Razzia (German) Roundup, similar to *Aktion;* used in Italy, France, Hungary, and the Netherlands.

rebbe (Yiddish, Hebrew) Hasidic rabbi who leads a sect, lit. "teacher."

Recht! (German) Right face!

revier (French) Infirmary.

rosario (Italian) Rosary.

Rosh Hashanah (Hebrew) The Jewish new year, a two-day holiday in the fall, lit. "head of the year."

Sanitater (German) Medical orderly.

Schein (German) Pass, permit.

schissel (Yiddish) Bowl, the container that served as a dish and single utensil for prisoners.

schlep (Yiddish) Drag.

Schneider Resort (German) Tailoring workshop.

Schneidersammelwerkstätte (German) Tailoring assembly workshop.

Schneiderstube (German) Tailoring room.

Schnell (German) Fast.

seder (Hebrew) Order of the ritual meal eaten on the first and second nights of Passover, lit. "order."

sedrah (Hebrew, Yiddish) The weekly *Torah* portion.

sefer, seforim (Hebrew) Book(s), also refers to a *Torah* scroll.

segulah (Hebrew) An amulet, protection against evil.

Selektion (German) Selection of those who would live or die in concentration camp; sometimes occurred in a ghetto prior to deportation.

seudah (Hebrew) Holiday feast.

Shabbat, Shabbos (Hebrew, Yiddish) The Sabbath, Saturday, the Jewish day of rest.

Shabbos Hagadol (Hebrew) The Sabbath before Passover, designated the Great Sabbath.

shalah monos (Yiddish) Sending of gifts, usually food, from one household to the other on the Purim holiday.

Shavuos, Shavuot (Hebrew) The Feast of Weeks, occurring seven weeks after Passover.

shehita (Hebrew, Yiddish) Ritual slaughter of fowl and kosher animals. The Yiddish verb is to *sheht*. Sometimes refers to a massacre.

sheitl (Yiddish) Wig worn by married Orthodox women to cover their hair.

shikker (Yiddish) Drunkard.

shiksa (Yiddish) Non-Jewish woman.

Sh'ma, Sh'ma Yisrael (Hebrew) The prayer, "Hear, oh Israel," which is the basic declaration of Jewish monotheistic faith. It is said three times a day and is also said before death.

shmatte(s) (Yiddish) Rag(s).

shmurah matzah (Yiddish, Hebrew) Matzah made by hand, from flour that has been watched from the moment of harvesting the wheat to prevent any moisture from touching it and leavening it.

shohet (Hebrew) Ritual slaughterer.

shpitzrute (Yiddish) A whip with a steel tip.

shteibel (Yiddish) Synagogue in a private house, lit. "little house."

shtetl(ekh) (Yiddish) Small town(s).

shtreim'l(ekh) (Yiddish) Fur-trimmed hat(s) worn by Hasidic Jews.

shtubhova (Polish) Prisoner in charge of a barrack in concentration camp.

shul (Yiddish) Synagogue.

shvitz (Yiddish) Sweat, steambath.

siddur (Hebrew, Yiddish) Prayer book.

signiora (Italian) A lady.

simhah (Hebrew) Joy, also refers to a joyous occasion such as a wedding or a *bar mitzvah*.

s'mikhah (Hebrew) Rabbinical ordination, lit. "laying on of hands."

Sonderkommando (German) "Special commando"; in concentration camps, work details that worked at the gas chambers and crematoria or at cremating corpses.

Stube (German) Room.

sukkah (Hebrew) The booth erected for the holiday of *Sukkot*.

Sukkot, Sukkos (Hebrew) The seven-day holiday of booths in the fall, when Jews erect a temporary dwelling that is used for meals, study, and sometimes even sleep. It commemorates the temporary dwellings used by the children of Israel during their wanderings in the desert after the Exodus, as well as temporary booths erected in the fields at harvest time.

szpera (Polish) Curfew. See also *Gehsperre Aktion*.

tallis, tallit(ot) (Hebrew, Yiddish) Prayer shawl(s); Yiddish plural, *taleisim*.

Tanakh (Hebrew) An acronym representing all the books of the Bible.

tefillah, tefillo(s) (Hebrew) Prayer(s).

tefillin (Hebrew) Phylacteries, worn by adult Jewish men during weekday morning prayers.

Tehillim (Hebrew) The Psalms, said daily and in times of stress.

Tisha B'Av (Hebrew) The ninth day of the Hebrew month of *Av*, commemorating the destruction of the first and second temples in Jerusalem, a day of fasting and mourning. Other tragedies in Jewish history are also attributed to this date.

Torah (Hebrew) The scroll of the five Books of Moses, read in sequential portions

every week in the synagogue. Also used as a generic term for all religious
Jewish studies.

Torah be'al peh (Hebrew) Oral teachings, the *Talmud*, and other rabbinic writings.

Tzena U'rena (Hebrew) Prayer book designed for women, with Yiddish translations and prayers specially composed in Yiddish for women.

tzore(s) (Yiddish, Hebrew) Trouble(s).

Umschlagplatz (German) Place of transshipping; in the Warsaw ghetto, the assembly point of transports to the death camps.

Vaad Hatzalah (Hebrew) Jewish Rescue Committee, based in Switzerland, active
in aiding resistance groups and rescue of Jews during the Holocaust.

Verzögerung (German) Delayed action fuse for a rocket or a bomb.

Volksdeutsche (German) Ethnic Germans living outside Germany; some collabo-
rated with the Germans.

Vorarbeiterin (German) Forewoman.

Waggon (German) Railroad car; refers to cattle cars.

Wehrmacht (German) The German army.

wysiedlenie (Polish) Resettlement, the German euphemism for deportation.

yahrzeit (Yiddish) The anniversary of a death.

yeshivah (Hebrew, Yiddish) Jewish elementary or secondary school.

Yiddishkeit (Yiddish) Jewishness, Jewish identity.

yimah shemo (Hebrew) May his name be erased.

Yom Kippur (Hebrew) Day of Atonement, a fast day observed ten days after the
Jewish new year; the holiest day of the Jewish calendar, which is spent in
prayer.

yom(im) tov(im) (Hebrew) Jewish holiday(s).

Zahlappell (German) Roll call in concentration camp.

zemirot (Hebrew) Hymns sung at home on the Sabbath and holidays.

zhid (Polish) Jew, derogatory term.

ziemlanka (Russian) A camouflaged dugout space in the forest that served as a living space for partisans.

Bibliography

Oral Histories and Archival Sources

Note: Unless otherwise specified, oral histories are from the Yaffa Eliach Collection, donated by the Center for Holocaust Studies, Museum of Jewish Heritage, New York.

Bay, Adele. Oral history interview.

Beilush, Theresa. Oral history interview.

Berke, Rozalia. Oral history file.

Borzykowski, Anshel. Oral history interview.

Burian, Andrew. Oral history interview.

Diament, Henri. Oral history interview.

Diament, Zanvel. "Memoir." In oral history file of Rywka Diament.

Ehrenreich, Dina Kraus. *Haggadah* (handwritten). Gift of Ludwig Ehrenreich, Zachary Ehrenreich, and Margaret Ehrenreich Heching. Museum of Jewish Heritage Collection, New York.

Evan, Harry. Oral history interview.

Finkler, Golda. Handwritten calendar and *siddur*. Loaned by Dr. Kaja Finkler. Museum of Jewish Heritage, New York.

Foxman, Abraham. Oral history interview.

Fuchs, Henry. Oral history interview.

Garfunkel, Rachel. Oral history interview.

Gelber, Michael. Oral history interview and file.

Glinzman, Regina, and Estelle Alter. Video history. Museum of Jewish Heritage, New York.

Gruber, Samuel. Video history. Museum of Jewish Heritage, New York.

Grunbaum, Rita. "Diary." Oral history file.

Horowitz, Ryszard. Oral history interview. Survivors of the Holocaust Visual History Foundation, Los Angeles, November 7, 1995.

Klein, Abraham. "Memoir" *(Zechor Yemot Olam)*. In oral history file of Edith Wachsman.

Levertov, Rachel. Oral history interview.

Lewis, Victor. Oral history interview.

Meed, Vladka. Oral history. USHMM Collection, Research Institute Record Group 50, Vladka Meed, call number RG50.030*0153. United States Holocaust Memorial Museum, Washington, D.C.

Meth, Rose. Copy of notes written in Neustadt-Glewe. Oral history file.

Podos, Jacob. Oral history interview.

RG1606. Oral history interview (name withheld by request of interviewee).

Rigler, Hannah Sara. Diary of Willie Fisher. Gift of Hannah Rigler. Museum of Jewish Heritage Collection, New York.

Rosenthal, Miriam. Oral history file.

Rothstein, Sara. Oral history interview.

Schwab, George. Oral history interview and file.

Silber, Sara. Oral history interview.

Stein, Sascha. Oral history interview.

van Ryk, Pepi. Oral history interview.

Wachsman, Edith. Oral history file.

Werdiger, David. Oral history interview.

Books, Articles, and Correspondence

Arad, Yitzhak. *Ghetto in Flames: The Struggle and Destruction of the Jews in Vilna in the Holocaust.* Jerusalem: Yad Vashem, 1980.

Arad, Yitzhak, Israel Gutman, and A. Margaliot, eds. *Documents on the Holocaust: Selected Sources on the Destruction of the Jews of Germany and Austria, Poland and the Soviet Union.* Jerusalem: Yad Vashem, 1981.

Bannett, Hannah (Marcus). *B'tzel Korato Shel Nazi.* Tel Aviv: Aleph, 1987.

Bauer, Yehuda. *A History of the Holocaust.* New York: Franklin Watts, 1982.

Berkon, Zenia. "Zichroinos fun Genia Berkon." *YIVO Bletter* 30 (winter 1947): 206.

Bezwinska, Jadwiga, ed. *Amidst a Nightmare of Crime: Manuscripts of Members of Sonderkommando.* Oswiecim: State Museum at Auschwitz, 1973.

Bezwinska, Jadwiga, and Danuta Czech, eds. *KL Auschwitz As Seen by the SS: Hoss, Broad, Kramer.* Oswiecim: State Museum at Auschwitz, 1972.

Blodig, Vojtech, and Ludmila Chladkova. *Ghetto Museum Terezin.* Terezin: Memorial Terezin, 1993.

Blodig, Vojtech, and Miroslav Karny. *Theresienstadt in der "Endlosung der Judenfrage."* Prague: Terezinska iniciativa, Panorama, 1992.

Bondy, Ruth. *Elder of the Jews: Jakob Edelstein of Theresienstadt.* New York: Grove Press, 1981.

Borzykowski, Tuvia. *Between Tumbling Walls.* Israel: Ghetto Fighters House, 1976.

Braham, Randolph L. *The Politics of Genocide: The Holocaust in Hungary.* New York: Columbia University Press, 1981.

C., Marta. "New Testimonies: Women's Resistance in Auschwitz." *The Voice of Auschwitz Survivors in Israel,* no. 34 (April 1986).

Czech, Danuta. *Auschwitz Chronicle, 1939–1945.* New York: Henry Holt, 1990.

Dagan, Avigdor, ed. *Jews of Czechoslovakia: Historical Studies and Surveys.* Vol. 2. Philadelphia: Jewish Publication Society, 1971.

———. *Jews of Czechoslovakia: Historical Studies and Surveys.* Vol. 3. Philadelphia: Jewish Publication Society, 1984.

Dawidowicz, Lucy S. *The War against the Jews, 1933–1945.* New York: Holt, Rinehart and Winston, 1975.

Diament, Zanvel. "Jewish Refugees on the French Riviera." *YIVO Annual* (1953).

Dicker, Herman. *Piety and Perseverance: Jews from the Carpathian Mountains.* New York: Sepher-Hermon Press, 1981.

Dobroszycki, Lucjan, ed. *The Chronicle of the Lodz Ghetto, 1941–1944.* New Haven: Yale University Press, 1984.

Ehrenburg, Ilya, and Vasily Grossman. *The Black Book.* New York: Holocaust Library, 1981.

Ehrmann, Frantisek. *Terezin, 1941–1945.* Prague: Council of Jews in the Czech Lands, 1965.

Eliach, Yaffa, and Brana Gurewitsch, eds. *The Liberators: Eyewitness Accounts of the Liberation of Concentration Camps.* New York: Center for Holocaust Studies, 1981.

———. *Oral History Manual.* Brooklyn, N.Y.: Center for Holocaust Studies, 1991.

Encyclopedia of Textiles. 3d ed. Englewood Cliffs, N.J.: Prentice-Hall, 1980.

Feig, Konnilyn. *Hitler's Death Camps: The Sanity of Madness.* New York: Holmes and Meier, 1981.

Frankl, Viktor. *Man's Search for Meaning: An Introduction to Logotherapy.* New York: Pocket Books, 1963.

Friedlander, Joseph, ed. *Pinkas Pruz'any.* Tel Aviv: United Pruziner and Vicinity Relief Committee/Pruz'ana Landshaft Association, 1983.

From the History of KL Auschwitz. Vol. 1. Oswiecim: State Museum at Auschwitz, 1967.

Gans, Mozes Heiman. *Memorboek: Plantenatlas van het leven der joden in Nederland van de middeleeuwen tot 1940.* Netherlands: Baarn, Bosch and Koening, 1971.

Goldstein, Bernard. *The Stars Bear Witness.* New York: Viking Press, 1949.

Groag, Trude. *Lieder Einer Krankenschwester, im Schleusenkrankenhaus L-124 im Ghetto Theresienstadt.* Handwritten, illustrated, and translated into Hebrew by Willi Groag. Israel: Beit Theresienstadt, 1989.

Groag, Willi. Letters to author, December 26, 1996, and February 4, 1997.

Gross, Solomon, ed. *Sefer Chrzanow: The Life and Destruction of a Jewish Shtetl.* Translated by Jonathan Boyarin. Roslyn Harbor, N.Y.: Chrzanower Young Men's Association, 1989.

Gutman, Israel. *The Jews of Warsaw, 1939–1943: Ghetto, Underground, Revolt.* Bloomington: University of Indiana Press, 1982.

———. *Men and Ashes: The Story of Auschwitz-Birkenau* (in Hebrew [*Anashim VaEfer: Sefer Auschwitz-Birkenau*]). Merhavia, Israel: Sifriyat Poalim, 1957.

———, ed. *Encyclopedia of the Holocaust.* New York: Macmillan, 1990.

Gutman, Israel, and Michael Berenbaum, et al. *Anatomy of the Auschwitz Death Camp.* Bloomington: Indiana University Press, 1994.

Herzer, Ivo, ed. *The Italian Refuge: Rescue of Jews during the Holocaust.* Washington, D.C.: Catholic University Press, 1989.

Hilberg, Raul. *The Destruction of European Jews.* Chicago: Quadrangle Books, 1961.

Huberband, Shimon. *Kiddush Hashem: Jewish Religious and Cultural Life.* Edited by Jeffrey S. Gurock and Robert S. Hirt. Translated by David E. Fishman. Hoboken, N.J.: Ktav, 1987.

Jackson, Livia Bitton. *Elli: Coming of Age in the Holocaust.* New York: Quadrangle, 1980.

Keneally, Thomas. *Schindler's List.* New York: Simon and Schuster, 1982.

Kieval, Hillel J. *The Making of Czech Jewry: National Conflict and Jewish Society in Bohemia, 1870–1918.* New York: Oxford University Press, 1988.

Klarsfeld, Serge, and Maxime Steinberg. *Memorial de la Deportation des Juifs de Belgique.* Paris: Beate Klarsfeld Foundation, 1982.

Kogon, Eugen, et al. *Nazi Mass Murder: A Documentary History of the Use of Poison Gas.* New Haven: Yale University Press, 1994.

Korbonski, Stefan. *The Polish Underground State.* New York: Columbia University Press, 1978.

Levy-Haas, Hanna. *Inside Belsen.* Sussex, U.K.: Harvester Press, 1982.

Lifton, Robert Jay. *The Nazi Doctors: Medical Killing and the Psychology of Genocide.* New York: Basic Books, 1986.

Lyle, Dorothy S. *Modern Textiles.* 2d ed. New York: Macmillan, 1982.

Mayer, Ernie. "Saving Jewish Lives Was a Moral Obligation." *Jerusalem Post Weekly,* November 5, 1974.

Mechanicus, Philip. *Year of Fear: A Jewish Prisoner Waits for Auschwitz.* New York: Hawthorne Books, 1968.

Meed, Vladka. *On Both Sides of the Wall: Memoirs from the Warsaw Ghetto.* Israel: Ghetto Fighters House, 1973.

Michaelis, Meir. *Mussolini and the Jews: German-Italian Relations and the Jewish Question in Italy, 1922–1945.* Oxford: Clarendon Press, 1978.

Milton, Sybil. "Women and the Holocaust: The Case of German and German-Jewish

Women." In *Different Voices: Women and the Holocaust,* edited by Carol Rittner and John Roth. New York: Paragon House, 1993.

Molho, Michael, and Joseph Nehama. *The Destruction of Greek Jewry: 1941–1944* (in Hebrew). Jerusalem: Yad Vashem, 1965.

Nomberg-Przytyk, Sara. *Auschwitz: True Tales from a Grotesque Land.* Chapel Hill: University of North Carolina Press, 1985.

Oberski, Jona. *Childhood.* New York: New American Library, 1978.

Obozy Hitlerowski na Ziemiach Polskich, 1939–1945. Warsaw: Panstwowe Wydawnichtwo Naukowe, 1979.

Perl, Gisela. *I Was a Doctor in Auschwitz.* Salem, N.H.: Ayer Co., 1984.

Pressac, Jean Claude. *Auschwitz: Technique and Operation of the Gas Chambers.* New York: Beate Klarsfeld Foundation, 1989.

Presser, Jacob. *Ashes in the Wind: The Destruction of Dutch Jewry.* Detroit: Wayne State University Press, 1988.

Richmond, Theo. *Konin: A Quest.* New York: Pantheon, 1995.

Ringelheim, Joan. "Women and the Holocaust: A Reconsideration of Research." In *Different Voices: Women and the Holocaust,* edited by Carol Rittner and John Roth. New York: Paragon House, 1993.

Rittner, Carol, and John Roth, eds., *Different Voices: Women and the Holocaust.* New York: Paragon House, 1993.

Roland, Charles G. *Courage under Siege: Starvation, Disease, and Death in the Warsaw Ghetto.* New York: Oxford University Press, 1992.

Rosenthal, Miriam. Letter to author, October 28, 1997.

Rotem, Simha (Kazik). *Memoirs of a Ghetto Fighter: The Past within Me.* New Haven: Yale University Press, 1994.

Roth, Cecil, ed. *Encyclopaedia Judaica.* Jerusalem: Keter, 1972.

Sendyk, Helen. *The End of Days: A Memoir of the Holocaust.* New York: St. Martin's Press, 1992.

Shelley, Lore, ed. *The Union Kommando in Auschwitz: The Auschwitz Munitions Factory through the Eyes of Its Former Slave Laborers.* Studies in the Shoah, vol. 13. Lanham, Md.: University Press of America, 1996.

Shirer, William L. *The Rise and Fall of the Third Reich: A History of Nazi Germany.* New York: Simon and Schuster, 1960.

Smolen, Kazimierz. *Auschwitz, 1940–1945: Guidebook through the Museum.* 6th ed. Oswiecim: State Museum at Auschwitz, 1976.

Szwajger, Adina Blady. *I Remember Nothing More: The Warsaw Children's Hospital and the Jewish Resistance.* New York: Pantheon Books, 1990.

Trunk, Isaiah. *Judenrat: The Jewish Councils in Eastern Europe under Nazi Occupation.* New York: Macmillan, 1972.

U.N. War Crimes Commission. *The Belsen Trial.* New York: Howard Fertig, 1983.

Vaclavek, Ludvik E. "Die Dichterin Gertrud Groag (1889–1979)." *Judaica Bohemica* 25 (1989).

Voigt, Klaus. "Jewish Refugees and Immigrants." In *The Italian Refuge: Rescue of Jews during the Holocaust,* edited by Ivo Herzer. Washington, D.C.: Catholic University Press, 1989.

Vorlaufiges Verzeichnis der Konzentrations Lager un Deren Aussenkommandos, 1933–1945. Arolsen: Comite International de la Croix-Rouge, Service International de Recherches, 1969.

Winick, Myron, ed. *Hunger Disease: Studies by the Jewish Physicians in the Warsaw Ghetto.* Translated by Martha Osnos. New York: John Wiley and Sons, 1979.

Yahil, Leni. *The Holocaust: The Fate of European Jewry*. New York: Oxford University Press, 1990.

Yerushalmi, Eliezer. *Pinkas Shavli: A Diary from a Lithuanian Ghetto* (in Hebrew). Jerusalem: Yad Vashem, 1958.

Zuccotti, Susan. *The Italians and the Holocaust: Persecution, Rescue, Survival*. New York: Basic Books, 1987.

Zuckerman, Yitzchak. *A Surplus of Memory*. Berkeley and Los Angeles: University of California Press, 1993.

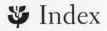
Index

INDEX

Stube, 83, 211, 213, 215. *See also* Simolaine, Franz

Odessa, Russia, 160

Oleander, Mrs., 300

Olmuetz (Moravia), 242–43, 244, 245, 255; *Kultusgemeinde*, 243

Olomuec. *See* Olmuetz

Omaha, Nebraska, 217

Oral history: of the Holocaust, xi–xiv; methodology for, xii–xiii, xx; thematic cataloging of, xiii

Orta (Italy), 121, 333 (n. 21)

Orthodox Jews, 11, 24, 25, 123, 185, 187, 278

ORT school, 77, 124

Oscka, Janusz, 293

Oswego, New York, 122

Oswiecim (Poland), 299

Palestine, 4, 9, 44, 63, 64, 72, 73, 74, 84, 107, 128, 145, 217; immigration certificates for, 5, 44, 45, 63, 74, 244, 267, 313. *See also* Britain, immigration policy

Palka, Stanislaw, 205

Palkovnik *(Natchalnik)*, 156

Paris (France), 4, 12, 13, 15

Pariser, Mr., 146

Parschnitz (camp), 89–90, 212

Partisans, xix, 29, 31, 78, 84, 91, 119–20, 135, 136, 261, 269–76; Czech partisan rebellion, 133, 135; entertainment, 274; Kirowsky *otrad*, 273; medical treatment, 273–74; raids, 226, 272, 273. *See also* Vilna ghetto, resistance

Passover *(Pesaḥ)*, 24, 29, 68, 135–36, 137, 138, 180, 184, 212, 275, 308, 314; *Haggadah*, 312

Pawiak prison, 285

Persia, 311

Pery, J., 18, 218, 241

Pesaḥ. See Passover

Pessah, Moshe, 28

Piemonte (Italy), 119–21

Pilsen, Czechoslovakia, 241

Pioneer Women, 125

Plaszow (camp), 98, 192, 238

Platenhof (Germany), 80

Podlavice (Slovakia), 135, 137

Poetry, 127, 256, 259, 309

Poland, 64, 157, 180, 244, 257

Polhora (Slovakia), 134

Police: German, 151, 260, 268; Hungarian, 189; Jewish ghetto, 86–87, 259, 268, 279, 280; Polish, 268, 291; Slovakian, 130

Polish army, 72, 288

Polish civilians, 80, 205, 240, 308

Polish Jews, 132, 191, 206

Polish language, 65, 210, 277, 278, 282

Political prisoners, 194

Ponar (camp/killing site), 38, 258, 324 (n. 20), 355 (n. 3)

PPR, 297, 365 (n. 19)

Prague (Czechoslovakia), 143, 200, 244; Palestine Office, 244

Prayer, 54–55, 58, 59, 62, 65, 80, 116, 131, 140, 199, 212, 268, 309, 313, 314; book, 311; Catholic, 119–20; *kaddish*, 248; *Modeh Ani*, 310; Psalms, 182, 197, 310; *Sh'ma Yisrael*, 116, 135, 212, 309, 310

Pregnancy, 6, 33, 69, 70, 90, 99, 112, 158, 192–96, 201, 255

Prisoners of war, 67, 68, 80, 83, 97, 287, 288; British, 151–54; Dutch, 233, 234

Prostitutes, 283

Protectorate of Bohemia and Moravia, 243

Providence, 63

Pruszkow camp. *See* Warsaw

Pruzhany (Poland), xiii, 226, 227, 267–71; strategic location of, 269

Pruzhany ghetto, 268–71, 307; escape from, 269–71, 273; food, 269; *Judenrat*, xiii, 268, 269, 270; religious life, 268–69

Pruzhany *Yizkor* book, xiii, 383

Pulverraum. See Union Werke factory

Putzig (Germany), 177

Pyrenees, 13

Radio broadcasts, 15, 129; BBC, 30–31

Radlow, Maria. *See* Warman, Marysia

Radviliskis (camp), 77

Rahm, Karl, 253

Rape, xv, xviii, 97, 157–58

Ratheiser, Kazik (Simha Rotem), 286

Rations: cards, 231; food, 58, 259

Ravensbruck (camp), 297, 305

Rechem, Richard, 241

Recipes, 24

Red Cross, 24, 71, 72, 80, 148, 174, 175, 196, 236, 242, 298. *See also* Theresienstadt

Red Cross hospital, 292, 293

Red Cross medal, 276

Redlich, Gonda, 249, 251

Reichenbach, Germany, 217

Reichman, Estia Englander, 211, 217

Reichsfeld, Heinrich *(Kapo)*, 192–93

Religious observance, 314; changes in, 18, 75, 108, 314

INDEX

Reno, Nevada, 159
Resistance, xvi; in Auschwitz, 297, 301; French, 12; Greek, 29; spiritual, 312
Revenge, 72, 143
Revuca (Slovakia), 128–30, 132–34, 137
Rhineland (Germany), 248
Riecka (Slovakia), 134–35
Riesengebirge (Sudetenland), 67
Riga (Latvia), 226, 262
Righteous Among the Nations, 161, 237, 284
Rigler, Hannah/Sara, xviii, xix, 145–61, 309, 313; photographs of, 165
Ritual slaughter (shehita), 54, 131, 137, 269, 307
Robota, Roza, xiii, 297, 302, 366 (nn. 15, 16)
Rosenthal, Miriam, xviii, xix, 187–203, 311, 314; photograph with family, 168
Rosmites family (photograph), 52
Rosner's Schneidersammelwerkstätte, 206
Roter, Masha (photograph), 52
Rothschild, Mrs., 248
Rothschilds, 116
Rothstein, Sara, 310
Rotterdam (Netherlands), 4, 19, 23, 230, 234
Rumania, 128
Rumkowski, Chaim, 86, 88, 171
Ruscova, Rumania, 180
Russia, 205, 217, 276
Russian army, 289
Russian language, 138, 155, 267
Russian occupation, 33–34, 53–54, 145, 267
Rymald, Hella Fabrikant, 66
Rymald family (photograph), 51

Sabbath (Shabbat, Shabbos), xviii, 9, 29, 34, 64, 68, 108, 115, 116, 117, 121, 129, 131, 132, 134, 137, 145, 180, 204, 206, 212, 216, 255, 311, 313; candles, 68, 108, 124, 136, 310, 311
Sabotage, 312; in Auschwitz, 300–302
Sachs, Tola, 216
Sacsl, Grete Lowy, 251–52
St. Leger des Vignes (France), 12, 13
St. Ottilien hospital, 158–59
St. Petersburg (Russia), 145
Saknowitz, Esther, 203
Salonika, Greece, 26–28, 73
Samulik, Josef, 273
Santa Ceasarea (Italy), 73
San Vittorio prison (Milan), 116
Saperstein, Regina, xiv, 301–2
Sawicka, Marysia, 284, 288. See also Righteous Among the Nations
Schaechter, Rafael, 253, 354 (nn. 53, 54)
Schein, Frieda Elbaum, 211, 215

Schindler, Emilie, 237–41; photograph of, 263
Schindler, Oskar, 224, 237–41
"Schindler's List," 224, 238
Schindler's List (film), 237
Schonbrun, Eva, 140–44, 312
Schonebrun (engineer), 240
Schonfeld, Solomon, 178
Scouts, Jewish, 14, 15
Scranton, Pennsylvania, 110
Second Generation, 294, 364 (n. 74)
Segall, Aviva, 76, 179, 262
Sephardic Jews, 26, 73
Sered (camp), 141
Sexual advances, xviii, 58, 59, 70, 155–57, 175, 200, 216, 275, 285
Shabbat. See Sabbath
Shabbos. See Sabbath
Shauman, Professor, 116
Shavli (Lithuania). See Siauliai
Shehita. See Ritual slaughter
Siauliai (Lithuania), 6, 10, 77–78, 84, 97, 145, 262, 329 (nn. 4, 5, 6); Kaukazas ghetto, 77, 145; Trakai ghetto, 77, 145
Siberia (USSR), 54, 158, 276
Siegel, Mr., 268, 269
Silber, Sara, xviii
Silberman, Rachel, xvii, 77–85, 309, 312, 313, 314; photographs of, 52
Silverstein, Leah (Lodzia), 289, 290
Silverstein, Leah (Lodzia), 289, 290
Simolaine, Franz, 215
Skonieczy, Waclaw, 279, 280–81
Slonim (Poland), 34
Slovakia, 96, 133
Slovak language, 133
Small, Brandla, 86–94, 314
Smuggling: across borders, 13–14, 16, 44, 84, 132; arms, 225, 259, 269–70, 279; calendar, 311; food, 37–38, 77, 225, 259, 279; gunpowder, 296–97; letters, 254; merchandise, 65–66
Sobibor (camp), xvii
Sobol, Mr., 123–24
Sobol, Mrs., 123–24
Sonderkommando. See Auschwitz
Sop, Helmut, 58–63
Sop, Tonia, 60–63
Sosnowiec (Poland), 65, 66, 67, 158, 206; transit camp, 208–9
Srodula (Poland), 67
SS, 60, 69, 72, 99, 154, 155, 170, 174, 176, 177, 182, 184, 190, 191, 192, 193, 195, 196, 197, 198, 199, 201, 210, 224, 238, 239, 240, 241, 295
SS Marine Fletcher, 159
Stalin's medal, 276

{ 394 }